TEXT AND INTERPRETATION

NEW TESTAMENT TOOLS
AND STUDIES

EDITED BY

BRUCE M. METZGER, Ph.D., D.D., L.H.D., D.Theol., D. Litt.

Professor of New Testament Language and Literature, Emeritus
Princeton Theological Seminary
and
Corresponding Fellow of the British Academy

VOLUME XV

TEXT AND INTERPRETATION

New Approaches in the Criticism of the New Testament

EDITED BY

P.J. HARTIN AND J.H. PETZER

E.J. BRILL

LEIDEN · NEW YORK · KØBENHAVN · KÖLN

1991

The paper in this book meets the guidelines for permanence and durability of the Committee on Production Guidelines for Book Longevity of the Council on Library Resources.

BS
2395
.T385
1991

Library of Congress Cataloging-in-Publication Data

Text and interpretation: new approaches in the criticism of the New
  Testament / edited by P.J. Hartin and J.H. Petzer.
      p.   cm.—(New Testament tools and studies, ISSN 0077-8842;
  v. 15)
    Includes bibliographical references and indexes.
    ISBN 90-04-09401-6 (alk. paper)
    1. Bible. N.T.—Criticism, interpretation, etc. I. Hartin, P.
J. (Patrick J.) II. Petzer, J.H. III. Series.
BS2395.T385   1991
225.6'01—dc20   91-11887
                                                                    CIP

        ISSN   0077-8842
        ISBN   90 04 09401 6

PREFACE

In 1985 Professor Bruce M. Metzger, former George L. Collord Professor of New Testament Language and Literature at Princeton Theological Seminary, visited and gave lectures at twelve academic institutions in South Africa. To mark the occasion a volume of essays by South African New Testament scholars was presented to Professor Metzger. The title of this publication was *A South African Perspective on the New Testament*, and it was published in 1986 by E. J. Brill in Leiden. This present book is meant as a sequel to the essays presented to Professor Metzger. The authors of essays in the current volume come from a wider range of scholars and represent a somewhat more diversified interest than that represented by the authors participating in the previous volume. As such the reader will get a somewhat different perspective of interest in the New Testament.

The editors would like to express their thanks to everyone who has contributed an article to this volume, to E. J. Brill for undertaking the publication of the book, and to Ms. U. Boonzaaier for help in proofreading the essays. The editors would like to extend a word of special gratitude to Prof. Bruce M. Metzger, editor of the series *New Testament Tools and Studies*, for accepting this book as part of the series.

Patrick J. Hartin and Jacobus H. Petzer
Pretoria, January 1991

CONTENTS

P.J. HARTIN and J.H. PETZER

INTRODUCTION

1. Hermeneutics

Being part of a rapidly changing society, wherein a process of definition and redefinition characterises everyday affairs, New Testament scholarship (and theology in general) in South Africa is also in a process of methodological definition and redefinition. Questions on how to interpret the New Testament, particularly regarding its role in a polarised and changing society, have up to now and are still dominating South African New Testament scholarship. Proof of this was, for example the 1988 annual meeting of the New Testament Society of South Africa. Under the general theme *Readings and Readers of Luke 12:35-48* all the papers presented at this meeting centered on different approaches to interpreting the New Testament (cf. *Neotestamentica* 22/2 of 1988). In the following year the Human Sciences Research Council held a conference with the title *Paradigms and Progress in Theology*, where, amongst other things, similar matters were addressed (cf. Mouton, Van Aarde & Vorster (eds.) 1988). In addition to these conferences individual articles by individual scholars, such as those by Vorster (1987), Lategan (1984) and Combrink (1986), complete the picture.

A common aspect of all these discussions on methodology in New Testament scholarship is that in the field of hermeneutics three poles stand out to which attention must be given: the *sender* (author) – the *text* – and the *receptor* (the reader). The history of hermeneutics has shown that at different stages and periods attention has tended to focus upon one of these poles to almost the total exclusion of the other. Today, more than at any other period in the history of interpreting the Bible, the number of approaches or methods is proliferating. Despite this proliferation, all the proposals in fact still fall under one of the three poles of sender-text-receptor.

It is the intention of this publication to give the reader an insight into the different approaches that have been adopted in more recent scholarship in the interpretation of the New Testament. Each article has a twofold aim: firstly, to situate the perspective adopted within the wider framework of interpretation and to make one aware of the context out of which this approach emerged. Secondly, in order to move from the realm of theory to practice each article has selected a particular New Testament text to illustrate how this approach can be worked out in reality.

A glance at the seventeen chapters of this book shows the breadth with which

New Testament scholarship, and in particular South African scholarship, is involved and interested. It is hoped that the volume will provide a readily accessible work by means of which one can gain insight into the various approaches that are being used today in New Testament interpretation. The bibliographies supplied at the end of each chapter have been so constructed in order to enable the scholar to pursue further any of the issues that have been raised.

This collection will thus answer a need that is commonly expressed and felt: while someone may be an expert in one particular branch of scholarship, it is not possible to become an expert in every branch. By presenting these chapters together in this collection, written by scholars chosen because of their expertise in the specific fields, it is hoped that the scholarship in these different areas will become readily accessible to a wider group.

The danger of presenting a work of this nature with so many different approaches is that they could be seen as so many competing methods. Consequently, one might wallow in the inevitable relativism that results and throw up one's hands in despair and ask: How am I to choose among so many competing theories? Or, perhaps the result will be to shrug one's shoulders, and to say 'So, what!' and walk away in frustration.

In no way are these approaches to be viewed as so many competing theories. Instead, each method has a particular function, a particular purpose in illuminating the text. Some approaches are more suited to particular types of texts than others, as the different authors themselves point out.

The image of a flashlight can help one to understand the various approaches more clearly. As a flashlight illuminates a certain segment of reality, so a stronger flashlight will illuminate a wider segment; or if the flashlight is shifted to focus attention on a different part of reality, so different aspects are revealed. The same is true of the various methods that are offered here. Like the flashlight, they illuminate the text with which they are dealing in different ways. The text that is illuminated reveals different aspects of its beauty depending upon the methods that are used. It is not to say that one is right and the other is wrong – each has a value. Some are more appropriate to a particular field. Others are more appropriate for a particular purpose.

As Ricoeur argues:

> (If) it is true that there is always more than one way of construing a text, it is not true that all interpretations are equal. The text presents a limited field of possible constructions. The logic of validation allows us to move between the two limits of dogmatism and scepticism. It is always possible to argue for or against an interpretation, to confront interpretations, to arbitrate between them and to seek agreement, even if this agreement remains beyond our immediate reach. (Ricoeur 1976:79)

In forging a path away from dogmatism and sceptism, the insights of Ricoeur, which the article of Draper develops and appropriates in a masterful way, are of great significance. To use the terminology of Ricoeur, the path lies along the route of following the dialectic of 'distanciation' and 'appropriation' (Ricoeur 1976:89). One moves firstly from the process of 'distanciation' or 'atemporalisation' of the text in which an 'Erklärung' of the text takes place which is beyond the actual horizon of the author of the text. From this world of disclosure one moves to that of 'appropriation' whereby one makes one's own, not the intention of the original author or even his understanding of himself or his own world. 'What has to be appropriated is the meaning of the text itself, conceived in a dynamic way as the direction of thought opened up by the text' (Ricoeur 1976:92). For Ricoeur this 'appropriation', in fact, coincides with Gadamer's understanding of 'the fusion of horizons'. The text remains the bridge by which the horizon of the author is fused with the horizon of the reader.

In the following chapters one will see how the focus of attention shifts from horizon of sender to that of the text and then to that of the reader. While each has, indeed, a value in its own right, they should all be seen as contributing together to a deeper understanding of the New Testament.

2. Sender

In the course of this century the approach to interpreting the New Testament, known as historical criticism, is the one that has received the attention, if not the acceptance, of most scholars of the New Testament. Such has been its influence and importance that even today it still remains the most widely adopted approach to the interpretation of the New Testament. In the opening chapter, *Through the Eyes of a Historian*, W. S. Vorster gives an insightful description of historical criticism in both theory and practice. He argues that two fields of interest concern historical criticism above all: firstly, to give an historical interpretation to the various writings of the New Testament; and secondly, to look at the historical context of Jesus and the early Christians who form the focus of attention of these writings.

Vorster emphasises that historical criticism is not to be viewed as a single method, but as a set of methods, or even better, as a specific way of thinking. He gives an illuminating description of the development of the historical-critical methodology in which he discusses its origins in source criticism, its development through form criticism, and the shift of emphasis after the Second World War into redaction criticism. Throughout Vorster gives carefully chosen examples from the New Testament to illustrate his point of view. To conclude the whole approach Vorster gives some valuable insights into exactly how one can speak about the New Testament as history or as a source for history.

3. Text

In focusing upon the text, consensus is necessary with regard to the text that is used. The text remains the starting point for any form of interpretation and without an established text all interpretation is fruitless. In *Eclecticism and the Text of the New Testament*, J. H. Petzer argues that eclecticism has become the major approach adopted in textual criticism at the present time. Proceeding from a definition of eclecticism in relation to New Testament texts, Petzer shows that the method is characterised by a threefold direction: (i) it aims at choosing the best reading in text critical problems; (ii) it makes use of a set of criteria to achieve this purpose; and (iii) it adopts an isolated and individual approach in order to solve textual problems. While drawing attention between different eclectic methods stemming from 'the set of criteria', Petzer distinguishes between the thoroughgoing eclectic methods, on the one hand, and the so-called reasoned eclectic methods on the other hand. He opts for the latter, which he claims is 'the most popular method in New Testament textual criticism today'. Petzer chooses Jesus' prayer for his crucifiers in Luke 23:34 as an illustration of this method, which ultimately enables him to evaluate the various readings of this passage.

P. J. Maartens, in a paper entitled *'Sign' and 'Significance' in the Theory and Practice of Ongoing Literary Critical Interpretation with Reference to Mark 4:24 and 25: A Study of Semiotic Relations in the Text*, continues the approach that centres attention upon the text itself. Using the field of semiotics, Maartens argues for a dialogue of relationships between the sign and the way it is literally represented: through this dialogue one comes to an interpretation of the text (Sign – Representation – Interpretation). The value for Maartens of the semiotic approach is that it enables the exegete to develop a critical consciousness and to venture beyond the field of one-dimensional consciousness. Such a critical consciousness enables the interpreter to avoid the dual pitfalls of a one-dimensional perspective on the one hand, and of adopting a methodological pluralism on the other hand, both of which hinder access to the interpretation of the text. Using Mark 4:24-25 as an example, Maartens illustrates how this literary critical dialogue directs the interpretation of the text past these two polarities of one-dimensionalism and pluralism. Every new generation becomes part of this dialogue contributing a new 'growth ring' to the history of exegesis. As Maartens says: '(It) is an open challenge to every generation to enter the dialogue and interpret the text relative to its historical situation'.

In the nineteen-seventies and the early nineteen-eighties an important change of direction took place in New Testament studies. This period saw a movement away from an exclusively historical conscious approach towards one that focused its attention upon the text as a literary work. It is to this change of direction that A. H. Snyman draws attention in his article *A Semantic Discourse Analysis of the Letter to Philemon*, in which he comments: 'Not the history of the text, but the text itself; not the situation behind the text, but the text as an autonomous object of study; not the intention of the author, but the intention of the text comes to the fore'. In the broad field of literary scholarship various approaches developed among theorists, who placed the text at the very centre of consideration. Snyman draws attention to three main approaches, namely French Structuralism, literary criticism and discourse analysis. The latter approach has received enthusiastic attention and support within South African New Testament studies, unifying scholarship within South Africa with almost every New Testament scholar making use of this approach within her/his research.

One can with justification say that discourse analysis is one field of New Testament scholarship where South Africa has made a significant contribution. Not only has it been accepted by more scholars as a group than anywhere else, but it was this unifying spirit that has enabled South African scholarship to make a significant contribution in this field. Snyman expresses well the direction of this method when he writes: 'The basic premiss of this method... is that meaningful relations not only exist between the words in a sentence, but also between larger parts of a text such as sentences, groups of sentences (clusters) and pericopes. It is therefore important to analyse the way a text is structured in order to grasp its meaning'.

A. G. van Aarde continues the perspective of focusing upon the text with his presentation *Narrative Criticism Applied to John 4:43-54*. He contrasts narrative criticism to the traditionally adopted approaches to the interpretation of the text where the New Testament is classified into four major literary types. Van Aarde maintains that such classifications are not very helpful. Instead, he argues that the gospel form should be approached from the viewpoint that the gospel is a narrative. This means that the gospel is to be examined from the perspective of that science which is concerned with narrative discourse. In order to illustrate this point, Van Aarde firstly presents a very lucid and detailed description of the science of narrative. He argues that the gospels must be understood as the products of a redactor-narrator who joins together at the same time two worlds: the world of Jesus is 'transposed' into the world of the early church and these two worlds fuse into one in the narrative presentation. Applying this detailed exposition of what narratology entails, Van Aarde argues convincingly that John 4:43-54 must be understood as a narrative in the sense that he has already defined.

A final contribution to the consideration of the text as the focal point of interest concerns the speech-act theory which focuses attention on the use and function of language. J. G. du Plessis, in his article *Speech-Act Theory and New Testament Interpretation with Special Reference to G. N. Leech's Pragmatic Principles*, argues that the 'vital nerves' of speech-act theory are situated in three phenomena. Firstly, there is the insight which goes back to J. L. Austin in which the function of language is not simply to make statements about something, but utterances are also seen to perform actions. The concern, then, that is expressed with utterances is not with their truthfulness or the conformity between what is said and the event itself, but with whether the utterance is successful or not. Secondly, H. P. Grice drew attention to the distinction that exists between what is said and what is meant. A third aspect of speech-act theory is to see human speech within the wider context of human action. These three phenomena are taken up into a wider context by G. N. Leech who pays attention to the concept of communication and the dynamics and constraints that are operative within it. Du Plessis argues that speech-act theory can have very fruitful results if it is applied in particular to Johannine studies and the Sermon on the Mount. By way of illustration of this approach to interpretation Du Plessis gives special attention to the parable of the vineyard and the tenants in Mark 12:1-12.

4. Receptor

The third pole to which the field of hermeneutics pays attention is that of the receptor. Recently in the South African context more and more attention has been devoted to the role of the reader in interpreting the New Testament. B. C. Lategan, in his contribution *Reception: Theory and Practice in Reading Romans 13*, sets the stage for the various contributions that deal with the receptor in this volume. After giving a broad outline of the development and background to reader-response criticism and reception theory over the past two decades, he gives a detailed explanation of the basic concepts which direct the whole approach. In applying this approach to the New Testament, Lategan argues that 'the importance of this approach is that it creates an intense awareness of the reading process and provides a framework within which the diverse aspects of this approach can be integrated'.

Choosing a passage (Romans 13:1-7) that is particularly relevant to the South African context, Lategan illustrates the practical application of reception theory for biblical material. In order to discover reader-clues to assist in the reading of the passage he resorts to three different approaches: discourse analysis, argumentative strategies and finally attention to the open spaces within the text. With the result emanating from this examination, Lategan turns his attention to the actual reader and examines four carefully selected readings, some of which, such as the *Kairos document*, have received significant importance in the South African context. In this way Lategan illustrates very successfully the reading strategies that were used in each of them.

A burst of new energy has thrust itself upon the biblical field of interpretation with the interest that rhetorical criticism has recently engendered in the text. W. Wuellner, the foremost proponent of this approach, in his article *Rhetorical Criticism*, situates rhetorical criticism against the history of interpretation and shows that as such it is not entirely new, since it is evident throughout the history of Christianity. However, there is a marked difference between the practice of former rhetorical criticism and what is practised today under this name. Previously the concern of rhetorical criticism lay in the realm of method in which interest was shown in such aspects as style, discourse analysis, speech-act theory, reader-response criticism (aspects that today would be considered under the umbrella term 'literary criticism'). Modern rhetorical criticism, on the other hand, aims at identifying the various techniques employed by the discourse and then to see how these techniques have been used to inspire the reader to implement the action that is being propagated by the text.

After an illuminating survey of the relationship of the history of rhetoric to biblical hermeneutics over the course of time, Wuellner presents four important features of modern practices of rhetorical criticism. John 11 (the Lazarus story) is selected as an example of how modern rhetorical criticism operates in relation to a biblical narrative. He shows that the rhetorical critic aims not at attaining a unity of meaning, but rather aims at illustrating an argumentative coherence within the narrative. The purpose of a rhetorical critic hence differs from that of hermeneutical exegetes.

Probably the area where the role of the reader dominates exclusively is the field of deconstruction where the receptor demonstrates total power over the text. In fact it must be the most radical of all the attempts at interpretation. The deconstructive activity is given attention in P. J. Hartin's article *Disseminating the Word: A Deconstructive Reading of Mark 4:1-9 and Mark 4:13-20*. Hartin is at pains to emphasise that deconstruction is by no means to be considered as yet another method of interpretation that, if correctly applied, will yield the right interpretation. Instead, deconstruction is an activity, a specific approach to texts and the way one reads them. In reading any text, then, the approach does not lie in trying to discover the hidden meaning lying within the text, but rather to see how the text itself unfolds, or disseminates itself. Instead of discovering meaning, deconstruction shows how meaning is deferred from one text to another. Traces of meaning appear in a text, and the reader endeavours to discover how these traces of meaning appear and disappear in the text and from text to text. In choosing the parable of the Sower (Mark 4:3-9) as an illustration of this activity, Hartin highlights the activity more clearly by contrasting it to the historical-critical method. While Hartin is somewhat critical of the approach of deconstruction and himself acknowledges that his appropriation of deconstruction is 'fairly conservative', he justifies his own approach from the very fact that deconstruction is not another method, but an activity that can with justification be appropriated in one's own way, within one's own context.

Fundamentalism is another approach to interpretation whereby the role of the receptor dominates the text. Here the world of the text and the world of the receptor are read on exactly the same level. The gulf that separates them is totally ignored and the New Testament is read through the spectacles of the present day. P. J. du Plessis, writing in his article, *Fundamentalism as Methodological*

Principle, draws attention to a rather surprising situation, namely that whereas the historical-critical method has dominated the scholarly scene for many decades, nevertheless fundamentalism actually influences the academic community in South Africa to a fairly large degree. For Du Plessis fundamentalism is not the expression of an individual church, but is to be found across the spectrum in almost all Christian churches. One main characteristic feature of fundamentalism is that in treating the Bible as the inspired word of God, the gift of inspiration is seen to preserve the authors from any factual errors whatever. These scholars adopt a rigidity and intolerant attitude that opposes and attacks any perspective or reading that is different from their own. Du Plessis in fact argues that in South Africa it is essential to move away from a fundamentalist approach and 'let the Bible be what it should be: universal and inclusive, a dynamic force as the ultimate communication between God and humankind'.

Interest in the world of the New Testamment is an area that has gained more and more attention in recent years and is exerting an influence upon all aspects of New Testament criticism. W. R. Domeris, in his article, *Sociological and Social Historical Investigation*, argues that the attempts in presenting a social description of the early Christian communities have been facilitated by the discovery of numerous texts relevant to the New Testament as well as by the archaeological discoveries from Syro-Palestine. Domeris gives a detailed presentation of the different models that have been adopted in sociological studies of the New Testament, before attempting to give his own approach.

Distinguishing between a social historical study and a sociological exegesis, Domeris provides an illustration of each by using John 9 and Luke 15 respectively. While he does not develop the point, Domeris shows the direction in which both sociological and social historical studies of the New Testament should move. They provide the stimulus and foundation for a contextualisation of the New Testament particularly in the context of South Africa.

5. Contextualisation

The role of the reader really comes into its own when the context of the reader is taken into consideration. In fact the study of the New Testament is never undertaken in a vacuum; there is always some context that influences it. In recent years the context of South Africa has become more and more a referential and influential point in studies that have been done by South African scholars. This is clearly evident from the remaining contributions, which form the bulk of this volume. This shows that South African New Testament studies are progressively orientating themselves towards the context and situation in which the scholar finds himself/herself. To see the New Testament as speaking to the situation of the reader, rather than viewing it as a document simply reflecting the world of its own time, is what is occupying the attention of more and more New Testament scholars.

J. A. Draper in his article, *'For the Kingdom is inside of you and it is outside of you': Contextual Exegesis in South Africa*, sets the stage for this approach. In discussing the heritage of scholarship within South Africa, Draper shows that the academic community in South Africa has been largely influenced by the scholarship emanating from Western Europe, using in particular the historical critical traditions, or in more recent times shifting attention away from the author to an analysis of the text itself. The difficulty, according to Draper, is that neither of these two approaches allows the Bible to have any meaning for the reader – it does not speak to the situation.

Using the approach advocated by the Kairos document ('Our Kairos impels us to return to the Bible and to search the Word of God for a message that is relevant to what we are experiencing in South Africa today', *Kairos Document* 1986:17), Draper argues for an interpretation that involves a 'reading from below'. With this in mind Draper sets as his goal the working out of a methodology for a contextual interpretation whereby those who are involved in striving for democracy in South Africa can draw meaning from the New Testament for their struggle. Draper proposes a number of important methodological theses that enable him to achieve this. In what certainly is an important contribution to the discussion, Draper, using Ricoeur's insights, shows how a dialectic operates whereby the reader in encountering the text actually moves from a situation of understanding and belonging to one of distanciation and explanation. The text challenges the reader to new insights and possibilities, which in turn produce a further journey to understanding and belonging within new contexts. Draper illustrates his approach aptly in reference to the parable of the Fig Tree in Luke 13:6-9.

S. van Tilborg in his article, *Ideology and Text: John 15 in the Context of the Farewell Discourse*, intends to present a definition of ideology that can serve as a research model for analysis. Re-interpreting Althusser's definition of ideology, Van Tilborg proposes to consider ideology as 'the linguistic representation of the linguistic relations of the individuals to the real conditions of existence'. By means of this definition Van Tilborg refers to one text, John 15, in order to illustrate, as he says, 'what must be done if one wants to bring out, interpretively, the ideology of the text'.

The decades of the seventies and the eighties have also been noted for a resurgence of studies devoted to the field of feminism and, in a wider context, to women's liberation. The influence of these studies has also been felt in South Africa, though to a lesser degree than elsewhere in the world, probably because the political liberation of the people of South Africa has been considered to be the more urgent matter. S. J. Nortjé, writing in her article, *On the Road to Emmaus – A Woman's Experience*, continues the contextual approach by reflecting and reading the Scriptures from a woman's perspective. Starting with the wider framework of feminist studies, Nortje shows how feminist theology has contributed important positive influences to the position that women exercise today both in society and in the church. In the interpretation of the Bible feminist approaches use experience as a hermeneutic tool. Turning to the narrative of the two disciples on their way to Emmaus (Lk 24:13-35), Nortje illustrates the woman's perspective in the reading of this narrative and at the same time reads it within the context of her situation within South Africa.

Studies on liberation theology have become more and more influential within the context of South Africa, and some important contributions in the field of liberation theology have been made by South African scholars. In a very penetrating study, *Reading Luke from the Perspective of Liberation Theology*, E. Scheffler illustrates how the perspective of liberation theology can be used in reading the New Testament. Again, this is a specific contextual approach that takes seriously the incarnation of the word in the life of the reader. Scheffler states his intention clearly when he says: 'My intention is rather to attempt to let the Gospel according to Luke dialogue with liberation theology'. After a brief introduction to liberation theology, Scheffler reflects on Luke 4:16-30 in the context of liberation theology and its appropriation in the context of South Africa. In particular he argues that the concept of liberation from suffering must be understood in its widest sense to incorporate all dimensions of suffering.

In the Third World many theologians have turned to historical materialism as a hermeneutic tool to assist them and their people in their struggle against economic and political oppression. W. R. Domeris, in his second contribution to this volume, entitled *Historical Materialist Exegesis*, argues that historical materialism can offer both a viable hermeneutic as well as a new Christian identity. After presenting the theoretical foundations of historical materialism, Domeris shows how one of its features as a hermeneutical tool within the South African context has been to wrest the Bible from the hands of the ruling class and to appropriate it as a tool for the working class in their struggle for liberation. Quoting Mosala, a South African scholar working with the categories of historical materialism, Domeris shows that the underlying perspective regarding the Bible is that it is the outcome of a 'ruling elite, which needs to be decoded in order to reveal the class struggle which ultimately gave it birth'.

In an important assessment of the historical materialist approaches, Domeris argues that they do not necessarily entail an uncritical acceptance of Marxist thinking. Using the thinking of Belo, Myers and Clevenot, Domeris demonstrates how the problem of atheism, the role of the church, and the place of the cross are dealt with by those attempting to use historical materialism within the context of interpreting the New Testament.

6. Conclusion

Each article in this volume is like a stone contributing its indispensable position to the whole construction. Each article enhances the beauty of the whole and without it one would experience a decided *lacuna*. It is hoped that this final product will meet the needs of those for whom it is intended.

BIBLIOGRAPHY

Combrink, H. J. B. 1986. The Changing Scene of Biblical Interpretation, in J. H. Petzer & P. J. Hartin (eds.). *A South African Perspective on the New Testament. Essays by South African New Testament Scholars Presented to Bruce Manning Metzger during his Visit to South Africa in 1985*. Leiden: Brill.

The Kairos Document: Challenge to the Churches. 1986. 2nd ed. Braamfontein: Skotaville.

Lategan, B. C. 1984. Current Issues in the Hermeneutical Debate. *Neotestamentica* 18, 1-17.

Mouton, J., Van Aarde, A. G. & Vorster, W. S. (eds.) 1988. *Paradigms and Progress in Theology*. Pretoria: Human Sciences Research Council. (Human Sciences Research Council Studies in Methodology 5.)

Ricoeur, P. 1976. *Interpretation Theory: Discourse and the Surplus of Meaning*. Fort Worth, Texas: Christian University Press.

Vorster, W. S. 1987. Op Weg na 'n Post-Kritiese Nuwe-Testamentiese Wetenskap. *Hervormde Teologiese Studies* 43, 374-394.

A.   SENDER

W. S. VORSTER

THROUGH THE EYES OF A HISTORIAN

1. Introduction

There are many reasons why the New Testament and aspects thereof should be interpreted and explained historically. In fact, historical interpretation of the New Testament is necessitated by the very nature of these writings.

The New Testament is a collection of ancient books, each of them written at a different time during the first and beginning of the second centuries C.E. Different purposes, different sociological contexts, different authors, and different recipients were responsible for the form in which we now have these writings. We do not possess a single original copy of any of these books, and in many cases we do not know who wrote them, for whom, or under what circumstances. It was long after they had been written that they were collected and canonised as the New Testament, or the second half of the Bible.

The origin, contents, transmission, reception and canonisation of the New Testament writings are only some of the factors that make the New Testament an object of historical interest. In addition there is also a past standing behind and a future standing in front of the individual texts. Some of them apparently represent the end phase of a process of oral transmission of tradition. The 'growth' of the inscripturated tradition is thus another aspect of historical interest, and so is the transmission of the written text through the ages. The writings of the New Testament are furthermore the products of human beings, reflecting the thoughts of people in whom we are interested. But they also reflect the processes of text production in early Christianity, which are obviously of great interest to us. They moreover serve as sources for the discovery of the past, including the recovery of persons, events and thought processes. And, last but not least, there is the interpreter who is also a historical figure, limited by his/her own time and context and knowledge all of which are historically conditioned. Taken together, all these factors make historical explanation, interpretation and construction with regard to the New Testament evident, and necessary.

Historical criticism of the New Testament concerns two fields of interest: (1) Historical interpretation and explanation of the individual writings or aspects of these writings. (2) The history of the people about whom the New Testament writings speak, that is Jesus and the early Christians. In this essay we shall concern ourselves with both aspects, although more attention will be paid to the first. Much of the material is based on an essay, that I have published elsewhere (cf. Vorster 1984). I have, however, reworked the material extensively.

2. What is historical criticism of the New Testament?

The term *historical criticism* often carries a negative connotation, especially with opponents to this approach. There is, however, reason to argue the opposite. In this essay the term will be used in the sense of discerning appreciation of histo rical phenomena in and concerning the New Testament. In this manner the term is used positively. That is not to deny the history of historical criticism from the early days of Reimarus (1694-1768) through the nineteenth and twentieth centuries and all the negative results that have been reached by New Testament scholars during this period. However, as I have indicated, the very nature of the New Testament calls for historical interpretation.

Historical criticism is more than a method, or a set of methods applied to historical phenomena. It is a way of thinking, an attitude and an approach to the past and past phenomena. In his well-known essay on historical and dogmatic method in theology, Troeltsch (1913:730) remarks that once the historical method is applied to biblical scholarship and church history, it operates like yeast. Everything changes and in the end the complete character of the theological method is changed. He insisted on the principles of *probability* (methodological doubt, or criticism), *analogy* and *correlation* in the historical study of the Bible; principles that still follow us like a shadow (cf. Harvey 1967:3ff; Stuhlmacher 1979:22ff). Our knowledge of the past is mediated by our historical judgements based on probability, analogies and the correlation between what we know and what might have been in the past.

Although the interest in historical investigation (historical criticism) of the Bible since the Reformation resulted in important studies, such as text editions, grammars, the nineteenth century's quest for the historical Jesus, and the sources behind the Gospels, to mention a few aspects, the beginning of the twentieth century marked a noticeable change in our understanding of the making of the Bible, the origins and the history of the primitive church, and so on. Like Troeltsch, others after him accepted the challenge of the discovery of the historical consciousness of man during the nineteenth century. By the middle of this century, historical criticism became widely accepted by New Testament scholars, and in many circles it was taken for granted that the methods applied in biblical research are those used by contemporary historians (Krentz 1975:33).

One should, however, not forget that historical thought is a way of thinking and that there are other ways of thinking too. Although historical thought is common to biologists, physicists, theologians and semanticists, who might think about their own subject in historical terms, each of these scientists also has his/her own particular way of thinking. Biologists think about reality as biologists. The same is done by physicists, theologians and semanticists.

To think historically, means to take seriously the difference and distance between one's own world and that of another who lived at an earlier stage, and to develop a willingness to enter into conversation with the (dead partners of the) past about something, somebody or some event (cf. Demandt 1979:463-78).

Historical thought is obviously based on theories and hypotheses that are human-made attempts to manipulate data for the purpose of explaining, be it the present or the past.

The history of historical criticism reminds us that there are constant shifts in theories. These shifts include shifts in the theory of history, historical interpretation and historiography (cf. Stern 1970), something that is not always realised in New Testament scholarship. It is therefore unsatisfying to speak of historical criticism of the New Testament as if it were one model, namely *the* historico-critical method (cf. Hengel 1973:85). This is illustrated by the many shifts from Von Ranke to the present (cf. Koselleck & Stempel 1973; Gilliam 1976; White 1975). Theories are devised to explain; they are systems of explanation that develop and are improved. Let us illustrate the point.

Historical criticism is always historical criticism current in the period of application or used by the interpreter in that period. Under influence of positivism, for instance, much attention was, and sometimes still is paid to *causality*, *genesis* or *origin* in New Testament scholarship. The reason being, so it is argued, that no written text can be explained without a proper knowledge of the author, his/her life and life setting, and the things that caused certain events and actions. Tremendous efforts have been invested in New Testament scholarship in constructing the original authors of New Testament writings, their lives, the *Zeitgeist* and their thoughts in order to explain these writings. This theory is based on the assumption that literature can only be understood through biography of the author (cf. Maren-Griesbach 1977:10ff; Wellek & Warren 1963:73). This is a theory of literature that has come under sharp attack and is rejected nowadays, although it is still maintained by many in New Testament circles.

Historical criticism is used in this essay in a broad sense. The term covers historiography, historical explanation and historical interpretation. One should, however, be clear about terminology because of the theories on which they are based. It is to my mind necessary to distinguish between historical interpretation, historical understanding (*Verstehen*), historical explanation (*Erklärung*) and historiography. In positivism there used to be no difference between the humanities and natural sciences. Everything was explained in terms of causality and genesis. Dilthey, on the other hand, propagated the idea that there is a great difference between the humanities and the natural sciences. In the first, phenomena are understood, while in the latter they are explained. However, let us remind ourselves that phenomena such as texts and the conduct of people are nowadays also explained and interpreted in the light of theories, for example, literary theories or sociological theories, and not only understood as Dilthey and his followers wished. Scientific investigation is based on theories, and theories form the framework within which phenomena are explained.

In view of the aforesaid, two things must be kept in mind. The first is that, given the fact that historical criticism is commonly accepted by New Testament scholars, it is necessary to be aware of shifts in the theory and practice of historical interpretation. Many of the methods and assumptions, as we shall see later, are based on theories of historical criticism that are no longer accepted. Secondly, it is a grave misunderstanding to assume that historico-critical methods used by New Testament scholars are necessarily the same as those used by contemporary historians. For this purpose, it will be necessary to relate aspects of historico-critical research to underlying theories and simultaneously to mention current views on relevant aspects of historical research with regard to literature. In the rest of the essay an attempt will be made at describing the different methods that are used in historical interpretation of the New Testament, and also to deal with aspects of New Testament historiography.

2.1 Historical interpretation of New Testament texts

2.1.1 On the assignment of meaning

Texts do not have meaning. Meaning is attributed to texts by an active interplay between text and interpreter. That explains why it is possible to interpret the same text in various ways depending on the method of interpretation. By consciously choosing a specific approach to literature, for example, a feminist or Marxist interpretation may be given of a particular text. On the other hand, one might approach a text with a specific problem in mind and interpret the same text psychologically or sociologically, or sociolinguistically. In each of these cases meaning is attributed to the text on the ground of a particular theory (cf. Van Luxemburg, Bal & Weststeijn 1982:75ff).

Historical interpretation is also interested in the meaning of texts and is obviously also based on a theory or theories of literature. Within this framework meaning is constituted by authorial intention, genetic contexts, extratextual reality and by the original readers.

The different aspects may be schematised as follows:

$$\text{extra-textual reality}$$
$$\downarrow$$
$$S \longrightarrow \text{TEXT} \longrightarrow R$$
$$\uparrow$$
$$\text{genetic context}$$

$\longrightarrow$ elements constituting the meaning of a text

The first thing that comes to mind when we think of the New Testament within the framework of this model is the fact that the interpreter is expected to do a lot of constructive interpretation. We have already said that we do not possess a single original copy of any text in the New Testament. So obviously the interpreter is expected to establish an authentic text. The method by which this is done is called Textual Criticism (cf. chapter 2 below). Since we nowadays have a number of critical editions of the New Testament, the task has become much easier for the historico-critical interpreter in this respect.

What we have are *contextless texts* that have to be interpreted historically. In each particular interpretation one has to establish who wrote the text, to whom, under what circumstances and about what. This is in short what is expected from the interpreter who wants to interpret a text historically. Many of these problems are dealt with in so-called *Introductions to the New Testament* where attention is paid to authors, receivers, places and purposes of writing of the individual books, and also in books about the history of the first century C.E. (*Zeitgeschichte*). In each particular case, however, the interpreter is expected to take into account all the (re)constructed detail in order to make sense of text.

Generally speaking the New Testament consists of narrative and argumentative texts. The Gospels, Acts and the Revelation of John are narratives, while the letters are argumentative texts. Both sets of texts offer different historical problems, and various methods are used to reconstruct information related to these matters.

Let us now turn to an example from an argumentative text in order to illustrate historical interpretation of a fragment of an argumentative text. Romans 13:1-7 forms part of the letter of Paul to the Romans. What Paul had in mind is dependent upon a number of things that the interpreter has to construct. There is no doubt that Paul wrote this letter after his conversion, and according to Romans 16:1 it is probable that he wrote the letter when he was in Corinth. In order to establish when this happened one has to take into account the chronology of Paul.

The only fixed point in Paul's life is derived from the Gallio inscription (cf. Kümmel 1965:177f). This inscription was found in Delphi during 1897, and is dated in the twenty-sixth acclamation of the Emperor Claudius. The probable date of Gallio's term as proconsul is spring 51 to spring 52. If the data in Acts 18:11f are correlated with the term of Gallio, it is possible to infer the probable date of the ministry of Paul in Corinth. Taking this as a vantage point, the different dates in Paul's ministry can be established. Paul's letter to the Romans is thus normally dated in 56/7.

The addressees are known from the letter. They are referred to as gentiles (cf. 1:5,13; 11:13), that is gentile Christians, in their relationship with Jewish Christians (cf. 4:1; 7:4-6; 9-11; 14:4-6, 13-23). The church of Rome therefore most probably consisted of gentile and Jewish Christians. Did Paul have Jewish Christians in mind when he wrote Romans 13:1-7? This is possible if we take into account the remark of Suetonius (cf. *Claudius 25*) in connection with the expulsion of the Jews (= Jewish Christians) from Rome. This took place in the year 49. But who were these people and what did they think? Were they Jewish Christians who lost their property when they had to leave Rome, returned to Rome after the death of Claudius in 54, and then had to be kept under the thumb? Were they anti-Roman charismatic Christians filled with the Spirit, regarding themselves as members of another world, indifferent to the Roman Empire? Were they perhaps revolutionaries who wished to overthrow Roman rule?

Romans 13:1-7 reflects the language usage and characteristicts of a Hellenistic Roman (constitutional) legal situation of the first century C.E. (cf. Friedrich, Pohlmann & Stuhlmacher 1976:135ff). In an attempt to construct the authorial intention, one also has to construct Paul's frame of mind. Did Paul write from an apocalyptic point of view with the expectation of the imminent return of the Lord coming to establish the kingdom of God? Or did he lay down principles for the ethical conduct of future generations?

From these various possibilities, of which I have mentioned only a few for the purpose of illustration, one has to recover a probable historical setting for a historical reading of the text. Because of the lack of external information from contemporary writings and other historical sources, it is very difficult if not impossible to reconstruct a historical setting for Romans 13:1-7 as Strecker (1972:27) and others have correctly pointed out. The same holds for the reconstruction of the authorial intention, the original recipients and what they thought about the matters referred to in the text.

Romans 13:1-7 is no exception to the problems involved in historical interpretation of the meaning of New Testament texts. The historical setting and the date of writing make quite a difference to the meaning that is ascribed to aspects of the Gospel of Mark, for example. Quite different situations are assumed by placing the Gospel in Rome, Syria or Galilee, and the same goes for dating the Gospel before or after the fall of Jerusalem. Similar problems occur when James, the brother of Jesus or another James is taken as the author of the letter of James, to mention a few examples.

The theory behind this approach is that it is possible to infer from a text the authorial intention, the historical situation referred to in that text, information about the subject matter and about the intended original recipients. Texts are regarded as windows through which the interpreter can see the reality to which they refer. This approach to literature has, however, been rejected by literary critics (cf. Wellek & Warren 1963). There is no direct route via the text to the mind of the author, the actual readers or the events referred to in the extratextual world of the text. That is why a historical interpretation of a text can never be called a *reconstruction* of the mentioned aspects. It always remains a construction of the interpreter based on probabilities, as we have illustrated above. The interpreter constructs the necessary information in order to make a historical interpretation and gives an interpretation within that framework. This is sound historical thinking and the most we can do with re-enacting the past.

Although the different historico-critical methods, or at least some of them, are also applied to argumentative material, they are normally used to analyse narrative material. That is because of the concept of the text which underlies the approach.

2.1.2 On texts and methods

2.1.2.1 What is a text?

There is reason to believe that most of the written narratives we find in the New Testament are based on sources, be they written or oral. According to Luke (1:1-4) the author of the Gospel made a thorough investigation into the things that had been handed down and written about Jesus before he wrote his story of Jesus. And Paul also tells us about the *tradition* that he had received concerning the death and resurrection of Jesus (cf. 1 Cor 15:3f). In addition, the Old Testament writings and other extracanonical writings are often quoted or alluded to (cf. the list of *Loci citati vel allegati* in the Nestle-Aland edition), which makes it all the more necessary to pay attention to the 'sources' on which the narratives are based and how they were used in compiling the final texts. If one furthermore takes into account the agreements among the synoptic gospels (see below), there seems to be enough reason to take seriously the view that these writings are based on sources, it is argued.

Historico-critical methodology started developing during the nineteenth century, and one should expect the underlying text theory to be from that period. The idea of *origin* and *growth* is basic to what a text is according to traditional historico-critical thought. New Testament narratives are the products of sources, which have not only been used by the compilers of these texts, but might have undergone changes and developments in the process of transmission and eventual inscripturation. In fact, the narratives originated from the sources, it is argued.

The first step in the development of historico-critical methodology was to devise a method by which the sources underlying a particular text could be discerned. Nineteenth century analysis of the New Testament bears witness to this stage. It was, however, realised that these sources underwent changes and that since they were transmitted orally, it was necessary to investigate the oral stage of tradition, the history of traditions, the transmitters of tradition, and the role of the setting which gave rise to particular forms in which the tradition was transmitted. After the Second World War, attention came to be paid to the purposes for which the final compilers of narrative texts, such as the gospels, used the material that they received. It is clear that the application and development of methodology had an influence on the concept of text of historico-critical methodology and that one should be aware of this. There is a clear difference between current views depending on insights from redaction criticism and, for instance, those of early practitioners of source criticism. The main idea, nevertheless remains. New Testament narratives are the products of communities and bear traces of processes of growth and development. With this in mind, let us now turn to the individual methods, which were mainly developed by German scholars for the interpretation of narrative material, but are nowadays commonly accepted by scholars who are involved in historico-critical study of the New Testament.

2.1.2.2 Source criticism

Source criticism is the more acceptable English equivalent for the German *Literarkritik*, which is sometimes translated by literary criticism. Since the purpose of *Literarkritik* is to determine the sources that have been used in a given text, it is inappropriate to use the term literary criticism, which is the name of a totally different discipline.

The main concern of source criticism is to determine the source/s that presumably lie/s behind a particular text. One of the major problems in this connection in the New Testament is the relationship between the so-called Synoptic Gospels, that is the Gospels of Matthew, Mark and Luke. They are called synoptic (seeing together) because they sometimes relate the same material in the same wording and in the same order.

Different solutions have been offered for the phenomenon of the striking agreements but also remarkable differences in *wording, order of material, style* and *contents* among the first three Gospels, since G. E. Lessing (1729-1781) first suggested that they are based on a common gospel *(Urevangelium)* that is no longer extant. J. G. Herder (1744-1803) proposed that the synoptic gospels were based on a series of oral traditions that the individual compilers of the gospels reworked for their own purposes. And in the same vein F. D. E. Schleiermacher (1768-1834) thought that the problem could be solved by assuming written and not oral sources behind the gospels.

These solutions assume a source or sources behind the synoptic gospels. Quite another model was proposed when it was suggested that there are signs of *literary dependence* among the synoptic gospels. I will mention two important hypotheses in this regard. Some scholars, following Griesbach, argue that Matthew is the oldest extant gospel. The Gospel of Mark is a shortened version of Matthew and its author also used Luke to compile his Gospel (cf. Farmer 1964). Contrary to this, the hypothesis that is commonly accepted is the so-called two-source hypothesis. Priority is given to Mark and it is argued that Matthew and Luke made use of Mark and an assumed sayings-source called Q. Q stands for

Quelle, that is 'source'. It is maintained by many that by accepting the priority of Mark and the existence of Q, one can best explain the differences and agreements among the synoptic gospels.

It makes quite a difference which hypothesis one prefers. To mention one problem in this regard: our construction of the development of ideas in early Christian thought is totally dependent on the solution of the synoptic problem. Since the Gospels of Matthew and Mark characterise Jesus differently, it is obvious that these differences would influence one's presentation of the development of Christology.

This is not the place to elaborate on the detail concerning these hypotheses. Suffice it to say that the synoptic problem is one of the most intriguing problems of New Testament scholarship and that it has certainly not been resolved. The most important synoptic relationships have conveniently been summarised by Sanders and Davies (1989:53f). They are the following:

* The triple tradition, that is, passages that occur in all three synoptic gospels.
* The placement of the material often agrees in the case of the triple tradition.
* More than ninety percent of the material of Mark is found in Matthew and more than fifty percent in Luke.
* In addition to *verbatim* agreements in the triple tradition, there also are substantial agreements between Matthew and Mark against Luke, but fewer between Matthew and Luke against Mark.
* The agreement between Matthew and Luke begins where Mark starts and ends where Mark ends. This also occurs in individual pericopes.

These observations emphasise the fact that Mark is closer to Matthew and Luke than Matthew is to Luke and *vice versa*.

In addition, it is remarkable that Matthew and Luke have a lot of material in common that is not found in Mark, most of which are sayings of Jesus. It is also remarkable that this material is not arranged in the same way in Matthew and Luke.

Source criticism is an attempt to explain, amongst other things, the agreements and disagreements of the synoptic gospels in wording, order, contents (e.g. omissions, doublets and misunderstandings), style, ideas and theology.

To enable scholars to study the relationships between the gospels, J. J. Griesbach already in 1774 published a critical synopsis in which the gospel material was arranged in parallel columns. We now have a large number of synopses of the synoptic gospels (cf. Sanders and Davies 1989:51f), each based on different assumptions. They allow us to investigate the different Gospels simultaneously.

Source criticism does, however, not only concern the synoptic problem in the New Testament. Literary relationships in New Testament texts are usually explained by the assumption of sources underlying texts. These relationships are of two kinds. First there are texts that seem to show a literary dependence upon other known texts. This is the case with the synoptic gospels, Colossians and Ephesians, 2 Peter and Jude, for example. In such cases the direction in which dependence lies has to be explained. There are, furthermore, single texts that are presumably based on unknown sources. In John 4:1, for example, it seems as if the author had used a source according to which Jesus and his disciples baptised people. In verse 2 he apparently corrects this view by asserting that Jesus himself did not baptise. Furthermore, because of the difference in vocabulary and the fact that John 20:30 seems to be a natural ending for the Gospel, it is often assumed that John 21 is based on another source not written by the same author who originally compiled the Gospel. Paul inserted hymns into his letters (cf. Phlp 2:5-11 and Col 1:15-20) and made use of pre-Pauline material in writing his letters (cf. 1 Cor 15, etc.). How does one determine whether an author made use of a source if he does not mention it, as is frequently the case of quotations of the Old Testament and so on (cf. 1 Cor 11:23ff)?

Sources are normally assumed when there are inconsistencies in a text (see the detailed discussion of Wenham 1985:144f). These include inconsistencies in the sequence of a text (e.g. breaks/seams and dislocations; cf. the relationship between Jn 14:31; 18:1 and Jn 15-17); stylistic inconsistencies (see the hymns in the infancy narrative of Luke); theological inconsistencies (cf. Rm 3:25-26 with Rm 1-2) and historical inconsistencies (e.g. doublets in the same document).

Originally source criticism was used to get as close as possible to the events being described in the New Testament, and in particular to the events in the life of Jesus. Especially in the nineteenth century it was maintained that the original sources behind the texts were closer to how things really happened, that is, to the historical events that are fundamental to Christian faith, and that special efforts should be made to determine and reconstruct these sources. This was part of the philosophy of history of that time and also of the concept of truth. The only truth is historical truth, that is truth which is based on facts (cf. Lührmann 1984:42). There are few scholars today who would still defend this view. The purpose of source criticism has shifted from the search for sources and 'reliable facts' to the explanation of the production of early Christian literature. It is therefore used nowadays in form critical and redaction critical studies to determine the tradition/s behind a written text.

2.1.2.3 Form criticism

In answer to the question where the authors of New Testament writings obtained their material, we have already noticed in our discussion of source criticism that much attention is paid to the use of sources in traditional historical criticism of the New Testament. Form criticism did not replace source criticism and still does not do so. It also concerns the origin of New Testament material, obviously from quite a different perspective, as we shall soon see.

Form criticism is a translation for *Formgeschichte*. The German term refers to the fact that form critics are interested both in the *forms* of material, which are found in the New Testament, and in their *pre-literary history*, that is, their oral growth and origin. Form criticism is therefore not only interested in the study of forms as the (English) term suggests. Forms *and* their history are the focal point in form-critical studies. Although scholars sometimes distinguish between the study of forms (form criticism) and the history of the traditions that constitute part of the content of a form (tradition history), it is difficult to do form criticism in the traditional sense of the word without studying the history of the traditions involved. This is clear from the standard works of R. Bultmann and M. Dibelius on form criticism. They should be regarded as the pioneers in this approach, although they built on the insights of their predecessors and contemporaries.

The publication of W. Wrede's book *Das Messiasgeheimnis in den Evangelien: Zugleich ein Beitrag zum Verständnis des Markusevangeliums* in 1906 brought to an end the idea that the oldest Gospel, that is the Gospel of Mark, was a chronicle of the life and works of Jesus. He illustrated how Mark portrayed Jesus to his readers by his theological construction of the secrecy and revelation of Jesus in the Gospel. That ruled out the idea that Mark's Gospel can be used as a basic history of the life of Jesus as had been believed in the nineteenth century. On page 41 of his book, *Kyrios Christos: Geschichte des Christusglaubens von den Anfängen des Christentums bis Irenäus*, which was published in 1913, W. Bousset furthermore drew attention to the need of investigating the 'laws' that regulate oral tradition and transmission. In 1919 three books were published that became classics in New Testament scholarship, one on source and the other on form criticism. In his book, *Der Rahmen der Geschichte Jesu: Literarkritische Untersuchungen zur ältesten Jesusüberlieferung*, K. L. Schmidt argued that the Gospel of Mark consists of small episodes that Mark edited and then put into a seemingly chronological and geographical framework. In *Die Formgeschichte des Evangeliums* M. Dibelius was the first to use the term *Formgeschichte* with regard to the study of the pre-literary oral forms of the gospel tradition. He went about constructively by assuming the missionary context and preaching as the life setting of most of the material in the gospel tradition. R. Bultmann worked analytically and in his book, *Die Geschichte der synoptischen Tradition*, concentrated on the history and characteristics of the forms of the Jesus tradition. Both regarded form criticism as a sociological approach in the first instance that helped the New Testament scholar to trace the history of the traditions we find in the New Testament.

When one pages through a synopsis and compares the introductions and endings of smaller units, such as parables, miracles or other narratives, one soon realises that the frameworks of the same stories are not always similar in all the Gospels. Matthew 18:10-14, for example, has it that Jesus told the parable of the

Lost Sheep to the disciples. But according to Luke 15:4-7, it was directed against the Pharisees. There also seems to be a limited amount of forms in which the gospel tradition was transmitted. These and many other details indicate that the individual units had their own life of transmission and that they were used in many different contexts by the primitive church depending on the needs of the church.

Taking their cue from the Old Testament scholar, Herman Gunkel, New Testament scholars such as Bultmann and Dibelius, soon realised that the content of the Jesus tradition, for example, was transmitted in certain forms and that there seemed to be a relationship between form, content and the situation in which a particular form originated. A major component of the teaching of Jesus appears in the form of parables, and his conflicts with opponents are normally narrated in the form of controversy stories, to mention two examples. It was argued that a particular setting in life (*Sitz im Leben*) is the occasion of a certain form. There seems to be a correlation between the form of the material and the occasion or setting out of which the material originated and was transmitted. Funeral notices, for instance, are normally occasioned by the death of somebody in a society. Similarly other sociological settings are responsible for other forms. Controversy stories or debates, for instance, can be traced back to internal strife in the primitive church or debates with opponents of the Christian sect at an early stage. In order to find a possible *Sitz im Leben* for a particular form it is helpful to relate the form to a particular activity of the primitive church, for instance, the cult, teaching, preaching or mission.

The purpose of form criticism is twofold. First it describes the genres, forms and formulas that occur in the New Testament. Secondly it focusses on the pre-literary history and growth of traditions and smaller literary forms, such as parables, miracle stories, birth stories and so on.

New Testament writings can be divided into four larger forms (*Gattungen*) or genres, namely gospels, a historical monograph (Acts of the Apostles), letters and an apocalypse. Each of these has its own characteristics that are important for the study of the particular writing. Incorporated into these larger forms are smaller ones (*Formen*) such as hymns, parables, miracle stories and so on. Then there are also formulas (*Formeln*) incorporated into the material that the authors of the New Testament writings used, such as credal formulas (cf. Rm 5:8; 10:9; 1 Cor 15:3). These could have formed part of early Christian catechesis. We also find confession formulas (Phlp 2:11) that could have been used at baptism ceremonies. There are furthermore liturgical formulas and texts such as acclamation (1 Cor 8:6) and praise formulas (Rm 16:25-27), prayers (Ac 4:24-26) and so on. These forms and formulas also indicate that the writings of the New Testament constitute part of the tradition of the church at an early stage of its development. Form criticism is interested in both the form and the prehistory of these larger and smaller forms. For reasons that are clear, the emphasis is on the Gospel tradition, although, as we have just seen, it is not restricted to that.

A number of *presuppositions* play a role in form criticism, of which the most important is the assumption that our written Gospels originated from oral tradition. During the time between the ministry of Jesus and the writing of the first Gospel, the sayings of Jesus and the stories concerning his words and works were circulated *orally*. It is also maintained that even the written sources that the authors of the Gospels might have used to compile their narratives originally circulated in oral form. They are folk or popular literature, and do not have the characteristics of literary texts in the classical sense of the term. The 'authors' of the Gospels can therefore not be regarded as real authors. The Gospels are the products of a process of evolution with the community as a collective institution, the generating force behind the process of transmission. Not individuals, but the community is the creative force behind the gospel traditions. They transmitted and even created the Jesus tradition that we now find in the written Gospels. The authors of the Gospels are regarded as compilers, collectors of traditions, tradents and exponents of their respective communities.

A further assumption is that it is possible to study the preliterary form of tradition, be it in written or oral form. It is assumed that the written Gospels reveal traces of oral transmission and that the New Testament scholar has the task of constructing the history of the transmission of traditions. This is done, amongst other things, by investigating how close a particular unit or pericope is to the 'pure form' of that particular form. Since miracles and other forms that we find in the Jesus tradition also occur in other writings of the same period, a particular form is compared to that in extracanonical literature in order to determine the characteristics of the so-called pure forms. A typical form critical argument would be that the miracle story of the Healing of the Paralytic in Mark 2:1-12 originally did not contain the saying concerning forgiveness. It may have been added by inserting the controversy about Jesus and the forgiveness of sins into the story. This resulted in a mixed form, that is, a miracle story mixed with a controversy story. It is argued that by comparing parallel accounts of the same unit of tradition, their wording, placement and context, it is often possible to trace the history of a particular unit to its possible original form. The parables of Jesus offer an excellent opportunity to apply this approach, since many of them occur in all three synoptic gospels as well as in the Gospel of Thomas.

Since it is furthermore believed that the original forms were initially circulated without their current narrative frameworks, and also transmitted in other frameworks, it is theoretically possible to distinguish redaction from tradition in order to get closer to the original form. Let us now turn to *preliterary forms* in the Jesus tradition.

It is obvious from the way in which Dibelius and Bultmann divided and treated the Jesus tradition that there is no such thing as a pure form and that it is possible to name the forms differently. This is not the place to enter into detail. A few remarks are nevertheless necessary.

Dibelius divided the material into paradigms, novellets, legends, myths and paranesis. Bultmann, however, divided the Jesus tradition into sayings (*logia*) and narrative material. This is also the division that to this day is followed to a greater or lesser extent by scholars. We shall give a short discussion of the different forms by which the tradition was transmitted. The *sayings tradition* will be dealt with first.

The term *apophthegm* was used by Bultmann for controversy stories, school debates and so-called biographic apophthegms. These small units normally refer to a short narrative containing a short and pointed independent saying as the hub of the particular story. Dibelius called them paradigms because of their exemplary function, while others preferred the term 'pronouncement story' (V. Taylor). These stories are best explained in the light of similar short narratives containing a saying, called *chreiai* (sg. *chreia*) which abound in Greek literature (cf. Robbins 1988 and Sanders & Davies 1989:146ff). A few examples of *chreiai* in the Gospels are the Healing of the Paralytic in Mark 2:1-12; the Call of Levi (Mk 2:14); the Question about Fasting (Mk 2:18-22); and others which indicate the importance of the pointed saying within the short narratives.

Another important group concerns the *figurative speech* of Jesus, which refers to his proverbs, overstatements (Mt 5:29-30), images (Mk 2:17), metaphors of all sorts, including similitudes (e.g. Lk 14:28-32), parables (Mt 20:1-16) and exemplary stories (Lk 10:30-37). The figurative speech of Jesus has been scrutinised intensively by form critics since the critical study of A. Jülicher, which put an end to the allegorical interpretation of this material by the church for a long period. Scholars such as T. A. Cadoux, C. H. Dodd and J. Jeremias did pioneering work in this connection and are worthwhile consulting. Especially with regard to the teaching of Jesus on the kingdom of God, and therefore with regard to the question of what Jesus taught, it is important to be aware of the problems involved in interpreting this material from a form critical perspective (cf. Jeremias 1970).

The *sayings of Jesus* also occur in different other contexts, such as dialogues (cf. Mk 13) and other narrative material. With regard to content and form these sayings are clearly recognisable. I am referring to wisdom sayings (Mk 9:49), prophetic and apocalyptic sayings that can be comforting (Lk 6:20-23), threatening (Lk 6:24-26), or admonishing (Mk 1:15). These sayings are uttered for the benefit of the church. There are also law sayings which are either apodeictic (Mt 7:6): 'Do...' 'Do not...', or casuistic (Mk 8:38): 'If... then...', in form. These sayings originated, according to the form critics, in catechetical contexts or they were used in polemics. The I-sayings constitute a special group (Lk 14:26). By these sayings Jesus revealed something about his person or his coming (Mk 2:17). Many of these were built on the model of the original I-sayings of Jesus and are therefore not authentic, as Bultmann and others have convincingly indicated. This obviously applies to the Jesus tradition in general and not only to the I-sayings. The primitive church used and reused the same sayings of Jesus and events in his life in many different situations for different purposes. That explains the diversity in the transmission of tradition.

The *narrative material* in the Jesus tradition is also the object of form critical studies. Bultmann divided this material in accordance with content.

Similar to other contemporary miracle workers, Jesus also performed miracles, and therefore the Jesus tradition has different *miracle stories*. These stories range from stories concerning exorcisms, healing miracles to nature miracles. Although the amount of detail differs, most of the stories have a common structure: there is a need and the need is eventually overcome. They are used to illustrate the authority of Jesus, and for apologetic and missionary purposes. Miracles stories performed by the followers of Jesus are also told in the Acts of the Apostles (cf. Ac 5).

In addition to miracle stories, the Jesus tradition also includes *historical narratives* and *legends*. These stories concern the infant narratives, baptism of Jesus, his entry into Jerusalem, the passion narrative, and the empty tomb narrative. It is very difficult to distinguish between what is historical and what is legendary in this material. Dibelius used the term legendary with regard to narratives that go back to inquisitiveness to know more about a person or an aspect of a person's life (cf. Lk 2:41-49). Myth, according to Dibelius, refers to supernatural events. The baptism of Jesus, his temptation and transfiguration are classified as legends by Dibelius.

Since form critics are also interested in theological reasons why traditions were transmitted in particular ways, the application of the method sheds light on theological trajectories in the primitive church.

Form criticism has been subjected to fundamental criticism. This is not the place to discuss the criticism. Let me conclude this section with a remark and references. The production of texts, the conception of what texts are, how authors use other and previous texts to make new ones, the role of oral tradition in the writing of New Testament texts and many other aspects of importance to form criticism have become a bone of contention (cf. Güttgemanns 1970; Sanders & Davies 1989:128ff and Vorster 1982:103f).

2.1.2.4 Redaction criticism

In the period between the two world wars scholars focussed on the smaller units and their prehistory even though persons like Bultmann already in his book on the history of the synoptic tradition drew attention to the Gospel writers as editors. After the Second World War there was a change of interest and a new method was applied to determine the theological purpose of the individual Gospel writers in their redaction of the Jesus tradition. The emphasis came to be placed on the Gospels as complete texts and not so much on fragments that the writers of the Gospels used in their compilation of their texts.

I have already referred to the works of Wrede and Schmidt, which in a certain way opened the possibility of investigating the role of the Gospel writers as editors and their individual theological intentions. Wrede emphasised Mark's theological scheme of the Messianic secret and Schmidt showed that the frameworks of the narratives about Jesus are not original. In addition, scholars such as R. H. Lightfoot, who, after his return to England from Germany where he studied under Dibelius, wrote a book on the function of the prologue of Mark, and E. Lohmeyer, who contended that the Gospel of Mark was built around geographical and theological themes. However, they were not taken seriously until the end of the Second World War as far as the Gospels as a whole were concerned.

In 1948 G. Bornkamm published an essay on the Calming of a Storm (Mt 8:23-27) in which he compared the pericope with its parallel in Mark 4:35-41. He argued that by placing the pericope after the Sermon on the Mount where Jesus was portrayed as the Messiah of the word, in this pericope he is shown as the Messiah of the deed. He also showed that imitation is an important theme in the previous as well as the following pericopes. These and other details, he maintained, indicated the importance of the redaction of the material by Matthew.

H. Conzelmann made a major contribution to the study of Luke with his book entitled, *Die Mitte der Zeit: Studien zur Theologie des Lukas*. He argued that Luke was not a reliable historian. On the contrary he was more of a historian who tried to portray the salvation history of the world in three periods: the time of Israel until John the Baptist; the time of Jesus, which is central, and the time of the church. According to him Luke was much more interested in showing the importance of Jerusalem in the history of salvation than in writing an accurate history.

Both these studies were based on the priority of Mark and therefore it was relatively 'easy' to determine the way in which Matthew and Luke used their sources and to point out the theological interests of the evangelists. In the case of Mark (and John for that matter) it is different if the two source hypothesis is accepted. Attempts to determine Mark's theological intentions and purpose were soon investigated.

W. Marxsen, who was the first New Testament scholar to use the term *Redaktionsgeschichte* as a name for the new method, maintained that redaction criticism is independent from form criticism. He was more interested in the methodological aspects of redaction criticism and wrote a book on *Der Evangelist Markus: Studien zur Redaktionsgeschichte des Evangeliums*. His book is an attempt to show in four separate studies on John the Baptist, Galilee, the term 'gospel' and Mark 13, that Mark independently reworked tradition for his own purpose and theological intentions.

These studies were the beginning of a renewed interest in the activities of the persons who were responsible for the final Gospels in their written form.

Detailed comparisons were made of how the evangelists altered their traditions, changed the order of material, added, omitted material, inserted the material in their own frameworks and so on, in order to put their own emphasis on the material.

By assuming that Luke used Mark, it can be argued that he changed the saying of Jesus in Mark 8:34 from:

If any man would come after me, let him deny himself and take up his cross and follow me.

to

If any man would come after me, let him deny himself and take up his cross *daily* (my italics) and follow me.

The insertion of 'daily' makes quite a difference to the meaning of the saying. This is but a small example of what is implied by the assumption that the evangelists used sources which they edited for their own purposes in order to portray Jesus in their own chosen way. Obviously the contributions of the evangelists cannot be restricted to minor changes in wording. It also concerns major changes in arrangement of material, such as the Sermon on the Mount in the Gospel of Matthew or the programmatic summary of the preaching of Jesus in Luke 4.

It is clear that traditional redaction criticism is based on detailed comparisons between different texts that presumably are dependent on detailed investigations of what could possibly be regarded as redaction where the sources are unknown. Whenever traditional material is isolated, however, it is possible to ask how a particular author interpreted the tradition by editing it.

The important question in redaction criticism is how did an author make use of a precursor text, be it a tradition, a complete text, or a quotation. Are there signs of editing of the precursor text or tradition? What are the characteristics of a particular writing in wording, style and thought? Is there any indication that these characteristics form part of the redaction of material? These questions are not only applicable in the case of Matthew and Luke, where it is assumed that they used Mark and Q, but also in all texts of the New Testament where it is presumed that an author used and interpreted tradition or other texts for his own purpose.

There have been major shifts in the theory and practice of redaction criticism during the past three decades. Although from the beginning there has been an emphasis on a holistic approach to texts in redaction criticism, the fact that the Gospels, for example, were still regarded as the products of a process of evolution, prevented scholars from taking the evangelists seriously as authors. In spite of their activities as editors, they kept on being tradents and exponents of the communities they represent. Mark is, for example, regarded as a conservative redactor who changed only slightly the traditions he received (cf. Vorster 1980 for a discussion of the problem). Only lately with the introduction of narratology have scholars started focussing on the internal structure and meaning of texts as wholes, and redaction critics have come to realise that they should pay more attention to the texts themselves than to their history of growth.

The result of redaction criticism is that scholars nowadays commonly speak of the theology of the different authors of New Testament texts, such as the theology of Mark, and so on.

At this point it seems necessary to make a critical remark about the methods we have now discussed. Traditional historical criticism of the gospel tradition has reached its limits. There is little that can be added to current hypothesis on the synoptic problem, or, for example, the relationship between the synoptics and the Gospel of John in view of traditional historical criticism. This is mainly due to the present state of evidence. Our sources are very limited. It is important to realise that there is such a problem as the synoptic problem, and it is imperative to make readers of the New Testament aware of it. When it comes to the methods we have treated, it becomes difficult to continue the process of 'disintegrating criticism'. The assumption that there is a direct continuity between the oral and literary phases of the gospel tradition, on the grounds of which the preliterary oral stages can be reconstructed in more than a speculative way, is no longer tenable (cf. Kelber 1983:1ff). Recovery of the preliterary forms and their meanings is well-nigh impossible – in view of our limited knowledge of the preliterary stages of the gospel tradition. Once oral tradition is inscripturated, it becomes completely changed. In a certain sense it is stripped of its past because all that remains in the written texts are traces of tradition without their preliterary contexts.

2.1.2.5 Historico-religio approach

We have noticed how important it is to understand a particular text within its own time and circumstances. In addition to socio-historical information, knowledge of religious ideas which were current in the area and period when a text was written is also of significance. Although Christianity has its origin in Judaism and started in Palestine, hellenistic religions and religious ideas are of great significance for the study of the religious world of the New Testament, because of the influence of Hellenism on the people living in Palestine and Asia Minor in the first century C.E.

At the turn of this century the religio-historical study of the New Testament was stimulated by a series of studies by members of the so-called *Religionsgeschichtliche Schule* of Göttingen (cf. Lüdemann & Schröder 1987). Gunkel (1910), one of the pioneers in this field, proposed the hypothesis that the 'religion of the New Testament' was influenced in its origin and development by foreign religions, and that these influences were transmitted into early Christian religion through Judaism. With regard to resurrection, for example, he asserts (1910:78) that Jewish ideas about resurrection (cf. 4 Ezr 7:29), with which the disciples were acquainted, should be understood against the background of dying and rising gods in non-Jewish religions and their influence upon Judaism. However this may be (cf. Vorster 1989), what is noteworthy is the fact that Gunkel and others assumed that the Christian religion was influenced in its beginnings by more religions than Judaism. 'Influence', 'background', 'motifs' and parallel thoughts and statements were basic to this approach in the early days of its application to the New Testament. It was maintained that to explain any religious idea, such as resurrection, one has to study the genesis of such beliefs by comparing parallel statements and motifs in different religions.

The purpose of religio-historical investigation has, however, been redefined (cf. also Berger & Colpe 1987). It is better to define it in terms of historical understanding and explanation of what people thought and believed when they spoke about religious phenomena. The main emphasis, in other words, is not on the searching for influence and genesis. It is an attempt to study patterns of thought with a view of understanding the thought world of the New Testament; that is, the religio-historical context of New Testament thinking about religious phenomena. Not what we think about baptism or life after death, but what people in the religio-historical context of the New Testament thought about these phenomena is important. This context is very large and includes Judaism, Hellenistic religions, such as the traditional Greek and Roman religions, mystery religions and gnosticism.

Each pattern of thought, each parallel statement or tradition should be studied in its original context, its reinterpretation(s) and in its use in the New Testament in order to establish what New Testament authors tried to communicate. It is of no use, for example, simply to establish that Jews and Christians believed in life after death or that immersions occur in the Qumran community and early Christianity. What is important is what they believed. In order to determine that one needs to investigate common thought patterns very carefully. What is more, one has to take into account that ideas often develop and are reinterpreted. Although the Pharisees, for instance, were Jews, their thoughts on a particular aspect of Jewish belief need not necessarily be the same as, say, the Maccabees, who were also Jews. That is why it is so important to establish what people thought at a particular time. Even when the Old Testament is quoted or alluded to in the New Testament, it is important to determine which version was used, a Hebrew or a Greek version, since the translation of the Hebrew text into Greek was also a transformation of Hebrew thought into Greek thought.

Religio-historical criticism helps the reader of the New Testament to understand and explain New Testament religious ideas historically, that is within the context of first century religiosity.

2.2. The New Testament and historiography

Historical criticism also concerns the history of the life and works of Jesus and the birth and growth of the primitive church, that is, the history of the persons and events concerned. In view of the lack of other sources, the New Testament and its writings are important for the construction of the history of the period concerned. Since I have dealt with the problem elsewhere I shall largely make use of the material and arguments I have advanced in that respect (cf. Vorster 1984). The first question we have to deal with is whether we can in any respect regard the New Testament or parts of it as history.

2.2.1 The New Testament as history

Very few scholars, if any, would nowadays claim that the New Testament or parts of it, which include the writings of Luke, are history books in the modern sense of the word. In spite of the fact that Luke is often regarded as a historian, albeit a Hellenistic historian (cf. Plumacher 1972), that does not mean that we can regard Luke's writings as history books of Jesus and the early beginnings of the church from Jerusalem to Rome. The following questions therefore immediately arise: What is history? And, how could Luke be regarded as a historian and his works not be history? It is often argued that there is a great difference between ancient (uncritical) historiography and 'modern' critical historiography, and that Luke as historian must be judged in terms of what can be expected of a historian of his age and not of a historian of the post-Enlightenment period (cf. Den Boer 1986; Van Unnik 1978). This is acceptable only if it does not lead to an uncritical acceptance of Luke's writings as 'factive' (historically true in the uncritical sense) and other non-canonical writings of the same kind as 'fictive'. Even in the first century historians were expected 'to say (exactly) what happened', 'to sacrifice to truth only' and to be 'fearless, incorruptible, free, a lover of free speech and the truth, as the comic poet says, calling figs figs and a boat a boat' (cf. Lucian, Πῶς δεῖ ἱστορίαν συγγράφειν 39,41). Even so, there is much more to the problem than simply to accept that Luke was a Hellenistic historian who kept to the rules of Hellenistic historiography, important as the comparison between Luke and his contemporary historians may be (cf. Güttgemanns 1983).

The crux of the matter lies in the relationship between history and language, irrespective of whether we are referring to the first or the twentieth century. I am referring to the problems of language and reference, text and reality, history and truth, objectivity in history and similar matters. These are the concerns of historians of life and works of Jesus and the beginnings of Christianity.

There is no possibility of regarding the writings of the New Testament or parts of them as 'history' in the modern sense of the word. That does of course not imply that there are not historical references, historical material, artefacts, so to speak, that can be used for historical construction in the New Testament. On the contrary, the writings of the New Testament are invaluable sources for the writing of the history of Jesus and the primitive church, as we shall see below.

2.2.2 The New Testament as a source for history

None of the writings of the New Testament were written specifically with a view to giving a historical survey of the words and deeds of Jesus or the birth and growth of the church and the birth of Christianity. And none of these present reality as it really happened. Even Luke-Acts, which comes closest to what may be called a history of Jesus and the primitive church in the ancient sense of the word 'history', is anything but historical in the post-Enlightenment sense of the word. And there is no other book of the New Testament that gives a historical survey of any person or event.

This does not imply that the writings of the New Testament cannot be used as sources for historical construction. On the contrary. Except for a few extra-canonical writings these are the only written sources we have to construct a history of the life and works of Jesus and early Christian beginnings. We are limited in more than one way. First of all there is a lack of sources and secondly our sources are totally insufficient as far as events and persons are concerned. What do we really know about 'the Twelve', Simon Peter, James the brother of Jesus, James and John the sons of Zebedee, Thomas, Joseph, Barnabas, Apollos, Paul and his helpers and the evangelists Matthew, John, Mark and Luke? There is, however, no reason for despair. Historical construction is in any case a painstaking undertaking in which 'fact' and 'fiction' struggle against each other in terms of *probability*. The nature of our sources and the nature of historiography explain the diversity in approaches and findings about Jesus and the origins of Christianity, including the history of the early period of the church.

The reasons why people are interested in historical construction and the purpose for which it is done are not always the same. This can be illustrated by the interest in the historical Jesus with regard to the so-called Old and New Quests. In the Old Quest people were interested in reconstructing the life of 'Jesus of Nazareth as he actually was' by means of the 'objective historical method' of the nineteenth century. 'Jesus of Nazareth' thus became the synonym for 'the historical Jesus' because the two terms coincided. As Robinson (1983:28) observes, 'For the twentieth century this is no longer obvious', because of a new view on the nature of history and the possibilities of reconstruction. In view of this, the term 'historical Jesus' came to refer to 'what can be known of Jesus of Nazareth by means of scientific methods of the historian' (Robinson 1983:29), that is, 'the historian's Jesus'. The 'historical Jesus' of the New Quest is therefore no longer 'Jesus of Nazareth as he actually was', since the hope to reconstruct such a Jesus is fiction. The history of Jesus survived only as *kerygma*. For this reason and also because of the historian's own historicity,

> ...it is easy to see that all that Jesus actually was is not likely to be fully grasped, objectively demonstrated and definitely stated by historical research in any given period (Robinson 1983:30).

The New Quest was, in view of the aforesaid, never intended as a renewed attempt to restore Jesus of Nazareth as he actually was. The purpose of the New Quest was: '... to test the validity of the *kerygma's* identification of *its* understanding of existence with Jesus' existence' (Robinson 1983:94). Or to put it differently, to test the continuity between the historical Jesus and the *kerygma* that we find in the New Testament (cf. Bultmann 1965:6ff). In order to avoid docetism, a New Quest was necessitated, it was argued, because the *kerygma* was concerned about the historicity of Jesus – the relation between the message of Jesus of Nazareth and the *kerygma* of the church.

It is clear from both these quests that historical inquiry was not and cannot be the foundation of Christian faith. It is not on the ground of the historicity of any matter mentioned in the New Testament that Christians believe. If the purpose of historical interpretation is regarded as the search for reasons to believe, historical investigation becomes disastrous. It is the *kerygma* of the church which forms the basis of faith, not historicity. On the other hand, one should keep in mind that 'historical events' seem to be very important to many post-Enlightenment Christians. Not everybody will be willing to accept Lessing's statement that *accidental truths of history can never become proof of necessary truths of reason* (cf. Peters 1977:229-34; Hartlich 1978:467-84). For many historical investigation provides confidence.

The difficulties of historiography concerning Jesus and the birth of the church, can further be illustrated by current investigations about Jesus. One of the problems with the gospel tradition, as we have seen, is the different contexts, forms and wording in which the Jesus tradition was transmitted. This is specifically true of the sayings of Jesus. One of the pioneers in the field of establishing the exact wording (*ipsissima verba*) of the sayings of Jesus was J. Jeremias, a New Testament scholar of Göttingen. He and others developed so-called criteria for the authenticity of the sayings of Jesus. In spite of these criteria and recent attempts to refine and improve these criteria (cf. Boring 1988), there is little consensus about what Jesus really said and how many of the sayings that bear his name in the Gospels are original. The problem is further complicated by the fact that it is clear that it will never be possible to construct the actual contexts of communication of the sayings of Jesus completely. Since the sayings are often transmitted in different contexts of communication by the evangelists, it is probable that the original contexts are lost for ever. On the other hand, since historiography is about probabilities and interpretation, possible frameworks for the teaching can be constructed, and has been done successfully. This is illustrated by the conviction that eschatology is an important formative factor in the teaching of Jesus, and especially with regard to his teaching about the kingdom of God.

Because of the difficulties mentioned, E. P. Sanders (1985), approached the problem of the life and works of Jesus from another perspective by focusing on the indisputable facts in the life of Jesus. These are:

(1) Jesus was baptized by John the Baptist.
(2) Jesus was a Galilean who preached and healed.
(3) Jesus called disciples and spoke of their being twelve.
(4) Jesus confined his activity to Israel.
(5) Jesus engaged in a controversy about the temple.
(6) Jesus was crucified outside Jerusalem by the Roman authorities.
(7) After his death Jesus' followers continued as an identifiable movement.
(8) At least some Jews persecuted at least parts of the new movement.

(Sanders 1985:11)

This is an improvement on the emphasis normally put on the sayings material, since the evidence is at least more secure for these so-called facts, and because it opens the field of inquiry. The problem, however, is that these facts are not self-explanatory and self-interpreting. They still have to be interpreted and put into a framework of understanding. That explains why D. J. Harrington (1987:36) has recently drawn attention to

> seven different images of Jesus that have been proposed by scholars in recent years, the differences relating to the different Jewish backgrounds against which they have chosen to locate their image of the historical Jesus.

These images include Jesus the Jew being any of the following: an eschatological prophet, a political revolutionary, a magician, a Hillelite or proto-Pharisee, an Essene, a Galilean charismatic or a Galilean rabbi. These images are the result of historical investigation and underscore the difficulties of constructing an image of Jesus of Nazareth.

Similar problems exist with regard to other aspects of the history of the birth and growth of the church. Our sources are scanty and insufficient. What are the roots of the church in Egypt, for example? Who were the first Christians in Rome and other centres in Asia Minor? Who were the so-called opponents of Paul? These and many other questions of importance for historians can be answered only partly. Suffice it to indicate that historical criticism is a challenging and an important endeavour of New Testament scholars to understand the sources and the beginnings of Christianity.

Historical construction is, however, not limited to historical facticity, as many would have it. The purpose of historical construction is to provide a background against which the writings of the New Testament can be read – and is read knowingly or unknowingly. Those who think that Christianity formed a mono-lithic unity from the beginning are sometimes stunned by the discovery that the New Testament contains diverse ideas about such important things as Chris-tology. We have already noticed above how important the priority of one or other Gospel is for the development of ideas in early Christianity. Part of the history of the primitive church is the sequence and order of events from Jesus to the evangelists and from the early apostles to Paul and eventually to his followers. That is why it is necessary to construct the history of the church and what the early Christians thought.

Although we do not have an exact picture of the early history of Christianity, it is usually held that primitive Christianity first became a Jewish sect. After-wards it became largely Gentile under the influence of Hellenism. This vague outline has to be filled out by constructions of the birth process and growth of a religious movement, but also of a thought process, namely the doctrine and be-liefs of that movement. It is traditionally being done in terms of Judaism versus Hellenism. This is obviously an oversimplification, as recent studies on the spread and influence of Hellenism have shown (cf. Vorster 1981:48-52). Despite the limited sources, our insights develop by testing the validity of hypotheses, re-visiting old problems and applying new methods.

During the last two decades historians of the New Testament era have ap-proached a number of problems of historical nature afresh by using insights of other disciplines such as sociology and anthropology. Although this has advanced research, the main problem that confronts us is the lack of sources. Many of these studies have broadened our vision and have stimulated scholars to rethink old axioms (cf. Theissen 1977). Even the study of the social history of New Testament times has profited from these new impulses (cf. Meeks 1983). In addition, much has been done to unlock the world of the New Testament in terms of archaeology of the ancient world. There seems to be a growing interest in archaeological evidence from Palestine and elsewhere and slowly, but surely a new picture of the social history of early Christianity is formed (cf. e.g. Lampe 1987).

3. Conclusion

In conclusion, it is important to address a few important aspects of historio-graphy – ideas about which have changed through the ages. I am referring to matters such as history and language, history and truth, and history and objec-tivity. We have already noticed with regard to the Old and New Quests that the purpose of historiography is different in the two approaches. Insights into the nature of historiography, and therefore also historical criticism, develop and change, and it is important for New Testament scholars to take note of these changes. The first question we have to address is what happens when 'facts' are described? Do we have a verbal representation or imitation of reality?

A history book does not offer a one-to-one correspondence between object and description, because language does not work in that way. What does it then offer? Historians normally select and arrange their material with respect to change in space and time. Historical description, in other words, is nothing else than narrative, human construction of past events and persons. Lévi Strauss's idea that history is never only *history of*, but always *history for* in the sense of being written with some ideological view in mind, is very attractive. He argues that to historise any structure, to write history, is to mythologise it (cf. White 1975:51). If history is a kind of narrative and narrative is the remaking of reality, matters such as text and reality, historical truth and objectivity become very interesting. Remaking of reality is not reality *an sich*.

What is historical truth? Truth is very often regarded as *correspondence* between an idea and an object,

> ...a statement is true if it corresponds to the facts, that is, if the statement expresses a relation which holds between the real object symbolised by those terms (cf. Gilliam 1976:244).

On the other hand truth can also be explained in terms of *coherence*, '...the locus of truth is internal to the world of historical idea, and its criterion is coherence'. Consider the following examples. The resurrection of Jesus is a historical truth only if he really had been raised from the dead (correspondence theory). Likewise the miracle stories can only be true if they really happened. We soon run into trouble with such a view of truth. What about the speeches in Acts and elsewhere in the New Testament (cf. the Sermon on the Mount!)? Are they true in the sense of a correspondence theory? Certainly not. But Lucian (Πῶς δεῖ, 58) already reminds us that,

> If a person has to be introduced to make a speech, it is especially important that his language suits his person and the subject, and that he speaks as clearly as possible.

'Factive' and 'fictive' are very misleading terms when it comes to historical truth and history as the remaking of reality. This has been realised long ago by ancient authors like Quintilian and Cicero (cf. Güttgemanns 1983:16ff).

Objectivity in historiography is related to the problem of historical truth because it also depends on one's views about historiography and philosophy of history. Because history is narrative, and narrative is told from a certain perspective for a specific purpose, one can hardly speak of objectivity in the sense of a correspondence theory. On the other hand, however, the historian is a member of a 'scientific community' and his findings and his narrative have to comply with the rules of the game. His results are subjected to control and scrutiny, and in that sense a 'set of rules' confirms its objectivity (cf. Nipperdey 1979:329-42; Junker & Reisinger 1974:1-46; Rüsen 1980:188-98).

These few introductory remarks illustrate the difficulties and the importance of historical criticism in the process of understanding and interpreting the writings of the New Testament. Historical criticism has come to stay. What changes are our insights into the nature of literature, history and historiography. That is why each reader of the New Testament, but especially New Testament scholars have to face the challenges of discovering the past of which Jesus of Nazareth, the birth of Christianity, and the history of early Christian writings form an important part, in order to discover the truth of their own existence.

BIBLIOGRAPHY

1. GENERAL

Demandt, A. 1979. Was heisst 'historisch denken'? *Geschichte in Wissenschaft und Unterricht* 30, 463-478.

Fuchs, W. P. 1979. Was heisst das: 'Bloss zeigen, wie es eigentlich gewesen'? *Geschichte in Wissenschaft und Unterricht* 30, 655-667.

Gilliam, H. 1976. The Dialectics of Realism and Idealism in Modern Historiographic Theory. *History and Theology* 15, 231-256.

Hartlich, C. 1978. Historisch-kritische Methode in ihrer Anwendung auf *Geschehnis*aussagen der Hl. Schrift. *Zeitschrift für Theologie und Kirche* 75, 467-484.

Humphreys, R. S. 1980. The Historian, his Documents, and the Elementary Modes of Historical Thought. *History and Theology* 19, 1-20.

Junker, D. & Reisinger, P. 1974. Was kann Objektivität in der Geschichtswissenschaft heissen, und wie ist sie möglich? in T. Schneider (ed.). *Methodenprobleme der Geschichtswissenschaft.* München: Oldenburg, 1-46.

Kosseleck, R. & Stempel, W.-D. (eds.) 1973. *Geschichte: Ereignis und Erzählung.* München: Fink.

Maren-Griesbach, M. 1977. *Methoden der Literaturwissenschaft.* 6. Aufl. München: Francke. (Uni-Taschenbücher 121.)

McCullagh, C. B. 1984. *Justifying Historical Descriptions.* Cambridge: Cambridge University Press.

Nations, A. L. 1983. Historical Criticism and the Current Methodological Crisis. *Scottish Journal of Theology* 36, 59-71.

Nipperdey, T. 1979. Kann Geschichte objektiv sein? *Geschichte in Wissenschaft und Unterricht* 30, 329-342.

Peters, C. H. 1977. How Important Are Historical Events for Religion? Reflection on G. E. Lessing's Philosophy of Religion. *Currents in Theology and Mission* 4, 229-234.

Rüsen, J. 1980. Zum Problem der historischen Objektivität. *Geschichte in Wissenschaft und Unterricht* 31, 188-198.

Stern, F. (ed.) 1970. *The Varieties of History. From Voltaire to the Present.* 2nd ed. London: Macmillan.

Van Luxemburg, J., Bal, M. & Weststeijn, W. G. 1982. *Inleiding in de Literatuurwetenschap.* 2nd ed. Muiderberg: Coutinho.

Wellek, R. & Warren, A. 1963. *Theory of Literature.* Harmondsworth: Penguin.

White, H. V. 1975. Historicism, History, and Figurative Imagination, in G. H. Nadel (ed.). *Essays on Historicism*, 48-67. Middletown: Wesleyan University Press. (History and Theory Beiheft 14.)

White, H. V. 1980. The Value of Narrativity in the Representation of Reality. *Critical Inquiry* 7, 5-27.

2. HISTORICAL INTERPRETATION OF THE NEW TESTAMENT

Aune, D. E. 1989. *The New Testament in its Literary Environment*. Philadelphia: Westminster.

Berger, K. & Colpe, C. 1987. *Religionsgeschichtliches Textbuch zum Neuen Testament*. Göttingen: Vandenhoeck & Ruprecht.

Bultmann, R. 1965. *Das Verhältnis der urchristlichen Christusbotschaft zum historischen Jesus*. Heidelberg: Winter.

Bultmann, R. 1970. *Die Geschichte der synoptischen Tradition*. 8. Aufl. Göttingen: Vandenhoeck & Ruprecht.

Conzelmann, H. & Lindemann, A. (eds.) 1975. *Arbeitsbuch zum Neuen Testament*. Tübingen: Mohr. (Uni-Taschenbücher 52.)

Dibelius, M. 1971. *Die Formgeschichte des Evangeliums*. 6. Aufl. Tübingen: Mohr.

Edwards, O. C. 1977. Historical-Critical Method's Failure of Nerve and a Prescription for a Tonic: A Review of Some Recent Literature. *Anglican Theological Review* 59, 115-134.

Epp, E.J. & MacRae, G. W. 1989. *The New Testament and Its Modern Interpreters*. Atlanta: Fortress.

Farmer, W. R. 1964. *The Synoptic Problem: A Critical Analysis*. New York: Macmillan.

Ferguson, E. 1987. *Backgrounds of Early Christianity*. Grand Rapids: Eerdmans.

Friedrich, J., Pohlmann W. & Stuhlmacher, P. 1976. Zur historischen Situation und Intention von Röm 13,1-7. *Zeitschrift für Theologie und Kirche* 73, 131-166.

Gunkel, H. 1910. Zum reiligionsgeschichtlichen Verständnis des Neuen Testaments. 2. Aufl. Göttingen: Vandenhoeck & Ruprecht.

Güttgemanns, G. 1970. *Offene Fragen zur Formgeschichte des Evangeliums: Eine methodologische Skizze der Grundlagenproblematik der Form und Redaktionsgeschichte*. München: Kaiser.

Hahn, F. (Hrsg.) 1985. *Zur Formgeshichte des Evangeliums*. Darmstadt: Wissenschaftliche Buchgesellschaft.

Harvey, V. A. 1967. *The Historian and the Believer: The Morality of Historical Knowledge and Christian Belief*. London: SCM.

Hengel, M. 1973. Historische Methoden und theologische Auslegung des Neuen Testaments. *Kerygma und Dogma* 19, 85-90.

Jeremias, J. 1970. *Die Gleichnisse Jesu*. 8. Aufl. Göttingen: Vandenhoeck & Ruprecht.

Kelber, W. H. 1983. *The Oral and the Written Gospel. The Hermeneutics of Speaking and Writing in the Synoptic Tradition, Mark, Paul and Q*. Philadelphia: Fortress.

Köster, H. 1980. *Einführung in das Neue Testament*. Berlin: De Gruyter.

Krentz, E. 1975. *The Historical-Critical Method*. London: SPCK.

Kümmel, W. G. (Hrsg.) 1965. *Einleitung in das Neue Testament*. 14. Aufl. Heidelberg: Quelle & Meyer.

Kümmel, W. G. 1970. *Das Neue Testament: Geschichte der Erforschung seiner Probleme*. 2. Aufl. Freiburg: Karl Alber.

Lüdemann, G. & Schröder. 1987. *Die Religionsgeschichtliche Schule: Eine Dokumentation*. Göttingen: Vandenhoeck & Ruprecht.

Lührmann, D. 1984. *Auslegung des Neuen Testaments*. Zürich: Theologischer Verlag.

Marshall, I. H. (ed.) 1977. *New Testament Interpretation: Essays on Principles and Methods*. Exeter: Paternoster.

Nations, A. L. 1983. Historical Criticism and the Current Methodological Crisis. *Scottish Journal of Theology* 36, 59-71.

Orchard, B. & Riley, H. 1987. *The Order of the Synoptics: Why Three Synoptic Gospels?* Macon: Mercer University Press.

Robbins, V. K. 1988. The Chreia, in D. E. Aune (ed.). *Greco-Roman Literature and the New Testament*. Atlanta: Scholars Press, 1-24.

Rohde, J. 1966. *Die redaktionsgeschichtliche Methode: Einführung und Sichtung des Forschungsstandes*. Hamburg: Furche Verlag.

Sanders, E. P. & Davies, M. 1989. *Studying the Synoptic Gospels*. London: SCM.

Strecker, G. 1972. *Handlungsorientierter Glaube. Vorstudien zu einer Ethik des Neuen Testaments*. Berlin: Kreuz.

Strecker, G. 1983. Neues Testament (NT), in G. Strecker (ed.). *Theologie im 20. Jahrhundert*. Tübingen: Mohr (Uni-Taschenbücher 1238), 61-145.

Stuhlmacher, P. 1979. *Vom Verstehen des Neuen Testaments: Eine Hermeneutik*. Göttingen: Vandenhoeck & Ruprecht.

Teeple, H. M. 1982. *The Historical Approach to the Bible.* Evanston: Religion and Ethics Institute.
Troeltsch, E. 1913. Ueber historische und dogmatische Methode in der Theologie, in E. Troeltsch. *Gesammelte Schriften. II. Zur religiösen Lage, Religionsphilosophie und Ethik.* Tübingen: Mohr, 729-753.
Tuckett, C. 1983. *Reading the New Testament: Methods of Interpretation.* London: SPCK.
Vielhauer, P. 1975. *Geschichte der urchristlichen Literatur.* Berlin: De Gruyter.
Vorster, W. S. 1980. Mark: Collector, Redactor, Author, Narrator? *Journal of Theology for Southern Africa* 31, 46-61.
Vorster, W. S. 1982. 'Formgeschichte' en 'Redaktionsgeschichte', in A. F. J. Klijn (ed.). *Inleiding tot de Studie van het Nieuwe Testament.* Kampen: Kok, 94-111.
Vorster, W. S. 1984. The Historical Paradigm: Its Possibilities and Limitations. *Neotestamentica* 18, 104-123.
Vorster, W. S. 1989. The Religio-Historical Context of the Resurrection of Jesus and Resurrection Faith in the New Testament. *Neotestamentica* 23, 159-175.
Wenham, D. 1977. Source Criticism, in I. H. Marshall (ed.). *New Testament Interpretation: Essays on Principles and Methods.* Exeter: Paternoster, 139-152.

3. HISTORIOGRAPHY AND THE NEW TESTAMENT

Boring, M. E. 1988. The Historical-Critical Method's 'Criteria of Authenticity': The Beatitudes in Q and Thomas as a Test Case. *Semeia* 44, 9-44.
Conzelmann, H. 1978. *Geschichte des Urchristentums.* Göttingen: Vandenhoeck & Ruprecht.
Den Boer, W. 1968. Graeco-Roman Historiography in its Relation to Biblical and Modern Thinking. *History and Theology* 7, 60-75.
Epp, E.J. & MacRae, G. W. 1989. *The New Testament and its Modern Interpreters.* Atlanta: Fortress.
Farmer, W. R. 1964. *The Synoptic Problem: A Critical Analysis.* New York: Macmillan.
Ferguson, E. 1987. *Backgrounds of Early Christianity.* Grand Rapids: Eerdmans.
Güttgemanns, G. 1983. In welchem Sinne ist Lukas 'Historiker'? Die Beziehung von Luk 1,1-4 und Papias zur antiken Rhetorik. *Linguistica Biblica* 54, 5-61.
Harrington, D. J. 1987. The Jewishness of Jesus. *Bible Review* 3, 32-41.
Lampe, P. 1987. *Die stadrömischen Christen in den ersten beiden Jahrhunderten.* Tübingen: Mohr. (Wissenschaftliche Unterzuchungen zum Neuen Testaments 2,18.)
Meeks, W. A. 1983. *The First Urban Christians: The Social World of the Apostle Paul.* New Haven: Yale University Press.
Mulder, M. J. (ed.) 1988. *Mikra.* Section 2, v. 1: *Text, Translation, Reading and Interpretation of the Hebrew Bible in Ancient Judaism and Early Christianity.* Assen: Van Gorcum. (Compendium rerum Iudaicarum ad Novum Testamentum.)
Plümacher, E. 1972. *Lukas als hellenistischer Schriftsteller: Studien zur Apostelgeschichte.* Göttingen: Vandenhoeck & Ruprecht.
Robinson, J. M. 1983. *A New Quest of the Historical Jesus.* Philadelphia: Fortress.
Robinson, J. M. (ed.) 1977. *The Nag Hammadi Library in English: Translated by the Coptic Gnostic Library Project of the Institute for Antiquity and Christianity.* Leiden: Brill.
Safrai, S. & Stern, M. (eds.) 1974. *The Jewish People in the First Century.* Section 1, vol. 1: *Historical Geography, Political History, Social, Cultural and Religious Life and Institutions.* Assen: Van Gorcum. (Compendium rerum Iudaicarum ad Novum Testamentum.)
Safrai, S. & Stern, M. (eds.) 1976. *The Jewish People in the First Century.* Section 1, vol. 2: *Historical Geography, Political History, Social, Cultural and Religious Life and Institutions.* Assen: Van Gorcum. (Compendium rerum Iudaicarum ad Novum Testamentum.)
Sanders, E. P. 1985. *Jesus and Judaism.* Philadelphia: Fortress.
Schürer, E. 1973-1987. *The History of the Jewish People in the Age of Jesus Christ (175 B.C - A.D. 135).* 3 vols. (A new English version rev. and ed. by G. Vermes, F. Millar and M. Goodman.) Edinburgh: T & T Clark.
Stone, M. (ed.) 1984. *Jewish Writings of the Second Temple Period.* Section 2, vol. 2: *Apocrypha, Pseudepigrapha, Qumran Sectarian Writings, Philo, Josephus.* Assen: Van Gorcum. (Compendium rerum Iudaicarum ad Novum Testamentum.)
Theissen, G. 1977. *Soziologie der Jesusbewegung: Ein Beitrag zur Entstehungsgeschichte des Urchristentums.* München: Kaiser.
Van Unnik, W. C. 1978. *Flavius Josephus als historischer Schriftsteller.* Heidelberg: Schneider.

Van Unnik, W. C. 1979. Luke's Second Book and the Rules of Hellenistic Historiography, in J. Kremer (ed.). *Les Actes des Apôtres: Traditions, Rédaction, Théologie*. Leuven: Duculot (Bibliotheca Ephemeridum Theologicarum Lovaniensum 48), 37-60.
Vorster, W. S. 1981. On the Origins of Christianity: A Religio-Historical Perspective, in W. S. Vorster (ed.). *Christianity among the Religions*. Pretoria: UNISA, 36-56.
Vorster, W. S. 1984. The Historical Paradigm: Its Possibilities and Limitations. *Neotestamentica* 18, 104-123.

B. TEXT

J. H. PETZER

ECLECTICISM AND THE TEXT OF THE NEW TESTAMENT

1. Introduction

Textual criticism has a twofold purpose, first and foremost to reconstruct the original version of a book and secondly, to interpret the documentary evidence of that book (i.e. the documents in which the text was transmitted) in the interest of reconstructing the history of the transmission of that text. Although these two purposes are interrelated and the first cannot be achieved without pursuing the second, the first has been dominating New Testament textual criticism right from its inception as a scholarly discipline in the eighteenth century. Even prior to that in the publication of texts by Erasmus, Beza, Stephanus, and others, the goals of the exercise were everytime formulated as being to supply a good representative of the original copy of the New Testament.

Whereas there was no real methodology in the scholarly sense of the word available to the initial editors of the text of the New Testament, the early development of a method by scholars such as Bengel, Semler and Griesbach illustrates that it was soon realised that the road to solving the riddle of the chaacter of the original New Testament leads through a sound reconstruction of the history of the text, particularly the earliest history (i.e. prior to the fourth century).

This direction was firmly established in the ninetheenth century by scholars such as Carl Lachmann, Tischendorf and Westcott and Hort, and in the twentieth century by scholars such as Streeter and Von Soden. All of these scholars were brilliant text historians, who substantiated their editions of the text upon manuscripts proven to be good representatives of the originals through detailed reconstructions of the history of the text. The general character of these methodologies was to choose the best manuscript among the existing and available manuscripts based upon its position in the history of the text, and to use this manuscript as the basis of the text.

For reasons not to be discussed here (cf. Petzer 1986), the pursuance of this ideal of an exclusively historical approach to the solving of the problems of the New Testament text was not to continue long beyond the turn of the century, and through the influence of scholars such as C. H. Turner, Lagrange, Kilpatrick and A. F. J. Klijn, New Testament textual critics started to develop a more eclectic approach to the solving of textual problems. Though somewhat radical in the beginning, eclecticism was developed by different scholars later in the century and gained ground until it today forms the most popular method in this discipline (cf. e.g. Epp 1976). It is for example the methodology used in the editing of the influential United Bible Societies' *Greek New Testament*, as well as the twenty-sixth edition of the *Nestle-Aland* text (presented by some of its editors as the new standard text.). (Cf. Petzer 1988 for a more detailed discussion of matters in the brief dicsussion above.)

Because of the dominant position of eclecticism in New Testament textual criticism in the fourth quarter of the twentieth century, the discussion in this chapter focuses on eclecticism. In the methodological part eclecticism as an approach and the different eclectic methods based upon this approach are considered. The so-called 'reasoned eclectic method' is then considered and illustrated in more detail in the practical part.

2. The methodology: Eclecticism as approach and method

2.1 The nature of eclecticism

Eclecticism is best defined by Epp in his article on the role of eclecticism in modern-day textual criticism. According to this definition an electic method is

> a method (1) that treats each text-critical problem (normally a single 'variation-unit') separately and largely in isolation from other problems, (2) that 'chooses' or 'selects' (*eklegomai*) from among available and recognised text-critical criteria those that presumably are appropriate to that particular text-critical situation, and (3) that then applies the selected criteria in such a way as to 'pick' or 'choose' (*eklegomai*) from one or another manuscript and thereby arrive at a text-critical decision for that particular variation-unit (Epp 1976:212; cf. also Aland 1977:22; Metzger 1966:348).

According to this definition an eclectic method is a method that is characterised by (1) the purpose of *choosing the best reading* in text-critical problems; (2) the use of a *set of criteria* to achieve this purpose; and (3) an *isolated, atomistic* or *individual approach* to variation-units, variant readings and criteria in the process of solving textual problems.

2.2 Applications of the eclectic principle

From the broad definition of eclecticism above it is clear that it is possible to apply the eclectic principle in different ways. Consequently, it is possible to distinguish between different eclectic methods. Based upon the contents of the 'set of criteria' one can distinguish between the so-called *rigorous* or *thoroughgoing* eclectic methods, on the one hand, and the so-called *general* (sometimes also called *reasoned*) eclectic methods on the other (cf. also Epp 1976:213).

2.2.1 Thoroughgoing eclecticism

Thoroughgoing eclecticism limits its set of criteria to criteria dealing with internal aspects, i.e. aspects of criticism that have to do with the habits of the author of a text and the habits of scribes. Underlying these methods is the notion that authors are consistent in aspects such as their use of language and their theology, and that scribes either knowingly or unknowingly attempted to alter more difficult readings to less difficult readings or that they were prone to a certain set of unintentional errors, resulting from misreading (or mishearing) the text. A set of criteria, based upon such matters, is then devised and applied to each variant reading in each instance of variation, the purpose being to determine which reading fits best into what the author could (stylistically and theologically) be expected to have written and/or what scribes could be expected to have altered in an attempt to ease out difficulties in the text or what scribes could have been expected to have misread.

The most rigorous application of this method is found in the work of those critics who apply criteria of internal criticism to textual problems in order to determine the original reading in each case of variation. It was used by C. H. Turner in his well-known series of articles on Marcan usage, and the implications thereof for the text of the Second Gospel (Turner 1924-1928; 1927). He was followed by George Kilpatrick, whose work culminated in the privately published *Greek-English Diglot* (Kilpatrick 1961-1964, cf. also Kilpatrick 1963; 1965; 1967). J. Keith Elliott, a former student of Kilpatrick, is currently a prominent supporter of this method. Elliott has done much to describe and defend the method theoretically and he is the only person to give a systematic outline of the criteria used in this method (Elliott 1968; 1972b; 1978). The use of this method by B. Weiss and in particular M.-J. Lagrange ought also to be mentioned, although both these scholars were less rigorous in their use of this method.

Although the criteria used in this method are themselves quite similar to criteria used in general eclectic methods, thoroughgoing eclecticism as a means of editing the text has been criticised fairly heavily in particular by supporters of the general eclectic methods (cf. e.g. Fee 1976; Flatt 1975; Metzger 1968:178). It is said that the method is methodologically biased for its disregard of documentary matters and that it therefore places too much emphasis upon internal aspects, which are viewed as being subjective and arbitrary. In addition the grounds for some of its criteria, e.g. the fact that an author is always consistent in style, have been questioned. Finally it is criticised for the circumstance that the application of the criteria sometimes results in the choice of readings that have only very weak external evidence, e.g. one or two late minuscules, in its favour. For these (and other) reasons this method is widely regarded as not able to solve the problems of the text of the New Testament in a convincing way. Notwithstanding this criticism, it must be said, on the other hand, that this method has called attention to the value and importance of internal evidence in the solving of textual problems. This is an aspect of the methodology that has been largely neglected by supporters of the traditional classical or genealogical approaches.

2.2.2 General eclecticism

Using the same principles and basic methodological outlines as thoroughgoing eclecticism, reasoned eclecticism broadens the set of criteria to include criteria dealing with external or documentary aspects together with internal aspects in its set of criteria. Underlying these methods is the notion that the reconstructed history of the text cannot and ought not be ignored in the final analysis of variant readings.

The basic premise of these methods is that manuscripts are the primary sources of our knowledge of the text and that it must be possible to relate the printed text to some manuscript or group of manuscripts that has historically been determined to represent the original text with greater accuracy than other manuscripts or groups of manuscripts. In other words, the printed text must be linked to existing manuscripts to have any claim of representing the original. For this reason the textual history, based upon an analysis of the documents and their relationship to one another, must be reconstructed and this reconstruction must lead to the identification of a best manuscript with which the text can be associated.

However, for reasons not discussed here, the 'best manuscript' is no longer regarded as such a trustworthy representative of the original text as was customary earlier, with the result that its readings are not followed as slavishly as was done earlier (cf. Petzer 1986). A second premise of these methods is consequently devised, i.e. that each variation-unit ought to be analysed *de novo* in order to see whether the readings of the best manuscript are supported by other criteria or whether other criteria point towards the originality of other readings in the unit.

To reconcile these two aspects, documentary history and other (internal) evidence in a single method, the results of the reconstruction of the history of the text are reinterpreted and reformulated so as to allow the textual critic to reconstruct the history of every variant reading in each variation-unit in isolation from the others (cf. Petzer 1988). By using aspects of the reconstructed history of the text in general, and by interpreting the documentary evidence in support of each reading in each variation-unit against the background of this general history, the critic attempts to reconsruct the history of each variation-unit individually. Based upon this reconstruction he then chooses the 'best reading' in each case of variation.

The method or the set of criteria, therefore, consists of two categories of criteria, though not always formally distinguished from each other. The first is *documentary* or *external evidence*. Its purpose is to determine which reading is supported by the earliest and best documents and it deals with aspects of the documentary history of the text. The second is *internal evidence*. Its purpose is to identify that reading that most probably gave rise to the others and it deals with aspects of the contents of the text and the idiosyncracies and customs of scribes. These two aspects are present in all versions of the general eclectic method and is what distinguishes it from the thoroughgoing eclectic method.

Within the general eclectic method it is, however, possible to make a further distinction between what may be called the *reasoned eclectic method* and the *local-genealogical method*. The main difference between these two methodologies regards the historical model underlying their use of external or documentary evidence. In the end it also has some consequences for the formulation of the method and the exact place of external evidence in the method.

2.2.2.1 Reasoned eclecticism

Reasoned eclecticism is the most popular method in New Testament textual criticism today. Though being used throughout the world, North American scholars, in particular Bruce Metzger, have done much to develop and formulate it. Metzger's formulation of the method in his well known introduction to New Testament Textual Criticism (Metzger 1968:207-211), repeated in the *Textual Commentary* (Metzger 1971:xxiv-xxviii), seems to have been taken over by quite a number of textual critics (cf. e.g. Fee 1982b; Ehrman & Plunkett 1983, to mention only two examples), and from the *Textual Commentary* it is clear that this was also the basic procedure upon which NA[26] and the UBS series of texts were based.

Characteristic of this method is the detailed distinction between the different kinds of evidence. The criteria for the consideration of external evidence is by definition very clearly distinguished from internal evidence so as to make it methodologically possible to consider the two kinds of evidence apart from each other. Within the criteria of internal evidence distinction is also made between those criteria directed at determining the transcriptional probability (having to do with scribal customs and idiosyncracies) of each reading and those criteria directed at determining the intrinsic probability (having to do with the author) of each reading. By definition external evidence is said to be more important than internal evidence, although there are some examples where internal evidence is allowed to tip the scale in the favour of some reading notwithstanding strong external evidence in favour of rival readings (cf. e.g. discussions on Lk 23:34; 1 Cor 13:3 in the *Textual Commentary*).

Underlying the consideration of external evidence is the reconstruction of the history of the text. The model followed in this method is based upon Westcott and Hort's model and only slight changes to that model are proposed, probed mainly by the evidence of the newly discovered papyri and alterations to the model earlier in the twentieth century. It boils down to the fact that Westcott and Hort's neutral text (ℵ, B) is no longer acknowledged as a neutral text. The neutral manuscripts together with P[75] and a few others are now considered to be part of a local text and called the proto- or early Alexandrian text, which implies that they are no longer viewed as such good representatives of the original as was the case in the Hortian model. In following Streeter, room is, secondly, being made for a fourth (local) text, the Caesarean text, which is placed somewhere between the Alexandrian and Western texts. The same place as in the Hortian model is assigned to the Western and Byzantine texts in the reasoned eclectic model. (Cf. Metzger 1968:211-219; Fee 1968; 1974a; 1974b; 1982a; Hurtado 1981; Ehrman 1986, to mention only a few discussions of historical matters)

Although being the most popular method today, this method has been criticised for a number of things (cf. e.g. Elliott 1968:1-11; 1975; Aland 1967). Methodologically speaking it has been criticised for not being eclectic in its practical application, since it results in almost every instance in the choice of the readings of at least one of the 'best manuscripts', i.e. the proto-Alexandrian manuscripts. Therewith it has been criticised for internal criteria not getting due consideration. Finally the historical model has also been criticised for keeping too close to Westcott and Hort's model, with the result that many of the papyri and other early manuscripts are forced into text-types to which they in fact do not belong.

2.2.2.2 The local-genealogical method

Unwilling to call the method he uses eclectic (cf. introduction to NA[26] pp. 5*, 43*), Aland prefers to speak of a 'local-genealogical method', the reason being that his method is focussed upon establishing a genealogy of readings at each place of variation in the text (which is merely another way of saying that the history of the variation-unit is to be reconstructed). Using the term 'local-genealogical' already in the introduction of NA[26], it was not until the appearance of the Alands' introduction that the method was described in more detail (Aland & Aland 1982:282-283).

From this description it is clear that the main difference between this method and the reasoned eclectic method is that it does not work with categories of criteria. The way in which it is formulated in the Alands' introduction makes it clear that they prefer to work with a number of broad general principles ('*Grundregeln*'), rather than detailed formulated criteria. The principles are, however, in general the same as those in the reasoned eclectic method, although the principles dealing with internal evidence are fewer and less developed than those used in the reasoned eclectic method. The result is that external evidence gets much more emphasis in this method than in the previously discussed method. In practice this method might be regarded as being closer to the old classical method, with its two branches, *recensio* and *emendatio*, than to the eclectic method.

The greatest difference between the two methodologies concerns, however, the historical model underlying the basic part of the method (cf. Aland 1981; 1982; Aland & Aland 1982:57-81). Whereas the reasoned eclectic method attaches itself to Westcott and Hort, Aland rather emphatically departs from Westcott and Hort. His main difference with Westcott and Hort, and therewith also the reasoned eclectic model, concerns the position of the papyri, the Caesarean text and aspects of the Western text. His premise is that the papyri do not fit well into text-types in Westcott and Hort's model, with the result that they seem to have mixed texts. (This is incidentally acknowledged by reasoned eclectics, cf. e.g. the classification of the papyri in Metzger 1968:247-255). Aland contends that this apparent mixture is in fact no mixture between text-types, since the papyri antedate the earliest manuscripts of the local text-types upon which Westcott and Hort's model was constructed. For this reason he concludes that the local text-types did not come into being before the third or fourth centuries. Prior to this period he identifies the period of the *Early text* ('Frühtext'), to which the majority of the early manuscripts belong, in which there are no local text-types and from which the local texts in the Hortian model developed. On the basis of their quality the manuscripts belonging to this early period may, however, be divided into 'qualitative text types', present in all the geographical areas where the text was transmitted. From these 'qualitative text-types' there developed in later centuries basically two local texts the Alexandrian (which was further developed through mixture and recensional activities and ended in the Egyptian text) and the D-text (the old Western text – the change of name being urged by the fact that the text did not originate in the West, as was thought for a long time, nor was it limited to the West in any geographical sense, cf. B. Aland 1986). There is an important difference between Aland and Westcott and Hort as regards the value of the Western text in that he does not acknowledge that the short Western readings (Western noninterpolations) are of any special value for the reconstruction of the original text. No Caesarean text is distinguished and the Byzantine text takes the same position as in the models of both Westcott and Hort and the reasoned eclectics.

This method and historical model of Aland have been on the table for less than a decade. It does not seem, however, to appeal to representatives of particularly the reasoned eclectic method. One may speculate that the lack of detail in the model might be one reason for it. Also the new concept of 'qualitative' instead of 'local' text-types may be somewhat strange to supporters of Westcott and Hort's model. The positive elements of the model, however, lie in exactly this aspect, i.e. the redefinition of the earliest text-types as being 'qualitative' and not local. It seems that this view does explain some aspects of the text of the papyri that the traditional model is not capable of explaining. However, the whole model will have to be spelled out in more detail before final judgements can be made.

3. The practice: Luke 23:34

The practical application and illustration of the text-critical method follows the broad outlines of the reasoned eclectic method. The main reason for this is the fact that the local-genealogical method, though very appealing indeed, has not yet been described in such terms that one may regard it as having reached any kind of finality. With Aland having explained that his main task in establishing the Institute at Münster was to gather the necessary material and that the analysis of that material is the task of the future generation (Aland 1985:61-62), one can expect the methodology described above, to be refined and rounded off in the years to come. This is particularly true with regard to the history of the text, which plays a major role in this method.

The method applied here to solve the problem of Jesus' so-called First Saying on the Cross (Lk 23:34), therefore, functions within the broad outlines of the reasoned eclectic method. It consists of two processes, the consideration of documentary evidence and the consideration of internal evidence.

A note as regards the nature and relation of these two processes is at this stage important. Because textual criticism is basically an historical discipline, i.e. working with an historical problem, its methodology should also be basically historical in nature. For this reason the first process in this methodology will always be the most important and the detail and accuracy with which the history of the readings in the variation-unit can be reconstructed, will in the end determine the success of the final decision.

3.1 Documentary evidence

The first step in the reconstruction of the history of a variant reading is to make an assessment of the documents in which the reading is found and to evaluate the historical value of these documents against the general outline of the history of the text.

In Luke 23:34 there are basically two variant readings (cf. IGNTP 1987, for full apparatus):

(1)   The inclusion of the disputed passage: ὁ δὲ ᾽Ιησοῦς ἔλεγεν, Πάτερ, ἄφες αὐτοῖς, οὐ γὰρ οἴδασιν τί ποιοῦσιν, appearing in documents such as ℵ*,c A C Db E L f1 (f13) 28 33 565 700 892 et al. it vg syrc copbo(mss) Diatessaron Hegesippus Justin Irenaeuslat Hippolytos Origenlat and many of the

later fathers.

(2)   The omission of the passage: P75 $\aleph^a$ B D* W Θ 0124 579 1241 it$^{a,b(c),d}$ syr^s cop$^{sa,bo(mss)}$ Cyril.

In assessing the documentary evidence wherein each reading appears, one will look primarily at the *date, geographical distribution* and *genealogical relationship* of the documents and the texts in the documents. To safeguard one from making merely mechanical judgements (i.e. choosing the reading of the proto-Alexandrian witnesses by default), the evidence of these three aspects of documentary evidence must be integrated with the intent of determining which reading has the earliest most independent (geographically and genealogically) witnesses in its favour. This part of the method is the cornerstone of the whole method and the more detail and certainty one can attain in this reconstruction of the documentary history of the readings in the variation-unit, the more trustworthy will one's final conclusions be.

Let us illustrate this procedure by looking at the documentary evidence of the readings in Luke 23:34.

The earliest documents containing the short reading (reading 2 above) date from the third century (P75 and the Sahidic version). Reading 1, on the other hand, has evidence from witnesses in the second century (Hegessippus, Irenaeus, Justin and the Diatessaron) in its favour. On its own it seems thus that the reading 1 has more in its favour than reading 2.

When the date of the witnesses is, however, integrated with the geographical distribution and genealogical relationships of the witnesses, this picture changes. Reading 2 was widely known early in the textual transmission. It appears in almost all the early Alexandrian witnesses, notably P75, B and the Sahidic version (which shows that it was known in Egypt in the 3rd century). It appears in some early Western witnesses, notably the early Latin witnesses **a** and **d** (both belonging to the European text of the *Vetus Latina*) as well as the Greek Codex Bezae (which suggests that it was known in Europe in the same time). It appears in the early Syriac tradition through its occurrence in the Synaitic Syriac version and the Syriac commentary of Cyril (which suggests that it was known in Syria at more or less the same time). Finally, it appears in the early sources of the Byzantine text through its occurrence in W. The geographical and textual diversity of the early evidence, which attests to the short reading, is impressive. Because of the independence of evidence in both genealogical and geographical sense, the common ancestor could be dated back at least a century or two. The evidence in favour of the short reading, however, shows a narrowing trend from the fourth century, until it virtually disappears in the Middle Ages, when it occurs only sporadically in manuscripts such as Θ, 579 and 1241.

The material evidence in favour of the long reading is, as has been said, earlier than that of the short reading and reaches into the second century. All these witnesses, however, belong to the same text-type. The evidence is thus genealogically limited. The pattern is more or less the same in the third century, with the reading occurring in Origen, Hippolytus of Rome, the Latin manuscripts c and e, which represent the earlier African form of the *Vetus Latina*, as well as the Curetonian Syriac version. All this evidence belongs to the Western text, with Origen the only exception. Origen is up to this point thus the only suggestion of evidence outside of the Western text and therefore the only suggestion of diversity in evidence. The occurrence of the reading in Origen could, however, be explained in terms of mixture (i.e. that the reading reached the regions where Origen lived, through the spreading of the Western text, from which he took it). Given the fact that the Western text is thought to have been the most widely used text-type in the second century, it seems that such an explanation is not altogether without substantiation. These genealogical limitations of the evidence in favour of the long reading brings about that it cannot be back-dated by the same principles as the previous reading was back-dated, with the result that it must be accepted that the chances are great that it originated sometime in the second century in the early sources of the Western text. From the fourth century onwards the evidence starts to diversify, and the long reading is found in witnesses of all the other text-types outside of the Western text. All this evidence can, however, in some way or another, be linked to the Western text.

The genealogical diversity in the evidence of the short reading, over against the genealogically limited nature of the evidence in favour of the long reading, brings about that one could conclude that the chances are much greater for the long reading to have had a secondary origin than the short reading. When it is viewed that the long reading appears in the Western text, with its distinctive tendency to interpolation, it makes the possibility of the long reading originating secondarily even greater, since it fits well into what characterises the textual tradition wherein it appears.

3.2 Internal evidence

After the assessment of external or documentary evidence there follows the consideration of internal evidence. It consists of two parts, the determination of the *transcriptional probabilities* of the readings and the determination of the *intrinsic probabilities* of the readings.

3.2.1 Transcriptional probabilities

In determining the transcriptional probabilities of each reading, one has to hypothesise as to what possible causes there might have been for a scribe to alter one reading to produce the other. Detailed studies of manuscripts and texts have shown that there are a number of common errors and changes that scribes often made in their work, such as the omission of a line, phrase or word because of *homoioteleuton*, or the addition of material from extra-textual sources, or changes made for dogmatic reasons (cf. Metzger, 1968:168-206; Royse 1981). To evaluate the transcriptional probabilities of a reading, one would analyse the readings in the variation-unit and attempt to see which of those readings fits best into the general causes of variation. In this way it is then determined which reading gives the best possible explanation for the origin of the other readings (cf. Nida 1981).

In the case of Luke 23:34 a number of possible causes for each reading can be put forward. In favour of the long reading are arguments such as that it could have been omitted because of the fact that the destruction of Jerusalem made it appear as if the prayer of Jesus was not heard by God, which was unacceptable to early Christianity (cf. e.g. Metzger 1971:180; Streeter 1924:138). It could also have been omitted because of anti-Judaism in the early church (cf. e.g. Von Harnack 1931:92-98; Streeter 1924:138). The prayer as a prayer for the Jews was then unacceptable to people who had strong anti-Judaic feelings. As such it seems that it is in accord with tendencies in Acts, where the 'ignorance-motif' was also removed because of anti-Judaism (Epp 1962; 1966). On the other hand, one can also hypothesise that there seems to have been such a general addition of extra-biblical *Jesus-logia* in the first and second centuries that the secondary addition rather than omission of these words seem to fit well into the general pattern in those centuries. One can also argue that the disputed text was added as a prayer for the Roman soldiers crucifying Jesus because of anti-Judaic tendencies in an attempt to apply the same principle to the Romans that is generally applied to the Jews in Acts and therewith emphasise the guilt of the Jews for the crucifixion, by aquitting the Romans. In this way the already anti-Judaic statement a few verses earlier in the same pericope (28-31) is being strengthened by the interpolator through the addition of a prayer asking for forgiveness not for them, but for the Romans, thus emphasising their guilt in Jesus' death by means of contrast.

As is clear from the preceding paragraph, this aspect of the method is very subjective and arbitrary. It rests mainly on hypothesis and speculation. In the case discussed above there is no way of methodologically distinguishing between the possibilities mentioned. An inventive mind can find even more reasons than these to explain the origin of either of these readings. It is this kind of subjectivity that makes most textual critics reluctant to base too much upon this kind of argument (cf. e.g. Fee 1976:177).

However, there are a few ways of at least limiting the total subjectivitiy of this practice. Detailed studies of tendencies in manuscripts, such as those done by Royse (1981) and O'Neill (1989), give some solid evidence as to practices in manuscripts, which, if applied thoroughly to discussions of variant readings, limits the possibilities of mere speculation. In addition the hypotheses could be viewed against the general background of the tendencies in and characteristics of text-types. If the reasons for the addition or omission of Luke 23:34, cited above, are viewed against this background, it becomes rather clear that the passage would probably not have been omitted because of anti-Judaism, because it is included in the same textual tradition known for anti-Judaic variation in Acts (i.e. the Western Text – cf. Epp 1966). Why would scribes keep the anti-Judaism in one instance and remove it in another? The opposite is true of the documents containing the short reading.

To apply these principles to the variation in our example seems to make the addition of the reading more probable than the omission. The addition of the reading is in accord with the general tendency in the early church, where the practice was to include rather than omit orally transmitted *Jesus-logia*. It is also in accord with the general trends in the Western text, which is in many respects a longer text than the Alexandrian and which is said to include much material from the tradition that is not thought to be original. It is also in accord with specific tendencies regarding the contents of that text-type, i.e. anti- Judaism, that is if it is taken as a prayer for the Roman soldiers, since it introduces the ignorance-motif as an excuse for the Romans in the same words as it appears in Acts in favour of the Jews. By removing those phrases in Acts and introducing them in Luke 23:34 seems to be two sides of the same coin.

3.2.2 Intrinsic probabilities

This brings us to the final matter, i.e. the determination of the intrinsic probabilities of each reading. The main question to be answered in considering this aspect is which reading has most likely been written by the author of the document. It involves matters such as the language, style and theology. The different readings in the text-critical problem under observation are analysed as to these aspects. The results are then compared to general trends in the rest of the book or author in which the variation occurs. The reading of which the features are best in accord with general trends in the rest of the work of the author has the best claims of being original. It is clear that this kind of argument rests on the basic assumption that an author is consistent in style and theology.

In the case of Luke 23:34 it is sometimes said that the fact that the word Πάτερ is used, shows that the *logion* was probably written by the author of the Third Gospel because it is a typical feature of Luke (cf. Von Harnack 1931:93). The reading seems at first sight also in accord with general Lucan theology, since there are parallel occurrences of the ignorance motif in Acts (3:17, 13:27).

However, that this evidence is even more subjective and speculative in nature than the previously discussed evidence is clear from a number of things. In the case of the use of Πάτερ above, one could just as well argue that it is an imitation of Luke's style by whoever added the passage. That this could have happened is indeed possible if it is kept in mind that only one word is involved and that an example of the Lucan use of that word appears in the immediate context (Lk 23:46).

Whether the theology of this reading is in accord with Lucan theology is also not so certain and depends upon interpretation. It could just as easily be shown why it is not in accord with Lucan theology if other matters are being emphasised. The fact that Jesus *prays* for forgiveness, has, for example, no parallel and seems in direct opposition to the way in which Jesus is generally pictured in the Third Gospel, i.e. as having the power to forgive vested in him.

It is clear that this kind of evidence is even more problematic than the previous. It is very often the emphases and accents of individual critics that make a given feature typical or not typical of an author (cf. e.g. Hull 1988). Recent developments in the theory of interpretation, which emphasise more and more the active role of the interpreter in the process of interpretation, substantiates this. Furthermore the fact that consistency is presupposed, is problematic in the light of the redaction history of the books in the New Testament. Any redactor changing aspects of books will naturally make changes in style and theology, and since we use the redacted books, and not the original author's texts, as our basis of analysis, it seems problematic to treat them as though they were not subject to redaction at all. Also questions of authorship make this a difficult way of working. Which books does one use, for example, to determine general Pauline style, and what does one do with changes in the stylistic patterns in Luke-Acts?

In the end one will only use this aspect of the method in a negative way, i.e. to determine if a reading, indicated by other evidence as being most probably the original, is *not* in accord with what is thought to be general style or theology. If enough strong evidence can be gathered in this way, it must lead to a re-evaluation of the other evidence, in an attempt to see if some mistake were not made there. On its own, however, this evidence can never be used to solve textual problems.

3.3 Conclusion

After all aspects of the method have been applied, one can make a final conclusion. The first part of the conclusion will be to state and describe which readings most probably originated secondarily in the redaction or transmission processes of the New Testament. One will also give the reasons for the choice of these readings, in other words, the full hypothesis concerning the origin of the readings under observation will be given. This will leave one reading that is most probably the original. What the relation of this reading is to the original text and the later redactional process cannot be determined by applying this method. The conclusion is therefore always a negative one, i.e. that it has text-critically been determined that all the readings apart from one are most probably *not* original to the original version of the book under observation, and that the one left over, *could* be original to the original copy of the book under observation. Whether it *is* (or whether it is the result of the early redaction of the book) must be determined by other means.

In this way one can now attempt to reconstruct the history of the readings in Luke 23:34. Original to the Third Gospel was probably an account of the crucifixion of Jesus without the disputed passage. The Gospel was consequently transmitted for some time without this reading in a wide geographical area. Since the second century, however, it had to compete with a version of the Third Gospel that included the disputed words, the origin and sources of which are unknown. One could speculate that it was for some time transmitted (orally) as a saying of Jesus until it reached the areas where anti-Judaistic sentiments found their way into the Western text of the New Testament sometime in the second century. It was then included in copies of the Third Gospel. For some time it was transmitted as part of the Third Gospel in these circles only, before it became introduced into other forms of the text. By the end of the third and beginning of the fourth century it was introduced into all the major text-types and through its introduction in the Byzantine manuscripts, started to dominate the text since the fourth or fifth centuries. Throughout the Middle Ages there seems, however, to have been some awareness of the problems of this reading through the sporadic occurrences of the short reading in witnesses such as Byzantine, late-Alexandrian and Caesarean manuscripts of the Middle Ages.

BIBLIOGRAPHY

Aland, B. 1986. Entstehung, Charakter und Herkunft des sog. Westlichen Textes untersucht an der Apostelgeschichte. *Ephemerides Theologicae Lovanienses* 62, 5-65.

Aland, K. 1967. Die Konsequenzen der neueren Handschriftenfunde für die neutestamentlichen Textkritik. *Novum Testamentum* 9, 81-106.

Aland, K. 1977. New Editions of the Greek New Testament. *Bulletin of the United Bible Societies* 108/109, 20-27.

Aland, K. Der neue Standardtext in seinem Verhältnis zu den frühen Papyri und Majuskeln, in E. J. Epp & G. D. Fee (eds.). *New Testament Textual Criticism: Its Significance for Exegesis. Essays in Honour of Bruce M. Metzger.* Oxford: Clarendon Press, 257- 275.

Aland, K. 1982. Der Textcharakter der frühen Papyri und Majuskeln, in H. Kunst (Hrsg.). *Bericht der Hermann Kunst-Stiftung zur Förderung der neutestamentlichen Textforschung für die Jahre 1979 bis 1981.* Münster: Hermann Kunst-Stiftung zur Förderung der neutestamentlichen Textforschung, 43-59.

Aland, K. 1985. Die Grundurkunde des Glaubens. Ein Bericht über 40 Jahre Arbeit an ihrem Text, in H. Kunst (Hrsg.). *Bericht der Hermann Kunst-Stiftung zur Förderung der neutestamentlichen Textforschung für die Jahre 1982 bis 1984.* Münster: Hermann Kunst-Stiftung zur Förderung der neutestamentlichen Textforschung, 9-75.

Aland, K. & Aland, B. 1982. *Der Text des Neuen Testaments. Einführung in die wissenschaftlichen Ausgaben sowie in Theorie und Praxis der modernen Textkritik.* Stuttgart: Deutsche Bibelgesellschaft.

Ehrman, B. D. 1986. *Didymus the Blind and the Text of the Gospels.* Atlanta: Society of Biblical

Literature. (The New Testament in the Greek Fathers 1.)

Ehrman, B. D. & Plunkett, M. A. 1983. The Angel and the Agony: The Textual Problem of Luke 22:43-44. *Catholic Biblical Quarterly* 45, 401-416.

Elliott, J. K. 1968. *The Greek Text of the Epistles to Timothy and Titus*. Salt Lake City: University of Utah Press. (Studies and Documents 36.)

Elliott, J. K. Rational Criticism and the Text of the New Testament. *Theology* 75, 338-343.

Elliott, J. K. 1975. The United Bible Societies' Textual Commentary Evaluated. *Novum Testamentum* 17, 130-150.

Elliott, J. K. 1978. In Defence of Thoroughgoing Eclecticism in New Testament Textual Criticism. *Restoration Quarterly* 21, 95-115.

Epp, E. J. 1962. The 'Ignorance Motif' in Acts and Anti-Judaic Tendencies in Codex Bezae. *Harvard Theological Review* 55, 51-62.

Epp, E. J. 1966. *The Theological Tendency of Codex Bezae Cantabrigiensis in Acts*. Cambridge: Cambridge University Press.

Epp, E. J. 1976. The Eclectic Method in New Testament Textual Criticism: Solution or Symptom? *Harvard Theological Review* 69, 211-257.

Fee, G. D. 1968. *Papyrus Bodmer II. Its Textual Relationships and Scribal Characteristics*. Salt Lake City: University of Utah Press. (Studies and Documents 34.)

Fee, G. D. 1974a. The *lemma* of Origen's *Commentary on John*, bk 10. An Independent Witness to the Egyptian Tradition. *New Testament Studies* 20, 78-81.

Fee, G. D. 1974b. P75, P66 and Origen: The Myth of Early Textual Recension in Alexandria, in R. N. Longenecker & M. C. Tenney (eds.). *New Dimensions in New Testament Study*. Grand Rapids: Zondervan, 19-45.

Fee, G. D. 1976. Rigorous or Reasoned Eclecticism – Which? in J. K. Elliott (ed.). *Studies in the New Testament Language and Text. Essays in Honour of George D. Kilpatrick on the Occasion of his Sixty-fifth Birthday*. Leiden: Brill (Novum Testamentum Supplements 44), 174-197.

Fee, G. D. 1982a. On the Inauthenticity of John 5:3b-4. *Evangelical Quarterly* 54, 207-218.

Fee, G. D. 1982b. Origen's Text of the New Testament and the Text of Egypt. *New Testament Studies* 28, 348-364.

Flatt, D. 1975. Thoroughgoing Eclecticism as a Method of Textual Criticism. *Restoration Quarterly* 18, 102-104.

Hull, R. F. 1988. 'Lucanisms' in the Western Text of Acts? A Reappraisal. *Journal of Biblical Literature* 107, 695-707.

Hurtado, L. W. 1981. *Text-Critical Methodology and the Pre-Caesarean Text. Codex W in the Gospel of Mark*. Grand Rapids: Eerdmans. (Studies and Documents 43.)

IGNTP: The American and British Committees of the International Greek New Testament Project (eds.) 1987. *The Gospel according to St. Luke*, v. 2.: Ch. 13-24. Oxford: Clarendon Press.

Kilpatrick, G. D. (ed.) 1961-1964. *A Greek-English Diglot for the Use of Translators*. London: British and Foreign Bible Societies.

Kilpatrick, G. D. 1963. Atticism and the Text of the Greek New Testament, in J. Blinzler, O. Kuss & F. Mussner (eds.). *Neutestamentliche Aufsätze. Festschrift für Prof. Josef Schmid*. Regensburg: Pustet, 125-137.

Kilpatrick, G. D. 1965. The Greek Text of Today and the *Textus Receptus*, in H. Anderson & W. Barclay (eds.). *The New Testament in Historical and Contemporary Perspective. In Memory of G.H.C. MacGregor*. Oxford: Blackwell, 189-208.

Kilpatrick, G.D. 1967. Style and Text in the Greek New Testament, in B. L. Daniels & M. J. Suggs (eds.). 1967. *Studies in the History and Text of the New Testament in Honor of Kenneth Willis Clark*. Salt Lake City: University of Utah Press (Studies and Documents 29), 153-160.

Metzger, B. M. 1966. Bibliographic aids for the study of the New Testament. *Anglican Theological Review* 48, 339-355.

Metzger, B. M. 1968. *The Text of the New Testament. Its Transmission, Corruption and Restoration*. 2nd ed. New York: Oxford University Press.

Metzger, B. M. 1971. *A Textual Commentary on the Greek New Testament*. New York: United Bible Societies.

Nida, E. A. 1981. The 'Harder Reading' in Textual Criticism: An Application of the Second Law of Thermodynamics. *The Bible Translator* 33, 430-435.

O'Neill, J. C. 1989. The Rules Followed by the Editors of the Text Found in Codex Vaticanus. *New Testament Studies* 35, 219-228.

Petzer, J. H. 1986. The Papyri and New Testament Textual Criticism – Clarity or Confusion? in J. H. Petzer & P. J. Hartin (eds.). *A South African Perspective on the New Testament: Essays by*

South African New Testament Scholars Presented to Bruce Manning Metzger during his Visit to South Africa in 1985. Leiden: Brill, 18-32.

Petzer, J. H. 1988. Shifting Sands: The Changing Paradigm in New Testament Textual Criticism, in J. Mouton, A.G. Van Aarde & W.S. Vorster (eds.). *Paradigms and Progress in Theology*. Pretoria: Human Sciences Research Council (Human Sciences Research Council Studies in Methodology 5), 394-408.

Royse, J. R. 1981. *Scribal Habits in Early Greek New Testament Papyri*. 2 vols. Berkeley. (Unpublished Doctoral Thesis.)

Turner, C. H. 1924-1928. Marcan Usage: Notes, Critical and Exegetical, on the Second Gospel. *Journal of Theological Studies* 25, 377-386; 26, 12-20; 26, 145-156; 26, 225-240; 26, 337-346; 27, 58-62; 28, 9-30; 28, 349-362; 29, 257-289; 29, 346-361.

Turner, C. H. 1927. A Text-critical Commentary on Mark 1. *Journal of Theological Studies* 28, 145-158.

Von Harnack, A. 1931. *Studien zur Geschichte des Neuen Testaments und der alten Kirche*. Berlin. (Arbeiten zur Kirchengeschichte 19.)

Westcott, B. F. & Hort, F. J. A. 1974. *The New Testament in the Original Greek*, v.2: *Introduction*. Graz: Akademie. (Reprint of the original in 1881.)

P. J. MAARTENS

'SIGN' AND 'SIGNIFICANCE' IN THE THEORY AND PRACTICE OF ONGOING LITERARY CRITICAL INTERPRETATION WITH REFERENCE TO MARK 4:24 AND 25: A STUDY OF SEMIOTIC RELATIONS IN THE TEXT

1. Introduction

It is the central thesis of this article that our knowledge of the meaning of a text is always perspectival. The various perspectives, or possibilities of interpretation, reveal the polymorphous character of the meaning of the text. The meaning of the text transcends all historically contingent interpretations. Although these interpretations provide readers with access to the meaning of artefact, the text nevertheless still remains a *corpus alienum*. The function of any literary theory is to make the meaning of the text accessible by providing a method of literary critical dialogue which leads to a multi-perspectival, yet historically contingent, interpretation.[1] The word 'critical' in the expression 'method of literary critical dialogue' cultivates an element of caution. A critical awareness is necessary to prevent the interpreter from slipping into one-dimensional consciousness that reduces the polymorphous *significance* of the artefact to one truth perspective only.

The relations between *sign* and *significance* in the title above facilitates an analysis of the text in structural theories, communication theory, reception theory and theory of metaphor contributing to the process of semiosis. The method of textual analysis designated as semiotics facilitates a critical dialogue of the relations between the *sign* and its literary *representation*, which leads to an *interpretation* of the text. The literary dialogue conducted in a semiotic analysis embraces numerous disciplines. Inevitably the semiotic interpretation as proposed by Eco (1976:73) takes its point of departure from a semantic representation of sentences. The semantic features of the text are specified in the Extended Standard Theory, especially as postulated by Katz (1972). The semantic analysis represents semantic features such as the *focus*,[2] *presupposition*,[3] *statement*,[4] *denotation*[5] and *connotation*.[6] At this point a

---

[1]   Theory constitutes method. According to Rauche (1983:29) method is the truth-function of knowledge. It follows that the function of theory is to give the exegete access to the text as study object. The function of literary theory is to explicate problematic phenomena in the text and to interpret the text.

[2]   The focus of a sentence is, according to Jackendoff (1972:230), the *new information* in the sentence. Compare Katz (1972:127-130) for further discussion.

[3]   The presupposition of a sentence is the *known information* which the reader can deduce from

semiotic analysis will cross its first frontier. As a literary method semiotics exceeds the limitations of modern linguistics confined to the limits of a sentence analysis. Subsequently, semiotics relates all structural relations between the *sign* and the *signified* in an ongoing literary critical dialogue. The semiotic method includes all devices of *foregrounding*,[7] both paradigmatic, e.g. metaphor, as well as syntagmatic *foregrounding*, e.g. parallelism and coupling. Semiotics further also includes the fulfillment of textual structures in the readers role as explicated by reception aesthetics.

I would like to explain my view of the role of various theoretical frameworks in the interpretation of a text by likening the meaning of a text to a growing tree. As the various layers of growth rings constitute a tree, so each new theoretical framework adds yet another interpretation to the layers constituting the meaning of the text. Seen in this manner, exegesis is the result, or should be the result, of an ongoing interaction between the various interpretations within each theoretical framework.

Unfortunately, too often today interpretation within a single theoretical framework is equalled to the meaning of the text, thereby reducing the meaning of the text to one-dimensional consciousness. Rauche (1986:4) identifies a current tendency in the humanities to merge practice and theory in functionalistic methods of scientific inquiry.[8] This approach has also invaded literary theory and criticism.[9] Jauss (1982:16) points out that

> the formal method... detached the literary work from all historical conditions and like the new structural linguistics defined its specific result purely functionally, as the sum-total of all the stylistic devices employed in it.

I would like to argue that literary criticism and interpretation should beware of such reduction. I attempt to show that interpretation can only gain by ongoing critical dialogue between different theoretical frameworks. I further intend to illustrate that semiotics facilitates a *literary dialogue*, which enables the exegete to

---

the content of each sentence.

[4]   The *statement* or *question*, as I have indicated elsewhere, is the content of each sentence, cf. Maartens (1980:5).

[5]   Denotation is the *cognitive* meaning or content of an expression, e.g. a *red traffic light* denotes 'danger'.

[6]   Connotation, according to Eco (1976:55), is a further signification that conventionally relies on a primary one, e.g. the connotation attached to a *red traffic light* is that any approaching traffic be brought to *a standstill*.

[7]   As indicated by me elsewhere (cf. Maartens 1980:8-19), *foregrounding* is the deliberate highlighting of sentence constituents as practiced in formalism.

[8]   Cf. Rauche 1985:4: The reduction of society to mere systems of social interaction or to the totalitarian functionalism in Marxism are prime examples.

[9]   Rauche (1985:4) considers in this regard the application of the analytical and structural methods to literary texts.

interpret beyond the limits of one-dimensional functionalistic consciousness. It is simultaneously necessary to cultivate a *critical consciousness* whilst conducting a literary dialogue. Only a critical dialogue will safeguard the interpreter from, on the one hand, the limitations of any single theoretical perspective and, on the other hand, the danger of committing a methodological pluralism. I shall subsequently consider the relations of *signifier* and *signified* in ongoing literary critical discussions that constitute a hermeneutic of semiotics. To appreciate such a literary critical hermeneutic of dialogue it becomes necessary to provide a brief survey of the development of theories that constitutes semiotics as literary critical method.

2. Methodological part: 'signs' and 'significance'

At the beginning of the twentieth century De Saussure (1915) contributed significantly to our understanding of semiotics. Hawkes (1977:123) quotes Saussure defining 'semiology' as 'a science that studies the life of signs within society...I shall call it *semiology* (from the Greek σημεῖον 'sign'). Semiology would show what constitutes signs, what laws govern them...'. The contribution of Saussure firmly rooted semiotics in structuralism. In Saussurean terms 'semiology' analyses the psychological and social conventions which constitute 'signs'. Saussure (1959:67) postulated the composition of a sign as follows:

> I propose to retain the word *sign* [*signe*] to designate the whole and to replace concept and sound image respectively by *signified* [*signifié*] and *signifier* [*signifiant*]; the last two terms have the advantage of indicating the opposition that separates them from each other and from the whole of which they are parts.

It further provides a methodological framework for the semantic representation of signs constituting the signified or *signifié* of the literary work of art. Saussure further regarded the relationship between the signifier and the signified as arbitrary. He (1959:67) explained the nature of the sign in the following way:

> The bond between the signifier and the signified is arbitrary. Since I mean by sign the whole that results from the associating of the signifier with the signified, I can simply say: *the linguistic sign is arbitrary*.

Culler (1981:22) rightfully shows that the theory postulated by Saussure explicates the system or *langue*[10] that underlies the literary work of art and that makes the artefact a meaningful production which he called *speaking*. Barthes

---

10   Saussure (1959:9) defines *langue* as follows: 'It is both a social product of the faculty of speech and a collection of necessary conventions that have been adopted by a social body to permit individuals to exercise that faculty'.

(1977:14) regards the former, *langue*, as 'the language, which is both institution and system'. In contrast to *langue*, Barthes (1977:14) defines *parole* or speech as 'essentially an individual act of selection and actualisation'. Semiology engages itself in an analysis of both the artefact and the conventions or systems that underlie the artefact. Semiology may consequently not be regarded as a mere performance analysis. Saussure also distinguished a *synchronic*[11] analysis from a *diachronic*[12] analysis. As Culler (1981:23) further indicates *synchronic linguistic analysis* concerns itself with the language 'system' as 'functioning totality', not with the historical provenance of its various elements or *diachronic linguistic analysis*. To facilitate a study of literary language as 'functioning totality' Saussure (1959:126), on the one hand, distinguished *associative relations* of signs, e.g. 'analogies such as *enseignement*, instruction, *apprentissage*, education or educate, internship and training'. On the other hand, Saussure distinguished *syntagmatic*[13] relations through which signs create larger units of communication e.g. all forms of extra-patterning such as parallelism or coupling. Barthes (1977:62) defines the *syntagmatic* level of language communication as the '(varied) combination of (recurrent) signs'.

In 1974 the International Association For Semiotic Studies at its first congress ruled in favour of the term 'semiotics' as the general designation for the discipline it promotes. Semiotics was the designation originally used by Charles Sanders Peirce (1834-1914), whose major contributions were posthumously published. Peirce postulated semiotic theory to constitute his epistemological method. Peirce (1974:123) designated the sign, or *representamen*, as

> something which stands to somebody for something in some respect or capacity. It addresses somebody, that is, creates in the mind of that person an equivalent sign, or perhaps a more developed sign.

Hawkes (1977:127) further indicates that Peirce called the object to which the *representamen* leads the *interpretant*. Van Zoest (1978:23) explicates semiosis as a dynamic process functioning in the following way:

> Drie elementen bepalen dus de aanwezigheid van een teken: het waarneembare teken zelf, datgene waarnaar het verwijst en een ander teken in de geest van de tekenontvanger. Tussen het teken en dat waarnaar het verwijst bestaat een relatie: het teken heeft een representatief

---

11   Saussure (1959:99) defines *synchronic linguistics* as follows: '*Synchronic linguistics* will be concerned with the logical and psychological relations that bind together coexisting terms and form a system in the collective mind of speakers'.
12   Saussure (1959:100) defines *diachronic linguistics* as follows: '*Diachronic linguistics*, on the contrary, will study relations that bind together succesive terms not perceived by the collective mind but substituted for each other without forming a system'.
13   Saussure (1959:123) designated language production on the horizontal level as follows: 'Combinations supported by linearity are *syntagms*'.

karakter. Teken en representatie leiden tot een interpretatie: het teken heeft een inter-
pretatief karakter. Anders gezegd: representatie en interpretatie karakteriseren het teken.

Peirce reserved the term *representation* for the signifying event proper. Van
Zoest (1978:23) explains further:

> Er is nooit interpretatie zonder representatie... Hoewel bij semiosis representatie en inter-
> pretatie allebei als even onafwendbaar aanwezig moeten worden verondersteld, is represen-
> tatie toch iets fundamenteler voor het tekenproces dan interpretatie. Dus: een tekenproces is
> het in functie brengen van een drievoudige relatie die niet (altans niet in de werkelijkheid,
> wel in de beschrijving uiteraard) kan worden teruggebracht tot een tweevoudige relatie,
> maar binnen die relaties is toch de representatieve fundamenteler dan de interpretatieve.

The interpretant is the image which establishes itself as 'aesthetic object' in the
mind of the person appreciating and interpreting the sign. Peirce further reserved the term *result* for the signifying action and the interpretative function
given to the sign. The term *denotatum* Peirce (1974:240) reserved for the result
of the semiotic action. Van Zoest (1978:23) continues to explain the relation
between *representation* and result as follows:

> De woorden 'representatie' en 'interpretatie' hebben het bezwaar dat ze een handeling kun-
> nen aanduiden en het resultaat van die handeling. Daarom is het goed dat voor die laaste
> betekenis (resultaat van een handeling) andere termen worden ingevoerd. Het resultaat van
> representatie heet dan denotatum. Misschien zou 'representatum' beter zijn geweest, maar
> waarom zich niet aansluiten bij een taalgebruik dat al ingang gevonden heeft? Het resultaat
> van interpretatie noemen we, met Peirce, de interpretant van het teken. Ook in dit geval con-
> formeren we ons dus aan een al eerder ingevoerd taalgebruik. De interpretant is dus dat te-
> ken dat zich uit een eerder teken ontwikkelt in de geest van de interpreterende persoon. De
> begrippen 'interpretant' en 'interpreterende persoon' moeten dus vooral niet als identiek
> worden opgevat.

Peirce further distinguished three types of signs: The three different signs which
Peirce (1974:142) distinguished are *qualisigns, sinsigns* and *legisigns*. A *qualisign*
is a sign which may be distinguished on the ground of some characteristic. A
qualisign is a quality which functions as a sign. Van Zoest (1978:26) chooses red
as a possible qualisign. In order to fulfill the function of a sign the qualisign
must be embodied in a definite contextual symbol. *Red* may be used as qualisign
to manifest socialism, love or danger. *Red* may signify *socialism* if embodied in
an appropriate flag. It may signify *love* if embodied in *roses*. *Red* signifies *danger*
if it is illuminated in a traffic light. A *sinsign* is a linguistic compound of a
singular sign. Sinsigns manifest in unconventional expressions. Sinsigns are
embodied in exclamations signifying pain, surprise or joy. Sinsigns may also
manifest in idiosyncratic mannerisms: a distinct way of laughing, coughing or
distinctly recognisable footsteps. Even the single occurance of an unique
metaphor constitutes the embodiment of a sinsign. A *legisign*, the linguistic

compound of *lex* and *sign*, designates the embodiment of a generally accepted rule, a general convention or a code. Traffic rules represent legisigns. Legisigns are also embodied in traditional gestures or punctuation rules in written language.

The corresponding relationship between the *representamen* and the interpretant determines the nature of the process of *semiosis*. Culler (1981:23) critically indicated that Peirce devoted much labour to a very complex yet taxonomic and speculative analysis of semiotics. His most influential contribution appeared in his so-called 'second triad'. In the second triad Peirce (1974:143) introduced his famous trichotomy: icon, index and symbol:

The *icon* distinctly manifests a relationship of resemblance between the sign and its object. Hawkes (1977:128) explains that the icon functions as a sign because in Peirce's terms it manifests 'a community in some quality or a correspondence with the object to which it refers'. Thus maps, diagrams, drawings, paintings and photographs are icons because their relationships to the objects they refer to constitute a resemblance of correspondence.

The *index*, according to Hawkes (1977:129), manifests a relationship between the sign and its object which is concrete, actual and of a sequential or causal kind. A knock on the door is an index of someone's presence. Similarly, smoke is an index of fire.

Finally, the *symbol* establishes, according to Hawkes (1977:129) a relationship between the signifier and the signified that is arbitrary. Symbols are determined by socio-cultural conventions. Waving, beckoning and nodding are ways of symbolic communication. Hawkes indicates further that symbols result from mutual consent and occur mainly in the language of the fluent speaker. Segers (1978:14) rightfully suggests that semiotics include 'all forms of communication insofar as this takes place by means of signs, based upon sign systems or codes'.

The distinction of Saussure between *langue* and *parole* corresponds to Eco's distinction (1976:4, 9) between *signification* and *communication*. Eco (1976:4) defines *signification* as 'a theory of codes' and *communication* as 'a theory of sign production'. As indicated by Ray (1984:4) Eco initially grants *signification* precedence over *communication*.

Eco (1976:8) distinguishes *signification*

> when the destination is a human being, or 'addressee' (it is not necessary that the source or the transmitter be human, provided that it emits the signal following a system of rules known by the human addressee), we are on the contrary witnessing a process of signification – provided that the signal is not merely a stimulus but arouses an interpretive response in the addressee.

Although Eco (1976:9) distinguishes signification from communication he maintains that 'every act of communication to or between human beings...

presupposes a signification system as its necessary condition'. Both the process of signification and the interpretive response in the addressee are facilitated by the existence of a *code*. The *code* is one of six elements that constitute the theory of communication.

Eco (1976:8) indicates that all cultural processes are regarded in the theory of semiotics as processes of communication. Semiotics explicates the interplay between sign and significance in the framework of the communication model postulated by Jakobson (1960). Jakobson (1960:353) distinguished the following language functions that constitutes verbal communication:

> The ADDRESSER sends a MESSAGE to the ADDRESSEE. To be operative the message requires a CONTEXT referred to ('referent' in another, somewhat ambiguous, nomenclature), seizable by the addressee, and either verbal or capable of being verbalized: a CODE fully, or at least partially, common to the addresser and addressee (or in other words, to the encoder and decoder of the message); and, finally, a CONTACT, a physical channel and psychological connection between the addresser and the addressee, enabling both of them to enter and stay in communication.

Jakobson postulated the above communication model on a linear base. The message, however, transmitted from an addresser to an addressee refers to something other than itself. Fiske (1982:37) indicates that Jakobson terms this 'third point of the triangle' the *context* of the message. Jakobson recognises two further factors, viz. the *contact* and the *code*. Fiske (1982:37) defines the contact as 'the physical channel and psycological connections between the addresser and the addressee'. The code Fiske (1982:37) defines as 'a shared meaning system by which the message is structured'.

Jakobson (1960:357) further distinguishes six functions of communication on the same linear base. Three of the six functions of communication concern us here: the *emotive*, the *conative* and the *referential* function.

The *emotive* function designates the relationship of the addresser to his message. Fiske (1982:37) explains:

> It is this function of the message to communicate the addresser's emotions, attitudes, status, class; all those elements that make the message uniquely his.

Guiraud (1975:6) further comments

> when we communicate...we express ideas concerning the nature of the referent...but we can also express our attitude toward this object: good or bad, beautiful or ugly, desirable or hateful, respectable or ridiculous.

The *conative* function designates the relationship of the message to the addressee. Fiske (1982:37) explains: 'This refers to the effect of the message on the addressee'. The goal of communication is to evoke some reaction from the reader. Guiraud (1975:7) indicates that the 'injunction may be addressed either to the intelligence or to the emotional sensitivity of the receiver'.

Guiraud (1975:6) regards the *referential* function as 'the basis of all communication'. The referential function designates the relationship of the message and the object to which it refers. The function of communication here is, as Fiske (1982:37) rightly shows, 'concerned to be 'true' or factual communication'. The referential function attempts to avoid any confusion between signifier and signified or, as Guiraud (1975:6) indicates, between message and encoded reality. The considerations on the referential function of communication returns our discussion to the subject of *codes*.

Segers (1978:25) rightly indicates that it is of primary importance to know 'in which language or in which code the text is encoded'. Knowing the code will enable the reader of a text to decode the textual signs and to give meaning to language and content of the message. According to Eco (1979:49) there are basically two different types of texts. Eco distinguishes 'closed' texts from 'open' texts. A 'closed' text is a text like James Bond, which is written in a code that aims at producing a predictable response from the average reader. Yet, simultaneously, such a closed text is paradoxically 'open', since the author assumes that it is able to communicate with any reader. A text that, on the other hand, is essentially ambiguous and challenges the reader with multiple possibilities of interpretation is an 'open' text. Eco (1984:49-50) defines 'openness' in the following way:

> In primitive terms we can say that they are quite literally 'unfinished': the author seems to hand them on to the performer more or less like the components of a construction kit. He seems unconcerned about the manner of their eventual deployment... At this point one could object...that any work of art, even if it is not passed on to the addressee in an unfinished state, demands a free , inventive response, if only because it cannot really be appreciated unless the performer somehow reinvents it in psychological collaboration with the author himself.

The ideal reader of the 'open' text fulfills a reader's role determined by the structures of the text. When the text conforms to a code that is presupposed by the reader and is consequently known to him, Lotman (1977:290), distinguishes an 'aesthetics of identity'. Lotman explains

> that here the rules of the author and of the audience are not one, but two phenomena in a state of mutual identity... Artistic systems of this type are based on a sum of principles which may be defined as the *aesthetics of identity*. It is based on the total identification of depicted phenomena of life with model-cliches that are known beforehand to the audience and operate according to a system of 'rules'.

Texts based on the aesthetics of identity share some characteristics in common with Eco's 'closed texts'. Lotman (1977:292), further distinguishes an 'aesthetics of opposition' when codes of the sender and the recipient differ. Lotman continues to explain:

> The other class of structures we find on this level are systems whose code is unknown to the audience before the act of artistic perception begins. This is the aesthetic of opposition rather than identity. The author sets his own, original resolution, which he believes to be the truer one, in opposition to methods of modeling reality that are familiar to the reader.

A text based on the 'aesthetics of opposition' deliberately thwarts the reader's expectations because the text does not conform to a code known to the reader.

Texts that are based on the aesthetics of opposition thus share characteristics common to Eco's 'open texts'. The literary critical dialogue conducted thus far progressed from signification to communication and more specifically the code of communication. In the communication theory the message communicated reaches its destiny in the response given by the reader. It is appropriate at this point of the discussion to show briefly the contribution of semioticians to the development of an *aesthetics of reception*.

Mukarovsky (1978:88) regarded the readers of different periods as 'perceivers' of the text. Mukarovsky distinguished between the literary work as *artefact* and the concretisation of the literary work as *aesthetic object* by the reader. Mukarovsky's distinction of an *aesthetic object* is comparable to Roland Barthes' classification of *reader roles* underlying the interpretation of a text. In some texts the reader is not only a recipient but also participant: the reader fulfills a function, he makes a contribution and is under obligation either to accept the text or to reject the text. In other cases the text makes no demands on the reader. Barthes (1974) identified two reader roles that respectively distinguishes two types of texts. The one group of texts he termed 'writerly texts' and the other group he termed 'readerly texts'. The *writerly text* Barthes (1974:5) maintains

> is a perpetual present, upon which no *consequent* language...can be superimposed; the writerly text is ourselves writing, before the infinite play of the world (the world as function) is traversed, intersected, stopped, plasticized by some singular system (Ideology, Genus, Criticism) which reduces the plurality of entrances, the opening of networks, the infinity of languages.

Hawkes (1977:112) indicates that readerly texts require virtually no activity from the reader. 'This reader', Barthes (1974:4) explains,

> is thereby plunged into a kind of idleness – he is intransitive; he is left with no more than the poor freedom either to accept or to reject the text: reading is nothing more than a *referendum*.

In readerly texts the relation between the signifier and the signified is 'clear, well-worn, established and compulsory'. In writerly texts, Hawkes explains (1977:114), the relation between the signifier and the signified is such that the

> signifiers have free play; no automatic reference to signifieds is encouraged or required...writerly texts presume nothing, admit no easy passage from signifier to signified, are open to the 'play' of the codes that we use to determine them.

It is to this category of texts that the text of the New Testament belongs. The New Testament reader not only engages in an appreciation of the aesthetic value of the text but produces meaning in the process of interpretation. It seems apparent that Eco's *closed texts* and Barthes's *readerly texts* share some characteristics in common. It is also clear that Eco's *open texts* and Barthes's *writerly texts* also share some common characteristics.

3. *Illustration: Mark 4:24-25*

I start off this dicussion of the semiotic relations in the text by following the functionalistic approach of a Prague structuralist framework, drawing on the work of Havránek (in Garvin 1964:10), Mukarovsky (in Garvin 1964:9-10) and Leech (1966:141).[14] Within this framework *foregrounding* as a literary device plays a major role in interpretation, *foregrounding* being the deliberate highlighting of literary language usage superimposed on the norm of standard language usage. The macro-structure of the four parables in Mark 4:1-33 is an extended chiastic structure with an *inner* and an *outer circle*.[15]

The four parables are organised as follows: The parables of The Sower and of The Mustard Seed constitute the *outer circle*[16] with the theme of *divine grace*.

---

[14]   Russian formalism attempted to combat the literary positivism of the nineteenth century. Eagleton (1983:2) traces the emergence of formalism back to the years before the Bolshevik revolution (1917). Roman Jakobson, among other formalists, later established himself in Prague. Hence Prague structuralism. The study-object of Prague linguists was 'literariness' (*literaturnost*) *vis-à-vis* literature in traditional literary scholarship. The Prague linguist Havránek (in Garvin 1964:10) defined literariness as 'deautomatised' language usage (*aktualisace*). Mukarovsky who subscribed to Havránek's theory, defined poetic language usage as 'an esthetically intentional distortion of the norm of the standard' (cf. Garvin 1964:9/10). Mukarovsky's esthetically intentional distortion becomes for Leech (1966:141) a unique deviation which he then reserves for syntagmatic foregrounding. Foregrounding is the deliberate highlighting of literary language usage superimposed on the norm of standard language usage.

[15]   In Lämmert's terms (1970:50) the 'prose structuring principles of prose composition' constitute an additive, correlative and contrastive arrangement of the four parables. The kingdom parables in Mark 4 are situated in larger unit (Mk 3:13-6:13). The common theme of 'a call to discipleship', apparent in: ...the appointment of the twelve (Mk 3:13-19), and...the mission of the twelve (Mk 6:7-13), demarcates the unit by an *inclusio*.

[16]   The *outer circle* of parables contrasts: A, the parable commonly known as The Sower (Mk

The parables of The Lamp and of The Growing Seed constitute the *inner circle*[17] with the theme of *divine initiative* in the manifestation of the kingdom. Mark 4:24-25 forms the centre of these two concentric layers. The identification of such a 'matrix'[18] in the text is of paramount significance in the 'semiotics of poetry' as proposed by Riffaterre (1978:4). The striking feature operative in Riffaterre's theory is the principle of semiotic unity. Riffaterre (1978:23) calls this matrix the *hypogram*.[19] All the signs in the macro-context referring to the hypogram must simultaneously be variants or transformations of the matrix. The matrix thus unites intertextual relations and all underlying lines of action. The proverb reads as follows:

24 Βλέπετε τί ἀκούετε
    ἐν ᾧ μέτρῳ μετρεῖτε μετρηθήσεται ὑμῖν   A
    καὶ προστεθήσεται ὑμῖν   B
25 ὃς γὰρ ἔχει, δοθήσεται αὐτῷ AB^1
    καὶ ὃς οὐκ ἔχει, καὶ ὃ ἔχει ἀρθήσεται ἀπ' αὐτοῦ AB^2

The micro structure is of interest for the significance of the statement made in the text. The proverb is introduced with the warning. The warning establishes a *legisign* exposing the reader to the eschatological time of decision making: 'Take heed of what you hear'. The remaining statement is contained in a highly structured text. There is an alliterative link, using Bloomfield's terms (1967:316) between *give* and *get* in the expression the measure you give (μετρεῖτε) will be the

---

4:3-20) to A^1, the parable of the 'Mustard Seed' (Mk 4:30-33). A, the parable of The Sower contrasts: the theme of the incompatibility of God's grace, manifest in the extra-ordinary harvest, to..., A^1: the theme of the universality of God's grace. The latter theme, again, is apparent in the parable of the Mustard Seed.

17   The *inner circle* of parables contrasts: B the parable of The Lamp (Mk 4:21-23) to B^1 the parable of The Growing Seed (Mk 4:26-19). B the parable of The Lamp particularises the theme of the divine initiative in the process of manifesting the Kingdom which is concealed. B^1 the parable of The Growing Seed concretises the theme of the divine initiative in the growth of the Kingdom of God.

18   Riffaterre defines the matrix as follows: 'The matrix is hypothetical, being only the grammatical and lexical actualization of a structure. The matrix may be epitomized in one word, in which case the word will not appear in the text. It is always actualized in successive variants; the form of these is governed by the first or primary actualization, the model. Matrix, model, and text are variants of the same structure.'

19   Riffaterre (1978:23) defines the *hypogram* as follows: 'In either case the production of the poetic sign is determined by hypogrammatic derivation: a word or a phrase is poeticized when it refers to (and, if a phrase, patterns itself upon) a preexistent word group. The hypogram is already a system of signs comprising at least a predication, and it may be as large as a text. The hypogram may be potential, therefore observable in language, or actual, therefore observable in a previous text. For the poeticity to be activated in the text, the sign referring to a hypogram must also be a variant of that text's matrix. Otherwise the poetic sign will function only as a stylistically marked lexeme or syntagm'.

measure you get (μετρηθήσεται). This alliteration establishes a causal relation between the decision made and the impending judgement. The proverb as a whole realises, in Jakobson's terms (1966:412), a double parallelism of which the symmetry is incomplete. The extra-patterning in the proverb exhibits an extended chiastic parallel through syntagmatic foregrounding: (AB)(AB^1) (AB^2). The warning of verse 24 that one should consider the consequence of one's decisions is concretised by an antithetical contrast: 'To him who has, more will be given; and from him who has not, even what he has will be taken away'. The verbs: μετρηθήσεται, προστεθήσεται, δοθήσεται, and ἀρθήσεται followed by the personal pronouns, are foregrounded in each stanza by moving them into sentence final position. The verbs are all *passiva divina*. The divine agent, ὑπὸ τοῦ θεοῦ, is deleted from the text.[20] A structural analysis, as illustrated here, now reaches the point of interpretation. Subsequently it should become clear how the formal method of *representation* finally leads to the *interpretant*. Let us take the divine passive as point of departure. God measures and adds, and allows to be taken away. God confirms the commitment and decisions of people in a way which surpasses all expectations. The proverb is a *midrash* on the parables. It unites all subordinate lines of action. It comments on the contrast between the harvest produced on good soil as opposed to the many losses suffered. Above all, the proverb signifies the abundance of divine grace manifest in the impending rule of God which ushers in the new age of the kingdom. The subject of the 'abundance of divine grace' will here constitute the *denotatum* of semiotic action.

As shown, such a structural analysis is relevant to the interpretation of the text. One of the significant assets is that a structural analysis ascertains the *code* of the text. It goes without saying that, on the one hand, the text conforms to the conventions of prose structuring principles. On the other hand, the deautomatised unconventionality of the above structure of the text can be explicated only in terms of the devices of foregrounding. The result of the structural analysis signifies the poetic structure, apparent in the abundance of parallelisms and metaphors, as a revelant aspect of the text of the gospels.[21] However, a structural analysis alone does not provide an adequate interpretation. Syntagmatic foregrounding reduces literary criticism to a functionalistic explication of the literary devices of extra-patterning and deviation. It reduces the inter-

---

[20]   The divine agent, present in the deep structure, is deleted in the derivation of the surface structure. The divine agent is recoverable from the context and available for the interpretation. A sentence constituent may be deleted subject to the recoverability condition of Bach (1974:100).

[21]   Consequently, an analysis of the structure of the Gospels requires not only an explication of the devices of narrative structure, but also of the devices of poetic language usage. I claim, therefore, that the structuring principles of prose composition, as well as the structuring principles of poetic language usage ought to be applied to give an adequate descriptive analysis of the structure of a text as complex as the text of the gospels.

pretation of the structure to a self-focussing textual relations. Post-formalists identify two major limitations in structural analysis. These objections are the following:

1. The main objection against Saussure's work is that it limits literary communication to the relation of signifier and signified on a single linear level. One-dimensional consciousness excludes what Kristeva (1980:66) terms as 'ambivalence' or plurality in meaning. Kristeva's notion of the plurality, or polymorphous character of the text derives from her concept of intertextuality. According to Kristeva (1980:66) the 'horizontal axis (subject-addressee)' and the 'vertical axis (text-context)' coincide in literary communication. Elsewhere, Kristeva (1984:59-60) defines *intertextuality* in the following way: 'The term inter-textuality denotes this transposition of one (or several) sign system(s) into another'. Whilst a text is the recipient of a system of structural codes it simultaneously participates in other texts with which it interacts. Hence the recognition of plurality and ambivalence in meaning production and interpretation.

2. The fact that foregrounding inadequately explicates the significance of the socio-historical dimensions of the text constitutes a grave limitation. Both acts of *encoding* and *decoding* are performed in historically contingent situations. According to Lotman (1977:295), the reader thus confines the text to familiar conceptions selected from the extra-textual environment. Lotman (1977:295) continues to show that extra-textual structures are determined by 'socio-historical, national, anthropological and psycological factors'.

Although subject to limitations, structural methods contributed to our understanding of textual devices and their significance for interpretation. Yet, a closer look at distinct features of a text, such as verse 24, suggests that the structure of the text is 'unfinished' and constitutes an 'open' text. The structure of the text of St. Mark shows traces of a 'writerly' text anticipating fulfillment in the role of the reader. The fulfillment of the textual structures in the reader's role is addressed in the reader orientated semiotics of Jauss (1977 and 1982) and Iser (1974 and 1978). The following observations demonstrate how the author elicits a response.

1. Intertextual relations link the expression in verse 24 'take heed what you hear...' with similar exhortations in verse 23: 'If any man has ears to hear, let him hear'. The latter exhortation is foregrounded by a parallel statement in verse 9. The text shows features characteristic of a writerly text which calls for fulfillment in the reader's response.

2. A closer comparison of the verbs shows a shift from the third person singular, 'if any man *has* ears', to the second person plural: 'Take heed what you hear'. This shift to the second person plural particularises the role of the reader. The reader is challenged to respond. Particularising the reader's role calls for the fulfillment of textual structures in the reader's response. Interpretation thus

needs to go beyond the one-dimentional consciouness of textual devices operative within the text. It becomes inevitable that we have to look for the fulfillment of textual structures in the reader's role.

I now turn to a post-structural reception framework to explore what the text/reader relations and the socio-literary dimensions of Mark 4:24-25 can add to the interpretation of this text.[22] In doing so, I draw on the work of Jauss (1982) and Iser (1978).

In Mark the conflict between Jesus and Judaism constitutes the textual structure of the reader's role. The journey to Jerusalem begins with five conflicts (Mk 2-3:6) and ends with an additive composition of the five conflicts (Mk 11:27-12:37). Jesus violates Jewish religious conventions and exclusivism (Mk 2:1-3:6, 3:16 and Mk 7). The causal plot of the narrative culminates in the rejection of Judaism (Mk 11:1-26 and 13:1). The Jesus of the implied author rejects Judaism (Mk 11:12-16) only to be rejected in turn (Mk 12:1-12). He comes to Jerusalem to judge Judaism only to be judged and condemned in turn (Mk 14:53-65 and 15:16-20). Jesus silences all misconceptions about his ministry (cf. the messianic prohibitions Mk 1:34, 44; 3:12, 8:30 and 9:9). He rejects the national political expectations of his disciples (Mk 8:29, 9:34 and 10:37) and the false acclamations of messianic pretendants.[23] Mk 9:9 and 10:45 hold the key to his ministry. The expression λύτρον ἀντὶ πολλῶν reinterprets Jesus' ministry retrospectively as that of the suffering righteousness. The passion predictions (Mk 8:31; 9:31 and 10:34) vindicate Jesus as the suffering righteous one. The image of the suffering righteousness belongs to the repertoire of the text.[24]

The structure of the latter paradigm correlates the teachings of discipleship (Mk 8:34f; 9:35ff and 10:38ff) and the passion sayings (Mk 8:31; 9:31 and

---

[22]   Reception theories, *vis-à-vis* structuralism, shifts the interest of literary criticism from the perspective of production to the perspective of the reader or the consumer. Holub (1985:12) traces the emergence of reception theories back to the changing historical conditions of 'a conflict ridden situation' in Germany of the mid-sixties. Mukarovsky (1978:88) designated the signified meaning of the text as the 'esthetic object' of the text. In reception theories Mukarovsky's aesthetic object becomes the object of study. In the theory of Jauss (1982:20,29 and 34ff.) the aesthetic object is explicated by the history of reception. Jauss uses the paradigm of Gadamer in fusing the two horizons of text and reader into the reception aesthetical object. For Iser (1978:112), who follows Ingarden, the aesthetical object is constantly structured and restructured in the reader's response. The reader's response fulfils the reader's role which is structured by the text. According to Iser (1978:34) the reader's role as textual structure constitutes the *implied reader*.

[23]   Cf. Petersen (1984:43-47) for a detail analysis of the sociopolitical context of messianic pretendants and the significance of their acclamations for the 'authorial readers'. Iser's comment (1978:55) on the context of speech acts is also of particular interest: 'They [speech acts] are linguistic utterances in a given situation or context, and it is through this context that they take on their meaning... The pragmatic nature of a text can only come to full fruition by way of the complete range of contexts which the text absorbs, collects and stores'.

[24]   A more elaborate analysis of the suffering righteous one as counter-determining context occurs elsewhere in Maartens (1986:82-87) with reference to Psalms 3, 5, 6, 18, 22, 26, 27, 28, 30, 31, 34, 35, 41, 43, 44, 49, 54, 56, 57, 59, 64, 69, 80, 89, 109, 110, 118 and 142.

10:33,34). The *suffering righteous one* as textual entity constructs an aesthetic object. It follows that the aesthetic object concretises in the theme of discipleship as the fulfillment the reader's role.

In verses 24 and 25 the implied author becomes explicit: The expression βλέπετε τί ἀκούετε is a perlocutionary speech act (cf. Searle 1977b:39ff and Iser 1978:57). It particularises an earlier call in verse 9 to obey the teaching of Jesus. A subsequent illocutionary speech act explicates the significance of the warning: 'The measure you give is the measure you get and more will be added to you'. All the divine passives which follow: μετρηθήσεται, προστεθήσεται, δοθήσεται, and ἀρθήσεται refer to the eschatological judgement of all men. In Mark 14:62 the author designates Jesus as the post-existential judge of mankind. The reader now begins to reduce the indeterminacies of the text. Mark 16:8 confronts the reader with the rule of the resurrected Lord. The real reader concretises the speech act in a situational frame which encompasses himself. His faith produces hope. The text re-enacts this hope: even in times of persecution, oppression and suffering, the hope of the implied reader perseveres. Faith endures because Jesus who suffered persecution and death is waiting at the destiny of the world. The gospel of this Jesus determines the destiny of faithful people. To their faith 'will be added' and 'more will be given'. The reader's consciousness fuses with the re-enacted Gospel in a self-realisation of destiny.

The 'aesthetic object' thus constructed in a/my reader's response also contributes a valuable perspective to the interpretation of Mark 4:24-25. Inasmuch as Iser (1978:25) is conscious of a possible meaning production that 'may lead to a whole variety of different experience and hence subjective judgments', he exercises self-restraint in interpretation. He attempts to establish 'an intersubjective frame of reference that will enable us to assess the otherwise ineluctable subjectivity of value judgments'. Reception aesthetics, however, levels subject/object relations between the observing subject and the represented object. Practised absolutely, it reduces interpretation to a one-dimensional existential consciousness. Such a conscious experience interprets the gaps left by indeterminacies in the text. Yet, 'indeterminacies' might only be overdeterminacies which are presupposed by the text and deleted as redundant. The subject/object relations in the text therefore require further attention. This can best be done within the framework of a descriptive analysis of the metaphoric language usage in Mark 4:24-25.

In Mark 4:24-25 the principal subject, in Black's terms (1962:28), is expressed in the words βλέπετε τί ἀκούετε. This expression is syntagmatically linked to μετανοεῖτε καὶ πιστεύετε in Mark 1:15 and the two expressions are therefore illocutionary correlatives. The *tenor* is the principal subject, namely *faith*, which is not available in the immediate context. *Faith* is therefore, in Miller's terms

(1971:128-134), the tenor of a suspended metaphor. The principal subject is metaphorised in the expression ἐν ᾧ μέτρῳ μετρεῖτε. In Reinhart's terms (1976:388) this is the focal expression.

The focal expression, ἐν ᾧ μέτρῳ μετρεῖτε, engages in reciprocal interaction with *faith* as principal subject. The principal subject *faith* stands in a relationship of identification to the focal expression ἐν ᾧ μέτρῳ μετρεῖτε. According to Abraham (1975:27), only the comparable semantic features are retopicalised and transferred to *faith* as principal subject. The retopicalisation of semantic features constitutes the *representation* of the *interpretamen*. The retopicalised semantic features articulate the *tertium comparationis*. The *tertium comparationis* is the result of the representation of the *interpretamen* and as such it constitutes the *denotatum* of the semiotic action. The retopicalised semantic features or denotatum, transferred to ἀκούετε in the expression βλέπετε τί ἀκούετε, may be explicated as follows: (human) (faithfulness) (decision) (trust) (commitment) (eschatological) (perspectiveness) (obedience) (hope).

In Miller's terms (1971:128) the verb metaphor, μετρεθήσεται is a submerged metaphor. The principal subject (or tenor) of a submerged metaphor is permanently suspended from text. The tenor of the verb μετρεθήσεται is the Son of Man (Mk 14:62) as exchatological judge. Μετρεθήσεται articulates the eschatological *judgement* executed and dispensed by the Son of Man. The retopicalised semantic features transferred from the vehicle μετρεθήσεται, to the principal subject *judgement*, may be articulated in the following semantic features: (divine) (justice) (righteousness) (faithfulness) (redemption) (proleptic) (eschatological dispensation) (destiny).

The conjunctive καί in the expression καὶ προστεθήσεται ὑμῖν is an epexegetical καί. The verb προστεθήσεται alludes retrospectively to the incomparability of divine grace evident in the extraordinary harvest of the sower. Προστεθήσεται retrospectively reinterprets μετρεθήσεται. The antithesis between δοθήσεται αὐτῷ and ἀρθήσεται ἀπ' αὐτοῦ concretises μετρεθήσεται. The antithesis contrasts the positive and negative consequences of divine judgement. Those who commit themselves to the gospel will abound in God's grace. Who exclude themselves from God's grace lose whatever share of the grace they may have enjoyed. The main thrust of the symbolism is to highlight the grace of God, which rewards its recipients surpassing all human comprehension.

4. Conclusion

The preceding three analyses confirm the thesis stated at the outset of this paper. Every theoretically founded analysis, subject to its own historical contingent situation, contributes a particular truth perspective to the interpretation of the text. A structural analysis of Mark 4:24-25 highlights the opposition between the disciples committed to the teaching of the kingdom of God on the one hand, and the Jews, Pharisees and scribes on the other hand, who exclude themselves from the grace of God. Whereas the former abound in the grace of God, the latter loose whatever share they had in the kingdom of God. The reception framework on the other hand, re-enacts the incompatibility of God's grace in the existential consciousness of the reader. The analysis of the metaphoric language usage then constitutes the proverb as an eschatological sign, and contributes the symbolism as expressed in the retopicalised semantic features to the interpretation of the text. The metaphoric signifier and its representation thus lead to an interpretation. This interpretation results in a consciousness that the reward of one who commits himself to the grace of God rises to a vindication that surpasses all human comprehension.

Such a comparative literary interpretation is produced by ongoing literary critical discussions in changing historical conditions. Hermeneutics is therefore illustrated as the science of literary critical dialogue. This dialogue is determined by the interrelations of the text and the extra-textual reality, or, what Iser (1978:80) calls, the repertoire of the text. The repertoire of the text provides guidelines for the 'dialogue' between the text and the reader, or what Jauss (1982:18) calls the 'aesthetics of production and of representation'. Text representation furthermore, establishes a history of reception. For Jauss (1982:20) this means 'that the understanding of the first reader will be sustained and enriched in a chain of receptions from generation to generation...'.

A hermeneutic of literary critical dialogue guides interpretation through the Scylla and Charybdis of functionalism and methodological pluralism. The escapism of methodological pluralism is counteracted by a critical dialogue of practice and theory in the ongoing interpretation of the text. The interplay of practice and theory in the dynamics of ongoing literary critical dialogue reaches beyond the limitations of one-dimensional consciousness. Every interpretation given in changing historical conditions contributes another layer to the 'growth rings' which compose the history of exegesis. The dynamics of ongoing literary critical dialogue projects interpretation into the future. Reading as an interpreting event engages all subsequent readers in the ensuing debate. 'Interpretation beyond functionalism' is an open challenge to every generation to enter the dialogue and interpret the text relative to its historical contingent or situation.

BIBLIOGRAPHY

Abraham, W. 1975. *A Linguistic Approach to Metaphor*. Lisse: Peter de Ridder Press.

Bach, E. 1974. *Syntactic Theory*. New York: Holt, Rinehart and Winston.

Barthes, R. 1974. *S/Z*. (Tr. by R. Miller.) New York: Hill and Wang.

Barthes, R. 1977. *Elements of Semiology*. 2nd imp. (Tr. from the French by A. Lavers and C. Smith). New York: Hill and Wang.

Black, M. 1962. *Models and Metaphors: Studies in Language and Philosophy*. Ithaca: Cornell University Press.

Bloomfield, M. W. 1967. The Syncategorematic in Poetry: From Semantics to Syntactics, in *To Honor Roman Jakobson*. The Hague: Mouton, 309-317.

Bronswaer, W. J. M., Fokkema, D. W. & Ibsch, I. 1977. *Tekstboek Algemene Literatuurwetenschap. Moderne Ontwikkelingen in de Literatuurwetenschap Geillustreerd in een Bloemlezing uit Nederlandse en Buitelandse Publikasies*. Baarn: Amboboeken.

Culler, J. 1981. *The Pursuit of Signs: Semiotics, Literature, Deconstruction*. London and Henley: Routledge and Kegan Paul.

De Saussure, F. 1959. *Course in General Linguistics*. (Ed. by C. Bally and A. Sechehaye in collaboration with A. Reidlinger. Tr. from the French by W. Baskin.) London: Peter Owen.

Eagleton, T. 1983. *Literary Theory: An Introduction*. London: Basil Blackwell.

Eco, U. 1976. *A Theory of Semiotics*. Bloomington: Indiana University Press.

Eco, U. 1979. *The Role of the Reader: Explorations in the Semiotics of Texts*. London: Hutchinson.

Eco, U. 1984. *Semiotics and the Philosophy of Language*. London: Macmillan.

Fiske, J. 1982. *Introduction to Communication Studies*. London and New York: Methuen.

Gadamer, H.-G. 1979. *Truth and Method*. (Tr. from the second edition (1965) of *Wahreit und Methode* by W. Glen-Doepel.) London: Sheed & Ward.

Garvin, P. L. (ed.) 1964. *A Prague School Reader on Esthetics, Literary Structure and Style*. Washington: Georgetown University Press.

Gombrich, E. H. 1960. *Art and Illusion*. Princeton: Princeton University Press.

Guiraud, P. 1975. *Semiology*. (Tr. by G. Gross). London and Boston: Routledge and Kegan Paul.

Hartshorne, C. & Weiss, P. (eds.). 1974. *Collected Papers of Charles Sanders Peirce*. 2 vols. 3rd imp. Cambridge, Massachussetts: The Belknap Press of Harvard University Press.

Havránek, B. 1964. The Functional Differentiation of the Standard Language, in P. L. Garvin (ed.). *A Prague School Reader on Esthetics, Literary Structure and Style*. Washington: Georgetown University Press, 3-16.

Hawkes, T. 1977. *Structuralism and Semiotics*. London and New York: Methuen.

Holub, R. C. 1984. *Reception Theory: A Critical Introduction*. London and New York: Methuen.

Iser, W. 1971. *The Implied Reader: Patterns of Communication in Prose Fiction from Bunyan to Beckett*. London: John Hopkins University Press.

Iser, W. 1978. *The Act of Reading: A Theory of Aesthetic Response*. London and Henley: Routledge and Kegan Paul.

Jackendoff, R. S. 1972. *Semantic Interpretation in Generative Grammar*. Cambridge, Massachussetts: MIT Press.

Jakobson, R. 1960. Closing Statement: Linguistics and Poetics, in T. A. Sebeok (ed.). *Style in Language*. Cambridge, Massachussetts: MIT Press, 350-377.

Jakobson, R. 1966. Grammatical Parallellism and its Russian Facet. *Language* 42, 399-429.

Jauss, H. R. 1977. Geschiedenis en Kunst, in W. J. M. Bronswaer, D. W. Fokkema & I. Ibsch (eds.). *Tekstboek Algemene Literatuurwetenschap. Moderne Ontwikkelingen in de Literatuurwetenschap Geillustreerd in een Bloemlezing uit Nederlandse en Buitelandse Publikasies*. Baarn: Amboboeken, 266-283.

Jauss, H. R. 1982. *Toward an Aesthetic of Reception*. The Harvester Press.

Katz, J. J. & Fodor, J. A. 1963. The Structure of a Semantic Theory. *Language* 39, 170-210

Katz, J. J. 1972. *Semantic Theory*. New York: Harper & Row.

Kristeva, J. 1980. *Desire in Language: A Semiotic Approach to Literature and Art*. (Ed. by L. S. Roudiez; tr. by T. Gora, A. Jardine & L. S. Roudiez.) Oxford: Basil Blackwell.

Kristeva, J. 1984. *Revolution in Poetic Language*. (Tr. by M. Waller, with and interoduction by L. S. Roudiez.) New York: Columbia University Press.

Lämmert, E. 1970. *Bauformen des Erzählens*. Stuttgart: J. B. Metzlersche Verlagsbuchhandlung.

Leech, G. N. 1966. Linguistics and the Figures of Rhetoric, in R. Fowler (ed.). *Essays on Style and Language*. London: Routledge and Kegan Paul, 135-156.

Lotman, J. 1977. *The Structure of the Artistic Text*. (Tr. from the Russian by G. Lenhoff & R. Vroon.) Michigan: University of Michigan.

Maartens, P. J. 1986. The Son of Man as a Composite Metaphor in Mk 14:62, in J. H. Petzer & P. J. Hartin (eds.). *A South African Perspective on the New Testament. Essays by South African New Testament Scholars Presented to Bruce Manning Metzger during his Visit to South Africa in 1985*. Leiden: Brill, 76-98.

Maartens, P. J. 1980. Mark 2:18-22: An Exercise in Theoretically-founded Exegesis. *Scriptura* 2, 1-54.

Miller, D. M. 1971. *The Net of Hephaestus: A Study of Modern Criticism and Metaphysical Metaphor*. The Hague: Mouton.

Mukarovsky, J. 1978. *Structure, Sign and Function*. (Tr. by J. Burbank & P. Steiner.) New Haven and London: Yale University Press.

Mukarovsky, J. 1964. Standard Language and Poetic Languae, in P. L. Garvin (ed.). *A Prague School Reader on Esthetics, Literary Structure and Style*. Washington: Georgetown University Press, 17-30.

Peirce, C. S. 1974. Elements of Logic, in C. Hartshorne & P. Weiss (eds.). *Collected Papers of Charles Sanders Peirce*. 2 vols. 3rd imp. Cambridge, Massachussetts.

Petersen, N. R. 1984. The Reader in the Gospel. *Neotestamentica* 18, 38-51.

Rauche, G. A. 1983. The Function of Method in the Constitution of Knowledge. *Journal of the University of Durban-Westville* 4, 25-33.

Rauche, G. A. 1985. *Theory and Practice in Philosophical Argument*. Durban: University of Durban-Westville. (The Institute for Social and Economic Research, Special Publication 1.)

Ray, W. 1984. *Literary Meaning: From Phenomenology to Deconstruction*. New York: Basil Blackwell.

Reinhart, T. 1976. On Understanding Poetic Metaphor. *Poetics* 5, 383-402.

Riffaterre, M. 1978. *Semiotics of Poetry*. Bloomington: Indiana University Press. (A Midland Book.)

Searle, J. R. 1977. What is a Speech Act? in J. R. Searle (ed.). *The Philosophy of Language*. London: Oxford University Press, 39-53.

Van Zoest, A. 1978. *Semiotiek: Over Tekens, hoe ze Werken en wat We ermee Doen*. Ambo, Baarn: Basisboeken.

A. H. SNYMAN

A SEMANTIC DISCOURSE ANALYSIS OF THE LETTER TO PHILEMON

1. Introduction

Since Zellig Harris first used the term 'discourse analysis' in 1952 up to Van Dijk's recent four volume publication, *Handbook of Discourse Analysis* (1985), it has come to be used with a wide range of meanings, covering various areas of interest for New Testament scholars. Consequently I want to begin this article by referring to some disciplines that have made discourse an object of investigation over the past four decades. This will be followed by a brief discussion of discourse analysis within the context of New Testament studies. The type of analysis practised in South Africa will then be outlined as a prelude to the final part of the essay, which is a practical application of this method to the letter to Philemon.

But what is meant by discourse analysis? According to Brown and Yule (1983:ix) their primary interest is 'to give an account of how forms of language are used in communication'. Van Dijk (1985: Vol I, xi) defines the term as 'interest for various phenomena of language use, texts, conversational interaction, or communicative events'. It is very difficult – almost impossible – to offer an adequate definition, owing to the multiple reasons why discourse is being studied by linguists and scholars from various other disciplines. It seems better to take a look at some of these disciplines – the main questions asked in each, the methods used and some of the principal practitioners – rather than to formulate an inadequate definition.

2. The study of discourse in various fields

All disciplines interested in communication regard discourse as part of their field: linguistics, sociology, psychology, literary criticism, structural criticism, semiotics, speech act theory, etc. As a result of this wide interest an enormous number of books, monographs and articles has been published during the last four decades, especially from the early seventies up to the present. No fewer than eleven hundred publications on the subject are listed in Van Dijk's publication of 1985. The following diagram may give an overview of the state of the art:

TYPES OF DISCOURSE ANALYSIS

	1	2	3
DISCIPLINE	Text-linguistics	Socio-linguistics	Literary linguistics
TYPE OF DISCOURSE ANALYSIS DONE	Text analysis	Conversational analysis	Stylistics Rhetorics Aesthetics
MAIN QUESTIONS ASKED	How is discourse organised as units?	How do humans interact with one another? How does discourse accomplish social goals?	How do texts optimise correlations of linguistic features?
VIEW OF TEXTS	As linguistic structures	As social and communicative acts	As creative language
TEXTS STUDIED	Written, oral All text types	Oral Conversation	Written Fiction
GENRAL CONCERNS	Information structure, FSP, Segmentation, Speaker orientation	Speaker/hearer negotiation of meaning	Writer's manipulation of language
THEORY & METHOD	Descriptive and general linguistics, Wellformedness, Criteria used, Ideal reader, Formal	Ethnomethodological, Social-psychological, Every-day, Empirical data, Inductive Real speakers/hearers	Aesthetics, Reader reaction Informal
UNITS OF ANALYSIS	Segmental parts language	Exchanges, Segmental and supra-segmental signals	Uncommon sound & word patterns, Tropes
CHARACTERISTIC VOCABULARY	Topic/comment, Cohesion, Tense sequences, Nominalisation, Proforms, Topicalisation, Anaphora, Word, Order, Functions,	Context, Focus, Cohesion, (Pro-) conv. strategies, Exchange structures	Key words, Style, Poetics, Verbal art, Interpretation, *Literaturwissenschaft*

Hierarchies

PRACTITIONERS	Longacre Hinds	Hymes Gumperz	Chatman Enkvist
	Halliday Givon	Sachs Schegloff	Fowler Ihwe
	Danes Dahl Grimes	Coulthard Winter	Hendriks Schmidt
	Sgall Dressler	Goffman Labov	
	Werlich Petöfi	Stubbs Schenkein	
		Bauman & Scherzer	

An important new branch of discourse analysis is the so-called psycho-linguistic approach. It deals mainly with text reception and perception. The question asked is: How are discourses processed by the mind? Written or oral texts (especially narratives) are studied as cognitive processes, the theory used being a cognitive theory. Van Dijk (1985:71-105) also includes a chapter on this approach written by Bower and Cirilo, in the first volume of his *Handbook of Discourse Analysis*.

Linguists who have paved the way for important advances in biblical studies during the past few years, however, are mostly found in the first column. One thinks of scholars like Robert E. Longacre (1983), who emphasised a comprehensive structural linguistics and a tagmemic approach to discourse structure. John Hinds (1978) wrote an excellent work on anaphora in the narratives of different languages, while F. Danes (1974) focused on syntax – especially word order – and the sequential layout of information in an ongoing discourse. Linguists such as M. A. K. Halliday (1976) had an important impact on the beginnings of discourse study by paying attention to notions like reference, substitution, ellipsis, conjunction and lexical cohesion. Of similar significance was the work of J. E. Grimes (1975) who described the history of linguistic discourse analysis up to 1975, the event types, participants, types of information in discourse, semantic/rhetorical relations, cohesion, reference, topicalisation, etc. T. Givon (1983) focused on the sequencing of subjects and the topics in discourse, while J. S. Petöfi (1979) paid attention to theoretical issues of discourse analysis and (in cooperation with E. Sözer - cf. Petöfi & Sözer 1983) to coherence and cohesion in texts. Egon Werlich (1976) gave a detailed analysis of written English discourse types. The publication of W. U. Dressler (1978) identifies scholars who developed different types of discourse analysis up to that stage, while the Handbook edited by T. A. van Dijk contains several contributions from general linguists and text-linguists, dealing with such topics as different discourse modes (jokes, argumentation, stories), different discourse types (interviews, meetings) and discourse levels (linguistic, paralinguistic, etc.).

All these publications on text-linguistics have a common core: they are first and foremost interested in how language works. They are mainly concerned with the structures and functions of linguistic units, and the interrelationships between the two. Their primary object of study is language, and the outcome must be a theory of language, of which discourse elements form an integral part. In this respect text-linguistics differs from all the other disciplines listed and described above. For them the study of discourse is a tool, a means to an end other than a theory of language. The socio-linguist, for example, may study discourse phenomena in order to advance our understanding of social order. The psycho-linguist views texts as cognitive processes and studies language use in order to gain insights about how knowledge is acquired and processed by the mind. The literary linguist is interested in the stylistic characteristics that give discourse an aesthetic value. In short, for these disciplines the study of discourse is not an end in itself. It is a convenient road to other non-linguistic aspects of human behaviour. For the text-linguist, however, discourse analysis is both the point of departure and the point of arrival, and it is on this approach to discourse that the remainder of this essay will focus.

3. Discourse analysis within the context of New Testament studies

Text-linguistic discourse analysis reached its height in the seventies and early eighties, coinciding with an important shift in the field of biblical studies: the movement away from an historical and towards a text-immanent approach to the New Testament. At the heart of this shift lies two different philosophies. On the one hand positivism, according to which the meaning of a text was sought in a genetic-causal process of origin and development. In historical exegesis the authors of the New Testament were seen as exponents of their time and the situations in which they lived; therefore their writings were the result of a process of development, which must be studied historically. The literary work was regarded as an historical document of a specific time, which needed to be described in terms of causality. The real object of study was not the literary work as such, but its origin, its *genesis* (Den Heyer 1979:89-90).

In the seventies this approach and the philosophy on which it based itself were challenged by various text-immanent approaches, with their focus on the text as a literary work. The underlying philosophy of these approaches is phenomenology, where the text is seen as a phenomenon that must be understood and explained in terms of itself. Not the history of the text but the text itself, not the situation behind the text but the text as an autonomous object of study, not the intention of the author but the intention of the text comes to the fore (Vorster 1982:128). Although this shift in the study of non-biblical literature took place as early as the turn of the century, its influence on biblical studies was not felt until the seventies. But it was a severe and important shift, with far-reaching implications for New Testament scholarship.

By the time this altered scholarly perspective made itself felt in the field of New Testament studies, there were various text-immanent approaches in circulation among linguists and literators. They may be classified in three groups, each with its own subdivisions: French structuralism, literary criticism and discourse analysis (Vorster 1982:133-134).

French structuralism has its roots in Russian formalism and Prague functionalism, where the autonomy of the text is emphasised with regard to its structure and function. Via Saussure, Trubetskoy, Jakobson and Mukarovsky, Vladimir Propp laid the foundation for modern structural text analysis. These scholars were not so much interested in the meaning of a text, but rather in the structures underlying the text – structures that create meaning. These structures have a universal character and are part of man's consciousness. The focus is on the so-called deep structure of a text, in contrast with the surface structure, which is the object of study in literary criticism and discourse analysis.

The second main category is literary criticism. Here one may refer to the analysis of (mainly) narrative texts in terms of plot (intrigue), characters, point of view and temporal and spatial relations. The analysis of a narrative discourse, for example, is primarily directed at the description of the characters' reciprocal relationships. Whatever the characters are doing in reciprocal relations can be visualised on five levels, namely the psychological, phraseological, temporal, spatial and ideological (Uspensky 1973). These five levels are linked to the position(s) that the narrator assumes in the narration. Another important notion in narrative discourse is 'point of view' or 'focalisation', that is the interaction between the situation of the narrator and the narrative discourse (Bal 1980:108-109; Genette 1980:186; Rimmon-Kenan 1983:74-77). There are numerous subdivisions under this rubric of literary criticism (the so-called New Criticism, Close Reading, etc.), but they all deal with the surface structure of the text and regard the text as an autonomous object of study.

This brings us to the third category of text-immanent approaches, namely discourse analysis. In addition to the text-linguists mentioned under column 1 above (Longacre, Hinds, Halliday, Givon, etc.), one may also refer to the work of W. J. Hutchins (1971), who emphasised the importance of selection and arrangement in communication; J. E. Grimes and N. Glock (1970), who illustrate the importance of discourse patterns; E. V. Paducéva (1974), stating that 'the coherence of a text within a paragraph is founded to a significant degree upon the repetition in adjacent phrases of the same semantic elements'; J. E. Jordan (1965) with his description of the four ways in which paragraphs may be structured on a central theme; T. S. Kane and L. J. Peters (1966) who define a paragraph as 'a structure of sentences unified by their common relation to a general conception', etc. All these scholars agree that the basic unit of communication is not the individual word or the separate sentence, but the discourse as a whole.

These developments had a profound influence on New Testament studies, especially on Bible translation and lexicography. The main figure here is

Eugene A. Nida, who put all translation work on a new track with his well-known *Toward a Science of Translating* (1964) and *The Theory and Practice of Translation* (1969, co-author C. R. Taber). The modern linguistic shift from the word to the sentence, and the fact that a sentence does not consist of a collection of individual words with no relation between them, form the basis of Nida's work – both in the field of Bible translation and in lexicography. His views on lexicography which are closely related to those of F. G. Lounsbury (1956), W. H. Goodenough (1956) and A. Lehrer (1974), are described in his *Componential Analysis of Meaning* (1975, 1979) and *Exploring Semantic Structures* (1975) and led to the recent publication in two volumes of the *Greek-English Lexicon of the New Testament, based on semantic domains* (1988, co-editors J. P. Louw, R. B. Smith and K. A. Munson).

The shift from word to sentence and from sentence to paragraph in modern text-linguistics also paved the way for a method to analyse the surface structure of the text of the Greek New Testament. In 1973 J. P. Louw published his 'Discourse analysis and the Greek New Testament' in *The Bible Translator*, followed by *Semantiek van Nuwe Testamentiese Grieks* (1976). With these publications he took the lead within the New Testament Society of South Africa in developing a method for discourse analysis, to be used by nearly all New Testament scholars in South Africa and finally finding its way abroad (Den Heyer 1979; Black 1987). The basic premise of this method – to be fully discussed under the next heading – is that meaningful relations not only exist between the words in a sentence, but also between larger parts of a text such as sentences, groups of sentences (clusters) and pericopes. It is therefore important to analyse the way a text is structured in order to grasp its meaning.

Louw's proposal for discourse analysis is further refined by the publication of *Style and Discourse* (Nida *et al.* 1983). The purpose of the book is 'to deal with the dimensions of discourse primarily in relationship to rhetorical features in the New Testament' (Nida *et al.* 1983:19). All the main figures (*schêmata*) in the New Testament are classified according to three basic principles: repetition, omission and a shift in expectancies. But more important: an attempt is made to describe their functions, that is, how and why an author employed them in communicating semantic content. Apart from this, attention is also paid to issues important to discourse analysis in general: progression and cohesion (12-17), types of texts or diverse genres (56-68), meaning of larger discourse units (80-82), types of signs (86-89), meaningful relations between structures (101-104), methods for the analysis of texts, with illustrations (110-144), etc. The last three chapters deal with the functions of communication and the interpretative process (145-152), various theories of literary analysis (153-164) and the implication of rhetoric for the translation of New Testament texts (165-171).

To summarise: All these so-called text-immanent approaches have two features in common: (i) They operate within a linguistic paradigm, which means that they regard language as a fundamental or basic category and not as a road to something else, for example history (Patte 1979:1); and (ii) they honour the autonomy of the text (Den Heyer 1979:91), that is, the text can be explained in terms of itself and need not be complemented by consideration of its genesis.

4. Colon analysis as method

The type of discourse analysis developed in South Africa and referred to in 3 may be called colon analysis. Numerous publications have emerged since Louw's article in *The Bible Translator* of 1973: Louw (1976; 1979), Combrink (1979), Du Toit (1980; 1981), Fryer (1984), etc; also editions of *Neotestamentica*, the official journal of the New Testament Society of South Africa: Volume 8 of 1974, 11 of 1977, 13 of 1979 and 16 of 1982. Colon analysis has been successfully applied to argumentative material like the Letters of Paul and long discourses in the Gospels: Louw (1979), Van Zyl (1987), etc. Its main contribution is to describe the cohesion of a text, thereby demarcating the paragraphs and determining its pivot point or central meaning.

The method operates on the text theory that a close link exists between the way a text is structured and its meaning. The structuring of phrases or sentences in clusters to form text-units, which in their turn have meaning for the text as a whole, takes place in various ways. It can be accomplished by conjunctions and other parts of speech (such as pronouns) by which a network of references is created. Repetition is also an important technique – repetition of both words and thoughts – as well as the arrangement of words in certain patterns (commonly known examples are *chiasmus* and *inclusio*). The result is a system of relations, which contributes in significant ways to the meaning of a text. To describe these relations and to determine the cohesion of a text is the principal objective of colon analysis.

A major problem in the development of the method was that some practitioners used it to answer questions for which it was never designed. One of the refinements of the method was the realisation of its limits. It can only be used to describe the structure or plan, the cohesion, of a text. Furthermore: the description must not be absolutised as though it represents *the* structure of a text (Deist 1978:260). It rather represents no more than the exegete's interpretation of the structure of the text, no matter how objectively he has been led by instructions from the text. And as far as the relation between deep structure and meaning is concerned, it is not so much structure that reveals meaning, but rather the other way round: the exegete structures his understanding of the text. Deep structure discovers or reveals nothing. It explains only how the reader understands the text. It is nothing more than a representation of the relations between constituents of sentences (Deist 1978:264). With these remarks Deist made an important correction by rejecting certain heuristic tendencies in the employment of the method.

It will be clear by now that colon analysis as a method is not without its share of problems and limitations. As is the case with all the types of discourse analysis up to the present, it has not yet developed a comprehensive theory of its own. Nor can it be presented as an exegetical method complete in itself. It is liable to the subjectivity of the interpreter. The analyst must continually guard against philosophical trends like structuralism and phenomenology, according to which the meaning of a text lies completely within the text itself (Jordaan 1986:415ff). Despite all these pitfalls, however, colon analysis has proved to be a viable method in demarcating pericopes, in revealing the structure or layout of a text and in following the trend of the argument.

After these general remarks about the history and development of the method, the question arises: What is colon analysis? To begin with: A colon is a syntactic unit with clearly marked external dependencies. In terms of meaning that goes beyond a single word, it constitutes the smallest semantic unit. It always has a central matrix consisting of a nominal element (subject) and a verbal element (predicate), each having the possibility of extended features. As long as all these features can be grouped under one N + V, it forms one colon (Du Toit 1977:1-10; Louw 1976:99-101). It is important to begin any exegetical study with the texts's syntactic features; they have priority since they constitute ways in which basic relationships between fundamental units are most clearly marked.

The syntactic analysis is followed by a grouping of cola into clusters or (as in this article) into pericopes on account of (mainly) semantic considerations. In doing this, logical and stylistic markers are also taken into account, because they contribute in various ways to the demarcation of a pericope and the formulation of its theme or pivot point.

In determining cohesion the so-called structure markers play an important role. They may be divided into two groups, the first being words belonging to the same semantic domain. An indispensable aid in this regard is the new dictionary of Louw, Nida et al. (1988), in that it is based on semantic domains. The second category is more traditionally grammatical and includes words marking a transition in the discourse, a change in person, an alteration in the mood of the verb, etc. In addition to these markers, Nida's exposition of the semantic relations between cola and larger discourse units is also valuable for the description of the structural pattern and the trend of the argument within a pericope. These semantic relations exist on all levels (that is, between cola, sentences, pericopes and chapters) and divide into relations which are coordinate (additive and dyadic) and subordinate (qualificational and logical) (Nida et al. 1983:102-103). Although this outline with its sub-divisions may not be completely exhaustive, it has proved to be adequate in explaining the most important semantic relations which exist between cola – whether on the level of individual cola or on the level of various groupings of cola.

Certain aspects of the method will receive more attention than others, depending upon the genre of the text being studied. What needs to be done in any colon analysis, however, is the division of the text into cola and the classification of words according to the various semantic domains. From this brief description of the method it is clear that colon analysis is nothing more than a type of semantic discourse analysis.

5. Pericope division in the Letter to Philemon

The Letter to Philemon has been selected for illustration because it is short and may therefore be discussed within the compass of a single article. In an attempt to illustrate the various ways in which this short letter has been divided into pericopes, the following six versions were compared (No commentry has been consulted, owing to the scope of the article: only translations and translation aids):

a. J. B. Philips, *The New Testament in Modern English.*
b. *Revised Standard Version.*
c. *Good News for Modern Man.*
d. *The New English Bible.*
e. *New American Standard Bible.*
f. *Die nuwe Afrikaanse Bybelvertaling.*

The divisions are presented in the following diagram:

Version	Verses
a.	1-3; 4-14; 15-21; 22; 23-25
b.	1; 2; 3 || 4-7; 8-14; 15-20; 21-22; 23-24; 25
c.	1; 2; 3 || 4-7 || 8-11; 12-14; 15-16; 17-20; 21-22 || 23-24; 25
d.	1-2; 3; 4-7; 8-10; 11-16; 17-20; 21-22; 23-24; 25
e.	1-3; 4-7; 8-20; 21-22; 23-24; 25
f.	1a; 1b-2;3 || 4-7 || 8-11; 12; 13-16;17-19a; 19b;20-22 || 23-24; 25

(The semi-colons and the double lines indicate breaks in the text: the semi-colons are used for minor breaks, the double lines for major ones. Major breaks are usually marked by superscripts).

It is clear from the diagram that certain divisions are widely agreed upon, while opinions on others diverge considerably. All the translations have a major or minor break between verses 3 and 4, as well as between verses 22 and 23. Most of them have breaks at the end of verses 7 and 24. Between verses 8 and

22, however, the Philips translation and the *New American Standard Bible* have only two pericopes, while the *Good News for Modern Man* has no fewer than five and the new Afrikaans translation six. It is these differences that I propose to address by means of colon analysis, thereby proposing a verifiable pericope division and formulating a theme or superscript for each pericope.

6. A colon analysis of the Letter to Philemon

The twenty-five verses of the letter also divide into twenty-five cola. When dividing a text into cola, certain verbs (which form the basis of a colon) may be supposed. The supposed verb in colon 1, for example is *write*, in cola 2 and 26 *be*, in colon 4 *pray* and in colon 8 *was*. This normally applies to stereotyped greeting formulae, terms frequently used in Paul's letters and various forms of the verb *to be*. Usually, however, the verbal elements are explicit in the text.

The twenty-five cola are:

1. Παῦλος δέσμιος Χριστοῦ ᾿Ιησοῦ καὶ Τιμόθεος ὁ ἀδελφὸς Φιλήμονι τῷ ἀγαπητῷ καὶ συνεργῷ ἡμῶν καὶ ᾿Απφίᾳ τῇ ἀδελφῇ καὶ ᾿Αρχίππῳ τῷ συστρατιώτῃ ἡμῶν καὶ τῇ κατ' οἶκόν σου ἐκκλησίᾳ·
2. χάρις ὑμῖν καὶ εἰρήνη ἀπὸ θεοῦ πατρὸς ἡμῶν καὶ κυρίου ᾿Ιησοῦ Χριστοῦ.

3. Εὐχαριστῶ τῷ θεῷ μου πάντοτε μνείαν σου ποιούμενος ἐπὶ τῶν προσευχῶν μου, ἀκούων σου τὴν <u>ἀγάπην</u> καὶ τὴν <u>πίστιν</u> ἣν ἔχεις πρὸς τὸν <u>κύριον ᾿Ιησοῦν</u> καὶ εἰς πάντας τοὺς <u>ἁγίους</u>,
4. ὅπως ἡ κοινωνία τῆς <u>πίστεώς</u> σου ἐνεργὴς γένηται ἐν ἐπιγνώσει παντὸς ἀγαθοῦ τοῦ ἐν ἡμῖν εἰς <u>Χριστόν</u>·
5. χαρὰν γὰρ πολλὴν ἔσχον καὶ παράκλησιν ἐπὶ τῇ <u>ἀγάπῃ</u> σου, ὅτι τὰ σπλάγχνα τῶν <u>ἁγίων</u> ἀναπέπαυται διὰ σοῦ, ἀδελφέ.

6. Διό, πολλὴν ἐν Χριστῷ παρρησίαν ἔχων ἐπιτάσσειν σοι τὸ ἀνῆκον, διὰ τὴν ἀγάπην μᾶλλον <u>παρακαλῶ</u>, τοιοῦτος ὢν ὡς Παῦλος πρεσβύτης, <u>νυνὶ</u> δὲ καὶ δέσμιος Χριστοῦ ᾿Ιησοῦ –
7. <u>παρακαλῶ</u> σε περὶ τοῦ ἐμοῦ τέκνου, ὃν ἐγέννησα ἐν τοῖς δεσμοῖς ᾿Ονήσιμον,
8. τόν ποτέ σοι ἄχρηστον
9. <u>νυνὶ</u> δὲ {καὶ} σοὶ [καὶ] ἐμοὶ εὔχρηστον,

10. ὃν <u>ἀνέπεμψά</u> σοι, αὐτόν, τοῦτ' ἔστιν τὰ ἐμὰ σπλάγχνα·
11. ὃν ἐγὼ ἐβουλόμην πρὸς ἐμαυτὸν <u>κατέχειν</u>, ἵνα ὑπὲρ σοῦ μοι διακονῇ ἐν τοῖς δεσμοῖς τοῦ εὐαγγελίου,
12. χωρὶς δὲ τῆς σῆς γνώμης οὐδὲν ἠθέλησα ποιῆσαι, ἵνα μὴ ὡς κατὰ ἀνάγκην τὸ ἀγαθόν σου ᾖ ἀλλὰ κατὰ ἑκούσιον.

13. τάχα γὰρ διὰ τοῦτο <u>ἐχωρίσθη</u> πρὸς ὥραν ἵνα αἰώνιον αὐτὸν <u>ἀπέχῃς</u>,
    οὐκέτι ὡς δοῦλον ἀλλὰ ὑπὲρ δοῦλον, ἀδελφὸν ἀγαπητόν,
14. μάλιστα ἐμοί, πόσῳ δὲ μᾶλλον σοὶ καὶ ἐν σαρκὶ καὶ ἐν κυρίῳ.

15. Εἰ οὖν με ἔχεις κοινωνόν, προσλαβοῦ αὐτὸν ὡς ἐμέ.
16. εἰ δέ τι ἠδίκησέν σε ἢ <u>ὀφείλει</u>, τοῦτο ἐμοὶ <u>ἐλλόγα·</u>
17. ἐγὼ Παῦλος ἔγραψα τῇ ἐμῇ χειρί, ἐγὼ <u>ἀποτίσω·</u> ἵνα μὴ λέγω σοι ὅτι καὶ
    σεαυτόν μοι <u>προσοφείλεις.</u>
18. ναί, ἀδελφέ, ἐγώ σου ὀναίμην ἐν κυρίῳ·
19. ἀνάπαυσόν μου τὰ σπλάγχνα ἐν Χριστῷ.

20. Πεποιθὼς τῇ ὑπακοῇ σου ἔγραψά σοι, εἰδὼς ὅτι καὶ ὑπὲρ ἃ λέγω ποιήσεις.
21. ἅμα δὲ καὶ ἑτοίμαζέ μοι ξενίαν,
22. ἐλπίζω γὰρ ὅτι διὰ τῶν προσευχῶν ὑμῶν χαρισθήσομαι ὑμῖν.
23. Ἀσπάζεταί σε Ἐπαφρᾶς ὁ συναιχμάλωτός μου ἐν Χριστῷ Ἰησοῦ,
24. Μᾶρκος, Ἀρίσταρχος, Δημᾶς, Λουκᾶς, οἱ συνεργοί μου.
25. Ἡ χάρις τοῦ κυρίου Ἰησοῦ Χριστοῦ μετὰ τοῦ πνεύματος ὑμῶν.

The following pericope division is thus proposed and then discussed:

```
Cola   1 - 2
       3 - 5
       6 - 9
      10 - 14
      15 - 19
      20 - 25
```

6.1 Cola 1-2

Neither of these two cola has an explicit verb, as already indicated. In the first colon the senders and recipients of the letter are mentioned, while colon 2 has the traditional salutation. As an introduction to the letter these two cola have many parallels in other Pauline letters (Rm 1:1 and 7; 1 Th 1:1; 2 Th 1:1-2; 1 Tm 1:1-2; 2 Tm 1-2; Phlp 1:1-2, etc.). This provides further evidence for demarcating cola 1 and 2 as a unit (Bratcher & Nida 1977:113-114).

6.2 Cola 3-5

The first verbal element in the letter, εὐχαριστῶ, separates colon 3 and what follows from the first two cola. It is followed by Paul's reason for thanking God, and the reason contains the semantic markers ἀγάπη, πίστις, 'Ιησοῦς Χριστός and ἅγιοι.

These markers are repeated in cola 4 and 5. Consequently, cola 3-5 may be described as a pericope where the point at issue is Philemon's love and faith. Philemon, however, is not the grammatical object of any verb in this section. This fact also isolates the pericope from cola 6 and 7, where Philemon is the object of the verb παρακαλῶ.

An interesting aspect of the structure of the pericope is that the reason why Paul thanks his God in colon 3, is expanded upon in cola 4 and 5. This expansion confirms that the terms ἀγάπη, πίστις, 'Ιησοῦς Χριστός and ἅγιοι in colon 3 are structured chiastically, that is, πίστις must be connected with 'Ιησοῦς Χριστός (as in colon 4), and ἀγάπη with ἅγιοι (as in colon 5). The chiasm emphasises that Philemon's love and faith constitute the pivot of the pericope: love for his fellow-believers and faith in Jesus Christ (Bratcher & Nida 1977:117-118; Louw 1986:142-144).

6.3 Cola 6-9

Colon 6 begins with διό, which separates it from the preceding three cola and at the same time draws an important conclusion from them. The verbal form παρακαλῶ in cola 6 and 7 further isolates this section (6-9) from cola 3-5 and 10-14, where it does not occur. For the first time Philemon becomes the object of a verb, thereby providing further evidence for the break between cola 5 and 6.

Why does the pericope end with colon 9? The answer is found in the parallel structure of the pericope (Beekman & Callow 1974:321). In colon 6 the person pleading on behalf of Onesimus, namely Paul, is qualified by the words τοιοῦτος ὢν ὡς Παῦλος πρεσβύτης, νυνὶ δὲ καὶ δέσμιος Χριστοῦ 'Ιησοῦ. In cola 7-9 the person on whose behalf Paul is pleading, Onesimus, is qualified as ὃν ἐγέννησα ἐν τοῖς δεσμοῖς 'Ονήσιμον, τόν ποτέ σοι ἄχρηστον νυνὶ δὲ [καὶ] σοὶ καὶ ἐμοὶ εὔχρηστον. The repetition of νυνί towards the end of each qualification further strengthens the parallelism.

The theme of the pericope may be formulated thus: I make a request to you on behalf of Onesimus. Διό, with which the pericope begins, indicates a conclusion based on Philemon's love and faith in cola 3-5. The basis for Paul's appeal is Philemon's love for his fellow-believers and his faith in the Lord.

6.4 Cola 10-14

It is clear from the comparison between the various translations above that the major differences occur in the demarcation of the pericope just discussed (cola 6-9, i.e. verses 8-11), and the present section (cola 10-14, i.e. verses 9-16). For what reasons may cola 10-14 be regarded as a separate unit?

First, on account of markers belonging to the same semantic domain(s). The relevant forms are ἀνέπεμψα (10), κατέχειν (11), ἐχωρίσθη and ἀπέχῃς (13). According to Louw and Nida (1988:187-191) the Greek terms ἀναπέμπω and χωρίζω belong to the semantic domain of 'Linear movement' (subdomain: leave, depart, flee, escape, send), while the forms κατέχω and ἀπέχω belong to the domain 'Possess, transfer, exchange' (1988:588 and 573). Furthermore: the utterance in colon 12 χωρὶς δὲ τῆς σῆς γνώμης οὐδὲν ἠθέλησα ποιῆσαι also implies that Paul sent Onesimus back. Cola 10-13 thus contain verbs or references to events which belong to the same semantic domains – prime evidence for demarcating a pericope.

The second consideration is the semantic relations between the cola. The pericope begins with the verb ἀνέπεμψα in colon 10. It is followed by two main verbs: ἐβουλόμην in colon 11 and ἠθέλησα in colon 12. Both these verbs are followed by parallel grammatical constructions: the infinitives κατέχειν (11) and ποιῆσαι (12), each followed by a purpose clause introduced by ἵνα. Both cola clarify the statement in colon 10: I am sending him back. Paul sent him back, although he would prefer to keep Onesimus with him. In terms of Nida's proposal, the relation between cola 11-12 and 10 is one of concession-result (Nida *et al.* 1983:103).

More complicated is the relation between colon 13 τάχα γὰρ διὰ τοῦτο ἐχωρίσθη πρὸς ὥραν ἵνα αἰώνιον αὐτὸν ἀπέχῃς and the preceding cola. Onesimus' running away is modified by the passive ἐχωρίσθη, suggesting that there was a divine purpose behind the event, namely that Philemon should have him back for ever (Bratcher & Nida 1977:127). We thus have a reason-result relation within colon 13, clearly marked by διὰ τοῦτο and ἵνα. But what is the relation between cola 13 and 10-12, especially with regard to the linking particle γάρ? According to Beekman and Callow (1974:323) colon 13 also supplies a reason for the introductory statement in colon 10 (I am sending him back). Paul is acting as he is because God has ordained a parting (ἐχωρίσθη) between Philemon and his slave in order that they might eventually be reconciled, not as master and slave, but as beloved brothers (13-14). For Paul to do otherwise would be to go against God's will.

The fact that Onesimus is no longer Philemon's slave, but his brother in the Lord, is stylistically emphasised by the climax in cola 13 and 14, qualifying αὐτόν in colon 13. The climax is: no longer a slave, but more than a slave: a beloved brother; a beloved brother to me, and therefore, even more so to you; a brother not only in the flesh, but also in the Lord! Colon 14 is thus closely linked to colon 13, and through colon 13 with the preceding three cola.

The superscript of cola 10-14 may read: I am sending Onesimus back as a beloved brother.

6.5 Cola 15-19

As in the case of colon 6, the particle οὖν in colon 15 draws a conclusion from the preceding section. This is the first reason for considering a break between cola 14 and 15. In cola 10-14 Paul has given certain information which has a bearing on the situation. On account of this he is going to put a few requests to Philemon.

The requests are made in the imperative mood. This provides a second reason for isolating colon 15 and what follows from cola 10-14. The moods of the Greek verbs in the preceding pericope were either indicative or subjunctive. Now we have a series of imperatives: προσλαβοῦ (15), ἐλλόγα (16), ἀνάπαυσον (19) and ἑτοίμαζε (21). The wish in colon 18 is in the optative mood (ὀναίμην), but semantically it is equivalent to a command: Let me have the benefit. Does this mean that the pericope extends to colon 21 or 22, as most translations suggest?

To answer the question, one must consider the persons involved and the issues at stake (Beekman & Callow 1974:324). The command in colon 15 is directed at Philemon and deals with the question of receiving Onesimus back. The same applies to the commands in cola 16 and 19. In colon 21, however, the command is directed at Philemon, but it is not concerned with the return of Onesimus. It is a command on behalf of Paul himself. The pericope thus ends with colon 19, strengthened by the change to the indicative mood ἔγραψα in colon 20.

Four of the finite verbs in the pericope belong to the same semantic domain: ὀφείλει and ἐλλόγα (16), as well as ἀποτίσω and προσοφείλεις (17). The domain and subdomain of ὀφείλει and προσοφείλεις are identical: 'Possess, transfer, exchange' (subdomain 'owe, debt, cancel') (Louw & Nida 1988:582), while the domain of ἀπότισω and ἐλλόγα is as that of ὀφείλει and προσοφείλεις the same but their subdomains differ (Louw & Nida 1988:575 and 583).

The semantic relations between the cola are not as logical as in the preceding pericopes. Colon 15 begins with a command to receive Onesimus back as if he were Paul himself. This is followed by two cola in which the semantic markers discussed above figure prominently and which deals with the problem: Does Onesimus still owe Philemon anything? If so, Philemon must charge it to Paul's account. Paul's request to Philemon is neither unconditional nor unfair. Cola 16 and 17 may thus be described as indicating the circumstances under which Philemon must receive Onesimus back (15) (Nida et al. 1983:102).

Cola 18 and 19 are also related to colon 15 in that Philemon by receiving Onesimus back, is doing Paul himself a favour. By welcoming Onesimus back just as he would welcome Paul (15), Philemon is cheering Paul up (18-19). In terms of Nida's proposal for semantic relations, colon 15 may be seen as the cause, with cola 18-19 the results (Nida et al. 1983:103). At the same time the semantic relation forms an inclusio, enclosing cola 15-19 stylistically.

The theme of the pericope may be formulated thus: Receive Onesimus back, just as you would receive me.

6.6 Cola 20-25

Colon analysis takes account of the main components of a typical Pauline letter. According to the majority of translations the conclusion of the letter begins with colon 23. This is possible, provided that cola 20-22 form part of the preceding pericope, or form a separate one. That they are not part of cola 15-19 has been shown above. They also do not form a pericope apart from cola 23-25 on account of the following two arguments:

(i) Paul usually concludes his letters with the verb γράφειν, as in colon 20. Examples are Gl 6:11, Rm 16:22, 2 Cor 13:10, 2 Th 3:17.

(ii) The issues in cola 20-25 are typical of the conclusions in other letters of Paul: arrangements to meet the adressees again (Rm 15:22-33, 1 Tm 4:9, 21 and Tt 3:12); greetings (Rm 16:1-23, 1 Cor 16:19-21, Phlp 4:21-22); and the final benediction (Phlp 4:23, 1 Th 5:28, 2 Th 3:18, etc.).

Owing to the various issues in the conclusion there is no cohesion based on semantic markers or relations between the cola.

7. The relations between the pericopes

Apart from the traditional introduction and conclusion (cola 1-2 and 20-25) the body of the letter may thus be divided into four pericopes. As already mentioned, the same relations between cola apply to all other levels, including clusters and chapters. An entire book, for example, may be organised in terms of reason-result: a series of chapters may lead up to a result, or the result may be stated and then followed by a series of reasons validating the result (Nida *et al.* 1983:104).

The relations between the four pericopes may be presented as follows:

Cola	Verses	Themes	Relations
3-5	4-7	Philemon's love and faith	Basis
6-9	8-11	I beseech you on behalf of Onesimus	Inference
10-14	12-16	I am sending him back as a brother	Basis
15-19	17-20	Receive him as you would receive me	Inference

The two inferences, read together, give the following overall theme: I beseech you to receive Onesimus back.

8. Conclusion

Colon analysis as part of text-linguistic discourse analysis inquires about the cohesion of a text in order to demarcate the pericopes in a verifiable manner and to describe the trend of the argument. Although new insights do not always result, it does make a contribution towards more reliable pericope divisions in cases where major differences of opinion occur. Pericopes can be further divided into so-called clusters, especially in extended discourses. The principles according to which this is done are the same as those illustrated in this article.

Colon analysis is not an heuristic, but a descriptive method. It represents nothing more than the reader's interpretation of the structure of the text – no matter how objectively he has been led by instructions from the text. It may be used to answer several questions, provided that they all pertain to the cohesion of a text. One of them is the division and entitling of pericopes – an important and difficult task for any Bible translator.

BIBLIOGRAPHY

Bal, M. 1980. *De Theorie van Vertellen en Verhalen. Inleiding in de Narratologie*. Muiderberg: Coutinho.

Beekman, J. & Callow, J. 1974. *Translating the Word of God*. Grand Rapids, Michigan: Zondervan Publishing House.

Black, D. A. 1987. Hebrews 1:1-4: A Study in Discourse Analysis. *Westminster Theological Journal* 49, 175-194.

Bratcher, R. G. & Nida, E. A. 1977. *A Translator's Handbook on Paul's Letters to the Colossians and to Philemon*. Stuttgart: United Bible Societies.

Brown, G. & Yule, G. 1983. *Discourse Analysis*. Cambridge: Cambridge University Press.

Combrink, H. J. B. 1979. *Structural Analysis of Acts 6:8-8:3*. Cape Town: DRC Publishers.

Culpepper, R. H. 1983. *Anatomy of the Fourth Gospel*. Philadelphia: Fortress.

Danes, F. (ed.) 1974. *Papers on Functional Sentence Perspective*. The Hague: Mouton.

Deist, F. E. 1978. Ope vrae aan die Diskoersanalise. *Nederduits-Gereformeerde Teologiese Tydskrif* 19, 260-71.

Den Heyer, C. J. 1979. *Exegetische Methoden in Discussie. Een Analyse van Markus 10:46-13:37*. Kampen.

Den Heyer, C. J. 1979. Struktuur-analyse. *Gereformeerd Theologisch Tijdschrift* 79, 86-110.

Dressler, W. U. (ed.) 1978. *Current Trends in Text Linguistics*. Berlin: De Gruyter.

Du Toit, A. B. 1980. Die Praktyk van Eksegese in die Lig van Nuwere Wetenskaplike Ontwikkeling, in *Die Nuwe-Testamentiese Wetenskap vandag*. Pretoria: Universiteit van Pretoria, 119-136.

Du Toit, A. B. 1981. Strukturale Eksegese en die Suid-Afrikaanse Redevoeringsanalise – Enkele Opmerkings aan die hand van Van Iersel se Analise van die Emmausverhaal. *Skrif en Kerk* 2, 3-14.

Du Toit, H. C. 1977. What is a Colon? *Neotestamentica* 11, 1-10.

Enkvist, N. & Kohenen, V. (eds.) 1976. *Reports on Text Linguistics: Approaches to Word Order*. Finland: Abo Akademi.

Fryer, N. S. L. 1984. *Discourse Analysis and Exegesis*. Kwadlangezwa: University of Zoeloeland.

Genette, G. 1980. *Narrative Discourse*. (Tr. by J. E. Lewin.) Oxford: Blackwell.

Givon, T. (ed.) 1983. *Topic Continuity in Discourse: A Quantitative Cross-language Study*. Amsterdam: Benjamins.

Goodenough, W. H. 1956. Componential Analysis and the Study of Meaning. *Language* 32, 195-216.

Grimes, J. E. 1975. *The Thread of Discourse*. The Hague: Mouton. (Janua Linguarum, Series Minor, 207.)

Grimes, J. E. & Glock, N. 1970. A Saramaccan Narrative Pattern. *Language* 46, 408-425.

Halliday, M. A. K. & Hasan, R. 1976. *Cohesion in English*. London: Longman.

Harris, Z. S. 1952. Discourse Analysis: A Sample Text. *Language* 28, 1-30, 474-494.

Harris, Z. S. 1963. *Discourse Analysis Reprints*. The Hague: Mouton.

Hinds, J. (ed.) 1978. *Anaphora in Discourse*. Edmonton, Illinois: Linguistic Research.

Hutchins, W. J. 1971. Semantics in Three Formal Models of Language. *Lingua* 28, 201-236.

Jordaan, G. J. C. 1986. 'n Kritiese Evaluering van die Suid-Afrikaanse Diskoersanalise. *Koers* 51, 401-418.

Jordan, J. 1965. *Using Rhetoric*. New York: Harper and Row.

Kane, T. S. & Peters, L. J. 1966. *A Practical Rhetoric of Expository Prose*. Oxford: University Press.

Lehrer, A. 1974. *Semantic Fields and Lexical Structure*. Amsterdam, London: North Holland Publishing Company.

Longacre, R. E. 1983. *The Grammer of Discourse*. New York, London: Plenum.

Lounsbury, F. G. 1956. A Semantic Analysis of the Pawnee Kinship Usage. *Language* 32, 158-194.

Louw, J. P. 1973. Discourse Analysis and the Greek New Testament. *The Bible Translator* 24, 108-118.

Louw, J. P. 1976. *Semantiek van Nuwe Testamentiese Grieks*. Pretoria: University of Pretoria. (New Afrikaans edition in 1986. Also translated and published in 1982 as: *Semantics of New Testament Greek*. Philadelphia: Fortress Press.)

Louw, J. P. 1979. *A Semantic Discourse Analysis of Romans*. 2 Vols. Pretoria: University of Pretoria.

Louw, J. P., Nida, E. A., Smith, R. B. & Munson, K. A. 1988. *Greek-English Lexicon of the New Testament, Based on Semantic Domains*. 2 vols. United Bible Societies.

Nida, E. A. 1964. *Toward a Science of Translating*. Leiden: Brill.

Nida, E. A. & Taber, C. R. 1969. *The Theory and Practice of Translation*. Leiden: E J Brill.

Nida, E. A. 1975a. *Exploring Semantic Structures*. München: Wilhelm Funk Verlag.

Nida, E. A. 1975b. *Componential Analysis of Meaning*. The Hague: Mouton.

Nida, E. A., Louw, J. P., Snyman, A. H. & Cronjé, J. v. W. 1983. *Style and Discourse with Special Reference to the Text of the Greek New Testament*. Cape Town: Bible Society of South Africa.

Paducéva, E. V. 1974. On the Structure of the Paragraph. *Linguistics* 131, 49-58.

Patte, D. 1979. *What is Structural Exegesis?* Philadelphia: Fortress Press.

Petöfi, J. S. (ed.) 1979. *Text vs. Sentence; Basic Questions of Text Linguistics*, 2 vols. Hamburg: Buske. (Papiere zur Textlinguistik 20.1 and 2.)

Petöfi, J. S. & Sözer, E. (eds.) 1983. *Micro and Macro Connexitivity of Texts*. Hamburg: Buske. (Papiere zur Textlinguistik 45.)

Rimmon-Kenan, S. 1983. *Narrative fiction, Contemporary Poetics*. London: Methuen.

Uspensky, B. 1973. *A Poetics of Composition. The Structure of the Artistic Text and Typology of a Compositional Form*. (Tr. by V. Zavarin & S. Wittig.) Berkeley: University of California Press.

Van Dijk, T. A. (ed.) 1985. *Handbook of Discourse Analysis*. 4 vols. London: Academic.

Van Zyl, H. C. 1987. *Matteus 18:15-20: 'n Diachroniese en Sinchroniese Ondersoek met Besondere Verwysing na Kerklike Dissipline*. Pretoria: University of Pretoria. (Unpublished Doctoral Thesis.)

Vorster, W. S. 1982. De Structuuranalyse, in A. F. J. Klijn (ed.). *Inleiding tot de Studie van het Nieuwe Testament*. Kampen: Kok, 127-152.

Werlich, E. 1976. *A Text Grammar of English*. Heidelberg: Quelle and Meyer. (Second revised edition, 1983.)

A. G VAN AARDE

NARRATIVE CRITICISM APPLIED TO JOHN 4:43-54

1. Narratology: general remarks

1.1 Terminology

1.1.1 Poetics

A prominent feature of modern literary theory is that the type of text dictates the exegetic method and approach. Traditionally, the New Testament is grouped into the following literary types: *gospel*, *acts*, *letter*, and *apocalypse*. For an ad hoc exegetical approach, this classification is not very serviceable. No exegetic models have been designed either to consider, methodologically, a gospel as a gospel, a letter as a letter, and so forth, or to determine, synchronously, their individual characteristics.

As far as the gospel form is concerned, much is currently being made of its narrative style as the poetics of the gospel form. The word 'poetics' comes from the Greek word ποιεῖν, meaning 'to make'. In literary theory the term 'poetics' implies the manner in which language is organised in a discourse – that is, the way in which a text is 'made'.

1.1.2 Narratology

The premise is that a gospel is a narrative and that it should therefore be analysed in terms of narratology, the science that concerns itself with narrative discourses.

The gospel form is characterised as 'narrative' because it contains the most elementary phenomena that comprise the essence of a 'narrative'. These are a *narrator*, a *story*, and a type of *reader*. The essence of the art of narration lies in the interrelationships between the narrator and the story, and between the narrator and the reader/listener.

1.1.3 Narrative

A narrative can thus be defined as a discourse in which language is organised in terms of characters who move in a particular structure of time and space, and which entails a chronological sequence of episodes with a causal relationship to one another (a plot). This narrative structure can be very simple or very complex.

1.1.4 Plot and intrigue

The plot of a narrative is, in other words, the structure of events or episodes of events (the sequential course of events). The study of plot is thus not the mere summation of the linear course of events, or episodes of events, in a narrative. It is only when we explain how elements in a narrative relate to other elements in the same narrative, and how they function together in an organised manner for the sake of a particular communicative effect, that the plot of the narrative amounts to a summation. An elementary and well-structured plot generally has a linearly sequential *beginning* that leads to a *middle* and an *end*.

The beginning of the plot introduces the action and creates expectations; in the middle the initial action is developed, and this presupposes an unravelling of the plot (denouement) which is worked out in the conclusion. Plot and characterisation are interdependent, since the events or actions in a narrative are determined by the reciprocal relations of characters (cf. 1.1.7). Since the successful or abortive conclusion of a narrative depends on the characters' reciprocal roles, suspense and intrigue are created in the plot. Intrigue is built by the relationship between elements of surprise and elements of suspense in a narrative.

As the plot develops, the expectations raised in the reader suggest an association on his part with the narrated characters – that is, sympathy or antipathy. The reader's uncertainty about what will happen to those characters with whom he particularly associates, creates expectation filled with suspense. The same happens when the reader is informed, but certain characters remain uninformed. When characters produce sudden surprises, the tension is heightened. Intrigue can thus be identified when, in the midst of the linear sequence of the narrated event, one can show a causality between the events or the episodes of events.

1.1.5 'Narrative point of view' and 'focalisation'

We have already suggested (cf. also 1.1.7) that a narrative discourse is constructed from the relations between the writer and the narrator, between the narrator and the (implied/idealised) reader, between the narrator and the narrated characters, between the (implied/idealised) reader and the narrated characters, and among the narrated characters themselves in their binary relations. All these relations affect the manner in which a writer presents (or structures) his narrative. This expression, 'manner of presentation', is referred to by the technical term *point of view* in narratology.

Point of view in literary criticism is often spoken of as the filter through which the narrator presents his narrative. It is like the position of a camera, which determines the angle from which a viewer sees an object. Those who hear or read a narrative depend on the narrator's viewpoint for the way in which they perceive the story.

Point of view is therefore a very serviceable concept that does justice to the interrelational communication between writer, narrative discourse and reader. It concerns the technical and perceptual dimension in a narrative, which causes a narrative discourse to appear as it does, and be read and interpreted by an implied reader in a particular manner. Thus, point of view no longer pertains to the technical angle of vision alone. The concept has changed. It has emerged as an ideological crux and force. It is much more concerned with who is narrating than with how observation takes place. This is indeed the reason that narratologists, because of a dissatisfaction with the traditional connotation attached to 'point of view', have drawn a distinction between *mood* and *voice*, and as a result have introduced the concept of *focalisation*.

Focalisation concerns *voice* and this relates to the way in which the narrator focuses, such as from the viewpoint of either a first-person or third-person narrator. Point of view is an aspect that, *inter alia*, involves *mood* and it has relevance only to the internal or external position of the narrator as regards the related events. An 'internal' narrative situation is, for example, one where a narrator is all-knowing and has ubiquitous access to the narrated events. An 'external' narrator's situation consists in the narrator telling the story as a mere objective observer. In both examples the narrator is not a character in the narrative. Since a narrator can also allow a character to tell his story, or he may even tell the story as an intratextual character, the earlier concept of focalisation has to be refined. On the basis of the distinction between *mood* and *voice*, a differentiation has been made between a character-focuser and a narrator-focuser respectively. The first refers to the *narrative mood*, where the narrator may tell his story through the main character or where the narrator himself poses as a character and tells his story from this angle.

However, whatever connotation is attached to the term 'point of view', in the art of narration it involves the relationship between an observing subject and an observed object. Viewed thus, all those who speak in a narrative feature as interpreters, and their views and diction are the result of the process of interpretation.

The term 'point of view' thus refers to two things: firstly, to the technical perspective (angle of vision) from which the narrator observes the narrated world and presents it to the implied/idealised reader; secondly, to the ideological perspective from which the narrator evaluates the narrated world, so that he observes it according his own perspective and technically presents it in a particular

manner. Many literary theorists avoid the second component. In their definition of 'point of view' they concentrate only on the narrative techniques, without
any mention of the narrator's ideological perspective, which is fundamental to
the techniques. Our approach takes account of the synthesis between idea and
technique. Because the gospels are religious texts, the narrator's ideological perspective is in reality his theological perspective.

To analyse narrative point of view is to abstract the narrator's ideological/
theological point of view from his narrative techniques. In a narrative the techniques of narration can be seen in the narrator's situation, the narrative tempo,
the narrative space and the narrated characters. The basic premise of any analysis of narrative point of view is therefore that, with an analysis of the techniques
of narration, the exegete can identify the underlying idea(s) in a story.

The most important matter to which analysis of narrative point of view leads,
is the question of whose perspective has been adopted by the narrator in his
ideological/theological evaluation and observation of the narrated world. Does
the writer allow the narrator to adopt a perspective that corresponds with his
own, or with that of the narrated world's normative system, as distinct from the
norms of the writer himself (and which may conflict with them)? Or does the
narrator adopt the perspective of one (or more) of the narrated characters? The
answer to this question indicates whether a narrative is simple or complex.

1.1.6 Ideology and social context

The term ideology can be understood either from the Marxist or from an ideal,
non-materialist viewpoint. Marxist tradition links the concept to situations in
which people find themselves with regard to economic production. Non-
materialistic tradition involves theories of idealism. Neither reality nor its
economic circumstances as it really is, is however reflected by either tradition.
Every ideology, in fact, represents an imagined distortion of reality. Texts as
imagined accounts of realities therefore belong to the sphere of ideology.
Within such literary theory frameworks the term ideology is used in narratology.
Using the concept of ideology, reference is made to the network of themes and
ideas that occur in a narrative as an imagined version of a specific reality.

All texts are in some way or other the products of real writers and are intended to be read and listened to by real readers and listeners. In verbal communication, such as in texts, there are always linguistic and perceptual dimensions.
The expression 'linguistic dimension' concerns the configuration of language
symbols in a text, and the text as a language symbol in a constellation of texts.
The perceptual dimension refers to a particular social context in a network of
textual themes and ideas. This dimension is thus no more than an evaluative
imagining of a particular social context.

In other words, while language (the linguistic dimension) is the communication code, a literary communication *record* (a text) presupposes an ideology (a network of themes and ideas) which is communicated and has meaning only in a certain social context. If the speech act takes the form of a narration, the ideological perspective (the evaluating point of view) is communicated by means of a narrative act. The ideological perspective (the perceptual dimension) in the communication act causes the speech act to be presented in the form of a narrative act, manipulating the reader in such a way that he/she agrees with the ideological perspective or rejects it. In a narrative discourse a writer thus communicates an ideology to a reader by means of a narrator in the form of a story.

In the process of communication there are consequently intratextual and extratextual components. The social context concerns the extratextual component. Its construction depends on a knowledge of other texts, of social and cultural codes, and of the sociocultural context of both the extratextual author and the extratextual reader. Extratextual factors however have exegetic relevance only in so far they manifest themselves in a specific text. The construction of the social context of a specific text depends on the text being read. However, the exegete need not undertake the construction of the social context only after analysis of the specific text. One can first construct a context and then read the text in that particular social context. It is of course taken for granted that the specific text will be interpreted meaningfully and coherently.

1.1.7 Narrative structure

When events in life that affect people (the social context) are imagined in ideological communication in a narrative record, this follows a specific narrative structure. The narrative communication contains at least four basic perspectives: the *writer* who compiles the story, the *narrator* who narrates the story, the *reader* who receives the story, and the *characters* who take part in the story. The analytical process in the exegesis of a narrative discourse as a communication record should thus be directed toward the unravelling of the following interrelations:

1. narrative discourse <-----> real reader
2. real reader <-----> implied writer
3. implied writer <-----> implied reader/listener
4. implied writer <-----> narrator
5. narrator <-----> narratee
6. narrator <-----> narrated characters
7. narrated characters in reciprocal dealings who move within a specific structure of time and space

Number 1 refers to the communication between the real writer and the intended real reader/listener. These are the people whose social context is imagined in the narrative discourse and which the exegete should be able to construe as far as possible to be able to interpret the text meaningfully as an act of communication. The exegete is of course also a real reader, but the nature of his concern with and influence on the reception of the narrative discourse is closely connected with his construction of the imagined social context of the real writer and the real reader/listener. This construction depends, among other things, on a knowledge of other texts, of social and cultural norms and of the socio-cultural context. The more the construction is done in terms of a designed sociological-scientific model, the better.

Numbers 3-7 involve the intratextual narrative arrangement. This arrangement has been expounded upon in many semeio-structurally oriented studies, in various theories. According to one of the theories there are three levels at which a narrative falls apart. These three levels are modelled on the basic structure of a narrative record, namely an implied writer who lets a narrator relate (the *narrator's situation* or the *narrative process*) what he (the narrator-focuser) or a character (the character-focuser) sees (the *story*) that character or other characters doing in a particular structure of time and space (the *narrative discourse*).

A text cannot be typed as a narrative if the events it contains do not constitute a linear, chronological series forming a story. Only when the events selected from the lives of people of a certain time and place are combined in a casual fashion into a series to develop a plot, has the *story* become a *narrative discourse*. The narrative discourse is the organised narrative available to the exegete as the real reader. The linear, chronological story is thus not directly available to the exegete. The *story* must be abstracted from the narrative discourse. The abstraction is hermeneutically important since the ideological perspective in a narrative record is construed from the techniques used to form a *story* in a *narrative discourse*. In the relationship between *story* and *narrative discourse* (the conversion of the former into the latter, or the abstraction of the former from the latter) one should be concerned with the identification of the narrator's ideological perspective.

The analysis of the *narrative discourse* is primarily directed at the description of what characters are doing in their reciprocal relations. This analysis is a precondition for the abstraction of the *story*. Whatever the characters are doing in their reciprocal relations can be visualised on five levels, namely the *psychological*, *phraseological*, *temporal*, *spatial*, and *idelogical* levels. These five levels are inextricably linked to the position(s) that the narrator assumes in the narrative. The angles from which the narrator tells the story determine the manner in which, and the ideological perspective(s) from which, the actions of the characters are presented.

The third part of the narrative record, beside the *story* and the *narrative discourse*, is thus the *narrator's situation* (narrative process). It is the interaction between the situation of the narrator and the narrative discourse that is usually described in terms of focalisation.

On the basis of the threefold classification of story, narrative discourse and narrative process, a narrative record represents a network of *time art*. While a narrative process (which takes time) results in a narrative discourse (which, in time, is read and which also offers codes in particular groupings of time); it above all gives substance to a story that can be construed from the discourse and in which something happens to someone in a certain position in time and space.

1.1.8 The hermeneutical purpose of the exegesis of a narrative discourse

A narrative's narrated world consists of a message (ideology/theology) communicated by a writer through a narrator to a reader. The message is communicated through the narrator supplying the (implied/idealised) reader with norms and guidelines for the evaluation. That is, the reader is manipulated by means of the narrative techniques on which the narrator builds the plot – the means by which he relates, in a chronological causality, episodes in which characters move in a particular structure of time and space.

The exegesis of a narrative discourse can be intended to involve the exegete (and eventually the exegete's listener/reader) in the narrator's ideological/theological perspective(s) which underlie the manner in which the narrative discourse is constructed. Hermeneutically, the exegesis of a narrative discourse concerns the fusion of the narrator's horizon of understanding (ideological/theological perspective) with that of the exegete. The exegete, as the real reader, becomes involved in a narrative because he is associated (positively or negatively) with the implied/idealised reader.

2. The poetics of the gospel form as narrative

2.1 A gospel is the literary product of a redactor-narrator

As soon as a narrative has been written, the text is divorced from its historical writer and it functions as a closed narrated world with its own architectonic design with intrinsic harmonious characteristics. The gospels are such literary works. But the gospels, by their very nature, cannot be compared with modern artistic narratives. The gospels are not entirely fictional texts in the sense of products of pure imagination (fiction). A gospel is the literary product of a redactor-narrator. Using, among other things, transmitted tradition, editorially processed in a re-interpretative and creative manner, the evangelists each communicate their own theological ideas by means of the narrative form, as story-tellers.

In the interpretation of narrative discourses the primary concern is not breaking into the real world of the historical reader, and the place and circumstances of writing, or the world of the historical reader and the place and circumstances of reception. Neither is the primary concern involved in the description of the early literal or pre-literal contextualisations of a narrative's tradition. Nevertheless, an investigation into the application of traditions in a gospel as a narrative discourse is not irrelevant, since the evangelist indeed produced his texts as a redactor-narrator.

The traditional *Redaktionsgeschichte* placed the emphasis on the redactor's influence on his sources. On the other hand, narratology is inclined to recognise the techniques of the narrative art. Narratology therefore has an eye on the circumstance that a redactor-narrator has created particular perspectives through his own contextualisation of traditions. The study of a narrator's redactional narrative technique is thus interested in the ideological motive underlying his phraseological redactive work.

Phraseology is the narrator's exercising of his options with regard to particular manners of speech sometimes referred to as 'diction'. The narrator's phraseological redactive work can be seen in his re-arrangement, modification, elimination, expansion and abbreviation of his sources. Sometimes the narrator does not succeed in fully assimilating his source into the broad narrative structure. This applies in particular to certain parables and miracle stories. Traces of the previous world of such traditional material can thus be seen in a gospel's narrated world. The two worlds can even come into conflict with each other.

In narrative exegesis preference is given to the narrated world of the macro-text, that is that of the gospel as a whole and not that of the source as a micro-text. Hermeneutically, the holistic context of a narrative is always the determinant. This also applies where a non-narrative discourse occurs as a microtext in narrative discourse. What this amounts to is that the genealogy in the Gospels of Matthew and Luke, and a letter in the Acts of the Apostles, are treated as an element of the respective narratives.

2.2 A gospel projects the world of the early church onto the world of Jesus

It was stated above that a narrative functions as a closed narrated world and that narrative criticism is not primarily concerned with penetrating the real world of the historical writer and the historical reader, as well as their circumstances. This statement does not in itself presuppose an a-historic interpretation of the text. What the remark implies is that narrative criticism is not historiography. Historiography is an attempt to construct the 'historical facts'. The narrative literature in the Bible is not intended to be historiography either, although narrative discourses, including those in the Bible, can be subjected to historiographical investigation. If someone should, for example, set oneself a goal of writing a history of Jesus or early Christianity, one would be obliged to undertake a historiographical investigation of – among other things – the Gospels. Such a researcher would however have to take into account that the poetics of a narrative will not allow one to use the narrative as a window through which to view the real world. A narrative is rather like a mirror, reflecting reality within the text.

Neither is it the primary aim of any kind of exegesis, within the living-space of the church as the believing community, to be historiographic. Its primary aim is the proclamation of the gospel. And this proclamation is not made successful by the proclaimer 'proving' the 'historical truth' of the Bible to one's listeners. Faith is not dependent on the historical authenticity of the Bible, either. Faith comes from God. Faith is not based on methodological or other scientific argumentation. This does not however mean that historical questions are irrelevant for exegesis.

In the transmission, conversion and re-interpretation of earlier traditions (oral and written), the Jesus era is transposed to the early church era in such a way that two historical worlds are simultaneously taken up as a narrative entity in the gospels. The story in a gospel thus concerns people and things from an earlier time, while the later period in which the gospel arose and was communicated is transparent in the text. A gospel thus simultaneously refers to two real worlds.

This can be compared with biblical scenes depicted in certain Mediaeval works of art. Biblical scenes were presented against Mediaeval backgrounds and biblical characters wore contemporary clothing. People from Mediaeval times were even depicted alongside biblical characters. In the Gospels the world of Jesus, the disciples and the others is generally the most transparent. Nevertheless, the world of the early church is more transparent in certain places. The one world is never manifested totally isolated from the other. The world of the early church and that of Jesus and the disciples are, in a dialectical sense, simultaneously taken up in the gospel as a narrative record. These two worlds are presented in accordance with the narrator's ideological/theological perspective.

Narrative exegesis as a communicative undertaking can therefore not set aside historical enquiry. The 'history' of Jesus and the 'history' of early Christianity are essential for the interpretation of the gospels as 'historical' accounts. It is however important to keep in mind that the construction of the social context of the New Testament is not in itself a methodological step in the analysis of the narrative act. On the one hand such knowledge is part of the competence with which the exegete *begins* to interpret the narrative, just as the exegete has pre-knowledge of the evolutionary history of the gospels in general. On the other hand the inter- and extratextual posing of questions plays a methodological role in the investigation of the intermediary relations between the implied writer/real writer and the implied reader/real reader (cf. Numbers

1-2 in Section 1.1.7 above).

To avoid going into detail regarding this methodological problem, one can take into consideration that the expressions 'the history of Jesus' and 'the history of the early church' do not imply that the brute facts are meant. Since the Gospels are the end product of a long and intricate process of transmission, and because they also project the post-Easter church, it is understandable that Jesus' words in the gospels cannot lead us directly back to the historical Jesus. The same is true as far as the early church is concerned.

There are at least four historical matters emanating from the pre-Easter period and which have served to project the post-Easter period. These are aspects that served the gospel writers as starting-points to address questions concerning the post-Easter church period, and give them meaning:

* Jesus' conflict with the scribes regarding the correct interpretation of the Torah projects, among other things, the post-Easter rift between the church and the synagogue that accompanied the reorganisation of Judaism at Jabneh.

* Jesus' calling God his Father, his astounding new interpretation of the Torah and his proclamation that the kingdom of God has arrived and that God desires to be unlimitedly present among people, projects post-Easter church ethics against the background of the delay of the Second Coming.

* Jesus' call that he should be followed projects various questions in the post-Easter church, for example the suffering and persecution of the Markan congregation, the neglect of the Matthean congregation to look after those in dire need, the status of the Lukan community against the backdrop of the missionary path through the world, and the struggle of the Johannine community to overcome the shocking idea that the man Jesus had come from God and was himself God.

* Jesus' claim that the Father had sent him and that he, in his turn, was sending his disciples in their turn, on one hand projected the authority with which the post-Easter church transmitted and proclaimed the reported words of Jesus and the kerygma concerning himself, and on the other hand the canonicity of New Testament writings in the early church.

2.3 A gospel is open-ended

A gospel is a narrative written from a post-Easter perspective. That is, it is written from a retrospective narrator's viewpoint. This retrospective viewpoint enables the narrator to give the plot of his story an open end. This means that the plot of a gospel continues after its apparent ending, and is only resolved in its implicit continuation. In other words, a gospel does not end with the conclusion of the Jesus era; it continues into the church period (refer again to the concept of *transparency* in 2.2).

It has already been shown that although the pre-Easter Jesus period is more transparent than the post-Easter church period, the two cannot be isolated and simply seen as linear sequences. There is a correlation between the pre-Easter Jesus period and the post-Easter church period. It would appear that the post-Easter church period linearly follows the pre-Easter Jesus period and that a gospel concludes with the beginning of the post-Easter church period. The fact is that the post-Easter church period does not extend briefly from Jesus' resurrection from the dead up to the beginning of the post-Easter church period. The time to which a gospel refers extends into the time of the gospel writer. It is the gospel writer's early-church situation which, as related in a specific gospel, is projected onto Jesus' world. This post-Easter church period in fact extends right up to the time of the modern reader. The end of a gospel is thus open, since after the epoch of Jesus came to an end, that of the church began and it will continue until the Second Coming.

It is indeed here, at the open end of the plot, that the persuasive power of a narrative lies. The implied writer wishes to win over the implied reader. This is done by drawing the reader into the narrative with the help of various narrative strategies and subjecting him to the manipulative position of the narrator. The story can thus be experienced and shared through affective reader involvement. In this respect the concluding episode of a narrative plays an important part.

The two worlds presented in the gospels – those of Jesus and the early church – can narratologically be studied by means of pointing out the temporal relations between the *narrative process* (*narrator's situation*) and the *story*. Four such temporal relations can be distinguished: *ulterior narration, anterior narration, simultaneous narration,* and the *intercalated narration.*

The story of Jesus and that of his disciples' journey from Galilee to Jerusalem in the Gospel of Luke, and in Acts regarding the journey of the apostles and the servants of the Word, accompanied by the Holy Spirit from Jerusalem to Rome, were written from a post-Easter perspective. That is, they are told from the retrospective viewpoint of a narrator (= *ulterior narration*), although the impression may be of an *anterior narration.* This angle of the narrator has enabled the implied writer to supply an open end to the plot of his narrative.

The intrigue in the plots of the Gospels of Matthew, Mark and John is continued after their apparent conclusion with the final Jerusalem episode, to be resolved only later in the mention of the onset of the Galilee episode (Antioch?), as a continuation of the plot (cf. Mt 28:16-20; Mk 13:9-13; 16:7-8 and Jn 21:1-25 resp.). The Jerusalem episode at the end of the Gospel of Luke is this narrative's open end, but in comparison with the other Canonical Gospels it is continued in a longer story as far as narrative time is concerned. This subsequent story is the travel narrative in Acts which does not begin at Galilee, but at Jerusalem, and has Rome as its open end. In other words, the different stories do not end with the conclusion of the Jesus period; they continue into the church period (cf., again, the idea of a transparency).

3. Narrative point of view analysis

3.1 The narrative process (narrator's situation)

3.1.1 The angle of the first-person or third-person narrator

In a *first-person narrative* the narrator is a character himself, and he refers to himself by the personal pronoun 'I' or 'we'. First-person narratives are often encountered in autobiographies.

In a *third-person narrative* the narrator is someone outside the narrative discourse and he *refers* to his characters by various names, such as proper names (e.g. Peter), personal pronouns (e.g. he/she) and by titles (e.g. Son of God).

3.1.2 Spatial narrator's situation

A third-person narrator can adopt an *omniscient point of view* (all-knowing) or a *limited point of view*. An omniscient, omnipresent narrator freely describes the actions and attitudes of the characters, as well as all events without himself or any other witnesses having been present. This narrative technique contributes to the fact that the implied reader experiences the narrator as being a reliable source.

When a narrator adopts a *limited point of view*, or a limited, focalised narrator's situation, he limits the 'omniscience' and 'omnipresence' to the actions and attitudes of a single character or, at the most, a small group of characters in a narrative. This narrator is therefore only able to describe events that concern himself. This spatial narrator's situation is generally found in first-person narrations, but not always. Both of these spatial narrator's situations can occur in combination in a narrative.

The narrator creates distance or proximity between himself and the characters by means of, respectively, an *omniscient point of view* or a *limited point of view*, as well as among the characters themselves and between the characters and the implied reader.

Investigation of the spatial narrator's situation has determined, among other things, that:
* a particular character acts in accordance with the ideological/theological perspective of the narrator and either becomes a 'vehicle' or an opponent of his theological/ideological perspective;
* the narrator can require the implied reader to distance himself from, or associate himself with, a particular character.

3.1.3 Psychological narrator's situation

As mentioned above, a narrator can describe the behaviour of his characters as well as all events in a narrative in an *external* or *internal* manner. The former means that a third-person narrator is generally not part of the narrated world that he narrates, thus he is external to the narrative discourse and is for that very reason able to adopt an *omniscient point of view*.

In contrast, a first-person narrator is generally a character in the narrative itself, thus part of the world of the narrative discourse and internal to the narrative discourse – that is, in and part of the narrative discourse. The narrator can thus only observe what he himself can physically see, and he therefore has a *limited point of view*.

The terms *internal* and *external* are however reserved in literary theory for the *psychological narrative situation* of the narrator. In the spatial narrator's situation, as far as the narrator/focaliser's distance from the narrated world of the narrative discourse is concerned, the psychological narrator's situation deals with whether a character is being described *from within* (that is, internally) or *from without* (that is, externally).

A narrator regards his characters as *external/from without* when he recounts the behaviour of his characters somewhat impersonally. His observations are expressed in phrases such as 'he [the character] said...', or 'he told them...'.

A narrator who, on the other hand, describes his characters *internally/from within* has, as it were, access to the inner consciousness, thoughts, feelings, emotions and sensory observations of his characters. A narrator such as this expresses his description of human behaviour in phrases using *verba sentiendi* such as 'he [the character] thinks', 'he feels', 'he was ashamed', 'he had fear in his heart', 'he knew', and so forth.

It is important to remember that a narrator – whether he has an *omniscient point of view* or a *limited point of view* – can make use of both of these psychological narrator's situations. The only difference is that an omniscient narrator can describe his characters in both ways if he wishes, while a limited narrator can only describe the characters in his immediate environment in both ways. The fact that the latter narrator has a *limited point of view* does not mean that he is limited in the sense that he can describe his characters only externally.

3.2 The narrative discourse

The narrative discourse is studied within the structure in which *characters* move and act (something happens to someone), in terms of their position at a specific *time* and in a specific *place*.

3.2.1 Time

3.2.1.1 Narrating time and narrated time

The aspects of *time* mentioned here essentially amount to two things – time that is *quantitatively fluid* (narrating time) and time that is *qualitatively set* (narrated time).

The former – *narrating time* – involves the time taken by the narrator in narration (text time) and the reader/listener to read/hear the narrative discourse (reading time). Narrating time is measured in minutes or in terms of the number of pages, sentences or words. An example of an investigation into narrative time is that into a change of pace between episodes in a narrative (a slowing down or speeding up). An example of such a study in the Gospel of Mark shows the following: in the first ten chapters of this gospel, Jesus moves from place to place, which brings about a speeding up of the narrating time. In the final six chapters all the events take place in and around Jerusalem. The narrator pauses at the crucifixion events, there is a slowing down, and the final events in Jerusalem are thus emphasised.

Narrated time, qualitative set time, in turn relates to two periods. One is that covered by the story from the first moment to the last. The other concerns the various departures from the course. These two interlinking periods to which narrated time has relevance are separately indicated as *story time* (the time of the story/*fabula*) and *plotted time* (the time of the narrative discourse/*suzjet*) (cf., again, 1.1.7).

The distinction 'story time' and 'plotted time' is largely based on the insights of the literary theorist Gérard Genette. He considers that a narrative consists in the three levels referred to in section 1.1.7, namely a story (*histoire*), a narrative discourse (*récit*) and a narrative process (*narration*). A narrative discourse (such as a gospel) comes about because a narrator, by narrating (a narrative process), retells a story (what happened) by putting it down as a narrative discourse. In this narrative process the narrator treats the time of the story dynamically, and thus presents its order in the narrative discourse in a different chronological sequence. There are thus discrepancies between the story time and the time of the narrative discourse. Our cultural conditioning has accustomed us to chronological 'story time'. Departures from the chronology therefore draw our attention and strongly contribute to the identification and development of the tension in the story. These departures, according to Genette, can be studied in terms of temporal order, duration and frequency.

(a) Temporal order: In a story events (largely the result of cause and effect) follow successively. We first get up (A), then we eat (B), then we go to work (C). The narrator can however present these as C-A-B in the narrative discourse. The sequence changes when we place events that happen later earlier on (*pro-*

lepsis = preview) or when we place events that should be at the beginning at the end of the narrative discourse (*analepsis* = flashback).

(b) Rhythm/duration: Genette distinguishes between four forms of rhythm, namely *ellipsis, summary, scène* and *pause.*

Ellipsis refers to an omission of events from the narrative discourse – events that did take place in the story. It can be assumed, for example, that a reference in a narrative discourse to the actions of a character like an apostle in a story has been preceded by a mention of the apostle's calling and legitimation, although it may not have been mentioned in the narrative discourse.

The *summary* refers to the phenomenon that, for example, a number of years in the story have been summarised in one paragraph in the narrative discourse.

In the case of the *scène* the tempo of the events in a story exactly matches that of the narrative in the narrative discourse. It is however also possible that the events are more amplified in the narrative discourse than the story itself would suggest. In this case there is thus a slowing down, because the story is more amplified in the narrative discourse.

The *pause* refers to the fact that an element that does not occupy much time in the story is dealt with extensively in the narrative discourse. Jesus' five sermons in the Gospel of Matthew, for example, are stationary. For example, the tempo of the story about Jesus' movements in Galilee, culminating in his journey to Jerusalem, is brought to a standstill by the Sermon on the Mount, but the narrative discourse reports on the sermon in detail.

(c) Frequency: Here Genette deals with the relation between the number of times that an event occurs in the story and the number of times it is told in the narrative discourse. An event can be related once, just as it occurs only once in the story, or be related more or fewer times than it appears in the story. Frequency, then, involves repetition. Previews and flashbacks, discussed under the heading 'temporal order' above, are sooner or later a repetition of an incident or episode already narrated, and enter therefore the domain that Genette calls frequency. Past and future references may occur within the framework of the story itself, or even extend beyond the beginning or end of the story.

By means of the threefold distinction already indicated between the narrating process, the story and the narrative discourse, contemporary literary theory concentrates on the circumstance that the narrator adjusts the pace of an event in a story in his narrative discourse. This, together with certain insights from literary theory known as Russian Formalism, stimulated the distinction between the study of *narrated time as story time* and *narrated time as plotted time.*

3.2.1.2 Narrated time as story time

The study of *story time* refers to the chronologically linear sequence from which the events in a narrative are abstracted, one after another, as they occur. This

study has three aspects:
* The reconstruction of the story time by abstracting it from the time of the narrative discourse. This abstraction describes the duration of the story, as it was before being adapted and processed by the narrator in the narrative discourse.
* The investigation of the chronological causality between (a) the *beginning*, *middle* and *end* of a narrative (Aristotle's analysis of plot) and (b) the different episodes comprising the 'beginning', 'middle' and 'end'. From the *beginning*, the narrator offers information introducing the rest of the narrated events, which are developed in the *middle* and culminate in the *end* (*denouement*). In other words, since an investigation into *story time* comprises, firstly, the period covered by the story and secondly, departures from the linear-chronological course of that period, it is necessary to abstract the story from the narrative discourse. A very simple method of doing so is to identify the beginning, middle and end of the story as well as the episodes comprising these three sections.
* The identification of the number of narrative-lines in a narrative discourse. A story presumes at least one sequence of episodes that causally extends from a *beginning* across a *middle* to the *end*, according to the Aristotelian perception regarding the linear and chronological arrangement of a plot. Eberhard Lämmert refers to this sort of consummated sequence as a *Handlungsstrang*. There are many narrative discourses with more than one line of action (narrative-line). Indeed, there may be an indefinite number of narrative-lines in a narrative discourse. In a *Rahmenhandlung* one of the narrative-lines is dominant (*übergeordnete Handlung*) and the others are subordinated (*eingelagerten Handlungssträngen*). If the narrative is a cohesive unit, the various subordinated narrative-lines should be in a structured way conjoined with or embedded into the main narrative-line. However, in spite of the contingency among the various narrative-lines, each of the subordinated sequences has to be self-reliant at least in respect of setting, time or characters. The principle underlying the conjunction or embeddedness (*Verknüpfungsprinzip*) can be addition, parallelism, repetition, flashback, anticipation, symbolisation, contrast, transparency, et cetera. Nevertheless, the exegete's pinpointing of the *Verknüpfungsprinzip* is one of the most important criteria to determine the narrator's ideological/theological point of view which causes the nature of his orchestration of events in the plot.
* The distinction between *narrated time* (= *erzählte Zeit/Welt*) and *time commented upon* (= *besprochene Zeit/Welt*). The latter is a departure from the linear course of the story time at the level of the narrative discourse through:
  - prospection (preview)
  - retrospection (flashback)
  - commentary
  - citation
  - translation
  - direct speech/extended discourse

- two (or more) narrative-lines (lines of action)

The reason for a narrator digressing from the linear course of events can be the desire (a) to supply the readers with additional information about his narrated characters and events and (b) to involve the implied reader in the narrated events (or a particular character). Since aspects of the narrator's *ideological/ theological* perspective are manifested especially in the *besprochene Zeit*, the time commented upon serves the implied reader as an important directive, according to which the narrative should be read.

3.2.1.3 Narrated time as plotted time

The study of *plotted time* differs from that of *story time* in that while the study of *story time* is chiefly directed at the reconstruction of the chronological story and the identification of all digressions on the level of the narrative discourse, the study of *plotted time* concentrates on the narrator's ideological/theological perspective in the narrative. The latter is thus searching for the reason why the course of events at the level of the narrative discourse is presented differently from that in the story. It is a study of the narrator's ideological perspective, which

* determines the chronology and causality between the different episodes;
* lies behind the digressions from the linear course of events;
* allows the different narrative-lines in a particular relation of meaning (*Ver-knüpfungsprizip*) to function together. Is this purely *parallelistic* or *anticipatory*? Is it not perhaps also:
  - analogous;
  - symbolic;
  - allegoric; or
  - in opposition?

The answer to this question lies largely in the identification of the narrator's *ideological/theological* perspective.

3.2.2 Space

Spatial arrangement in narrative material is tied to the temporal sequence of a story. A painting can be observed from left to right and from right to left without its inherent topography losing its focus. A narrative cannot be perceived in this manner. Unlike a painting, narrative material must be perceived first in its linear temporal sequence, and then with regard to its spatiality, which is inseparably related to the former.

Our use of the term *space* includes everything in a narrative that possesses spatiality. It can include the following:

* Space is the *place* in which characters find themselves. In the Synoptic Gospels, for example, Galilee and Jerusalem are important designations of place.
* Space can also be the *appurtenances of place*, for example the temple in Jerusalem and the curtain hanging in the temple.
* Space is also the *manner* in which a place is presented. The turbulent waves and the wind that died down (Mk 4:37,39) are good examples of this.
* Space is also the explicit or implicit *emotional value* (atmosphere) associated with the place. The expressions 'outside into the darkness' and the 'gnashing of teeth' in the parable of the Wedding Feast (Mt 22:13), for example, not only describe the *manner* in which reference is made to the place outside the hall of the wedding feast, but also the *emotions* associated with that place.
* *Non-spatial concepts* are sometimes – as in metaphorical narratives – represented as spatial. The comparison of the kingdom of God with a man scattering seed in his field (Mk 4:26-29) is an example of this.

The concept of spatiality thus comprises more than mere place. The manner in which the narrator presents the various spaces in his narrative also contributes to the different meanings and functions that should be attached to these spaces.

With a view to identifying these functions, a distinction should be made between *space as local setting* and *space as scope of ideological/theological interest*. It can be typified respectively as *scope* and as *focal space*. The difference between the two can be expressed as follows:

Should the narrator create a link between characterisation and spatial imagery, space functions as focal space. In other words, as soon as space is filled by characters or the dialogue of characters, it no longer functions as mere local description. Thus, should one of the characters become closely involved with space, it became focal space because it contributes to characterisation.

Research into emotive space in a narrative therefore, as with research into narrated time as plotted time, concentrates on the principle of order behind the structuring of space in the story. There is thus a certain relationship between *focal space* and the ideological/theological perspective of the narrator. For this reason *focal space* is always shown as being structured, and related to the functional role that it fills with regard to characterisation – for example: the portrayal of milieu and atmosphere, symbolic value and the role of functional character himself.

It is therefore clear that *focal space* reveals the narrator's ideological perspective(s), as well as that (those) from which the narrator presents the narrated characters. In this context it often indicates either a trend towards consensus or a counter trend. *Galilee* ('Galilee of the Gentiles' – cf. Mt 4:15) and *Jerusalem* ('killer of the prophets and messengers of God' – cf. Mt 23:37) represent such a counter trend, with regard to interests.

3.2.3 Characterisation

In a narrative there are two basic types of character, namely a *simple character* (flat character) and a *complex character* (rounded character). A simple character embodies a straightforward ideological perspective throughout the narrative. The complex character, however, presents the surprise element. A complex character often acts contrary to expectations. He often demonstrates a degree of hesitancy, inner doubt and discord in his actions and attitude. He creates conflict in the story and – as far as the reader is concerned – gives rise to tension.

Taking note of the narrator's *phraseology* throws light on his characterisation in particular and, consequently, his ideological and theological perspective(s). In this context phraseological choices means 'speech characteristics'.

Broadly, characters fulfill the following *actantial functions* and behavioural relations: protagonists, objects (addressees), antagonists, helpers, arbitrators. The *protagonist* is the principal character (i.e. Jesus in the Gospels); the *objects* are the persons at whom the values of the protagonist are aimed (i.e. the followers of Jesus); the *antagonists* are those whose efforts are aimed at the failure of the mission of the protagonist (i.e. the Jewish leaders); the *helpers* are the characters who attempt to help the protagonist in his mission (i.e. the twelve disciples); the function of the *arbitrator* is not apparent in the Gospels, with the possible exception of the Holy Spirit. The functional role of the arbitrator is usually the resolving of conflict between two opposing characters through a third party, who gets opponents to agree or to accept the third party's will.

Some characters fulfill a 'decorative' role that is not critical to the development of the plot. On the contrary, the literary function of such characters changes as the 'plot' develops. Sometimes they furnish the implied reader with norms against which to judge the main characters. Sometimes they function as *pars pro toto* in terms of other characters.

The exegete discovers the perspective(s) of the narrator, chiefly by analysing the perspectives from which the characters are presented. The ideological perspective of the narrator is put into focus by the way in which the perspectives of the various characters function in relation to one another.

Naming is an important means that a narrator can use to express the perspectives of the characters in their binary relations. As far as the Gospels are concerned, one can think especially of names which are used as 'titles' (e.g. Son of God, Son of Man). In German technical literature dealing with research into the Gospels, titles that designated theological functions were previously referred to as *Würdeprädikationen*.

By using different titles for a single character a narrator can show the perspectives of other characters who, individually (or sometimes together) express a perspective on that character (and the other characters) through the typical name for the character.

Psychological observation of the characters by the narrator is a subdivision of 'narrator's commentary' – an aspect of particular importance in the study of *besprochene Zeit* (cf. 3.2.1.2), and which overlaps what is termed a 'psychological narrator's situation' (cf. 3.1.3).

The narrator's commentary on the character's emotions, sensory observations, feelings, thoughts, insights and so forth, serves the implied reader as an effective evaluative guide on how to read the narrative from the narrator's ideological/theological perspective. Contributory factors are the identification of voice inflections, such as sarcasm and irony, which are shown through psychological observation.

3.2.4 The ideological perspective

Boris Uspensky refers to this part of the narratalogical investigation as the identification of the *narrative point of view on the ideological level*. According to Uspensky, the narrative point of view (cf. 1.1.5) is investigated by studying the narrator's perspective(s) as manifested explicitly or implicitly in the narrative. It can take the form of a study of the interrelations between the different perspectives from which the narrator presents the various characters. The study can involve the question of which characters are the vehicle(s) of the narrator's perspective. It can also comprise an investigation into the manifestation of the narrator's perspective at various levels in the story, such as the level of *characterisation* (which has much to do with 'psychology' and 'phraseology' – cf. 3.2.3) or the levels of *time* and *space*. The ideological level is basic to the other levels.

Uspensky explains the relationship between the *ideological* and the other levels, such as the 'phraseological', 'temporal, and spatial' levels, in the light of the concepts of *surface structure* and *depth structure* that play an important part in Structuralism. These two concepts are thus used here unlike in the narratology of Gérard Genette (cf. also Mieke Bal, Rimmon-Kenan, Ina Gräbe and others). There the surface structure relates to the narrated discourse (*récit*) and the depth structure to the story (*histoire*) which can be abstracted from the narrative discourse (cf. 1.1.7). Nevertheless, what it involves somewhat resembles what applies to Structuralism. A distinction is made between the plane of observation (the 'surface structure') and the plane of fundamental intentions (the 'depth structure').

The narrative point of view on the ideological level can thus be considered the *idea* that comprises the fundamental principle from which the narrative and its elements are constituted. These elements have been summarised above as *time, space* and *characterisation* – the eventual form of the narrative.

Briefly, the study of the ideology in a narrative discourse amounts to the systematisation of the thematic lines that have become evident in the investigation. Thus it can be determined (1) that the narrated characters are presented from a certain perspective, for example, from an analogic or counter perspective and

(2) which characters agree with the narrator's ideological perspective.

In the investigation of narrative point of view the latter is probably the most important matter that can be discerned on the ideological level. Does the author allow the narrator to adopt a perspective that agrees with his own as author, or does he allow it to agree with the normative system of the 'narrated world', in contrast (and perhaps in conflict) with that of the author? Or does the narrator adopt the perspective of one (or many) of the narrated characters?

Earlier in this article (cf. 2.1) reference was made to the *simple* nature of the Gospels. The simplicity of a gospel as a narrative is manifested in the narrator's *ideological perspective* corresponding with the perspective of the author, and in particular in its simultaneous agreement with the perspective of the protagonist. As a result all events, characters and so forth in the Gospels are constantly being presented from one particular perspective – that is, from that of one character, namely Jesus. Such a character is sometimes referred to as the 'viewpoint character'. The *ideological perspective* of the narrator is evident in whatever the 'viewpoint character' does, says, thinks, and so on – and in the manner in which he acts and speaks. This perspective is reflected in every episode in the story, since the perspectives from which the other characters are narrated, as well as other *phraseological, psychological, temporal* and *spatial* data, are subordinate to it, linked to it and serve as its substructure.

As far as the Gospels are concerned, what it amounts to is that the perspectives of the characters (the Jewish leaders, the Jewish multitude, the gentiles, John the Baptist and the disciples) should be evaluated in terms of the perspective from which the protagonist, Jesus, is narrated. Sometimes another character, who features as the main character in a specific episode, such as the Good Samaritan (Lk 10:30-35), serves as an example of the character who functions as the overall protagonist in the narrative. The example can, from the holistic context, therefore be part of what are called above either the 'helpers' or the 'decorative characters'. Here, as far as the Gospel of John is concerned, one thinks, for example, of the beloved disciple but also of the royal official in John 4:43-54 (cf. 4).

A complex story demonstrates a multiple-evaluation narrative point of view. In other words, a complex story can have various ideological perspectives, which together can manifest an intricate network of relationships. Uspensky calls such a story a 'polyphonic narration'. In a 'many-voiced' narrative such as this, the narrator can successively adjust his position. The narrator's perspective can vary, for instance, with the different levels (*phraseological, psychological, temporal* and *spatial*) in a narrative. In a complex narrative the narrator's perspective can coincide with that from which a particular character is being presented, and in the next episode with that from which another character is presented. The narrator's perspective can even change in a single episode. A number of variations are thus possible and narratives can therefore show degrees of simplicity or complexity.

4. Narrative point of view analysis of John 4:43-54

4.1 Is John 4:43-54 a narrative?

John 4:43-54 is a narrative, since the discourse organised within it is in terms of *characters* (such as Jesus and the royal official) who move in a particular structure of *time* and *space* (such as from Samaria to Galilee), and there is a chronological sequence of episodes which have a causal relationship (*plot*) (the movement to Cana, the meeting with the official, and the conclusion).

4.2 Analysis of the 'surface structure'

4.2.1 The narrative process (narrator's situation) (cf. 3.1)

4.2.1.1 First- or third-person narrative angle (cf. 3.1.1)

This pericope is a third-person narrative, that is, a narrator outside the text refers in the third person to the characters in the narrative. Some, indeed, are made to communicate by means of direct speech, but this does not change the narrator's angle.

4.2.1.2 The narrator's spatial situation (cf. 3.1.2)

The narrator has adopted both an 'omniscient point of view' and a 'limited point of view' in this section. The 'omniscient point of view' is evident from his references in verse 45 to the Galileans who were also attending the Passover Feast. The 'limited point of view' is most evident after verse 46b, particularly in the character of the royal official. The narrator in this way wishes to show that he expects the implied reader to associate himself with the character of the official. Apart from the royal official, it is Jesus in particular who acts as the 'vehicle' of the narrator's ideological perspective. Jesus' 'omniscient' perspective is not, however, so closely associated with that of the narrator that they are indistinguishable.

4.2.1.3 The narrator's psychological situation (cf. 3.1.3)

The 'omniscient point of view' is evident from verse 44: 'For Jesus himself had said...', as opposed to the 'limited point of view' in verse 50: 'The man believed....'

4.2.2 The narrated discourse (cf. 3.2)

4.2.2.1 Time (cf. 3.2.1)

4.2.2.1.1 Narrating time (cf. 3.2.1.1)

This pericope comprises twelve verses. Verses 1 to 4 tell of Jesus' journey from Samaria to Galilee, and then to Cana in Galilee. This is followed by a stationary section in the eight verses dealing with the meeting between Jesus and the official.

4.2.2.1.2 Narrated time

4.2.2.1.2.1 Narrated time as 'story time' (cf. 3.2.1.2)

The *beginning* of the story extends from John 4:43 to 44, where Jesus' journey from Samaria to Galilee is related. The *middle* extends from verse 45 to verse 53, and this has two scenes. First there is Jesus' arrival in Galilee, and then his visit to Cana. The second scene follows in Cana with the arrival of the royal official and his meeting with Jesus. This section – extending from verses 46b to 53 – can be subdivided into two smaller scenes, namely the meeting in Cana, and then the official's return home and what happened here. The *end* of the story comes in verse 54, where it is pointed out that Jesus' second miracle had also taken place in Cana.

The narrated time is sometimes alternated with *besprochene Zeit*, such as in verse 44 where, by means of commentary, reference is made to the antagonism of Judea. This also applies to the reference in verse 45 – the Galileans' reception of Jesus – because they were also attending the Passover Feast. The same applies to verse 46, with a reference to the first miracle in Cana. Verse 54, as well, contains a reference to the second miracle.

4.2.2.1.2.2 Narrated time as 'plotted time' (cf. 3.2.1.3)

In this narrative we have identified the following scenes:

* The arrival in Galilee
* The reception in Galilee
* The arrival in Cana
* The meeting with the official
* The journey to Capernaum
* Conclusion.

To establish the ideological perspective that determined the chronology and causality of the above scenes, one should remember the departures from the linear sequence. As far as the transition from the first to the second episode is concerned, Jesus' reference to his own country indicates a contrast between Judea and Galilee. Although he is rejected in his own country, he is welcomed in Galilee. The following section in the *besprochene Zeit*, namely Jesus' action at the Passover Feast as the reason for his warm reception, simultaneously alludes to Jesus' later words regarding the seeing of signs and wonders as preconditions for believing. Jesus then leaves for Cana and, again, the departure from linear time is important. The reminder that Jesus' first miracle had taken place there was important to the fact that Jesus was again on his way to Cana.

Since Cana is pertinently mentioned as a place in Galilee, the Galilean base becomes not only the *scope* (cf. 3.2.2) within which Jesus performs his miracles, but it functions as *focal space*. This reveals the ideological perspective of the Galileans: their reception of Jesus (vs. 45), unlike that of the Judeans, is based on the witnessing of miracles. Conversely, the first episode in Cana stressed Mary's unconditional faith in the circumstances (cf. Jn 2:1-12).

When we look at the 'narrating time' of the following two episodes, which occupy seven of the twelve verses, it is clear that it is very important to the narrative. Two complete narrative-lines (*Handlungssträngen* – cf. 3.2.1.2) can be identified here, namely:

* The official comes to Jesus after hearing that he is in the vicinity, as his child is ill (*beginning*). This is followed by the discussion between them (*middle*). The man believed Jesus and went home (*end*).
* He met his slaves (*beginning*). This was followed by the discussion with the slaves (*middle*). Both he and his household believed (*end*).

These narrative-lines thus together carry a certain tension. The verb 'believed' gives no indication of whether the one 'belief' excludes or perhaps complements the other. That is, whether faith without visible signs is worth less than that resulting from visible signs. Viewed thus, the latter must be complemented by the former to be true faith. Did the official at first simply believe that his son had been healed and, only when he had experienced the miracle, subsequently believe that Jesus was the Son of God? It appears that the *Verknüpfungsprinzip* (linking principle, nexus) between the two parallel narrative-lines is not in opposition, but rather analogic. The second seems to confirm the first. But it is more than a mere question of confirmation. The narrator's ideological perspective becomes evident. Faith is more than accepting Jesus as a worker of miracles. The miracles serve to confirm the true identity of Jesus as God become man (Jn 1:14), as having been sent by the Father, as the Logos. Faith involves overcoming the *Anstoß* and this can only be done by believing the 'word' (gospel) of Jesus, by going (being sent) so that the faith is able to spread even further, as it did through the household of the official.

The end of the narrative, a further digression from the linear sequence, is linked to the previous reference to Cana, where the first miracle had taken place (Jn 2:1-12).

4.2.2.2 Space (cf. 3.2.2)

Jesus left Sychar in Samaria for Galilee, where he was cordially received. Both Galilee and his own country – in which he had not been welcome – serve as *focal-spaces*. This, then, delineates the atmosphere in which the story takes place. There is a contrast between Jesus' own country and Galilee, an antagonistic Judea as opposed to a welcoming Galilee.

Cana also serves as *focal space*, since the first miracle took place there. The fact that Cana is again mentioned creates tense expectation in the reader. The water turning to wine serves as an appurtenance. The distance between Cana and Capernaum serves also as *focal space*. In other words, the distance serves as *focal space*, indicating that the miracle took place over a distance.

From the *focal spaces* the characters seem to portray a tendency to consensus with the narrator, except for the inhabitants of Judea, who tend towards opposition. These trends are related to their acceptance or rejection of Jesus. An important question that is raised by the statement that the miracle took place over some distance is that of faith without visible signs.

4.2.2.3 Characterisation (cf. 3.2.3)

Jesus is the *protagonist* in the narrative, the inhabitants of Jerusalem the *antagonists*, and the inhabitants of Galilee the *helpers* (including the royal official). The protagonist acts as the 'vehicle' for the narrator's ideological perspective. Certain other *namings* also play a part. In verse 44 Jesus is described as a prophet. According to the narrator's perspective, Jesus' true identity is however described throughout the Gospel of John as the one who comes 'from above' and not 'from below' (cf. Jn 3:31). It was precisely this *Anstoß* that the Judeans could not overcome, Jesus being regarded by some as a 'prophet', at most (cf. Jn 7:40). Other Judeans openly rejected this possibility (cf. Jn 4:44 with Jn 7:41). Since Jesus had come from Galilee (Jn 7:41) they could not accept him as the Christ. The Samaritans, on the other hand, did accept him (Jn 4:25-26), as the Saviour not only of the Jews (Jn 4:22), but also of the world (Jn 4:42). The

Galileans also accepted Jesus (Jn 4:45) but merely as a worker of miracles (Jn 4:48). The designation 'royal official' (βασιλικός) (vs. 46) stresses the fact that this Galilean official was an outcast in the eyes of the Jewish nation and leaders. He, however acts as a 'helper' of the protagonist against the antagonists. As a Galilean, he overcomes (like Mary and John the Baptist in a particular Jewish situation earlier in the Gospel of John, and the Samaritan woman in a universal non-Jewish situation) the *Anstoß*, and believes in Jesus. His faith, on the one hand, does not depend on the witnessing of miracles, and, on the other, it spreads outwards and his entire household is able to share in it.

4.3 Analysis of the 'deep structure': The ideological perspective

The following themes can be identified in this narrative:
* Jesus is warmly received in Galilee in contrast with the antagonism of Judea.
* The miracle relates to the first miracle in the same place.
* The miracle took place over a distance.
* Coming to faith without seeing visible signs and wonders.
* Visible signs and wonders, according to the Gospel of John, serve merely as confirmation of the true identity of Jesus (cf. Jn 3:2). *Jesus' words are thus in themselves worthy of belief.*

The *ideological/theological perspective* of the narrator can be summarised as follows: Jesus must be accepted in faith, and be confessed as the Son of God. This must be the result of hearing words (the gospel) without witnessing signs and wonders. The royal official is presented in this narrative from an analogic perspective and the inhabitants of Judea (Jerusalem) from a counter perspective. The *ideological/theological perspective* of the protagonist (Jesus) coincides with that of the narrator. The implied reader is manipulated to associate with the action of the royal official, and to disassociate himself both from the inhabitants of Jerusalem who either reject (Jn 4:44) or accept (Jn 7:41) Jesus as a prophet, and from the Galileans in general, who receive him as – at most – a worker of miracles.

The intrinsic trust one should place in the 'hearing of words' (the gospel) is strongly emphasised. Within the context of the Gospel of John as a whole, the beloved disciple fulfills an important role: apparently, in the Johannine community this disciple was a symbol of reliable tradition regarding Jesus' identity (cf. Jn 19:35 and 21:34). This is the message to the Johannine community: *the intrinsic truth of the Gospel can be trusted and believed.*

BIBLIOGRAPHY

Bal, M. 1980. *De Theorie van Vertellen en Verhalen. Inleiding in de Narratologie.* Muiderberg: Coutinho.

Blok, W. 1960. *Verhaal en Lezer.* Groningen: Wolters.

Brink, A. P. 1987. *Vertelkunde. 'n Inleiding tot die Lees van Verhalende Tekste.* Pretoria: Academica.

Chatman, S. 1978. *Story and Discourse. Narrative Structure in Fiction and Film.* Ithaca: Cornell University Press.

Combrink, H. J. B. 1983. The Structure of the Gospel of Matthew as Narrative. *Tyndale Bulletin* 34, 61-90.

Culpepper, R. A. 1983. *Anatomy of the Fourth Gospel. A Study in Literary Design.* Philadelphia: Fortress.

Culpepper, R. A. 1989. Commentary on Biblical Narratives. Changing Paradigms. *Foundations and Facets Forum* 5, 87-102.

Du Rand, J. A. 1986. Plot and Point of View in the Gospel of John, in J. H. Petzer & P. J. Hartin (eds.). *A South African Perspective on the New Testament. Essays by South African New Testament Scholars Presented to Bruce Manning Metzger during his Visit to South Africa in 1985.* Leiden: Brill, 149-169.

Genette, G. 1980. *Narrative Discourse.* (Tr. by J. E. Lewin.) Oxford: Blackwell.

Gräbe, I. 1986a. Narratologiese Ondersoek en Eksegese van die Boodskap van die Evangelies. *Hervormde Teologiese Studies* 42, 151-168.

Gräbe, I. 1986b. Die Gelykenis van die Barmhartige Samaritaan. Narratiewe Tegnieke en Vergelykingskonstruksies. *Hervormde Teologiese Studies* 42, 265-281.

Kingsbury, J. D. 1988. *Matthew as Story.* (2nd rev. and enlarged ed.) Philadelphia: Fortress.

Kurz, W. S. 1987. Narrative Approaches to Luke-Acts. *Biblica* 68, 195-220.

Lämmert, E. 1972. *Bauformen des Erzählens.* 5. Aufl. Stuttgart: Metzlersche Verlagsbuchhandlung.

Lanser, S. S. 1981. *The Narrative Act. Point of View in Prose Fiction.* Princeton: Princeton University Press.

Lintvelt, J. 1981. *Essai de Typologie Narrative. Le 'Point de Vue'. Théorie et Analyse.* Paris: Libraire José Corti.

Lotman, J. M. 1975. Point of View in a Text. *New Literary History* 6, 413-419.

Matera, F. J. 1987. The Plot of Matthew's Gospel. *Catholic Biblical Quarterly* 49, 233-253.

Petersen, N. R. 1978a. 'Point of view' in Mark's Narrative. *Semeia* 12, 97-121.

Petersen, N. R. 1987b. *Literary Criticism for New Testament Critics.* Philadelphia: Fortress.

Petersen, N. R. 1980. Literary Criticism in Biblical Studies, in R. A. Spencer (ed.). *Orientation by Disorientation. Studies in Literary Criticism and Biblical Literary Criticism Presented in Honor of William A. Beardslee.* Pittsburgh: Pickwick, 25-50.

Potgieter, J. H. 1988. *'n Narratologiese Ondersoek van die Boek Jona.* Pretoria: University of Pretoria. (Unpublished Doctoral Thesis.)

Prince, G. 1982. *Narratology. The Form and Function of Narrative.* Berlin: Mouton.

Ressequie, J. L. 1982. Point of View in the Central Section of Luke (9:51-19:44). *Journal of the Evangelical Theological Society* 25, 41-47.

Rhoads, D. 1982. Narrative Criticism and the Gospel of Mark. *Journal of the American Academy of Religion* 50, 411-434.

Rhoads, D. & Michie, D. 1982. *Mark as Story. An Introduction to the Narrative of a Gospel.* Philadelphia: Fortress.

Rimmon-Kenan, S. 1983. *Narrative Fiction. Contemporary Poetics.* London: Methuen.

Stanzel, F. K. 1986. *A Theory of Narrative.* (Tr. by C. Goedsche.) Cambridge: Cambridge University Press.

Sternberg, M. 1985. *The Poetics of Biblical Narrative. Ideological Literature and the Drama of Reading.* Bloomington: Indiana University Press.

Tannehill, R. C. 1980. The Gospel of Mark as Narrative Christology. *Semeia* 16, 57-95.

Tannehill, R. C. 1984. The Composition of Acts 3-5. A Narrative Development and Echo Effect, in K. H. Richards (ed.). *Society of Biblical Literature 1984 Seminar Papers.* Chico: Scholars Press, 217-240.

Tannehill, R. C. 1985. Israel in Luke-Acts. A Tragic Story. *Journal of Biblical Literature* 104, 69-85.

Tannehill, R. C. 1986. *The Narrative Unity of Luke-Acts. A Literary Interpretation*. Philadelphia: Fortress.

Uspensky, B. 1973. *A Poetics of Composition. The Structure of the Artistic Text and Typology of a Compositional Form*. (Tr. by V. Zavarin & S. Wittig.) Berkeley: University of California Press.

Van Aarde, A. G. 1982a. Die Vertellersperspektief-analise. 'n Literatuurteoretiese Benadering in die Eksegese van die Evangelies. *Hervormde Teologiese Studies* 38, 58-82.

Van Aarde, A. G. 1982b. *God met Ons. Dié Teologiese Perspektief van die Matteusevangelie*. Pretoria: University of Pretoria. (Unpublished Doctoral Thesis.)

Van Aarde, A. G. 1986. Plot as Mediated through Point of View. Mt 22:1-14 – A Case Study, in J. H. Petzer & P. J. Hartin (eds.). *A South African Perspective on the New Testament. Essays by South African New Testament Scholars Presented to Bruce Manning Metzger during his Visit to South Africa in 1985*. Leiden: Brill, 62-75.

Van Aarde, A. G. 1987. Immanuel as die Geïnkarneerde Tora. Funksionele Jesusbenaminge in die Matteusevangelie as Vertelling. *Hervormde Teologiese Studies* 43, 242-277.

Van Aarde, A. G. 1988. Narrative Point of View. An Ideological Reading of Luke 12:35-48. *Neotestamentica* 22, 235-252.

Vandermoere, H. 1982. *The Structure of the Novel*. Leuven: Acco.

Van Eck, E. 1986. Die Funksie van Ruimte in die Narratologie. *Hervormde Teologiese Studies* 42, 339-349.

Van Eck, E. 1988. Galilea en Jerusalem as Narratologiese Ruimtes in die Markusevangelie: 'n Kontinuering van die Lohmeyer-Lightfoot-Marxsen Ketting. *Hervormde Teologiese Studies* 44, 139-163.

Van Eck, E. & Van Aarde, A. G. 1989. Narratological Analysis of Mark 12:1-12. The Plot of the Gospel of Mark in a Nutshell. *Hervormde Teologiese Studies* 45, 778-800.

Vorster, W. S. 1986. The New Testament and Narratology. *Journal of Literary Studies* 2, 52-62.

Vorster, W. S. 1988. Oor die Nuwe Testament, Vertelkunde en Prediking. *Hervormde Teologiese Studies* 44, 164-177.

J. G. DU PLESSIS

SPEECH ACT THEORY AND NEW TESTAMENT INTERPRETATION WITH SPECIAL REFERENCE TO G. N. LEECH'S PRAGMATIC PRINCIPLES

Introduction

In 1962 an unassuming work by J. L. Austin, *How to do things with words* (Austin 1975), based on a series of lectures held at Harvard University in 1955, was published posthumously. A little more than a quarter of a century later the field of research generated by it has become so vast and has branched out into so many different areas of specialisation that it has become impossible for the individual researcher to cover or evaluate the whole terrain.

I am going to proceed as follows: First I want to draw attention to that which – to my mind – has been the vital nerves touched by Austin's theory (which has become known as 'speech act theory') and which has elicited the flood of books and papers. The idea is not to become bogged down in too many details, leaving the uninitiated reader overwhelmed by the *plethora* of terminology.

I do not have a comprehensive introduction in mind that will enable the reader to 'practise' speech act theory. Apart from the fact that such a pretence would be out of step with the vastness and intricacies of the field, it would also be unrealistic to expect that experts in various areas in New Testament research will leave those fields of expertise to become practitioners of speech act theory (although I do hope to make a few converts for an exciting approach to exegesis).

Rather, the purpose is to make the reader perceptive to those phenomena addressed by the 'theory'. Speech act theory gives insight into practical human reasoning and as such a clear(er) perception of the perception of the phenomena on which speech act theory focuses will help to enrich the process of analysis, even if the technicalities of the theory are not incorporated in an analysis. By extending and/or intensifying the perception of the exegete in this way a general insight into speech act theory can be fruitful for those working with different methods: phenomena are thrust upon the attention of the exegete that otherwise could have escaped him.

Buss (1988:125) has pointed out that speech act theory can potentially contribute either to a theoretical reconceptualisation of the process of exegesis or to a refinement of exegetical procedures in their application to specific passages. My interest lies with the second of these two – in contrast to the thrust of the papers in *Semeia* 41 of 1988, which was devoted to speech act theory, but which focused on the nature of religious and biblical language from the vantage point of speech act theory.

After having sketched the central phenomena on which speech act theory focuses, I shall then give in more detail an exposition of a specific development
within the field, namely that of G. N. Leech, which may be viewed as a radical
reinterpretation of speech act theory (Dillon, Coleman & Fahnestock 1985:446-
460). Leech's theory will also serve as the basis for the application to the exegesis of Mark 12:1-12 in the second part of the essay.

The exposition of speech act theory in this essay is done with Leech's theory
in view. As a result of this some aspects of the research and of prominent contri-
butors to the theory in general – especially the work done by by J. R. Searle
(1969; 1979; 1983) – will not receive the attention they deserve in a straightforward discussion of the theory.

The first part of the essay will be concluded with references to the main areas
of research within the theory and its influence in New Testament research.

PART 1: THEORETICAL ORIENTATION

1. Austin, Grice and the vital nerves

1.1 From 'saying' to 'doing'

Austin, trying to escape from the sterility into which linguistic philosophy had
fallen with its stress on the analysis of propositional statements, focused attention on a second, important function of language, namely the fact that utterances do not mainly make statements about a given state of affairs, but that utterances may also *perform* certain *actions* (thus Austin's term, 'performative').
Note for instance in the preceding sentence the word 'make' in 'make a
statement'.

Austin (1976:235) gives the following example of what he means by performative:

> Suppose, for example, in a marriage ceremony I say, as people will, 'I do' – (sc. take this wo-
> man to be my lawful wedded wife)...it would be absurd to regard the thing that I say as a re-
> port of the performance of the action which is undoubtedly done... I am not reporting on a
> marriage, I am indulging in it.

When we look at utterances from the point of view of their performative function we are not (in the first place) concerned with their veracity (as in the case
when we analyse propositional statements), but whether they are successful or
not, in Austin's terms: 'felicitous/infelicitous'. From there the stress on conditions for felicity, which is an important theme in Austin's theory.

In trying to answer what precisely the act is which is performed when making a performative utterance Austin refers to three different aspects. In the first place it is simply an act of producing language (the '*locutionary*' act). Secondly the speaker enacts his intention. The utterance gives expression to the purpose of the speaker. The speaker may for instance be thanking, apologising, warning, and so forth. This aspect of an utterance is called the '*illocutionary*' act. Thirdly Austin identified the effect that an utterance has. By producing language (the locution) with a specific purpose (illocution) the speaker attains a specific effect or consequence with his utterance. This is called the '*perlocution*'. The perlocution refers to the action(s) of the addressee (Cloete 1984:3).

Let me explain the distinction between the illocution and perlocution with the following example: The utterance 'Beware, the car!' is said with the purpose of warning (illocution) and the effect of the utterance (perlocution) may be that the addressee will avoid walking in front of a car.

We may also identify the intended perlocution (a distinction not made by Austin, cf. Van Coller & Van Jaarsveld 1984: Inleiding): The speaker *wants* the addressee to avoid the car. The distinctions illocution and perlocution have proved to be extremely influential.

In making distinctions between locutions, illocutions and perlocutions Austin focused attention on the aspects of meaning which link language with its context, that is the pragmatics of verbal meaning. Austin (1975:108) identified the locutionary aspect with 'meaning' in the traditional sense. The illocutionary and perlocutionary together add a new dimension.

The illocutionary aspect adds the element of 'force' (e.g. begging, warning, praising, etc.) to the concept of meaning (Austin 1975:1) and the perlocutionary the element of effect or result (or even intended effect or result) which may be non-verbal.

The difference between meaning in the traditional sense and the added components of illocution and perlocution can be illuminated by the following example: We all know the reaction to and utterance expressed with the words: 'I understand what you are saying, but I don't know why you are saying it' (cf. Du Plessis 1987:33). 'I understand what you are saying' refers to the 'sense' of an utterance, i.e. the meaning the words and phrases have within the specific language system. 'I don't know why you are saying it' refers to the purpose of the communication and the effects of the utterance as communication, that is the pragmatic meaning.

An analysis of meaning is not complete until this last aspect has been treated. With these distinctions Austin opened the way for a renewed interest in the pragmatics of language and communication (a field earlier pioneered by Peirce, cf. Peirce 1931-58). This is one of the vital nerves touched by Austin's philosophy.

1.2 The gap between what is said and what is meant

Some five years after the publication of Austin's lectures, H. P. Grice delivered the Wiliam Jones lectures at Harvard which were published only eight years afterwards (Grice 1975, reprinted 1982). With this contribution Grice infused the debate on the pragmatic aspects of meaning with new vigour.

Grice focused the attention on the prerequisites or principles that must be adhered to for speech to be used in such a way that a conversation (seen as a series of utterances or speech acts) may be conducted successfully (Du Plessis 1985:17). In this way Grice's work develops a theme reminiscent of Austin's felicity conditions (although he does not refer to Austin), with its emphasis on the success or failure of an utterance as a speech act, rather than focusing on the truth or untruth of the utterances.

More important is that Grice's work contributed to our understanding of how utterances imply specific perlocutions and how we may gauge intended perlocutions.

In trying to describe the conditions governing conversations Grice's interest was aroused by the fact that speakers often seem to 'mean' more than what they actually say. He uses the following example:

> Suppose that A and B are talking to a mutual friend C, who is now working in a bank. A asks B how C is getting on in his job, and B replies 'Oh quite well, I think; he likes his colleagues, and he hasn't been to prison yet' (Grice 1982:409).

Grice argues that A might well want to know at this point why B referred to C not having been to prison yet. Whatever B implied with his remark (e.g. 'that C is the sort of person likely to yield to the temptation provided by his occupation'), it is clear that it is distinct from what B actually said (Grice 1982:409).

To describe this phenomenon Grice chooses the term 'implicature'. Implicature comes into being when the speaker willingly and blatantly does not cooperate with his addressee as could be expected of him. It is, for instance, when the speaker does not cooperate in giving enough information (or conversely in giving more information than is necessary) that a gap between what is meant and what is said comes into existence (Grice 1982:414).

Grice postulated a Cooperative Principle governing the conversational relationship between speaker and addressee if the conversation between the two is to succeed, despite the gap between what is said and what is meant. The cooperative principle consists of various maxims arranged according to four categories.

The first category is that of 'quantity,' obliging the speaker not to give too little or too much information. The second category is that of 'quality', obliging the speaker not to speak without sufficient evidence and to be conscientiously truthful. The third category is that of 'relation', imploring the speaker to be relevant, and the fourth, 'manner' relating not to what is said, but to how it is said (e.g. not obscure, not ambiguous, etc., Grice 1982:411).

Recalling Grice's initial example of the conversation about C not yet having been in jail, the concept of conversational implicature may now be explained as follows:

> In a suitable setting A may reason as follows: '(1) B has apparently violated the maxim 'Be Relevant' and so may be regarded as having flouted one of the maxims regarding perspicuity; yet I have no reason to believe that he is opting out from the operation of the CP; (2) given the circumstances I can regard his irrelevance as only apparent if and only if I suppose him to think that C is potentially dishonest; (3) B knows that I am capable of working out step 2. So B implicates that C is potentially dishonest' (Grice 1982:414).

What Grice has done is to initiate research into the factors that influence our ability to decipher what is said (or written) 'between the lines'. If Austin touched a vital nerve in focusing our attention in a sophisticated way on the fact that words execute actions (in other words helping us to realise that there is a difference between what is said and why it is said), Grice touched the vital nerve of the gap which often exists between what is said and what is meant. Our attention is focused on the important fact that the vital things 'said' in conversation are often left 'unspoken'. To understand and interpret properly we must be able to read and understand the *invisible* text properly.

1.3 A theory of speech and a theory of human action

The third phenomenon upon which speech act theory focuses our attention is that human speech is part of the larger domain of human action.

Austin was conscious of the fact that verbal and non-verbal behaviour are linked. When discussing his felicity conditions he comments thus:

> First of all, it is obvious that the conventional procedure which by our utterance we are purporting to use must actually exist. In the examples given here this procedure must be a verbal one, a verbal procedure for marrying or giving of whatever it may be, but *it should be borne in mind that there are many non-verbal procedures by which we can perform exactly the same acts as we perform by these verbal means* (Austin 1970:237 – my emphasis).

The implication of talking about speech *acts* goes even further than these remarks of Austin. Thinking of speech as action forces us to relate this form of human action to other forms of human action. We are teased with the idea to fit a theory of speech acts into a wider theory of human action in general. We are reminded that speech may only be understood properly if we have a comprehensive view of human behaviour. Of course knowledge of the speech 'act' may in turn help to enrich our knowledge of the general patterns of human behaviour.

It was especially Jürgen Habermas (cf. Habermas 1970) who tried to relate the ideas of Austin as fleshed out by Searle to a general theory of human action. His approach proved especially influential in New Testament studies as Edmund Arens (Arens 1982) attempted to interpret the parables of Jesus with Habermas' key concept of 'kommunikatives Handeln'.

The connection between speech action and human action in general also helps us to consider the ideology hidden in human verbal behaviour. Pratt (1986) argued recently that the ideology encapsulated in the description of the conversational conventions of speech act theory warrents closer scrutiny. This is an exciting new development, relating speech act theory closer to the broader social reality, introducing the issue of power and authority into reality.

2. Geoffrey N. Leech's reinterpretation of speech act theory

In his book *Principles of Pragmatics* G. N. Leech (Leech 1983) attempted an extension of speech act theory. He admits that the view of meaning as illocutionary force as it was developed by Austin and Searle and meaning as conversational implicature as it was formulated by Grice have been the strongest influence on his own theory (Leech 1983:x). His approach, however, incorporates and modifies the views of his predecessors from the perspective of communication as a problem-solving activity:

> A speaker, *qua* communicator, has to solve the problem: 'Given that I want to bring about such-and-such a result in the hearer's consciousness, what is the best way to accomplish this aim by using language? 'For the hearer there is another kind of problem to solve: 'Given that the speaker said such-and-such, what did the speaker mean me to understand by that?' (Leech 1983:x).

This conception of communication entails that the speaker is seen 'as trying to achieve his aims within the constraints imposed by principles and maxims of 'good communicative behaviour" (Leech 1983:xi).

The main motivation for talking (or communicating) is defined by Leech (1983:17) as the illocutionary force of an utterance. The regulative factors that ensure that conversation, once it is under way, will not follow 'a fruitless and disruptive path', is called the rhetorical force by Leech. Grice's cooperative principle is included in this concept together with other principles, notably that of politeness and irony.

The rhetorical force conveys the meaning of an utterance regarding the speaker's consideration for his audience. It indicates how the speaker adheres to the social goals which ensures that his audience remains attentive and well disposed towards the speaker until he has attained the main purpose of his communication.

The illocutionary force and the rhetorical force combine to form the prag-

matic force of the utterance. This is more or less the intended perlocution of the
utterance.

By relating perlocutionary force (purpose or communicating) and rhetorical
force (principles of cooperation, politeness, irony...) forges the ideas of Austin,
Searle and Grice into a new unity.

Leech (1983:104-107) further elucidates the effects of specific illocutions on
the social goals or rhetorical force by undertaking a reclassification of illocutionary acts (in the process demonstrating the deficiency of Searle's classification).

He finds four different classes (Leech 1983:104): (a) those illocutions that
are competitive with the social goals, such as ordering; (b) those that are convi-
vial to the social goals, such as congratulating; (c) illocutions that are collabora-
tive (i.e. indifferent to the social goals), such as instructing; and (d) those that
are conflictive with the social goals, such as threatening.

Leech (1983:42) redefines some of the maxims of the cooperative principle
as formulated by Grice. Regarding the Maxim of Relation Leech states that the
speaker should advance his own and the audience's goals with his utterance.
The Maxim of Manner stipulates that the speaker's utterance should give a
clear indication of his illocutionary force (his main purpose for communicating).

One of Leech's most important contributions is his exposition of the Politeness Principle, and because it will play the major role in our application of the
theory on Mark 12:1-2, I give a more extensive rendition of this principle.

Leech (1983:132) analyses the Politeness Principle and its constituent
maxims as follows: The Tact Maxim requires the speaker to say something that
minimises the cost to the other or conversely that maximises the benefit to the
other; the Generosity Maxim requires minimal benefit to self or maximum cost
to self; the Approbation Maxim requires minimal dispraise of other or maximum praise of other; the Modesty Maxim requires minimal praise of self or
maximum dispraise of self; the Agreement Maxim requires minimum
disagreement between self and other; the Sympathy Maxim requires minimum
antipathy between self and other or maximum sympathy between self and other
(cf. also Du Plessis 1987:36).

By relating the analysis of meaning to the social goals for communicating and
stressing the relation between illocutionary force and the rhetorical force's
social goals Leech made the pragmatic facet of communication more accessible
to analysis. He furthermore provides a conceptual 'grid' that proves very applicable in practical analysis/exegesis.

Unfortunately this extremely brief exposition will have to be sufficient (for
further comments on Leech's theory cf. Du Plessis 1985:16-40; 1987:34-37;
1988:311-313).

I now turn to a cursory overview of some of the areas of research in speech
act theory.

3. Areas of research and application in New Testament scholarship

3.1 Areas of research

Searle (1969; 1979) developed the ideas of Austin, and by paying attention to issues such as the nature of a performative and the classification of illocutionary acts and verbs, he became more or less responsible for the 'received theory'.

Research continued in basically three different terrains: the philosophical issues involved in the theory, purely linguistic aspects and the nature of fictional or literary speech.

Interestingly enough there is not so much work available where the results of the theory have been implemented in actual analysis. Exceptions are, for instance, Eaton (1983), Stern (1984) and especially the outstanding work done by South African literary scientists and collected in Van Coller and Van Jaarsveld (Van Coller & Van Jaarsveld (eds.) 1984). The essays in this volume are textbook examples of how enriching analysis can be that is done on the basis of speech act theory.

3.2 Speech act theory in New Testament studies

Speech act theory entered New Testament research through the field of parable research. Already in 1970 Thiselton presented the theory in an article on Fuchs' interpretation of the parables. In 1977 Aurelio used speech act theory extensively in his interpretation of the parables. His approach was developed by Arens (1982) who introduced the notions of Habermas (1970) regarding speech and human action. My own work (Du Plessis 1985; 1987; 1988) follows the trend of Aurelio and Arens, but focuses on the analysis of specific texts by using the theory as reinterpreted by Leech.

In the rest of the field of New Testament studies speech act theory has not received the same detailed attention at all. Snyman (1983) and Jacobs (1985) used the theory to analyse portions of 1 Corinthians. Botha (1989) used the theory extensively in his analysis of John 4:1-42 to try and formulate a more functional definition of style.

Apart from these works, in which analyses of specific texts are made with the help of the theory, the theory is also used for broader speculation regarding the nature and purpose of exegesis and character of religious language. These were the issues focused on in *Semeia* 41, as mentioned earlier. Very often one forgets to describe the position of biblical language *vis à vis* that of litarary fictional discourse (cf. the arguments *contra* offered by me in Du Plessis 1984).

To my mind the real future of speech act theory in New Testament research does not lie with these broader philosophical issues, but in the support the theory gives to the exegesis of individual texts. Especially in the fields of Johannine studies and the Sermon on the Mount a rich harvest may be reaped.

PART 2: PRACTICAL APPLICATION

4. The parable of the vineyard and the tenants and the ensuing conversation (Mark 12:1-12)

In traditional exegesis of the parable little attention has been paid to the larger unit including both parable and subsequent discourse. As a matter of fact the subsequent discourse which includes the quotation from Psalm 118:22-23 has been treated more or less as an appendix to the parable.

Our attention is focused on the shape of the discourse in the final form of the redaction. I will attempt to show that the parable in itself is still an incomplete part of the discourse and is completed only by the discourse as a whole (together with the quotation of Psalm 118:22-23). In what follows I will closely follow the exposition as given in my unpublished doctoral dissertation (Du Plessis 1985).

The parable and the subsequent discourse are calculated by Jesus (as presented by Mark, of course) to anatagonise his opponents systematically and to emphasise his own unique position in the dealings between God and his people. The enmity reported at the conclusion (cf. 12) is the inevitable sequel to the way in which the conversation is conducted by Jesus.

In the parabolic narrative Jesus sketches an antagonistic relationship between God and the chosen religious supervisors of Israel. This is a transgression of the Politeness Principle in Jesus' dealings with the religious leadership. Those who are supposed to care for and support God's cause are told that they are his opponents.

At the same time Jesus narrates a progression in God's dealings with the supervisors: instead of sending slaves, the point has been reached in which he sends a special envoy (here 'son' need and should of course not be interpreted in a specialised christological sense – the point is the distinction between the previous envoys and the present one and the stress upon the ultimate urgency of this action).

The process of patiently attempting to recover God's share has reached its end. A final decision must be reached with the mission of the ultimate and exceptional envoy. It is the focus on the exceptional nature of the envoy that gives the clue to the identification of the 'son' as referring to Jesus, not the mentioning of 'son' as such.

From the perception of the opponents of Jesus (who have been accused by him by means of the parable in excessive and aggravating terms) the distinctive use of 'son' as a designation for Jesus himself confirms his arrogance. This is the function of the sending of the son in the parable. From the point of the internal logic of the narrative it is an incomprehensible action, reflecting on the prudence of the father. Biser (1965:139) speaks of the father's 'Arglosigkeit'. Derrett (1974:431, 432) does not want to call it 'implausible', but admits that the sending of the son subsequent to the messengers is 'remarkable'. What is certainly implausible is Jeremias' attempt at giving an explanation to let it appear unremarkable (Jeremias 1972:71ff).

The parable is, however, not constructed as an aesthetic object, but as a story to engage the audience in confrontation. The episode of the sending of the son is an indication that the parable refers to a reality outside the parable-world and that it is constructed for a pragmatic purpose. The mission of the son is recounted in the parable narrative to enrage the opponents and to provide a link with the subsequent conversation.

The parable thus ends with Jesus flouting the Politeness Principle by describing the religious authorities as enemies of God (the maximising of dispraise of the other). He leaves them, though, with the consolation that even he foresees that the confrontation between them will end in his demise (maximising the cost to himself).

In the first instance Jesus transgressed the Approbation Maxim of the Politeness Principle. By praising himself as the ultimate envoy of God, he transgressed the Modesty Maxim of the Politeness Principle. The circumstance of the tenants is for the moment left undecided.

Without the terminology: At the end of the parable the religious leaders will feel enraged because Jesus assumes a privileged position in God's dealings with Israel, while at the same time he presents them as the villains of the story, but they will at least have the satisfaction that he will be vanquished by them.

The first part of the 'explanation' follows now (9). It is introduced with a rhetorical question by Jesus (also in Luke, but not so in Matthew). The theme of conflict between Jesus and his opponents is developed with the answer.

The tenants (i.e. the religious leaders) are going to be judged and punished by God. The giving away of the vineyard to others is a secondary theme. It adds to what the criminal behaviour of the tenants is going to cost them. With this first explanation Jesus flouts another maxim of the Politeness Principle.

At the end of the parable itself he has supported the Generosity Maxim by having minimised the benefit to himself and maximised the cost to himself (presenting himself as being killed). At the same time he has minimised the cost to the others by leaving their fate undefined, thus keeping the possibility open that they could remain victorious despite their liquidation of the final envoy.

Now Jesus asserts (in Matthew it is the audience) that the religious supervisors will also be defeated. Their hope of a possible triumph is extinguished by the explanation. Jesus flouts the Tact Maxim by accruing cost to the addressees. Initially, at the end of the parable, they were only dispraised, now they are warned of the eventual cost of their behaviour. At the end of the narrative they could still view themselves as *infamous victors*. Now they are depicted as both infamous and *vanquished*.

The only consolation left to them is that their opponent, Jesus, in his own words, describes himself as being their victim and succumbing to them. The Politeness Principle Maxim of Generosity is being upheld. This is the slender thread by which the rhetorical force still operates between Jesus and his opponents.

It is this last surviving positive rhetorical element that is taken away with the mentioning of the quotation from Psalm 118. The opponents are likened to the builders who have rejected the eventual cornerstone (this is in line with the isotopy of the passage: they were the ones who rejected the emissaries of the owner). The one rejected in the parable is primarily God, but He is rejected through his rejection of his emissaries. The ultimate emissary is the son (as interpreted above), that is Jesus. The quotation speaks of initial rejection that is followed by eventual victory: the stone obtains a key position in the building (indicative here of God's work – his people perhaps?).

With the quotation Jesus removes the last remaining consolation for his opponents. Their rejection will not result in his final demise. He will be victorious. Jesus is not only transgressing the Maxim of Modesty (which he did in the parable itself with the reference to himself as the unique and ultimate emissary of God), but also the Generosity Maxim, which, up to now, has been maintained. With the quotation Jesus maximises the benefit to himself.

The opponents are left without any consolation. Every vestige of the rhetorical force with which the conversation between Jesus and the opponents could have been kept going has been dismantled. Jesus has systematically destroyed every bridge between himself and his opponents.

Mark (as Matthew) adds verse 23 of Psalm 118 to the quotation. This asserts that God will be the One who accomplishes the reversal of fortunes of the 'cornerstone'. This makes the close affinity between Jesus and God even more explicit.

The fact of the quotation is significant within the thrust of the conversation. It constitutes the final outrage, from the perspective of the opponents. It is a quotation from a so-called 'Messianic' psalm. It is therefore a psalm that gives expression to the people's hopes that they as a rejected nation will eventually be vindicated by God. The religious leaders are of course representative of this rejected people and their aspirations. By making use of the Messianic psalm, their hopes are dashed by Jesus. They are once again designated as enemies of God. Those hoping that God would change their fate, and that He would vindicate them, are told by Jesus that this hope is applicable precisely to the one whom they despise and reject.

It is also possible to see in the use of the quotation from the Messianic psalm a reproach by Jesus to his opponents. The theology of the Messianic expectation rested upon the assumption that the God of Israel cares for the despised and the rejected. It is in the name of that theology that Jesus now vindicates his position before his opponents. They who hope for the vindication of the despised and rejected Israel (within the context of Roman rule) should have recognised the real rejected one. Jesus is asserting that he is in line with the fundamental logic of Israel's thought.

The quotation is part of the explanatory passage, but is itself couched with imagery (Marin 1980:54). The nature of the son's/cornerstone's vindication remains obscure. It is a provocative formulation. The secret of Jesus' victory is not revealed.

The provocative and outrageous way in which Mark presents Jesus' conduct of the conversation binds the various disparate elements together. Marin (1980:54), who analysed the passage from a structuralist point of view, found the discourse subsequent to the parable narrative not integrated into a single isotopy with the parable. The above should prove otherwise. It is especially the isotopy of rejection and acceptance that remains constant.

The pragmatic force of the conversation is Jesus' rejection of his opponents and their antagonisation. This was done by a systematic flouting of the rhetorical principles in which the parable with its illocutionary force of accusation and condemnation was embedded.

The reader is confronted with the absolute control that Jesus exerts in the face of adversity, even creating adversity on purpose. He is not going his way unintentionally floundering into conflict with the religious authorities. He is shown as calculating and, even in his rejection, completely in control.

The illocutionary force of this parable and its subsequent discourse is that of accusation and condemnation. The rhetorical force conveys disregard for any comity between speaker and addressees. The pragmatic force is one of bitter confrontation. The concluding verse (12) reports the success of this pragmatic force.

The parable and its subsequent discourse is clear to the opponents. The Maxim of Manner is adhered to. The opponents understand the illocutionary force correctly as accusing and condemning. This clarity is, however, of no advantage to them. The flouting of the Politeness Principle realises the dark and sombre purpose of judgement.

BIBLIOGRAPHY

Allwood, J. 1977. A Critical Look at Speech Act Theory, in O. Dahl (ed.). *Logic, Pragmatics and Grammer*. Göteborg: University of Göteborg, Dept. of Linguistics, 53-69.

Arens, E. 1982. *Kommunikative Handlungen: Die paradigmatische Bedeutung der Gleichnisse Jesu für eine Handlungstheorie*. Düsseldorf: Patmos.

Aurelio, T. 1977. *Disclosures in den Gleichnisse Jesu: Eine Anwendung der Disclosure-Theorie von I. T. Ramsey, der modernen Methaphorik und der Sprechakte auf die Gleichnisse Jesu*. Frankfurt: Lang. (Regensburger Studien zur Theologie 8.)

Austin, J. L. 1975. *How to Do Things with Words*. New York: Oxford University Press.

Austin, J. L. 1976. Performative Utterances, in *Philosophical Papers*. London: Oxford University Press, 233-252.

Bach, K. & Harnisch, L. M. 1979. *Linguistic Communication and Speech Acts*. Cambridge, Massachussetts: MIT.

Biser, E. 1965. *Die Gleichnisse Jesu: Versuch einer Deutung*. München: Kösel.

Botha, J. E. 1989. *A Study in Johannine Style: History, Theory and Practice*. Pretoria: University of Pretoria. (Unpublished Doctoral Thesis.)

Buss, M. J. 1988. Potential and Actual Interactions between Speech Act Theory and Biblical Studies. *Semeia* 41, 125-134.

Cloete, T. T. 1984. Taalhandeling en die Literatuur, in H. P. van Coller & G. J. van Jaarsveld (eds.). *Woorde as Dade: Taalhandelinge en Letterkunde*. Durban: Butterworth, 1-14.

Dahl, O. 1982. The Contract Game. *Theoretical Linguistics* 9, 3-10.

Derrett, J. D. M. 1974. Allegory and the Wicked Vinedressers. *Journal of Theological Studies* 15, 426-432.

Dillon, G. L., Coleman, L. & Fahnestock, J. 1985. Review Article: Discourse Analysis, Principle of Pragmatics, Pragmatics. *Language* 61, 446-460.

Du Plessis, J. G. 1984. Some Aspects of Extralingual Reality and the Interpretation of Texts. *Neotestamentica* 18, 80-93.

Du Plessis, J. G. 1985. *Clarity and Obscurity: A Study in Textual Communication of the Relation between Sender, Parable and Receiver in the Synoptic Gospels*. Stellenbosch: University of Stellenbosch. (Unpublished Doctoral Thesis.)

Du Plessis, J. G. 1987. Pragmatic Meaning in Matthew 13:1-23. *Neotestamentica* 21, 42-56.

Du Plessis, J. G. 1988. Why Did Peter Ask his Question and How Did Jesus Answer Him? Or: Implicature in Luke 12:35-48. *Neotestamentica* 22, 311-324.

Eaton, M. 1983. James' Turn of the Speech Act. *British Journal of Aesthetics* 23, 333-345.

Grice, H. P. 1982. Logic and Conversation, in R. J. Fogelin. *Understanding Arguments*. New York: Hartcourt, 407-421.

Habermas, J. 1970. *Zur Logik der Sozialwissenschaften: Materialen*. Frankfurt: Suhrkampf.

Jacobs, L. D. 1985. *Taalhandelinge en Strategieë in 1 Korinthiërs 1-4*. Bloemfontein: University of the Orange Free State. (Unpublished M.A. Dissertation.)

Jeremias, J. 1972. *The Parables of Jesus*. London: SCM.

Leech, G. N. 1983. *Principles of Pragmatics*. London: Longman. (Longman Linguistics Library 30.)

Leonardi, P. & Sbisá, M. 1984. Introduction. *Journal of Pragmatics* 8, 1-7.

Marin, L. 1980. *The Semiotics of the Passion Narrative*. Pittsburg: Pickwick.

Mertens, T. H. 1986. Habermas en Searle: Kritische Beschouwingen bij de Theorie van het Communicatieve Handelen. *Tijdschrift voor Filosofie*. Maart.

Patte, D. 1988. Speech Acts Theory and Biblical Exegesis. *Semeia* 41, 85-102.

Peirce, C. S. 1931-58. *Collected Papers*, v. 1-8. Cambridge: Massachussetts: Harvard University Press.

Pratt, M. L. 1977. *Toward a Speech Act Theory of Literary Discourse*. Bloomington: Indiana University Press.

Pratt, M. L. 1986. Ideology and Speech Act Theory. *Poetics Today* 7, 59-72.

Searle, J. R. 1969. *Speech Acts: An Essay in the Philosophy of Language*. Cambridge: Cambridge University Press.

Searle, J. R. 1979. *Expression and Meaning: Studies in the Theory of Speech Acts*. Cambridge: Cambridge University Press.

Searle, J. R. 1979. *Intensionality: An Essay in the Philosophy of Mind*. Cambridge: Cambridge University Press.

Searle, J. R., Kiefer, F. & Bierwisch, M. (eds.). 1980. *Speech Act Theory and Pragmatics*. Dordrech: Riedel.

Snyman, A. H. 1983. Vrae, Vraagstelling en Vraagappélle, in M. C. J. van Rensburg (ed.). *Kongresreferate by die 19de Nasionale Kongres van die Linguistevereniging van Suider Afrika*. Bloemfontein: University of the Orange Free State.

Stern, C. 1984. Dulcinea, Aldonza and the Theory of Speech Acts. *Hispania* 67, 61-73.

Thiselton, A. C. 1970. The Parables as Language Event: Some Comments on Fuch's Hermeneutics in the Light of Linguistic Philosophy. *Scottish Journal of Theology* 23, 437-460.

Thomas, J. A. 1985. The Language of Power: Towards a Dynamic Pragmatics. *Journal of Pragmatics* 9, 765-783.

Van Coller, H. P. & Van Jaarsveld, G. J. (eds.). 1984. *Woorde as Dade: Taalhandelinge en Letterkunde*. Durban: Butterworth.

Wendland, E. R. 1985. *Language, Society and Bible Translation: With Special Reference to the Style and Structure of Segments of Direct Speech in the Scriptures*. Cape Town: Bible Society of South Africa.

White, H. C. 1988. Introduction: Speech Act Theory and Literary Criticism. *Semeia* 41, 1-12.

White, H. C. 1988. The Value of Speech Act Theory for Old Testament Hermeneutics. *Semeia* 41, 41-64.

C. RECEPTOR

B. C. LATEGAN

RECEPTION: THEORY AND PRACTICE IN READING ROMANS 13

PART 1

1. Introduction

A prominent feature of literary studies during the past two decades has been the emergence of the reader. This reader appeared in many guises and assumed a wide variety of roles. The impetus behind all these developments is a fascination with the intricacies of the reading process. As a distinctive approach it has become known on the Continent as *reception theory*, while in North America the usual term is *reader-response criticism*. It is closely related to the concept of audience criticism, but also to some aspects of narrative analysis, speech act theory and rhetorical criticism. In an even wider context, it has connections with other approaches that feature in this book, such as discourse analysis, semiotics, socio-linguistics, sociological exegesis and contextualisation.

The common thread, which binds these diverse approaches together, is the interest in the effect of language-in-use. The gradual shift from the historical, via the structural to the pragmatic aspects of language can be traced on various levels and appears in many different forms (cf. Lategan 1984). It forms part of a fuller understanding of the communication process. This process is not only in the hands of the author or sender to control and to manipulate. It needs the co-operation of an audience or a reader, which often goes his or her own way. Language is not only a vehicle to convey information or to express meaning. More often than not it is an instrument in getting things done. Language usage ultimately has to do with power relationships. It can be used to foster understanding, but also to persuade and to manipulate – and therefore it is open to ideological abuse.

As in the case of so many exegetical methods, reception theory has its origin in literary studies where it was developed as a tool for the critical analysis of literature. It was only at a later stage that its usefulness for the interpretation of biblical material was realised, resulting in a number of studies written from this perspective.

There are several reasons for the attractiveness of reception theory for biblical scholars. It restores a sense of integration and continuity after the atomistic dissection of the text by form- and redaction criticism, it invites participation by the 'ordinary' reader (cf. Van Iersel, Dormeyer), breaking through the exclusive privilege of the critic (cf. Fowler), who for so long has dominated the business of interpretation. It promises a return to the historical dimensions of the text after the synchronic and a-historical attitude of structuralism – understanding reading not as an abstraction or as a theoretical exercise, but as an event that takes place in a concrete historical setting. Finally, it offers an opportunity to become involved in the praxis and power play of interpretation (cf. Wuellner) after the abstract theorising of reading in the study.

However, the usefulness of this approach for the interpretation of biblical texts may be deceptive, as we shall soon see. Because everyone is a reader of some sorts, the concept of the reader is both simple and familiar, offering a natural and obvious point of entrance to the reading process. At the same time, we are discovering that this process is in itself an extremely complicated matter. It is the meeting place of a whole network of relationships, influenced by a wide variety of factors and forces. It is therefore necessary to sketch in broad outline the wider context out of which reception theory has developed, before we discuss some of the basic characteristics of the method and illustrate how it can be applied to New Testament texts.

2. The wider context of reception theory

In terms of origins, a distinction can be made between *reader-response criticism* and *reception theory*. The former is a concept prevalent in North America, the latter was developed in an European context. *Reader-response criticism* is an umbrella term which brings together literary critics from diverse backgrounds. The common denominator is their opposition to the New Critical emphasis on the 'text itself', that is, on the autonomous status of the text as text and their concentration on the ways in which the text interacts with readers. *Reception theory*, on the other hand, is a much more coherent movement, most prominently represented by the so-called School of Constance with Robert Jauss and Wolfgang Iser as its principal exponents.

The rise of reception theory or the 'aesthetics of reception' (Jauss) was preceded by four other related developments. Firstly, studies in the sociology of literature emphasised that not only the production of a work of art or its inherent qualities are worthy of investigation, but also and especially its effect on society. Similar ideas came from a second quarter, that of philosophical hermeneutics, where Gadamer developed his concept of the 'effective-history' (*Wirkungsgeschichte*) of a text. An individual does not exhaust the meaning potential of a text, but his or her interpretation is relativised and complemented by other readings of the text. If fact, these different readings form a history of its own which influences the predisposition of the individual reader even before he or she actually encounters the text – whether the reader is aware of this influence or not. The concept of 'effective-history' prepared the way for the third influence, namely the idea of writing a history of literature in terms of the reception of texts. Jauss, its major exponent, understands such an undertaking as the prerequisite for an 'aesthetics of reception'. The aim is to provide some explanation for the success or failure of certain texts during certain periods in history and in doing so to establish a basis for the evaluation of texts. A fourth and very powerful influence came from the ideas of the Prague structuralists. In developing and revising certain concepts of Russian formalism, a clear distinction was maintained between the text as stable structure and the realisation of that structure by the reader. By seeing the work of art as a complex sign which mediates between the artist and the receiver, the social dimension of reception became prominent. This line of thought was taken up and explored further by the School of Constance. From quite a different angle, reception was also influenced by insights deriving from *speech act theory*. Here too the focus was on the effect achieved by language usage.

In its turn, concepts developed by reception theory proved to be fruitful for many other related areas of research. The following are the most prominent: Theoretical studies have been complemented with a vast amount of empirical work where the actual reception of texts by various types of readers is monitored under controlled conditions. This has developed into a specialised field of research. Sociology of knowledge has emphasised the historical relativity of knowledge, that is the effect which the position of the observer, i.e. the observer's place in history and in the social network, has on the observer's perception of reality. Critical hermeneutics gave rise to the development of 'materialistic' readings of texts, where both production and reception are understood in terms of the interaction of socio-economic forces. Psychological studies of the reading process have made use of reception insights, while communication theory as a whole has benefitted from this interchange. In the earlier stages of development, the work of Iser represented the only significant link between reader-response theory and reception theory. However, as a result of the ongoing exchange of ideas, the different schools and traditions can no longer be separated so easily.

3. Basic concepts

Against this backdrop, we can now look at some basic concepts of reception theory. Fundamental to the whole approach is the Prague distinction between the text as 'artefact' and as 'esthetic object' (cf. Mcknight 1985:16, 27, 37). The text has two modi of existence. On the one hand, it is a network of signs that has the appearance of an independent 'object'. On the other hand, it only functions as a text when it is actualised or realised by a reader. The text needs a reader. This 'actualisation' of the text is the second modus of existence that should be distinguished carefully from the first. The tussle between text and reader is at the heart of reception theory. All other aspects are in some way tied to the relationship between these two modi of existence.

First of all, each text presupposes a specific kind of reader. The features of this anticipated reader can (usually) be inferred from the text. The text of Mark presupposes a reader who at least knows Greek, who is fairly familiar with conditions in first-century Palestine, etc. But, in the course of reading, the text also increases the competence of its reader, providing him or her with additional information, like details about the personalities of the characters or clues to the development of the plot.

> ...a well-organized text on the one hand presupposes a model of competence coming, so to speak, from outside the text, but on the other hand works to build up, by merely textual means, such a competence (Eco 1979:8).

Whether the actual reader has the required competence or whether he or she follows the instructions of the text, is a completely different matter. Reception theory therefore makes a basic distinction between 'real' and 'implied' readers. This distinction is at the same time the dividing line between two main streams in this type of research: empirical studies based on the evidence of actual readings and theoretical reflection on the reading process as part of literary criticism.

The implied reader as theoretical construct was first introduced by Iser. Subsequently, it has been modified and expanded in many ways. Basically, it is a heuristic tool to draw out the explicit and implicit communicative strategies of the text in order to follow the anticipated realisation of the text as closely as possible. From the author's point of view, it is an image of the intended reader; from the reader's point of view, it is a device to gain a clear understanding of the author's instructions to the reader. In other words, it is a pose adopted by the (real) reader for rhetorical purposes (Fowler 1990:II/20-21).

The real reader is a historical person, the implied reader a textual construct. But further distinctions are possible. An author may make use of a narrator in the text to tell his/her story – which has as counterpart the narratee. In this way the implied author can distance him- or herself from the narrator, and expect the same from the narratee and implied author. In his Groot Marico stories, Henry Charles Bosman makes use of Schalk Lourens as narrator, who spins his yarns to an unnamed narratee – someone who would presumably be gullible enough to take the tall stories of the old farmer at face value. But behind their backs and over their heads, the implied author winks knowingly at the implied reader and they secretly share the humor and irony of all that 'Oom Schalk' is divulging. As Chatman (1983:256) shows with the example from John Barth's *Menelaid*, this form of imbedding can be extended almost indefinitely. However, the basic scheme is as follows:

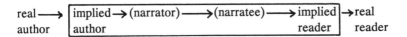

real⟶ | implied→ (narrator) ⟶ (narratee) ⟶ implied | →real
author | author   reader | reader

The implied reader is therefore 'inside' the text, being a textual feature. Some (like Petersen) prefer to talk of an 'encoded reader'. The implication is that for the characterisation of this reader we are completely dependent on what can be gleaned from the text itself. How intensive and complete this scrutiny of the text will be depends again on what level the reading process is taking place. To put it differently, the implied reader can either be envisaged as a naive or as a very sophisticated reader – and the kind of reading that will follow will differ accordingly. Fowler (1990:II/21) shows that the (naive) reader and the critic find themselves in a continuum, with various possible intermediate positions. Dormeyer (1987) distinguishes at least four types of readers and reading:

Type of reader:	naive	understanding	critical
Mental activity:	experience	reflection	analysis
Textual function:	confirmation	alteration	neutrality
Effect:	enjoyment	mediation	distancing

Depending on how the realisation of the text is envisaged, reader types have been expanded to include, *inter alia*, the informed reader, the model reader, the superreader, the new reader, the resistant reader and the wilful misreader (cf. Fowler 1983:31). In the interpretation of specific New Testament texts, readings are usually offered from the perspective of the critical or fully informed reader (cf. Fowler, Kelber, Rhoads, Resseguie, Tannehill, Kingsbury, Culpepper). A significant exeption is the study of Van Iersel, who, without denying that he has access to all the information available to the critical reader, offers a reading of Mark consistent with the perspective of the implied reader, that is, the reader 'that the author has created through the way in which he wrote his book' (1989:12).

When reception theory is applied to New Testament texts, specific problems arise. It must be kept in mind that the basic concepts of this approach have been developed in the context of the 'Gutenberg galaxy'. Are these concepts not by definition ill-suited for documents which have their origin in an ancient oral-aural environment? The debate on orality has underlined the differences between aural and visual appropriation and the special needs of gospel interpretation, for which 'audience' and 'hearers' would be much more suitable categories. Even if it is true that the Gospels eventually ended up in written documents and that letters were part of the emerging New Testament right from the beginning, it cannot be denied that the hearing/reading process was very different for the first receivers of these documents than for modern readers, for whom the text has assumed, because of its availability and perfect reproduction, more and more the dimensions of a fixed object.

Despite these drawbacks, reception theory has one important advantage when dealing with New Testament literature. Because it conceives of reading as an *event*, it presupposes a *temporal* and *sequential* flow of information during the reading process, which appropriates the original situation of aural reception much closer than the repetitive and cumulative nature of critical analysis.

In order to follow this sequential flow of information, the present reader operates on a different level of the text where he or she can move to and fro and assume different positions. This is what Iser has aptly described as the 'wandering viewpoint' of the reader. Various textual perspectives are open to the reader – that of the narrator, the characters, the plot and the implied reader. In moving backwards and forwards between these perspectives, different segments of the text are brought into the foreground, while others become marginal. In presenting these different options, the text can fulfill a mediating function between the reader's horizon and that of the text.

The present reader can therefore never be a virginal reader. Neither can he or she emulate the first or original reader of the text. There is a certain artificiality in the re-enactment of the reading experience by the biblical interpreter. It involves retracing steps, reconsidering choices, trying out of different alternatives. It has the artificiality of a director requesting his cast to play the same scene with a different emphasis or to experiment with an alternative ending. But the aim remains to find, by trial and error, the most adequate or satisfying rendering of the text.

The fact that the text permits, even invites different readings, brings us in contact with another important concept of reception theory, namely the indeterminacy of the text. Although a wide variety of clues may be offered to the reader – on the linguistic, rhetorical and conceptual level – to guide the production of meaning, there still remains a measure of openness or indeterminacy. What is revealed in the text is at the same time accompanied by what remains concealed. It is this dialectic between what is explicit and what is implicit, between the known and the unknown, which sets the reading process in motion. According to Iser, the text contains certain deliberate 'gaps' or 'open spaces'. These structured blanks spur the reader to action and entice him or her to supply the missing information in order to make sense of what is said. In this way the text requires an input from the reader and makes the reader co-responsible for the realisation of the text as meaningful discourse.

The interaction between text and reader has given rise to the question which of these two is really in control of the reading process. But if it is kept in mind that the role of the reader is a theoretical construct without any independent existence apart from the text, it becomes a non-question. That is also why, in the long run, it becomes problematic to keep intratextual and extratextual readers neatly separated. The 'implied reader' as such illustrates the problem. Although originally conceived as a means to account for the presence of the reader without having to deal with real readers, it does become the point of entrance for the real reader in so far as it represents the stance which the latter attempts to adopt. Iser is therefore forced to define the implied reader both as a textual structure (*Textstruktur*) and as a structured act (*Aktstruktur*). This dual definition of the concept of the implied reader enables Iser to move to and fro from text to reader, but also gave rise to the criticism that he can do so only because the relationship between these two aspects remains vague.

Fowler (1990:II/24-25) is therefore more to the point when he writes:

> Therefore, who is 'the reader' in reader-response criticism? First, it is I, as a critical reader. And it is I, as a supposed ideal reader, a role I shall play by formulating and putting forth a composite ideal reader created out of the best that has been thought and said by my critical community. But that ideal reader, individual and composite, can only be a heuristic abstraction contrived from the countless implied readers implied by countless texts, chief among them here the Gospel of Mark. To put it as simply as possible, the critical reader of Mark has an individual persona (mine), a communal persona (the abstracted total experience of my critical community), and a textual persona (the reader implied in the text at hand).

It is exactly at this point where deconstruction levels its strongest criticism against the concept of the reader, by insisting that the idea of the stability of the text is an illusion and nothing but a form of foundationalism. It is no doubt true that any statement about the text or the reader in the text is dependent on a prior reading of the text. In that sense all such statements are relative. But to shift the centre of control from the text to the interpretative community, as Fish proposes, is only a partial solution. The critical presuppositions of community or guild of which the reader forms part no doubt have a strong or even decisive influence of the way the individual reads. But – as Fowler indicates (1990:II/29 note 39) – certain questions remain unanswered. For example: 1) How critics in the same interpretative community can disagree; 2) how critics in different communities can agree; 3) how a new community can come into existence.

But recognition of the role of the interpretative community opens an important perspective on the pragmatic implications of language usage, on the exercise of power through language and its ideological abuse. These social dimensions of language are closely linked to the important issue of contextualisation – an aspect of the reading process that is in urgent need of further exploration, but which will take us beyond the scope of the present essay.

In view of the limitations of reception theory, can it still make a positive contribution to the interpretation of New Testament texts? The importance of this approach is that it creates an intense awareness of the reading process and provides a framework within which the diverse aspects of this process can be integrated. It is designed to activate the rhetorical potential of the text and to facilitate the transition from the theoretical to the pragmatic aspects of textual communication. In the second part, we shall try to illustrate its application to a problematical passage from Romans.

PART 2

4. Reading Romans 13:1-7

The practical application of reception theory to biblical material has up to now been focused almost exclusively on narrative texts. The Gospel of Mark especially has attracted a variety of readings from this perspective (cf. e.g. Kermode, Fowler, Van Iersel, Rhoads & Michie, Kelber, Best, Breytenbach), but also Luke (Tannehill), Matthew (Kingsbury, Patte and Phillips) and John (Culpepper) have received attention. Analyses of non-narrative material are less frequent – cf. Petersen's treatment of Philemon as a narrative, Wuellner's rhetorical analysis of sections of Paul's letters and Betz's rhetorical commentary on Galatians.

None of these interpretations take readings of actual readers into account. In what follows, an attempt will be made to combine a theoretical analysis of Romans 13:1-7 with some actual readings of the passage. We shall first try to establish the reader instructions of the text and then compare these with the actual reader reception of our sample readings.

Generally speaking, theoretical analyses deal with the question of how a text could be read or how a text should be read. That is, they deal with the possibilities or with the perceived prescriptions of the text. It is quite a different matter when we try to ascertain how texts in actual fact are read. An answer to this question can only be attempted when sufficient data on actual receptions is available. In the case of biblical texts, evidence of such 'readings' could be the use of the Old Testament in the New, the different versions of the gospel story by the evangelists, the formation of the canon, commentaries on specific books or on the same text, to name just a few. These different types of data all present their own problems. Because of difficulties related to availability and control, empirical reception research in general has concentrated on the study of contemporary readings, producing a vast amount of material (cf. Groeben 1977; Holub 1984:134-46).

In contrast, very little contemporary empirical research has been undertaken so far on the reception of biblical texts (cf. Lategan and Rousseau 1988). The present study is an attempt to take a further exploratory step in this direction. The aim is to analyse the actual reception of the text of Romans 13:1-7 in a South African context and to study the strategies employed in these readings. Three readings will be discussed briefly – the Kairos Document, Nürnberger and Du Toit. As a 'control text' a reading by Jüngel in a West-German context will be used. The small sample of South African readings is placed against the wider backdrop of a collection of recent readings of Romans 13, including examples from Eastern and Western countries, from Greek Orthodox to Reformed contexts, and from the First and Third Worlds. These readings were collected for and discussed in the SNTS seminar on the Role and the Reader at its Cambridge meeting in 1988 (cf. bibliography for further details).

5. Theoretical considerations[1]

5.1 The pragmatic effect of Romans 13

Romans 13:1-7 is indeed a provocative text, judging by the seemingly endless stream of readings and interpretations over the centuries (cf. Friedrich *et al.* 1976 for a overview of the different positions). Its *Wirkungsgeschichte* reflects a remarkably wide sphere of influence, including fields of law, political philosophy, public administration, education, politics and many others. Often its effect has been indirect. Luttikhuizen (1988), for example, shows how it found its way into the constitutions of political parties. But the main arena, where pragmatic consequences of this text remains a hotly debated issue, is in the relationship between church and state. In any situation where the state exerts its power over institutions and individuals, the potential for conflict exists. How does the church interpret Romans 13 when it finds itself in disagreement with the policies and actions of the government of the day? How should the individual understand this passage when his or her conscience forbids him or her to obey a specific law? On the other hand, this is one of the most frequently quoted passages by those in authority when their own legitimacy and authority are questioned.

It would seem, therefore, that no 'innocent' reading of the passage is possible. When attempting to analyse some of these readings, it is important to keep in mind that all empirical reader research takes place within a specific theoretical framework (cf. Groeben 1977, and for the approach employed here, Lategan and Rousseau 1988). The actual reading can be analysed either from the perspective of the text or of the actual reader. Both are important to understand what happens when Romans 13 is read. From the perspective of the text, what are the instructions given to the reader? How open or closed is the text? Whose interests are served by the text? From the perspective of the reader, how are these instructions followed? What are the presuppositions of the reader? Why does he or she actualise the text in this way?

The actual readings of the text can be analysed and evaluated only if we have a clear understanding of the contours of the text itself, of its structure, of the

---

1   What is presented in par 5-7, forms part of an essay 'Reading Romans 13 in a South African context', due to be published by the Human Sciences Research Council in the collection B. C. Lategan (ed.) 1990. *Reception and Beyond. Theory and Practice in South African Reader-Oriented Studies*. Pretoria: HSRC.

semantic options it offers, of the directions given to the reader. Inherent in all reading is the dilemma that an analysis of the text as proposed here is possible only on the basis of the analyst's own reading. The following statements about reader instructions, therefore, do not claim to have 'objective' status, but are meant to serve as basis for our own reading of other readings.

5.2 Reader clues in Romans 13:1-7

When searching for reader clues in the sense of the previous paragraph and exploring the ways in which a text could or should be read, a wide variety of possible procedures present themselves to the interpreter. These techniques may be designed for analysis on the linguistic, literary or theological level of the text. Each of these procedures forms part of a wider methodological framework that provides the rationale for and purpose of the specific technique. In the context of this contribution, it will not be possible to discuss these methodological approaches in any detail, as our main purpose is the analysis of actual readings of Romans 13. We shall, therefore, restrict ourselves to three of these possible approaches and illustrate how they might be used to uncover the reading potential of our text, namely a discourse analysis based on syntactic units, a rhetorical analysis of the argument in the passage and a consideration of the 'gaps' left in the text. For the first two, extensive use is being made of a study by Jan Botha entitled *Obedience to the Authorities? The Reception of Romans 13:1-7.*

5.2.1 Discourse analysis

When analysing the discourse structure of our passage with the help of colon divisions (following Louw 1979:32), the following picture emerges:

ROMANS 13:1-7

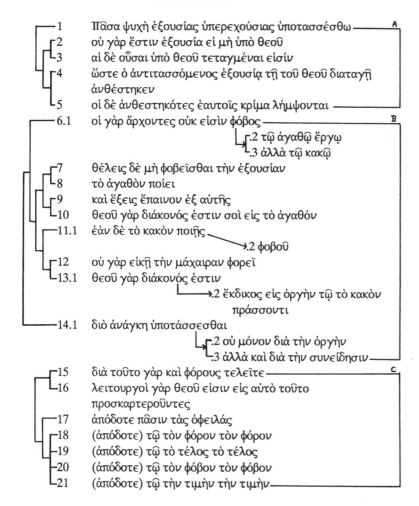

```
┌─1      Πᾶσα ψυχὴ ἐξουσίας ὑπερεχούσας ὑποτασσέσθω ─────── A
│ ┌─2    οὐ γὰρ ἔστιν ἐξουσία εἰ μὴ ὑπὸ θεοῦ
├─┤ └─3  αἱ δὲ οὖσαι ὑπὸ θεοῦ τεταγμέναι εἰσίν
│ ┌─4    ὥστε ὁ ἀντιτασσόμενος ἐξουσίᾳ τῇ τοῦ θεοῦ διαταγῇ
│ │        ἀνθέστηκεν
│ └─5    οἱ δὲ ἀνθεστηκότες ἑαυτοῖς κρίμα λήμψονται ──────┘
┌─6.1    οἱ γὰρ ἄρχοντες οὐκ εἰσὶν φόβος ──────────────── B
│               ┌.2 τῷ ἀγαθῷ ἔργῳ
│               └.3 ἀλλὰ τῷ κακῷ
│ ┌─7    θέλεις δὲ μὴ φοβεῖσθαι τὴν ἐξουσίαν
│ └─8    τὸ ἀγαθὸν ποίει
│ ┌─9    καὶ ἕξεις ἔπαινον ἐξ αὐτῆς
│ └─10   θεοῦ γὰρ διάκονός ἐστιν σοὶ εἰς τὸ ἀγαθόν
│ ┌─11.1 ἐὰν δὲ τὸ κακὸν ποιῇς
│ │               →.2 φοβοῦ
│ ┌─12   οὐ γὰρ εἰκῇ τὴν μάχαιραν φορεῖ
│ └─13.1 θεοῦ γὰρ διάκονός ἐστιν
│               →.2 ἔκδικος εἰς ὀργὴν τῷ τὸ κακὸν
│                     πράσσοντι
└─14.1   διὸ ἀνάγκη ὑποτάσσεσθαι
                ┌.2 οὐ μόνον διὰ τὴν ὀργὴν
                └.3 ἀλλὰ καὶ διὰ τὴν συνείδησιν ─────── C
 ┌─15    διὰ τοῦτο γὰρ καὶ φόρους τελεῖτε ──────────────
 └─16    λειτουργοὶ γὰρ θεοῦ εἰσιν εἰς αὐτὸ τοῦτο
           προσκαρτεροῦντες
 ┌─17    ἀπόδοτε πᾶσιν τὰς ὀφειλάς
 ┌─18    (ἀπόδοτε) τῷ τὸν φόρον τὸν φόρον
 └─19    (ἀπόδοτε) τῷ τὸ τέλος τὸ τέλος
 ┌─20    (ἀπόδοτε) τῷ τὸν φόβον τὸν φόβον
 └─21    (ἀπόδοτε) τῷ τὴν τιμὴν τὴν τιμήν ───────────────
```

An analysis of this kind reveals a wide variety of stylistic features. For the purpose of our discussion, only a few are highlighted (for a more extensive discussion, cf. Botha 1988:2-9):

* The repetition of γάρ, ἐξουσία and διάκονος lends a thematic coherence to the passage.
* On the strength of syntactic markers, the passage can be separated into three distinctive clusters (A, B and C). The position of ὑποτάσσειν in colons 1 and 14 marks the beginning and end of the first two clusters and the end of the

more theoretical part of the argument. In the same sense the function of the parallelism in 6-13 and the reversal of it in 14 binds cluster B together as a unity. The combination of *anadiplosis* and *paranomasia* in 18-21 marks the climactic end of the passage (Botha 1988:7).

Cluster A states the basic proposition of the passage: Authorities should be obeyed because they receive their authority from God. *Cluster B* outlines two possible attitudes to the proposition made in A: Doing right and living without fear of the authorities, or doing wrong and facing the consequences. (These options rest on the assumption that authorities reward what is right and punish what is wrong.) Both prudence and conscience dictate the former course of action. *Cluster C* spells out the practical implications of the conclusion reached in B.

According to Botha (1988:4), A is a generic statement which is specified in a double sense: theoretical in B and practical in C (cf. also Pelser 1988:10-11).

5.2.2 Argumentative strategies

If argumentation implies the 'contact of minds', another way of discovering reader clues in an argumentative text like Romans 13 would be to analyse the presuppositions underlying the passage. Of special importance are the so-called 'givens' – those premises which the author assumes will be unquestionably shared by his reader and on which he can base his argument or appeal for the reader's concurrence. Botha (1988:10-11) distinguishes the following universal convictions or presuppositions in the paraenetic section 12:1-15:13:

* God exists, He rules the universe and He has the final authority.
* God has established authorities, therefore they have authority.
* Governing authorities are servants of God.
* Governing authorities carry the sword (they could punish/kill – or commend – people).
* Taxes must be paid to the governing authorities.
* Everyone knows what is right/good and wrong/bad behaviour.
* Everyone must submit him- or herself to the governing authorities.

The intriguing question is whether we can identify the kind of context in which this set of convictions will fit. If the specific historical situation is not recoverable any longer (cf. Strecker 1972:27), can the rhetorical situation be reconstructed? This concerns both the intratextual and intertextual context. Although opinions differ, there are good reasons to believe that Romans 13 is compatible with Pauline paraenetics as a whole (cf. Friedrich *et al.* 1976:148-

150). As far as the extratextual historical situation is concerned, some would opt
for a synagogal/Old Testament setting (cf. Friedrich *et al*. 1976:145), but
following the line of, amongst others, Stroebel (1956, 1964), the vocabulary of
Hellenistic-Roman administration seems undeniable. This would also account
for the very general nature of most of the presuppositions in our passage that
could be shared by a universal audience, by Romans and Christians, by ancient
and modern readers alike.

At the same time, there is also a movement from conviction to persuasion,
from a universal to a particular audience (to use the terminology of Perelman)
taking place. The very open statement on the status of authorities is gradually
qualified by the introduction of the διάκονος-theme.

> Thus, we could say that Paul meets his audience on familiar ground...and in his argument he
> wants to move them to a new understanding of the nature of the authorities' authority and
> because of that, also a new understanding of the nature of their submission to the authorities
> (Botha 1988:11).

The transition referred to in the previous paragraph is strengthened by reader
clues on other levels of the text. One example – the shift from a universal to an
elite audience is paralleled by a change in the use of *pronomia*. In cluster A the
third person form is used (ὑποτασσέσθω over against the ὑποτάσσεσθε of
variant readings), while in B and C, the second person form appears (θέλεις,
ποιῇς, τελεῖτε, ἀπόδοτε), indicating a closer association with the reader. As is
the case elsewhere in Paul's letters, he makes very effective use of textual space
to distance or to associate himself with his reader(s) (cf. Lategan 1987).

A last important point as far as Paul's audience is concerned – the injunc-
tions of Romans 13 are directed at subjects, not addressed to *authorities*. For a
rereading in a new context, this has important consequences, as we shall pre-
sently see.

5.2.3 Open spaces

The concept of blanks and vacancies has been developed by Iser to account for
the participation of the reader in the realisation of the text. Blanks refer to suspended connectability in the text (Iser 1980:115), which prompts the reader to
organise the interacting textual segments as they project themselves upon
another in the reading process (114). Vacancies refer to nonthematic segments
within the referential field of the wandering viewpoint. These are not part of the
text as such, but are to be implemented by the reader's ideational activity (115).

Voelz (1988:1-2) has reminded us that Iser developed these concepts with
primarily the reading of narrative texts in mind and that they are not necessarily

useful for the analysis of argumentative texts. He shows that the 'openness' in a text like Romans 13 is due essentially to different forms of ambiguity. He distinguishes three types of ambiguity:

(1) Ambiguity of breadth of semantic range of words – 'furniture' includes both 'chair' and 'table.' In the case of Romans 13, examples of these 'broad' terms would be ἐξουσία, κακός, ἀγαθός, διάκονος.

(2) Ambiguity of referent of words, which can be the result of the first kind of ambiguity. Here the question is not what is included in a specific word, but to what it refers.

(3) Ambiguity of macrostructural arrangement. What is the central thought of a specific paragraph? What is the pivotal statement(s)? These are the types of questions to which procedures like discourse analysis try to find answers, but a degree of ambiguity still remains.

What we are dealing with here are different forms and different degrees of indeterminacy in the text. It is this indeterminacy that activates the participation of the reader, which entices him or her to close the 'openness' of the text, by supplying the missing information or realising one of the possibilities offered by the text.

When we look in what way the imaginative co-operation of the reader is required in the realisation of Romans 13, the text reveals some interesting features.

The first of these is the remarkably open or unmarked character of many of the words in our passage. ἐξουσία, κακός, πᾶσα, ἀγαθός, διάκονος, ὑποτασσέσθω, συνείδησις, φόβος, λειτουργός are all open and can be filled in a wide variety of ways. ἐξουσία, for example, is so unmarked that it is not even clear what form or what level of authorities are included in this reference. Louw & Nida (1988 II:92) list at least eight nuances in the New Testament alone, all referring to 'authority' or 'power' in an unspecified way. In colon 2, it is used without an article, keeping its reference completely open and general. αἱ δὲ οὖσαι in colon 3 is used without any qualification, creating an all-inclusive effect. οἱ ἄρχοντες in colon 6 continues this open trend, leaving room for all possible referents.

The unqualified reference to authorities is paralleled by the all-inclusive way in which subjects are introduced – cf. πᾶσα ψυχή in colon 1. But also other concepts in our passage strengthen its unrestricted and general character. ἀγαθός and κακός in cola 6, 8 and 11 represent a very wide range of possible actualisations – and carry the assumption that the reader knows what is good and bad. As Luttikhuizen and Havelaar show, the σοί εἰς τὸ ἀγαθόν of colon 10 is 'open to quite diverse interpretations. In the words 'for your benefit' every political party may project its own ideal about what is good for people'. An interesting parallel is 1 Corinthians 12:7, where the phrase πρὸς τὸ συμφέρον in a very similar way invites a variety of actualisations, because of its unspecified nature.

There are clear indicators that would encourage an open reading of our passage. But this trend – remarkably enough – is countered by an opposite movement, that is one of narrowing down the concept of authority by a series of qualifications – it is διάκονος of God and it is a διάκονός σοι εἰς τὸ ἀγαθόν.

The plurality in the form of marked/unmarked reference is related to a plurality of semantic possibilities, which leads to a remarkable series of bifurcations in the passage. The linking of God with the powers that exist, has a double effect. Firstly, authorities are sanctioned as instituted by God and should, therefore, be obeyed. Secondly, this linkage not only sanctions authorities, but at the same time relativises them, by implying that they are accountable to God. The linkage provides the textual basis and stimulus for two diametrically opposed readings. The one insists on the divine right and obligation to obey authorities. The other insists on relativising the power of authorities by making them accountable to God. Examples of both these readings can be found in actual recorded readings.

6. Reader reception of Romans 13:1-7

Having established a rather crude grid of possible reader clues by using these three approaches, we can now have a look at the actual reader reception in some selected readings. Every reading proceeds from a certain *Vorverständnis* and takes place against a certain *Erwartungshorizont*. The first concept was developed by Bultmann. The latter was introduced by Gadamer and has recently taken up again by Jauss. Although related to the *Vorverständnis*, the 'horizon of expectation' does not refer only to the pre-understanding of the reader, but especially to the active expectation with which he or she encounters the text. But even so, the *Erwartungshorizont* remains too general to be very useful in analysing actual readings and is in need of further clarification. A number of factors make up this horizon of expectation. At least the following should be taken into account:

(1) The ideograph or rhetorical vision of the reader or the interpretative community. The former concept was developed by McGee and refers to a symbol of ideological orientation.

> In political texts ideographs are used to represent the characteristic views and commitments of a community. Specimens are such words and expressions as 'freedom', 'the voice of the silent majority', 'no-nonsense policy', 'solidarity', 'equality'. The way in which these terms are used suggests that each member of a community understands every nuance of meaning in them. By comparing the usage of specific ideographs (and the hierarchical connections be-

tween the ideographs) we would be able to define the differences between political parties
(and between communities) (Luttikhuizen & Havelaar 1988:1).

The concept of a 'rhetorical vision' has been developed by Bormann.

A rhetorical vision can be defined as a composite view or fantasy about the character of the
world which cannot in itself be verified but which does provide meaningful interpretations of
how people and things exist in the world. The political function of a rhetorical vision is to
catch up large groups of people in a symbolic reality. To a large extent the rhetorical vision
of a community determines how the group and each member acts and how events are interpreted (Luttikhuizen & Havelaar 1988:1).

These concepts come close to Bultmann's idea of the *Vorverständnis* with which
the reader approaches a text, but carry with them a collective overtone. The
ideograph is the formal articulation of the interpretative community's beliefs.
More precisely – by these symbols, members of the same interpretative community identify each other, like bees from the same swarm. At the same time,
the selfunderstanding of the community is reinforced by the repetition of the
symbols.

(2) Closely related to the rhetorical vision is *the authority or importance with
which the text is viewed by the reader or interpretative community.* Where authority
is not an issue, the appropriation of the text is also much freer. But the problem
of resistant readings is directly related to the importance the reader attaches to
the text, as is clearly illustrated by the various readings of Romans 13.

(3) The evaluation of the situation of the reader (as perceived by the reader). In
reading Romans 13 this is clearly illustrated. If the reader perceives his situation
as being a democracy (e.g. Du Toit), he reads in a specific way. If the situation is
perceived to be undemocratic (Kairos), a different reading follows. Although it
is generally accepted that Romans 13 is written under and referring to a non-
democratic situation, it can be read 'under democratic pre-suppositions'
(Jüngel, Nürnberger). In this way Nürnberger forces a democratic reading on a
text written in an undemocratic context and so gains an understanding of how it
could be read in a different setting. Note also that there is a difference between
the evaluation of the actual situation and the pre-suppositions of the reader
him- or herself.

(4) The life experience of the reader. Quite apart from the question what the
reader's ideolect is, past experiences can influence the reader, e.g. encounters
with the authorities, protection/persecution by law, life under different political
systems (free enterprise/socialist – in themselves loaded terms).

(5) The reading experience of the reader. Not only is it important to distinguish
between first and later readings of the same reader, but all other reading experiences of the reader must be taken into account. Here the whole problem of
intertextuality comes into play – in a more restricted sense in the qualification

of the text by the immediate context of Romans 13, by Romans as a whole, Pauline and Deutero-pauline texts, the New Testament and canon in a ever widening circle to include all previous reading experiences of the reader.

(6) The role of the audience – not of the original text, but of the reading. For whom is the reader reading? For him- or herself, for the own group who shares the same ideolect, or for an opposing audience, who could be either hostile or the target for persuasion or rebuke (cf. THK reading, Kairos).

In analysing actual reader uptake, we shall briefly discuss four readings – three from South Africa (the Kairos Document, Nürnberger and Du Toit) and one from the Federal Republic of Germany (Jüngel). This is done against the much wider background of the collection of readings listed in the bibliography.

Texts may contain directions for their intended readers, but are these fol lowed in the actual reading? As Luttikhuizen and Havelaar show, the *Erwartungshorizont* of the real reader plays an important role. In this sense, all (recorded) readings are texts on texts. They can be analysed in the same way as the texts that generate them and they reveal the same presuppositions and assumptions about their intended or implied readers. Let us look at some of the features of these readings.

6.1 Nürnberger

The pragmatic context of Nürnberger's reading is what he describes as a situation of escalating violence, caused by structural imbalances in society. These imbalances cannot be redressed as long as those in power maintain their position, *inter alia* by appealing to Romans 13 as the reason why subjects should submit to the authority God has placed over them. Nürnberger's aim is to question the right of oppressive rulers to appeal to Romans 13 (41). His reading is, therefore, intended as a counter-reading to an existing reading.

In offering his reading, Nürnberger accepts an important presupposition of his opponents, namely that Romans 13 has as audience those in authority – a presupposition that is not supported by the textual indicators (cf. 5.2 above). Whether he himself is convinced that this is the case or whether he merely adopts this position in order to argue with his opponents on their own ground, is not clear. What is clear, is the logic of his argument: Yes, Romans 13 does apply to the rulers, but not in the way my opponents would like us to believe.

In order to verify his claim, Nürnberger fills in the open space of εἰς τὸ ἀγαθὸν to his own advantage. It enables him to argue that the authorities form part of God's redemptive action to redeem this world. In this grand design, the authorities have a special purpose, 'namely to further the good and *to combat evil in social terms*' (42).

The words printed in italics are Nürnberger's own addition, which is the result of a 'mirror reading' of the immediately preceding phrase. 'Social terms' as such do not occur in the text, but form part of his strategy to extend the scope of the text beyond its original setting. He has to grant that Romans 13 'presupposes the existing authoritarian state of its time' (43). But its meaning must also be tested in different contexts. The reading strategy Nürnberger employs to do this, is to introduce a new set of presuppositions, which is foreign to the text as such, but which produces new meaning. He reads Romans 13 'under democratic presuppositions' (44, 45). This is a good example of an 'ideograph' (Luttikhuizen & Havelaar 1988:1) that accurately describes Nürnberger's *Erwartungshorizont*.

This *Erwartungshorizont* leads him to the conclusion that the sword of authority 'ultimately belongs to the ruled' (45).

> If the rulers become guilty and do not subject themselves to the scrutiny of the ruled, they forfeit the right to use the sword and this right returns to the primary authority. They then, not the existing rulers, are entitled to use force to curtail evil – even the evil committed by the rulers (45).

In order to restrict the legitimacy of using force by the ruled against the rulers, Nürnberger in the end has to qualify his conclusion by introducing a series of conditions for a 'just revolution', derived from the tradition of the 'just war' (45-47).

6.2 The Kairos Document

The Kairos Document (KD) approaches Romans 13 from very much the same position as Nürnberger, but applies a different strategy. It also counters what it judges to be an illegitimate reading of the passage. The reading is that of 'State Theology', which attempts to justify the status quo and which the KD describes as follows: 'It blesses injustice, canonises the will of the powerful and reduces the poor to passivity, obedience and apathy' (3). (In the KD both 'State Theology' and 'Church Theology' are renounced in favour of the development of a 'Prophetic Theology.')

One of the pillars of 'State Theology' is the use of Romans 13 'to give an absolute and 'divine' authority to the State' (3). Such a reading, amongst other features, understands Romans 13 as being addressed to the authorities, and specifically, to the state. In countering, the KD does not start off by disputing this premise, but follows a different tack. The strategy is to narrow down the general nature and timelessness of the statements made in our passage. In other words, the intention is to close down the gap in the text as far as possible. This is done by bringing the context into play on two levels:

Firstly, by stressing the historical context and the specific circumstances of the Christian community in Rome. The passage is addressed to a particular community which had its own particular problems (4). The Roman Christians were not revolutionaries, but enthusiasts who believed Christians were exonerated from obeying the state at all (5). Romans 13 addresses this misconception and cannot have universal or timeless validity. 'Consequently, those who try to find answers to the very different questions and problems of our time in the text of Romans 13:1-7 are doing a great disservice to Paul'. (5)

Secondly, by placing the passage in the wider context of the Bible. From Pharoah to Pilate examples can be found to illustrate that God does not demand obedience to oppressive rulers (4). The state can even become the servant of Satan (Rev 13), and obedience is expected only to the kind of state that serves God 'for your benefit' (5). (Draper (1988) also uses the context to soften the statements on authority by referring to the letter opening, where Paul relativises his own authority by relating it to its divine origin.)

According to the KD then, 'State Theology' is an example where the reading is determined not by the text, but by the reader (5).

6.3 Du Toit

Very interesting is a reading by D. A. du Toit (1987), which runs counter to the preceding two readings and which provides a good example of the influence of the perspective of the reader. The text unfortunately is not available in English and I shall list only some of its main features. The basic difference is caused by the way in which the reader evaluates his own pragmatic situation and the social context in which he or she writes. Whereas Nürnberger judges the situation to be one of escalating violence caused by structural imbalances (cf. 3.1 above), Du Toit sees it as one which still contains basic democratic elements and which is still open to reform (71, 77). Accordingly, his reading strategy differs. Theoretically, he concedes all the points made in the two preceding readings concerning the ministering duty of the state, the limits of its power, the danger of abusing power and even the ethical justification of revolution in extreme circumstances. This possibility remains a theoretical option (78). Du Toit is addressing an audience who themselves do not contemplate violence, but still have the power to influence the course of events. His rhetoric is very revealing. All negative examples are drawn from the opponents' behaviour, illustrating the unacceptable consequences of their position ('structural violence' (73-4), 'liberation movement' (75) are bracketed, intervention in a democratic state is 'unnecessary' (77), etc.). The reading, therefore, favours the positive exercise of power (73) and the language abounds in power terminology: 'The power of the sword must be exercised against all internal and external threats' (71), 'the sovereignty of the state' (71), 'inviolable' (74), 'unacceptable' (71), etc. The reading is made not only from a specific perspective, but also addressed to a specific audience.

6.4 Jüngel

A complex and penetrating reading comes from Jüngel, who responds to a wide spectrum of reader instructions and develops a few strategies of his own. We shall look at a few of these.

Jüngel understands the significance of distinguishing clearly who the intended audience of Romans 13 is – the ruled and not the rulers (14, cf. also 5.2 above). What can be said about the latter can only be inferred indirectly from the text and lies outside its immediate focus.

As with other readings, the wider context of the letter is stressed: chapter 13 follows on chapters 1-12, where the indicative of the gospel is established as the basis for the imperative of chapter 13 (16-17). Jüngel also interprets this chapter as directed against 'urchristliches Enthusiasmus' (22-23).

The concept of service (4) is pivotal for the chapter as a whole. But service is to be understood not only as the criterion and purpose of good government, but as the basis and essence of its authority (24). The reference to conscience likewise has explosive potential, and became the stimulus for criticism of and resistance to the state (31).

Very revealing are the presuppositions which Jüngel expects to share with his audience. 'We' have come of age or strive to do so, living as part of a free parliamentary democracy (12). This differs considerably from the situation of Paul under Roman rule or from the authors of the KD, for whom revolt is not merely an academic possibility. Later on, Jüngel's audience is narrowed down even further to 'wir Deutsche' (34). But this also forms the basis for his rhetorical strategies. He is writing to people who have experienced the results of the abuse of power (34), who have an inborn mistrust of authority (13). He is, therefore, able to use argumentative strategies which are based on these presuppositions and introduce them by appealing to these shared beliefs: 'offensichtlich' (21); 'deshalb' (22); 'es mag uns nicht schmecken' (26); 'glasklar' (28); 'keine Frage' (31), and so forth. Like Nürnberger, Jüngel is reading under democratic presuppositions (35).

7. Conclusion

The analysis of these sample readings gives an indication of the reading strategies employed either to affirm or to oppose this problematic pericope. First three general remarks:

Firstly, it would seem that there is not an insignificant agreement between readers on the pivotal points and crucial transitions in the text. All readings accept that the text is dealing with the relationship between authorities and subjects and with the need of obedience to the authorities. Divergence starts where ambiguous or open spaces occur in the text. This, on the one hand, strengthens confidence in the communicative ability of the text, but, on the other hand, illustrates how a high occurrence of *Unbestimmtheiten* inevitably generates a spectrum of readings.

Secondly, the seemingly unqualified call to obedience results in two basic types of reading – either an affirmative or a resistant reading. As we have seen in 5.1 above, no innocent reading of the passage is possible. The choice depends largely on the *Erwartungshorizont* of the reader, with all its components as explained in 6 above. The examples offer an insight into how the interaction between *Erwartungshorizont* and text takes place.

Thirdly, an important factor in all the readings is the audience to whom the new reading is addressed. The convictions that the reader (who by now has become a writer) shares or expects to share with his or her audience has a major influence on the shaping of the argument and persuasive strategy he or she adopts. Much can be learnt about the audience from the structure and point of the argument, the assumptions that are taken for granted and that form the basis of appeal and other features of the actual reading.

Against this background, we can now be more specific about the strategies readers employ in dealing with this provocative text and the way in which affirmative or resistant readings are generated.

7.1 The basic assumption of the affirmative reading is that the passage is universal in its scope and that it provides guidelines for the fundamental relation between subject and authority, between church and state. Although the addressees are the believers as subjects, inferences are drawn for the conduct, powers and responsibilities of authority and the state.

In the South African context, the affirmative reading is further dependent on a specific evaluation of the present situation as being essentially democratic or open to reform (Du Toit).

7.2 Resistant readings are achieved by using different strategies to relativise the seemingly unqualified call to obedience. The following moves were found:

7.2.1 The intertextual move. Romans 13 is relativised by placing it in the wider context of the letter (the different nature of the paraenetic sections in Romans 12 and 13:8ff, the relativisation of his apostolic authority by Paul himself – Draper), of other sections of the New Testament (Acts, which expects obedience to God rather than to man; Revelation 13, which show the demonic side of the state – Kairos), or of the Bible as a whole (Pharaoh as oppressive ruler – Kairos).

7.2.2 The evaluative move. The hegemony of 'the state' is broken by introducing a criterion to distinguish between good and bad government.

7.2.2.1 The first criterion is drawn from Romans 13:4, that is, whether the authority is a servant (διάκονος) and whether authority serves the common good (σοί εἰς τὸ ἀγαθόν). Only those authorities that meet these criteria are worthy of obedience (Nürnberger, Jüngel). For Jüngel, the reference to the conscience in Romans 13:5 is of great significance, because it carries with it the potential for criticism and resistance to the state.

7.2.2.2 The second criterion is the fact that all authority is instituted by God and, therefore, accountable to Him. Those who do not fulfill this responsibility cannot claim obedience to themselves.

7.2.3 The interpolation move. A drastic measure is to declare the passage to be so unpauline in spirit or so incompatible with the rest of his thought that it could only be a *Fremdkörper* that was inserted into the text at a later stage.

7.2.4 Relativisation by restricting the universal scope of Romans 13. This, in a certain sense, is the opposite of the intertextual move. Instead of widening the scope of the passage, it is restricted to a specific situation (the circumstances of the Christian community in Rome) or a specific problem (revolutionaries contemplating the overthrow of the regime or enthusiasts disregarding worldly authorities) (Kairos).

7.2.5 Reading Romans 13 under different presuppositions. A novel way to escape the restrictions of the passage is to emphasise the horizon of the contemporary reader and to read 'under democratic presuppositions' (Jüngel). This enables the reader to bring different questions to the text and to draw different conclusions about its contemporary implications.

7.2.6 Redefining the authorities. Taking the reading under democratic presuppositions even further, Nürnberger comes to the conclusion that the sword of authority ultimately belongs to the ruled. They are those who have to judge whether the government of the day really rules for the common good. By redefining the authorities of Romans 13 in this way, Nürnberger is, in fact, affirming the call to obedience. But that also leads him to accept the possibility of a just revolution, which in the South African situation has implications of its own.

These provisional results on the basis of a few readings in a specific pragmatic context give some indication of what can be expected of a reader approach when dealing with argumentative texts. (For details of narrative texts treated in this way, cf. par. 4 above.) The next step would be to compare what has transpired here with the results of readings of Romans 13 drawn from other contexts and different historical periods, but that would take us far beyond the confines of this contribution (cf. Botha).

BIBLIOGRAPHY

1. GENERAL LITERATURE

Eco, U. 1979. *The Role of the Reader: Explorations in the Semiotics of Texts*. Bloomington: Indiana University Press.
Grimm, G. 1977. *Rezeptionsgeschichte: Grundlegung einer Theorie*. München: Fink.
Groeben, N. 1977. *Rezeptionsforschung als empirische Literaturwissenschaft*. Kronberg: Athenäum.
Holub, R. C. 1984. *Reception Theory: A Critical Introduction*. London: Methuen.
Iser, W. 1974. *The Implied Reader: Patterns of Communication in Prose Fiction from Bunyan to Beckett*. (Tr. from German, 1972.) Baltimore: John Hopkins.
Iser, W. 1978. *The Act of Reading: A Theory of Aesthetic Response*. (Tr. from German, 1976.) Baltimore: John Hopkins.
Jauss, H. R. 1970. *Literaturgeschichte als Provokation*. Frankfort: Suhrkamp.
Jauss, H. R. 1975. Der Leser als Instanz einer neuen Geschichte der Literatur. *Poetica* 7, 325-344.
Kussler, R. 1979. Zur Einstellung südafrikanischer Studienanfänger im Fach Deutsch gegenüber den Deutschen. Ergebnisse einer empirischen Untersuchung in literaturdidaktischer Absicht. *Sociologia Internationalis* 17, 215-34.
Suleiman, S. & Crosman, I. (eds.) 1980. *The Reader in the Text: Essays on Audience and Interpretation*. Princeton: Princeton University Press.
Tompkins, J. P. (ed.) 1980. *Reader Response Criticism*. Baltimore: John Hopkins.
Van Dijk, T. A. 1981. *Studies in the Pragmatics of Discourse*. The Hague: Mouton.

2. BIBLICAL MATERIAL

Baird, J. A. 1969. *Audience Criticism and the Historical Jesus*. Philadelphia: Westminster.
Brown, R. E. 1979. *The Community of the Beloved Disciple: The Life, Loves and Hates of an Individual Church in New Testament Times*. New York: Paulist.
Crossan, J. D. 1980. *Cliffs of Fall: Paradox and Polivalence in the Parables of Jesus*. New York: Seabury.
Culpepper, A. 1983. *The Anatomy of the Fourth Gospel: A Study in Literary Design*. Philadelphia: Fortress.
Detweiler, R. (ed.) 1985. *Reader Response Approaches to Biblical and Secular Literature*. Decatur: Scholars. (Semeia 31.)
Dormeyer, D. 1987a. Das Verhältnis von 'wilder' und historisch-kritischer Exegese als methodologisches und didaktisches Problem. *JRP* 3, 11-126.

Dormeyer, D. 1987b. *Anfragen zu Norman R Peterson, 'Prolegomena to a reader-oriented study of Paul's Letter to Rome'.* Unpublished response presented to the SNTS Seminar on The Role of the Reader in the Interpretation of the New Testament, Göttingen.

Du Plessis, J. G. 1985. *Clarity and Obscurity: A Study in Textual Communication of the Relation between Sender, Parable and Receiver in the Synoptic Gospels.* Stellenbosch: University of Stellenbosch. (Unpublished D.Th. Thesis.)

Du Toit, D. A. 1987. *Staatsgesag en Burgerlike Ongehoorsaamheid.* Cape Town: Lux Verbi.

Ebeling, G. 1971. *Einführung in theologische Sprachlehre.* Tübingen: Mohr.

Elliott, J. H. 1981. *A Home for the Homeless: A Sociological Exegesis of I Peter, Its Situation and Strategy.* Philadelphia: Fortress.

Fowler, R. M. 1981. *Loaves and Fishes: The Function of the Feeding Stories in the Gospel of Mark.* Chico: Scholars. (SBL Dissertation Series 54.)

Fowler, R. M. 1983. Who Is 'The Reader' of Mark's Gospel?, in P. J. Achtemeier (ed.). *SBL 1983 Seminar Papers.* Decatur: Scholars Press, 1-16.

Fowler, R. M. 1986. Reading Matthew Reading Mark: Observing the First Steps toward Meaning-as-Reference in the Synoptic Gospels, in K. H. Richards (ed.). *SBL 1986 Seminar Papers.* Atlanta: Scholars Press, 1-16.

Fowler, R. M. 1988. *Wriggling off the Hook: Strategies of Resisting Authoritarian Readings of Romans 13:1-7.* Paper prepared for the 1988 SNTS Seminar on the Role of the Reader in Cambridge.

Fowler, R. M. 1990. 'Let the Reader Understand': Discovering the Rhetoric of Mark. (Forthcoming).

Friedrich, J., Pöhlmann, W. & Stuhlmacher, P. 1976. Zur historischen Situation und Intention von Röm 13, 1-7. *Zeitschrift für Theologie und Kirche* 73, 131-166.

Jewett, R. 1981. *Letter to Pilgrims: A Commentary on the Epistle to the Hebrews.* New York: Pilgrim.

Kee, H. C. 1977. *Community of the New Age: Studies in Mark's Gospel.* Philadelphia: Westminster.

Lategan, B. C. 1987. Reader Clues in the Text of Galatians. *Journal of Literary Studies* 3, 47-59.

Lategan, B. C. & Rousseau, J. 1988. Reading Lk 12:35-48: An Empirical Study. *Neotestamentica* 23 (forthcoming).

Lategan, B. C. & Vorster, W. S. 1985. *Text and Reality: Aspects of Reference in Biblical Texts.* Philadelphia: Fortress.

Lundin, R., Thiselton, A. C. & Walhout, C. 1985. *The Responsibility of Hermeneutics.* Grand Rapids: Eerdmans.

McKnight, E. V. 1985. *The Bible and the Reader: An Introduction to Literary Criticism.* Philadelphia: Fortress.

Meeks, W. A. 1983. *The First Urban Christians. The Social World of the Apostle Paul.* New Haven: Yale.

Petersen, N. R. 1985. *Rediscovering Paul: Philemon and the Sociology of Paul's Narrative World.* Philadelphia: Fortress.

Staley, J. L. 1985. *The Print's First Kiss: A Rhetorical Investigation of the Implied Reader in the Fourth Gospel.* Berkeley. (Dissertation.)

Theissen, G. 1979. *Studien zur Soziologie des Urchristentums.* Tübingen: Mohr.

Wuellner, W. 1977. Paul's Rhetoric of Argumentation in Romans: An Alternative to the Donfried-Karris Debate Over Romans, in K. P. Donfried (ed.). *The Romans Debate.* Minneapolis: Augsburg, 252-274.

Wuellner, W. 1987. Where is Rhetorical Criticism Taking us? *Catholic Biblical Quarterly* 49, 448-463.

3. READINGS OF ROMANS 13

Barraclough, R. 1985. Romans 13:1-7: Application in Context. *Colloquium* 17, 16-22.

Botha, J. 1988. *Obedience to the Authorities? The Reception of Romans 13:1-7.* (Unpublished paper read at a Western Cape regional meeting of the New Testament Society of South Africa in April 1987 in Stellenbosch.)

Draper, J. 1988. 'Humble Submission to Almighty God' and its Biblical Foundation: Contextual Exegesis of Romans 13:1-7. Paper read at the 1988 annual meeting of the New Testament Society of South Africa.

Du Toit, D. A. 1987. Die Christen en Burgerlike Ongehoorsaamheid, in D. A. du Toit (ed.). Staatsgesag en Burgerlike Ongehoorsaamheid. Cape Town: Lux Verbi, 70-79.

Gale, H. M. 1952. Paul's View of the State. Interpretation 6, 409-414.

Grundlagen der sozialethischen Orientierung der Tschechoslowakischen Hussitischen Kirche. Beschluss des VI. Konzils der THK vom 16. 8. 1981. Prag: Zentralrat der THK.

Haddon, W. 1979. Towards a Theology of the State, in D. F. Wright (ed.). Essays in Evangelical Social Ethics. Wilton: Morehouse-Barlow, 85-102.

Hultgren, A. J. 1976. Reflections of Romans 13:1-7: Submission to Governing Authorities. Dialog 15, 263-269.

Jüngel, E. 1986. 'Jedermann sei untertan der Obrigkeit ...' Eine Bibelarbeit über Römer 13,1-7, in E. Jüngel, & H. Simon. Evangelische Christen in unserer Demokratie. Gütersloh: Gütersloher Verlagshaus, 8-37.

The Kairos Document. 1986. 2nd ed. Braamfontein: Skotaville, 3-8.

Louw, J. P. 1979. A Semantic Discourse Analysis of Romans. 2 vols. Pretoria: University of Pretoria.

Luttikhuizen, G. & Havelaar, H. 1988. The Interpretation of Romans 13:1-7 in Four Political Parties. Paper prepared for the 1988 SNTS Seminar on the Role of the Reader, Cambridge.

Nürnberger, K. 1987. Theses on Romans 13. Scriptura 22, 40-47.

Ogle, A. B. 1978. What is Left for Caesar? A look at Mark 12:13-17 and Romans 13:1-7. Theology Today 35, 254-264.

Pelser, G. M. M. 1988. The Christian and the Ruling Authorities according to Romans 13:1-7. (English translations of an article originally published in Hervormde Teologiese Studies 42 (1986), 515-533.)

Stroebel, A. 1956. Zum Verständnis von Röm. 13. Zeitschrift für die Neutestamentliche Wissenschaft 47, 67-93.

Stroebel, A. 1964. Furcht, wem Furcht gebührt. Zum profangriechischen Hintergrund von Röm. 13,1-7. Zeitschrift für die Neutestamentliche Wissenschaft 55, 58-62.

Webster, A. F. C. 1981. St. Paul's Advice to the Haughty Gentile Christians in Rome: An Exegesis of Romans 13:1-7. St. Vladimir's Theological Quarterly 25, 259-282.

W. WUELLNER

RHETORICAL CRITICISM AND ITS THEORY IN
CULTURE-CRITICAL PERSPECTIVE: THE NARRATIVE
RHETORIC OF JOHN 11

Modern rhetorical criticism came into its own mainly in the United States of America about the time James Muilenburg (1969) gave his Society of Biblical Literature presidential address in 1968 in praise of rhetorical criticism as method. Since then we have experienced the development of a Muilenburg school of rhetorical criticism, mainly in studies of the Hebrew Bible. Betz's lecture of 1974 at the meeting of the Societas Novi Testamenti Studiorum, followed by his commentary on Galatians (Betz 1975; 1979), generated a similar interest in rhetorical criticism as method for New Testament studies. Kennedy's study (1984) put the method in the context of some rhetorical theory. Amos Wilder was another major contributor to the revival of rhetoric in Anglo-American exegesis (Wilder 1971).

Rhetorical criticism today, in its revitalised form, is not the same as we know it throughout most of Christian history. Traditional rhetorical criticism was mostly concerned with method – a concern still very much with us and widely used, oftentimes synonymously with, and indistinguishable from, literary criticism, stylistics, discourse analysis, text linguistics, speech act theory, reader response-criticism, and the like.

The critical study of texts as rhetoric is determined by the basic perception of the discipline of rhetoric, ancient or modern, as the critical study of two interrelated aspects: (1) the text's discursive techniques, and (2) the functioning of these techniques employed to provoke, or to increase, the support of minds, on the part of the readers, to the action presented for approval. What has paralysed and nearly obliterated rhetorical criticism is the preoccupation with the first of these two aspects at the expense of the second. To distinguish the two aspects is necessary in theory; to separate the two, in theory or practice, is disastrous.

Rhetorical criticism still faces the same challenges it has faced throughout its checkered history: how to combine and balance these two aspects. For the last four hundred years we have seen in Western culture mostly gross imbalance and witnessed the devastating results of breaking up the combination of the two aspects. Without a clear position on rhetorical *theory*, the currently revived interest in rhetorical criticism as *method* will not help us in freeing rhetoric within biblical exegesis from the debased state it endured for so long, oftentimes unwittingly.

PART I

1. The history of rhetoric and its relation to biblical hermeneutics

Rhetorical criticism applied to biblical exegesis has a long history. There are many continuities of rhetorical critical conventions, especially in the area of rhetorical criticism as method or stylistics, but there are also significant discontinuities and new beginnings. The history of rhetoric has been 'the history of a continuing art undergoing revolutionary changes' (McKeon 1987:20).

1.1 Late Antiquity

By the time Christianity began its interaction with antiquity's rhetorical culture, as Judaism had done before and alongside the church, rhetoric had already undergone several changes and transformations. The earliest writings of the Christian tradition, the letters of Paul, already reflect a sharp conflict between rival representatives or interpreters of the faith, each informed by competing rhetorical traditions (Betz 1986; Forbes 1986).

One of the most important contributions of recent scholarship in the history of rhetoric is this: All appearances (of ancient rhetorical textbooks, or of modern interpretations of ancient textbooks, such as the often quoted Lausberg 1960, or the synoptic history of classical rhetoric by Murphy 1983) to the contrary, there never existed a uniform or unified system of classical rhetoric. Rather, we find an ongoing and unresolved struggle for redesigning the institutional structure of rhetoric, as in Isocrates' fight against the sophists on the one hand, and the Academy on the other (Cahn 1987).

The institutionalisation of rhetoric as part of the educational system (*paideia*) as one of the three 'liberal arts' (the *trivium* of grammar, dialectics/logic/philosophy, and rhetoric) encouraged the notion, consolidated by centuries of scholarship, that classical rhetoric was a more or less fixed 'system'. Rhetoric was, indeed, taught at least, if not practised (as grammar and philosophy were so taught), namely as a closed system whose rules were easily teachable and passed on, like dogmatic truths in a catechism. However, only recently have we come to appreciate the realisation that 'classical' rhetoric and its legacy consisted of a wide diversity of theories and practices, each 'more or less defined by...values and functions of culture' (Kennedy 1980:8).

Another important contribution of modern scholarship in the history of rhetoric is this very point just quoted from Kennedy. What may be true of ancient Greece and Rome, that rhetoric could depend on 'a common value set as criteria for selecting...the...means for resolving common problems' confronting society (Cushman & Tompkins 1980:51), was challenged, however, in the cultural conflict between 'Athens and Jerusalem'. This conflict arose either between classical antiquity and Judaism or Christianity respectively, or as clash of indigenous cultures resisting the homogenising forces of cultural, political, racial, or gender ideologies. A variation on this theme will reappear in the reform movements of medieval and modern Christian traditions. The modern rhetorical critic of biblical texts has learned to discern the common value sets embodied in biblical texts as premises of arguments for the vindication and affirmation of divine truths. It is this aspect which forces rhetorical criticism to be genuinely, and constructively, *critical*.

Kennedy (1984:8-19) finds historical justification for approaching the New Testament in terms of Greek ideas of rhetoric in the ubiquity of rhetoric in antiquity. The modern critic, however, needs to recognise that 'classical rhetoric was developed to account for discourse in a different, and perhaps simpler, social context' (Miller 1989:112) and to reevaluate efforts of simply restoring the original domain of classical rhetoric.

We have become increasingly aware of the intimate relation between rhetorics and hermeneutics as it existed from antiquity into the Middle Ages and the early stages of the 16th century Reformation and Counter-Reformation (Eden 1987; Evans 1980; 1984; 1985). Modern discussions have renewed the exploration of the relationship between rhetoric and hermeneutic (Hyde & Smith 1979; Magass 1985; Mailloux 1985; Mosdt 1984; Rickman 1981; Schrag 1986; Todorov 1975).

1.2 Middle Ages, Humanism, Renaissance, Reformation, Counter-Reformation

Rhetoric continued to play a crucial role in the interpretation of the Bible, whether as part of the traditional *lectio divina*, or as part of the *via moderna* cultivated by the emerging European universities beginning in the 12th century.

One of the developments that affected sacred and secular hermeneutics was the virtual identification of poetics and rhetorics in the Renaissance (Vickers 1987). Kennedy called this phenomenon 'letteraturizzazione', which signifies

> the tendency of rhetoric to shift its focus from persuasion to narration, from civic to personal contexts, and from discourse to literature, including poetry (Kennedy 1980:5).

This shift and subsequent bifurcation into what Kennedy calls 'primary' and 'secondary' rhetoric is still operative in distinctions between "rhetoric' as a *kind* of text and 'rhetoric' as a *function* of texts of any kind' (Chatman 1989:48).

Another development, with consequences still affecting us today, is the emergence of (a) the study of culturally indigenous rhetorics in the wake of the vernacular movements in the late Middle Ages, and (b) the ensuing conflict between Western rhetorics (whether Greek or Latin, or the vernacular versions) and non-Western rhetorics. The latter was experienced in two ways: In the clash between (a) Greek or Latin and Hebrew (Rabinowitz 1985), and (b) European cultures (including the Jewish diaspora) and the conquering Arab, Moslem culture (Vickers 1988:473 note 44 for literature). Colonial and missionary expansion led to the imposition of Western rhetorics on non-Western cultures, but also the first awareness of alternative theories and practices of rhetoric.

A third and fateful development of rhetoric in the 16th century was the educational reform advocated by Peter Ramus, which affected exegesis profoundly for centuries (Meerhoff 1986). Ramism influenced biblical exegesis at the very time that missionaries went world-wide to found Western centers of learning. Ramism's effect was the institutionalisation of the bifurcation mentioned earlier; it brought the separation of the study of thought or content from the study of form or feeling. Ever since we have remained preoccupied in the West with theology (or ethics) at the expense of religion or aesthetics.

During this period a fourth development became influential and has remained so ever since: alongside the prevailing traditional concerns with the rhetoric of the Bible as a whole, there arose an interest in the distinctive features of the rhetoric to be found in individual books or authors. A related, but distinct development is the emerging differentiation between secular and sacred hermeneutics.

1.3 Hostility to and death of rhetorics in the eighteenth and nineteenth centuries

It may be more than coincidence that with the rise of historical (= scientific or modern) criticism rhetoric became marginalised to the point of near extinction or at least increasing irrelevance, in contrast to its fifteen hundred year-long central importance to exegesis. From Melanchthon in the early sixteenth century to Johann August Ernesti, the German Cicero, in the eighteenth century, some distinctive professors of biblical exegesis came to occupy simultaneously also university chairs in rhetoric – but not any more in the late eighteenth century and beyond! Vickers explained the near eclipse of rhetorical studies since 1750 as due to the post-Romantic hostility to rhetoric. Whatever the cause(s) of this eclipse, the records of studies published speak for themselves: all the way into the twentieth century publications of exegetical works dealing with Scripture's rhetoric became increasingly sporadic.

It may also be more than coincidence that, at the very time we hear pronouncements about the decline and end of the hegemony of historical criticism, we witness the renaissance of rhetoric. But the modern, scientific approach to rhetoric has lately been challenged by postmodernism (Griffin 1989; Lyotard 1984).

1.4 Rebirth or reinvention of rhetoric today

Classicists such as A. Wifstrand (Sweden), W. Jens (Germany), and G. A. Kennedy (USA) in our generation have contributed greatly to the rediscovery and renaissance of rhetorical studies in biblical exegesis. So have scholars from other disciplines, such as philosophy, linguistics, semiotics, to name only a few. There have been more books, dissertations, and essays published related to rhetorical criticism of biblical texts in the decade of the 1980's than in several centuries prior to this! But the legacies of the past are still with us and haunt us. All is not well with rhetorical criticism today as it faces up to its massive task of defining, or redefining, its proper domain.

One of the main features of modern rhetoric is its focus on the practical intentions, or practical force with motivating action, as constitutive of rhetorical discourse. This is the concern for the text's 'rhetorical situation' or its intentionality or exigency (Brinton 1981; Scott 1980). Biblical texts (like any other text or rhetorical discourse) are approached as having arisen in response to practical problem, i.e. problem about what to do (Cushman & Tompkins 1980:52-3).

Another feature is the recognition of the text's rationality. Kennedy spoke of the 'striking result' of his study of New Testament rhetoric which was the 'recognition of the extent to which forms of logical argument are used in the New Testament' (Kennedy 1984:159). For Cushman and Tompkins this rationality of rhetorical discourse makes readers/interpreters 'recognise the rhetorical exigencies confronting them (and) understand the relationships between such exigencies, audiences, and the constraints involved'. Moreover, such rationality lets readers/interpreters not only discern the possible ends and all the available means for achieving the ends, but also examine 'the best ends and the most efficient means for achieving them' (Cushman & Tompkins 1980:53-4). Modern rhetoric, which is more than the revival of classical or traditional rhetoric, had one of its pioneers in Perelman and his school (Perelman 1969; Meyer 1986) with a strong focus on the rationality employed in rhetorical argumentation as distinct from logical demonstration.

A third feature that distinguishes modern rhetorical criticism belongs to the efforts of what Eagleton (1983:205-6) sees as the reinvention of rhetoric, or what Bakhtin (1981:267) saw as part of the mandate of restoring rhetoric 'to all its ancient rights'. This feature focuses on the biblical 'discursive practices' and 'grasping (them) as forms of power and performance' or 'as forms of *activity* inseparable from the wider social relations between writers and readers' (Eagleton).

2. Rhetorical criticism: theory and method

2.1 Theories of rhetorical criticism

A theory based on *traditional* rhetoric was outlined by Kennedy (1984:3-38). It features some diachronic and one or two synchronic aspects of rhetorical criticism (cf. outline in Wuellner 1987:455-58).

  Its main features are: (1) Definition and selection of rhetorical unit(s); (2) Identification of rhetorical situation or intentionality, and of rhetorical genre; (3) Discernment of the rhetorical structure or disposition; (4) The analysis of the stylistic means employed for the intended action; (5) Assessing the interaction of all these elements and components as a whole which is supposed to be argumentatively and persuasively coherent. A similar traditional theory of rhetoric is operative in the works of Betz (1979), Jewett (1986), Hughes (1989), Watson (1988), and others.

  A theory based on *modern* rhetoric would follow one of three lines: 1. the Anglo-American theories of argumentation, sharpened by the reception of Perelman's *New Rhetoric* (for application to Pauline studies, cf. Wuellner 1986:54-72); 2. the Continental theories of literary rhetoric (e.g. Genette; cf. Harlos 1986); 3. the largely American theories of rhetoric as part of social science hermeneutics. More eclectic in their approaches are Mack (1989) and Moore (1989). Johanson (1987) works with a combination of text linguistics and rhetoric, as advocated also by Siegert (1985).

2.2 Four features of modern theories and practices of rhetorical criticism

Before outlining the features, it may be helpful to distinguish the two senses in which rhetorical criticism has come to be used: (1) the rhetoric *in* a given biblical text as the overt and discernible intentionality and appeal of the text, regardless of the text type or literary genre; (2) the rhetoric *of* a given biblical text, where rhetoric stands for that aspect of the text as a whole, or text as an integral act of communication and appeal to action. In the latter sense, rhetoricity becomes synonymous with textuality (Winquist 1987).

  I have selected the following four features of modern theories and practices of rhetorical criticism:
1. 'The turn toward argumentation' (Mack 1989), and the designation of arguments as a text-type distinct from narrative and description, with each of the text-types ready to be 'of service' to each of the others (Chatman 1991). Hence we come to approach religious narrative as narrative rhetoric, or rhetorical narrative (Sternberg 1985). Perelman (1969:11-62) defines argumentation not just in terms of its persuasive intent, but more pointedly in terms of argumentation's

practical force, i.e. in terms of commitment or action.

2. Closely related to the first is the focus on the text's rhetorical intentionality or exigency. Modern rhetoric thus comes to be associated more closely with the philosophy of action than with the philosophy of language.

3. The social, cultural, ideological values imbedded in the argument's premises, *topoi*, and hierarchies (e.g. old and wise as superior to young and foolish; civilised vs. primitive; culture vs. nature; maleness as strong and rational vs. femaleness as weak and emotional; etc). It is in this area that rhetorical criticism operates truly as criticism, whether as imaginative criticism, practical criticism, or ideological criticism (e.g. gender roles).

4. The rhetorical or stylistic techniques (Perelman 1969:185-502) are seen as means to an end, and not as merely formal, decorative features. Alter (1989:77-205) calls them the modalities of literary expression that are accessible to analytic attention. This includes the concerns for the work's structure, disposition, and argumentative coherence. The *functional* aspects of these 'techniques', as the formal resources of literary expression in the service of intentional writing and reading, are highlighted by Snyman (1988).

2.3 The dialectic between modern and postmodern rhetorical criticism

The dialectic is determined by two forces at work in our midst: on the one hand, the continuing commitment to scientific scholarship (whether in the use of linguistics, semiotics, social sciences, cybernetics, or whichever 'science' seems suitable for a science of rhetoric); on the other hand, the discontinuous effect of postmodernism's critique of presumed objective scientific neutrality; of postmodernism's reenchantment of science (Griffin 1989), or the effects of the politics of scientific interpretation (Rabinowitz 1987:173-231).

The area where this dialectic has been felt most keenly is in the difference with which feminist criticism has been handling what Alter (1989:14), too, acknowledges as the subversive power of such rhetorical text-types as narrative or argument (Bal 1987; for a critique, cf. Alter 1989:221-227). For Alter, as for Frye (1981:199-233), the Bible's rhetoric accounts for 'multiple readings and the bog of indeterminacy' (Alter 1989:206-238).

Another way of characterising the difference between modern and postmodern approaches to rhetoric is the perception of texts. In most traditional and modern rhetorics, texts merely express and transmit knowledge, social relations, and the self in contrast to the postmodern notion of texts by which knowledge, social relations and the self get *constituted*. In the latter case rhetoric is more concerned about the substance of social belief; in the former more about the forms of the text.

3. Is rhetorical criticism a method, or more than that?

As method, rhetorical criticism comes into focus primarily on *one* issue: The text's potential to persuade, to engage the imagination and will, or the text's symbolic inducement. The appeal of rhetorical criticism over other methods lies in its promise of explaining the text's power (Kennedy 1984:158). Two inter-related aspects inform the practice of rhetorical criticism. The method has to account for *two* constraints (and not just for one – the textual constraint): There are the two interrelated aspects of rhetorical theory – the text as artifact and its textual function(s) – at the level of the text as analysable object, with all its textual constraints. This includes the materiality or technology of its medium: oral or visual; cheirographic or typographic; etc. What distinguishes rhetorical theory from text theory and literary theory is the priority of concerns for the text's intentionality to 'move' the reader.

Rhetorical criticism as method approaches the text at this level as a construct with a persuasive intentionality that has its own integrity, coherence, and textual constraints as a rhetorical unit, with a discernible beginning and ending, connected by some action or argument (Kennedy 1984:34). The multifarious context in which every text is embedded is only partially analysable in terms of social and cultural codes to be found in every text-type, as in all language use. Rhetorical criticism redefines the problem of reference by virtue of 'its reliance on community, convention, and persuasion' (Miller 1989:114). It is this context-factor that distinguishes rhetorical criticism as a method from literary criticism.

The experiential dimension on which most literary works turn (Alter 1989:206), or the text's power (Kennedy), cannot be reduced, however, to the study of the textual constraints through which that power, that experiential dimension, is expressed. But what rhetorical criticism as method can do is to rule out what Alter calls weak or wrong readings (e.g. misjudging irony; failing to note the subversive quality of the text; etc). On the other hand, what rhetorical criticism cannot rule out is that critics working on the same text come up with different interpretations of the text's intentionality or rhetorical genre, as in Betz's reading of Galatians as forensic, Kennedy's plea for the deliberate genre, and now proposals for the epideictic genre, and finally and not surprisingly the rising discontent with the whole legacy of the three Aristotelian genres.

There are two constraints on the reading and interpretation of texts: one posed by the text itself; the other by the reader. The constraints assert themselves at different times in the three temporal moments in the act of reading or interpretation: *before* reading (Rabinowitz 1987); *while* reading (Alter 1989); *after* reading, such as when communities, scholarly or ecclesial, adjudicate among interpretations by individuals or groups (Bleich 1975:80-95). Traditionally rhetorical criticism as method is almost exclusively concerned with the textual constraints *while* reading. This is the indispensable 'rhetorical analysis of the

most vigilant and patient sort' (Miller 1989:81). Vigilance and patience with the
text have led us to distinguish between a narrative's mimesis or showing, and its
diegesis or telling; between text and context. Facing us is the task of 'mediation
between the rhetorical study of literature...and the now so irresistibly attractive
study of the extrinsic relations of literature'. Exegesis of Scripture, like the interpretation of any other imaginative literature, brings us to an encounter with
something that, though embedded within a *literary* (as distinct from *ordinary*)
language, 'is irreducible by historical, sociological, or psychological methods of
interpretation' (Miller 1989:81).

Traditionally rhetorical critics distinguished between the convincing and persuasive dimensions of texts as argument (Perelman 1969:26-31). For biblical
exegesis that means the distinction between convincing textual argumentation
that presumes to gain the adherence of every believer (with belief defined by
norms of culture) and persuasive textual argumentation that claims validity only
for believers-readers in a special rhetorical (not just *historical*) situation. Even
while reading within the textual constraints we are nowadays aware of constraints more refined, more subtle, more conducive to full *inter*-action with the
text than merely 'understanding', i.e. standing under, the text's message.

Modern theory has widened the scope, beyond the temporal limits *while*
reading, by emphasising the inescapable constraints imposed both *before* and
after reading. Miller sees here 'the implications of a rhetorical study of literature
for our political and ethical life' (1989:84). So does Booth in his study of *The
Company We Keep* (1988).

A further extension of rhetorical criticism, peculiar to the postmodern era, is
the invited reflection on the rhetoric of scholarship. The *rhetoric* of shared critical inquiry is perceived as different from the *logic* of shared scholarly work. The
latter has been characteristic of scientific modernism also in the field of biblical
studies, as manifest in the histories of scholarly biblical societies such as the
New Testament Society of South Africa, Society of Biblical Literature, Societas
Novi Testamenti Studiorum, and the like. On this extended level rhetorical criticism is reconceived as rhetorico-political activity (Lentricchia 1983:145-63).

4. Rhetorical criticism and its relation to other methods

The history of rhetoric has shown that the reduction of rhetoric to poetics has
been but one of the ways of getting and keeping rhetorics restrained and de-
generate. The same tendency reappears today in the Muilenburg legacy of reducing rhetorical criticism to stylistics or literary criticism, or in bringing
rhetorical criticism in conjunction with text linguistics (Johanson 1987) or with
discourse analysis, as Snyman points out in his essay in this volume. Likewise,
rhetorical criticism as method cannot be reduced to serving only, or even mainly, the study of the text's semantic contents or message.

Nor is rhetorical criticism reducible to social description, as tends to be the orientation in Mack (1989), for whom one of the promises of rhetorical criticism is its contribution to the analysis of social formation. This is not to deny that social factors are very important for rhetorical criticism. Indeed, beyond the social there is also the larger complex of the ideological, which appears equally unavoidable and inescapable for rhetorical criticism, if with Ricoeur (1986) we perceive ideology as the rhetoric of basic communication, as the rhetoric of what 'goes without saying'. But rhetoric cannot be reduced to a social science, nor to linguistics, speech act theories, or a communication science. Rhetoric does indeed overlap with one or another of various sciences, but the realm of rhetoric has its own integrity and its own constraints.

PART II

5. An example of rhetorical criticism: the narrative rhetoric of John 11
(the Lazarus story)

5.1 Plot as argument. Rhetorical unit(s) of narratives

We start with the conceptualisation of story as argument or as a conflict of value positions (Fisher 1987), as exemplified in the Lazarus story (Jn 11). As a rhetorical unit the story has its own beginning (with the dual setting of Jesus in forced hiding 10:39-42, and the request for help 11:1-3; both located in a named and unnamed Bethany!) and its own ending (with Jesus's return to forced hiding 11:54-57). As clearly definable rhetorical unit it both contains within itself smaller rhetorical units (e.g. 11:5-16) and is contained within other rhetorical units preceding (what led to the forced hiding, and, as 11:37 signals, the healing of the blind man in Jn 9) and rhetorical units following (as signalled by the narrator in 11:2, the anointing of Jesus for his own burial in Jn 12). This intertwining of rhetorical units is 'building up a structure which embraces the whole (narrative)' (Kennedy 1984:34).

5.2 Intentionality or rhetorical situation

The intentionality of the text is manifest in the introduction of a conflict of values which comes early in the dissociation of the reality of God's glory from the appearance of sickness and death (11:4). Argumentation by dissociation

is always prompted by the desire to remove an incompatibility arising out of the confrontation of one proposition with others, whether one is dealing with norms, facts, or truths (Perelman 1969:413).

To narrate (or argue) dissociatively (cf. Perelman 1969:411-459) is done 'on behalf of another outlook and another criterion of reality' (Perelman 1969:436). To bring death and glory in conjunction thus functions like an oxymoron; its plausibility is paradoxical.

5.3 Disposition and rhetorical structure

The structure and disposition of the story, as argument for the plausibility of the value and action it calls for, shows up in the following plot structure as argumentation: after the exordial introduction of the case at hand, namely the split jury over the validity of the claim made by, and for, Jesus as God's agent ('agent' as cultural code, cf. Harvey 1987), with 'many believing' but others forcing Jesus and the believers into hiding, the 'case' is stated clearly at the outset in nearly propositional form (11:4).

The narrative unfolds as argumentation for the plausibility of this paradox, whose aim is to 'move' the characters *in* the story, and the reader *of* the story, to 'believe' as the acceptance of 'another outlook and another criterion of reality'. Like the characters *in* the story, some do become convinced, others do not, and others still, though witnessing the events, remain unreported (e.g. the disciples) as to their belief or new outlook.

5.4 Style and rhetorical techniques

The stylistic means, appropriate to achieving the desired ends of gaining or stabilising plausibility for the oxymoron of glorification through death, are richly textured. A series of internal monologues, or narration of mental events (as distinct from physical or verbal events) shape the surface of the narrative: John 10:41 and John 11:4, where 'saying' equals 'thinking/affirming', do for the exordium of the argumentation what John 11:9-10 does for the first argument, namely Jesus' interaction with his disciples; what John 11:41-42, the prayer, does for the resumed argument with Martha (11:38-42); what John 11:47-48 does for the second to last argument, the reaction of the unconvinced jury (11:46-53); and what John 11:56, the musing Temple crowd at Passover, does for the final argument (11:54-57), which leaves the story without a conclusion, thereby generating new momentum for resuming the unresolved, unfinished narrative.

One of the stylistic means is the choice of the *katachresis/abusio trope* in John 11:4. The glorification of God in bringing dead Lazarus to life is also bringing

the living Jesus to his 'glorious' death. The ensuing first argumentative development offers a verbal action with his disciples, and the physical action of (once
more) coming out of hiding (as before, e.g. 5:13; 6:15; 7:1-13) and returning to
the public sphere, the sphere of life and death (11:5-16). This first argument is
characterised by the use of the trope of irony by Jesus and underscored by the
narrator's comment (11:13). Thomas' concluding appeal (11:16) ends on a figurative note. The conflict of values is obvious; the resolution of the conflict is not
only not obvious, it is downright unacceptable, given the contingency of the
disciples' untimely death and the certainty of Jesus's own death as the hour of
glory.

Irony, explored by Kenneth Burke as one of the 'four master tropes', is one
the distinctive rhetorical devices used in Jn 11, indeed throughout John. Its
power is 'that it so forcefully engages us in what we read...it jolts us with in-
congruity or nudges us with meaning or a value or a commitment...irony is like
the Incarnation itself' (Duke 1985:155).

Repetitions (among other 'figures') mark the second (11:17-27 Martha) and
third (11:28-37 Mary and the commiserating Jews) argumentative sequences.
The oxymoron (11:25 believers shall live though they die) keeps the focus of the
argumentative situation on the *verbal (inter)actions* between Jesus and the believer, both inside and outside of the narrative world, rather than focusing on
the miracle itself. The *katachresis* continues into the climax of the plot, the narrative denouement which, though bringing Lazarus to life and getting him un-
shrouded (11:38-45), also introduces the expected, because foretold, intensifica-
tion of efforts of bringing Jesus to death and getting Jesus shrouded (11:46-57).
Paradoxically, not Lazarus's resurrection, but his death brings about the (implausible) glorification of God, just as Jesus brings God's glorification to fullest
expression and completion on the cross, not on Easter!

5.5 Argumentative coherence

To look for unity or overarching meaning, as hermeneutical exegetes are prone
to do (e.g. Beker 1980 on contingency and coherence of the gospel), is quite different from the concern of the rhetorical critic for argumentative coherence.
Besides coherence as property of the Johannine narrative – with its textual con-
figurations, textual ruptures, protagonist interacting with antagonists – there is
coherence as perceived or generated by the reader and the critic, especially in
narratives like the Lazarus story which is full of jolts, ruptures, and inconsistencies (e.g. no telling or showing of who subsequently did untie the resurrected
Lazarus, or any reactions by the disciples, Mary or Martha or even Lazarus himself).

The coherence of the narrative strategy of John 11 can be seen in such
seemingly incoherent appearances as (i) the textual gaps, like those just out-

lined; (ii) the textual surplus features, such as the seemingly superfluous adverbial or adnominal qualifiers in John 11:1-2, 11:18, or the body and face wrapping in John 11:44, to name only a few; and (iii) thematisation and closure, with intended allusion to other texts (for Old Testament 'codes' in John, cf. Roth 1987) as clues for God's action in history, and of representatives of God's own people habitually responding to God's agent ambiguously.

The subversive effect of the coherence of the Lazarus story gets recognised both *while* reading John 11, as well as *before* reading John 11 as result of the experience, or remembrance, of texts like John 1-10, or by experiences readers/ interpreters bring with themselves of morbid or moribund (social, institutional) structures outside of the text (Kelber 1988).

BIBLIOGRAPHY

Bakhtin, M. M. 1981. *The Dialogic Imagination*. (Ed. by M. Holquist.) Austin, Texas: University of Texas Press. (University of Texas Press Slavic Series 1.)

Bal, M. 1987. *Lethal Love: Feminist Literary Readings of Biblical Love Stories*. Bloomington: Indiana University Press.

Beker, J. C. 1980. *Paul the Apostle. The Triumph of God in Life and Thought*. Philadelphia: Fortress.

Betz, H. D. 1975. The Literary Composition and Function of Paul's Letter to the Galatians. *New Testament Studies* 21, 353-379.

Betz, H. D. 1979. *Galatians: A Commentary on Paul's Letter to the Churches in Galatia*. Philadelphia: Fortress. (Hermeneia.)

Betz, H. D. 1986. The Problem of Rhetoric and Theology according to the Apostle Paul, in A. Vanhoye (ed.). *L'Apôtre Paul. Personalité, Style et Conception du Ministère*. Leuven: Leuven University Press (Bibliotheca Ephemeridum Theologicarum Lovaniensum 73), 16-48.

Bleich, D. 1975. *Readings and Feelings: An Introduction to Subjective Criticism*. Urbana, Illinois: National Council of Teachers of English.

Booth, W. C. 1988. *The Company We Keep. An Ethics of Fiction*. Berkeley, Los Angeles, London: University of California Press.

Brinton, A. 1981. Situation in the Theory of Rhetoric. *Philosophy and Rhetoric* 14, 234-248.

Cahn, M. 1987. Der Ort des rhetorischen Wissens. Kunst und Natur bei Isokrates. *Berichte zur Wissenschaftsgeschichte* 10, 217-228.

Chatman S. 1989. The 'Rhetoric' of 'Fiction', in: J. Phelan (ed.). *Reading Narrative. Form, Ethics, Ideology*. Columbus, Ohio: Ohio State University Press, 40-56.

Chatman, S. 1991. *Coming to Terms: Verbal and Cinematic Narrative*. Ithaca, New York, London: Cornell University Press. (Forthcoming.)

Cushman, D. P. & Tompins, P. K. 1980. A Theory of Rhetoric for Contemporary Society. *Philosophy and Rhetoric* 13, 43-67.

Duke, P. D. 1985. *Irony in the Fourth Gospel*. Atlanta: Knox.

Eagleton, T. 1983. *Literary Theory. An Introduction*. Minneapolis, London: University of Minnesota Press.

Eden, K. 1987. Hermeneutics and the Ancient Rhetorical Tradition. *Rhetorica* 5, 59-86.

Evans, G. R. 1980. *Old Arts and New Theology: The Beginnings of Theology as an Academic Discipline*. Oxford: Clarendon.

Evans, G. R. 1984. *The Language and Logic of the Bible: The Earlier Middle Ages*. Cambridge, London, New York, Sidney: Cambridge University Press.

Evans, G. R. 1985. *The Language and Logic of the Bible: The Road to Reformation*. Cambridge, London, New York, Sidney: Cambridge University Press.

Fisher, W. R. 1987. *Human Communication as Narration: Toward a Philosophy of Reason, Value, and Action*. Columbia, South Carolina: University of South Carolina Press.

Forbes, C. 1986. Paul's Boasting and Hellenistic Rhetoric. *New Testament Studies* 32, 1-30.

Frye, N. 1981. *The Great Code. The Bible and Literature*. New York, London: Harcourt Brace Jovanovich.

Griffin, D. R. 1989. *The Reenchantment of Science: Postmodern Proposals*. Albany: SUNY Press. (Constructive Postmodern Thought.)

Harlos, C. 1986. Rhetoric, Structuralism, and Figurative Discourse: Gérard Genette's Concept of Rhetoric. *Philosophy and Rhetoric* 19, 209-223.

Harvey, A. E. 1987. Christ as Agent, in L. D. Hurst & N. T. Wright (eds.). *The Glory of Christ in the New Testament. Studies in Christology in Memory of George Bradford Caird*. Oxford: Clarendon, 239-250.

Hughes, F. W. 1989. *Early Christian Rhetoric and 2 Thessalonians*. Sheffield: Almond. (JSNT Suppl. 30.)

Hyde, M. J. & Smith, C. R. 1979. Hermeneutics and Rhetoric: A Seen but Unobserved Relationship. *Quarterly Journal of Speech* 65, 347-363.

Jewett, R. 1986. *The Thessalonian Correspondence: Pauline Rhetoric and Millenial Piety*. Philadelphia: Fortress. (Foundations & Facets: New Testament.)

Johanson, B. C. 1987. *To All the Brethren. A Text-Linguistic and Rhetorical Approach to I Thessalonians*. Lund: Almquist & Wiksell.

Kelber, W. H. 1988. Gospel Narrative and Critical Theory. *Biblical Theology Bulletin* 18, 130-136.

Kennedy, G. A. 1980. *Classical Rhetoric and Its Christian and Secular Tradition from Ancient to Modern Times*. Chapel Hill, North Carolina: University of North Carolina Press.

Kennedy, G. A. 1984. *New Testament Interpretation through Rhetorical Criticism*. Chapel Hill, London: University of North Carolina Press.

Lausberg, H. 1960. *Handbuch der literarischen Rhetorik*. Munich: Hueber.

Lentricchia, F. 1983. *Criticism and Social Change*. Chicago: University of Chicago Press.

Lyotard, J.-F. 1984. *The Postmodern Condition: A Report on Knowledge*. (Foreword by Fredric Jameson.) Minneapolis: University of Minnesota Press. (Theory and History of Literature 10.)

Mack, B. L. 1989. *Rhetoric and the New Testament*. Minneapolis: Augsburg Fortress. (Guides to Biblical Scholarship.)

Magass, W. 1985. *Hermeneutik, Rhetorik und Semiotik. Studien zur Rezeptionsgeschichte der Bibel*. Konstanz: University of Konstanz. (Unpublished Dissertation.)

Mailloux, S. 1985. Rhetorical Hermeneutics. *Critical Inquiry* 11, 620-641.

McKeon, R. 1987. *Rhetoric: Essays in Invention and Discovery*. (Ed. by M. Backman.) Woodbridge, Colorado.: OxBow Press.

Meerhoff, K. 1986. *Rhétorique et poétique au XVIe siècle en France. Du Bellay, Ramus, et les autres*. Leiden: Brill. (Studies in Medieval and Reformation Thought 36.)

Meyer, M. 1986. *From Logic to Rhetoric*. Amsterdam, Philadelphia: Benjamins Publishing Co. (Pragmatics and Beyond VII:3.)

Miller, J. H. 1989. Is There an Ethics of Reading? In J. Phelan (ed.). *Reading Narrative. Form, Ethics, Ideology*. Columbus, Ohio: Ohio State University Press, 79-101.

Moore, S. D. 1989. *Literary Criticism and the Gospels. The Theoretical Challenge*. New Haven, London: Yale University Press.

Mosdt, G. W. 1984. Rhetorik und Hermeneutik: Zur Konstitution der Neuzeitlichkeit. *Antike und Abendland* 30, 62-79.

Muilenburg, J. 1969. After Form Criticism, What? *Journal of Biblical Literature* 88, 1-18.

Murphy, J. J. (ed.) 1983. *A Synoptic History of Classical Rhetoric*. Davis, California: Hermagoras Press.

Perelman, C. & Olbrechts-Tyteca, L. 1969. *The New Rhetoric. A Treatise on Argumentation*. (Tr. by J. Wilkinson & P. Wever.) Notre Dame, London: University of Notre Dame Press.

Rabinowitz, I. 1985. Pre-Modern Jewish Study of Rhetoric: An Introductory Bibliography. *Rhetorica* 3, 137-144.

Rabinowitz, P. J. 1987. *Before Reading. Narrative Conventions and the Politics of Interpretation*. Ithaca, London: Cornell University Press.

Rickman, H. P. 1981. Rhetoric and Hermeneutic. *Philosophy and Rhetoric* 14, 100-111.

Ricoeur, P. 1986. *Lectures on Ideology and Utopia*. (Ed. by G. H. Taylor.) New York: Columbia University Press.

Roth, W. 1987. Scripture Coding in the Fourth Gospel. *Papers of the Chicago Society of Biblical Research* 32, 6-29.

Schrag, C. O. 1986. *Communicative Praxis and the Space of Subjectivity*. Bloomington, Indiana: Indiana University Press. (Studies in Phenomenology and Existential Philosophy.)

Scott, R. L. 1980. Intentionality in the Rhetorical Process, in E. E. White (ed.). *Rhetoric in Transition*. Pennsylvania State University Press, 39-60.

Siegert, F. 1985. *Argumentation bei Paulus gezeigt an Römer 9 bis 11*. Tübingen: Mohr. (Wissenschaftliche Untersuchungen zum Neuen Testament 34.)

Snyman, A. H. 1988. On Studying the Figures (*schemata*) in the New Testament. *Biblica* 69, 93-107.

Sternberg, M. 1985. *The Poetics of Biblical Narrative. Ideological Literature and the Drama of Reading*. Bloomington: Indiana University Press. (Indiana Literary Biblical Series.)

Todorov, T. 1975. Rhétorique et Hermeneutique. *Poétique* 23, 289-415.

Vickers, B. 1987. Rhetoric and Poetics, in *Cambridge History of Renaissance Philosophy*. Cambridge: Cambridge University Press, 715-745.

Vickers, B. 1988. *In Defense of Rhetoric*. Oxford: Clarendon.

Watson, D. F. 1988. *Invention, Arrangement, and Style: Rhetorical Criticism of Jude and 2 Peter*. Atlanta: Scholars Press. (SBL Dissertation Series 104.)

Wilder, A. N. 1964. *The Language of the Gospels: Early Christian Rhetoric*. New York: Harper & Row. (Reprinted in 1971 as *Early Christian Rhetoric: The Language of the Gospels*. Cambridge, Massachussetts: Harvard University Press.)

Winquest, C. E. (ed.) 1987. *Text and Textuality*. Decatur, Georgia: Scholars Press. (Semeia 40.)

Wuellner, W. 1986. Paul as Pastor. The Function of Rhetorical Questions in First Corinthians, in A. Vanhoye (ed.). *L'Apôtre Paul. Personalité, Style et Conception du Ministère*. Leuven: Leuven University Press (Bibliotheca Ephemeridum Theologicarum Lovaniensum 73), 49-77.

Wuellner, W. 1987. Where is Rhetorical Criticism Taking Us? *Catholic Biblical Quarterly* 49, 448-463.

Wuellner, W. 1989. The Rhetorical Structure of Luke 12 in its Wider Context. *Neotestamentica* 22, 283-310

P. J. HARTIN

DISSEMINATING THE WORD: A DECONSTRUCTIVE READING OF MARK 4:1-9 AND MARK 4:13-20

Preface

Prefaces, along with forewords, introductions, preludes, preliminaries, preambles, prologues, and prolegomena, have always been written, it seems, in view of their own self-effacement. Upon reaching the end of the *pre-* (which presents and precedes, or rather forestalls, the presentative production, and, in order to put before the reader's eyes what is not yet visible, is obliged to speak, to predict, and predicate), the route that has been covered must annul itself. But this subtraction leaves a mark of erasure, a *remain(s)* that is added to the subsequent text and that cannot be completely summed up within it (Derrida 1981a:9).

A preface, a *prae* + *fari*, a before the speaking (Sykes 1982:809), denotes an activity leading into the body of a text, but at the same time it already understands the ending of the text. In fact it brings together the edges of the beginning with the edges of the ending of the text. At the same time there is no real beginning or end, as every text is, as it were, 'more like a fabric with loose ends than a hemmed cloth' (Taylor 1984:178). A preface draws attention to certain loose ends at either side of the text and shows the direction of these ends running throughout the text.

Homo ludens (Nethersole 1988:248) is the best image to capture the activity of deconstruction. Whereas Niebuhr (1963:47-51) characterised the human person in different activities in relationships to the world and to God, *homo ludens* illustrates the human person in activity with the text and with the world. This gives expression to the notion of Barthes' *jouissance*. 'The Text, on the other hand, is linked to enjoyment [*jouissance*], to pleasure without separation' (Barthes 1979a:80). One is meant not simply to enjoy reading and rereading the text. It goes further; it means that one must play the text, one must allow the text to unfold and let itself go (Barthes 1979a:80).

The attempt will be made to illustrate the deconstructive approach by contrasting it to the historical-critical approach in interpreting the New Testament. Reading the text of Mark 4:1-9 with the intertext of Mark 4:13-20 as well as the other synoptic intertexts of Matthew 13:1-9, Luke 8:4-8 and Matthew 13:18-23 and Luke 8:11-15 allows one to view certain aspects of the deconstruction activity in operation.

Elsewhere my approach to deconstruction has been labelled 'fairly conservative' (Smit 1988:458). However, a classification in this way fails to understand the very nature of deconstruction. It does not have a uniform method. Instead, it is an activity that shies away totally from becoming yet another method that is

simply applied as a means for acquiring the right interpretation. I have en-
deavoured to approach a text of Scripture with this activity in mind. The aim is
to see how I can use this activity of deconstruction within the limits of my own
intertext as a biblical studies scholar. In this perspective it is not my intention to
take over this activity uncritically, but rather to see its limits within the confines
of my own context. As almost every exponent of this deconstructive activity
operates in her/his own way – for, let it be repeated again, the deconstructive
activity is not a method – I feel that I am at liberty to play the game in my own
way as well. The aim is to illustrate the *modus operandi* of the activity and not so
much to endorse it *in toto*.

1. What is the deconstructive activity?

The best attempt to define the activity of deconstruction has been given by Leavey (1982:43) whereby he characterises the deconstruction of Derrida as containing four protocols:

> In four protocols, this essay approximates how Jacques Derrida's deconstruction works. Each
> protocol approaches from a different direction the strategies Derrida uses in deconstruction:
> (1) *In a certain way* and *strategy* define part of Derrida's close readings of Western tradition.
> (2) According to Paul de Man, Derrida is an Archie Debunker. (3) *Reversal* and many forms
> of *reinscription* constitute the twofold 'process' of deconstruction. (4) *Double invagination* de-
> fines the *narrative* structure of deconstruction's double science.

Basic to the whole approach of deconstruction is that it is to be viewed as a
strategy. In no sense is it a method, but it adopts a specific approach to the understanding and reading of texts. 'The Text must not be thought of as a defined
object...In other words, *the Text is experienced only in an activity, a production*'
(Barthes 1979a:74-75). Consequently, no text is a rounded off unity. It appears
much like a cloth with frayed edges. These edges can interface with the frayed
edges of any other text. 'Every text, being itself the intertext of another text,
belongs to the intertextual' (Barthes 1979a:77).

Every text presents itself as the rewriting of a previous text:

> Writing does not express the individual intention of an original author. To the contrary,
> writing stages a play of repetition in which apparent production is actual reproduction. All
> writing, in other words, is rewriting (Taylor 1984:16).

The role of the author with regard to the text assumes an important direction.
Deconstruction liberates the text entirely from the hegemony of an author.
Once a work has been written the text thereafter acquires an independent exis-
tence. 'The Text, on the other hand, is read without the father's signature'
(Barthes 1979a:78). Consequently, the author can approach the text only in the
same way in which any other interpreter approaches the text. The fact that

he/she is the father/mother of the text gives him/her no special authority with
regard to the text and its interpretation.

In reading or rewriting any text the approach is not to uncover the hidden
meaning residing within a text. Instead every text is viewed as plural.

> This does not mean just that it has several meanings, but rather that it achieves plurality of
> meaning...thus it answers not to an interpretation, liberal though it may be, but to an explo-
> sion, a dissemination. The Text's plurality does not depend on the ambiguity of its contents,
> but rather on what could be called the *stereographic plurality* of the signifiers that weave it
> (Barthes 1979a:76).

Instead of trying to uncover the archimedes point in a text, the approach endeavours to show how the text itself unfolds, explodes, disseminates. Meaning is
not to be discovered in a text. Instead, one tries to see how meaning is deferred
from one text to another. Traces of meaning appear in a text and the reader endeavours to see how these traces of meaning appear and disappear, and how
meaning in this way is ultimately deferred (Taylor 1984:179).

When De Man (1979:128-129) refers to Derrida as 'Archie Debunker' he is
comparing him to the TV character Archie Bunker. '...asked by his wife whether
he wants to have his bowling shoes laced over or laced under, Archie Bunker
answers with a question. He asks: 'What's the difference?' Being a reader of
sublime simplicity, his wife replies by patiently explaining the difference
between lacing over and lacing under, whatever this may be, but provokes only
ire. 'What's the difference?' did not ask for difference but meant instead 'I don't
give a damn what the difference is".

When comparing Derrida to Archie Bunker De Man in fact shows Derrida as
playing a similar game. He asks questions, but in doing so he refuses to be tied
down by the rules of logic. He remains free to interpret and to read the text in
whatever way he wishes. 'Derrida debunks criticism and the ontotheological
presumptions making it possible' (Leavey 1982:47).

Metaphorical language lends itself to the deconstructive activity. The
parables of Jesus are to be viewed as belonging to this metaphorical language.
'Reading a parable, therefore, is a *metaphora*, a passage, a journey, a pil-
grimage. *Imitatio* to follow the footprints of' (Taylor 1982a:121). The details
within a parable are there to draw one along towards the horizon towards which
it is tending. The details point not to themselves but beyond themselves to the
horizon of the passage (Taylor 1982a:118).

Taylor (1982a:120-121) further defines a parable in this way: 'Parable: 'an
ambiguous transition between one and another". The parable projects a world
into which it attempts to translate the hearer.

> Since the world it describes deforms the 'received' world, it constitutes nothing less than an
> invitation to live in that world, to see the world in that way, to take up one's abode within a
> totality of significations that is different from the everyday world.

A parable is not, as in the mind of the supporters of the historical-critical method, to be seen as containing an archimedes point which it is the task of the interpreter to discover and to unlock. Instead, one strives to see how the signifiers present in the story point beyond themselves to the horizon of the passage.

> The parable and the painting draw the eye, by means of a skilfully arranged soft focus on objects in the foreground, to the horizon by virtue of which those objects gain their places and faces. Thus, the objects in the foreground previously released again become the object of attention, but within a new horizon and undergirded and protected by fresh integrity (Taylor 1982a:118).

In place of discovering the *tertium comparationis* that is seen to contain the meaning of the parable, the deconstruction activity views the meaning of the parable as being continually deferred. Every rereading of the text gives a new reflection of the parable. Each time the figurative details of the story are seen to point beyond themselves to a new horizon that becomes part of the text, and in its turn a new horizon or meaning is opened up and then ultimately disappears. In this sense meaning is deferred.

2. The text (Mark 4:3-9; 14-20)

The intention here is to illustrate how the historical-critical view approaches this text and to contrast this with what would be the approach adopted by a deconstructive reading of this text.

2.1 The parable of The Sower (Mark 4:3-9)

2.1.1 An historical-critical understanding of this parable

What has become almost an axiom in the historical-critical method is to uphold a distinction between the figurative usage of the parable and the allegory (Connick 1974:203). While the parable focuses the interest of the interpreter along the path of the discovery of the overall thrust of the parable, the allegory focuses attention on every small detail within the parable, which is seen to contain a hidden reference or meaning. The parabolic method of interpretation and teaching is seen to have its origins in Judaism alone, and the teaching of Jesus is seen to be moulded within this framework. 'Among Jewish teachers the parable was a common and well-understood method of illustration, and the parables of Jesus are similar in form to Rabbinic parables' (Dodd [1935] 1980:16).

On the other hand the allegorical interpretation given to the parables of

Jesus is a development and transformation of Jesus' parables within the world-view of Hellenism. This took place during the apostolic period wherein the apostles and early preachers adapted the teaching of Jesus to the world of their hearers. In adapting this teaching they made use of other teaching methods belonging to the world of their hearers. This development saw the adoption of the allegory as a mode of figurative speech. In some cases the parables of Jesus were transformed into allegories by which every single detail in the parable was given a significance and meaning of its own. This development of the interpretation of the parable in an allegorical way was judged unanimously as being invalid and was rejected out of hand:

> In the Hellenistic world, on the other hand, the use of myths, allegorically interpreted, as vehicles of esoteric doctrine, was widespread, and something of the kind would be looked for from Christian teachers. It was this, as much as anything, which set interpretation going on the wrong lines (Dodd [1935] 1980:16).

This judgment and condemnation of the allegorical approach is common to most historical-critical interpretations of the parable. The historical-critical method judges this procedure as invalid and a distortion of the mind of the author, and in this instance the mind of the person of Jesus, who originally taught the parable. The whole purpose of the historical-critical method has been to ascertain as far as possible what the actual teaching and words of Jesus were. The interest is not simply to ascertain what the evangelist Matthew, Mark or Luke intended (this is at times a centre of interest, as in the case of redaction criticism). The aim more particularly is to establish the teaching as it appears in the mind of Jesus.

For this reason attention is focused upon the actual parable of The Sower, attributing it to the person of Jesus, while the allegorical interpretation is generally rejected and discarded. 'In order to grasp the point of The Sower we shall have to disregard the interpretation which transforms it into a Christian allegory' (Connick 1974:216). Connick goes on to note that the allegory does transform the meaning: 'This interpretation shifts the emphasis from the eschatological to the exhortative' (1974:216). The focus of the parable of The Sower is seen to be in the eschatological dimension: the establishment of God's kingdom. Despite the numerous, and frequent failures (as is evident in the different failures of the seed in growing), finally God's kingdom will come (as is evident in the rich harvest that finally emerges from the seed).

> What Jesus really sets forth is another contrast parable. It concerns the coming of the kingdom. First he suggests the manifold frustrations to which the sower's labor is liable the sun-baked soil, the thorns, the weather, the plundering birds. Then, by way of contrast, he describes the glorious grain standing in the field awaiting the harvest. The yield is unusual...As bystanders watched the sower, much of the labor seemed futile and fruitless. Failures were frequent. But Jesus is confident. He knows that God has made a beginning. In spite of every failure the kingdom will inevitably come (Connick 1974:216).

The parable is retold in an almost identical way in each of the Gospels with only minor differences. The text starts with the statement that Jesus is teaching in parables (Mk 4:2). The account opens with the picture of a farmer sowing seed in his land. The feeling of expectation is engendered by the description, but immediately this is met with the frustrations and the failures that this action encounters. For the bystanders the feeling of expectation is replaced by the feeling of futility. Contrasted to the natural feeling of the bystanders is the feeling of confidence betrayed by Jesus. He shows the ultimate result as the production of a harvest which is beyond compare.

2.1.2 A deconstructive approach to the parable

No explanation is given here to the account. It is presented as a parable, and hence requires the hearer to use her/his mind to search the account for an explanation: 'He who has ears to hear, let him hear' (Mk 4:9). Reading this parable intertextually with other parables, one sees how so many of the comparisons initiated by Jesus in his parables concern the kingdom of God. While no direct reference is made here to the kingdom of God, one sees the trace of the expectation of the coming of the kingdom of God appearing and disappearing throughout this parable when it is read intertextually with the rest of the parables in this chapter (Mk 4).

At the commencement of the parable the expectation of the establishment of God's kingdom is in the forefront. It is awaited eagerly, just as one awaits with eagerness the sower's results from his sowing of the seed. Faced with initial bad results from the sowing of the seed, a feeling of failure emerged, which can be traced as well into the comparison with the establishment of God's kingdom. But, finally, this feeling of failure is replaced by a feeling of confidence and joy in the final success that is attained. Just as the outcome of the harvest surpasses all expectations aroused at the beginning, so too the kingdom of God is to be awaited with the certainty and assurance that far surpasses every expectation.

It is in this contrast of feelings that a trace of the absence-presence of the kingdom is perceived. In the actual event of sowing the presence of the kingdom is expected as imminent, but this presence is experienced as absence in the failures that are encountered. The feeling of confidence and certainty on the part of Jesus re-awakens the trace of the presence of the kingdom. The presence of the kingdom is seen to be something that is inevitable, notwithstanding every failure that appears to re-inform its absence.

2.2 The application of the parable of The Sower (Mark 4:14-20) (with Matthew 13:19-23 and Luke 8:11-15 as intertexts)

Much more of a difference is evident in the application of the parable offered by the three Gospels. This shows that the parable has been reread and reinterpreted in the course of time. Rather than reject this interpretation outright, as occurs in so many approaches of the historical-critical method (because it is judged not to come from Jesus), I believe that a deconstructive approach offers an important perspective with that to view it. This is a clear illustration of what happens to every text which is read again. It is reinterpreted in a new vein according to the new contexts and these become the text's intertexts in which it finds itself.

The new text is seen to replace the previous text which it rereads. In doing so it gives a new direction, a new interpretation. Rather than opting for a position whereby one interpretation is judged to be right, the other wrong, the categories in this sense of right and wrong are rejected. In its place one observes the natural and very normal process by which all interpretation is seen as a rereading of a previous text and in the process a new text is produced. This is exactly what has transpired here with the interpretation of the parable of The Sower. However, in the interpretation offered, not just one new text is produced, but three emerge, as is evident in each one of the Gospels. Although there are close similarities among the three, which shows that they must each depend upon a common source, this common source has been altered somewhat to show evidence of the hands of the individual evangelists. This can be observed in the following chart.

SOWER SOWS

THE SEED (=THE WORD) IN THE HEARERS

	Mark 4:14-20	Matthew 13:19-23	Luke 8:11-15
THE HEARERS	*EXPLANATION*	*EXPLANATION*	*EXPLANATION*
i. Along the path	*Satan* takes away the word	*Evil one...*	*Devil...*
ii. Rocky ground	*Persecution* causes them to fall away	*Persecution*	*Temptation*
iii. Thorns	*Desire* for riches and *cares* of the world	*Delight* in riches and *cares* of the world	*Cares* and riches and *pleasures* of life
CONTRAST	*CONTRAST*	*CONTRAST*	*CONTRAST*
iv. Good soil	Hearers	Hears the word and	Hears the word and
	ACCEPT IT	*UNDERSTANDS*	*HOLDS IT FAST*
	RESULT	*RESULT*	*RESULT*
	30, 60, 100	100, 60, 30	brings forth fruit patiently

The interest of this investigation is not with the small differences that are in evidence in each of these texts. Rather, the interest focuses on the way the text has been reread in new contexts. An identification is given to the seed as being the word of the kingdom and by way of illustration the response to this word is illustrated. A sharp contrast is portrayed in the first three responses from that of the final response.

In each of the Gospels a different contrast is expressed in the final comparison. For Mark the contrast is made with the hearers who accept the word. For Matthew the emphasis is placed on those who understand it, while in Luke the emphasis lies on those who hold it fast.

Behind this contrast in all three texts appears the trace of an exhortation. The hearers are exhorted to pay heed to and to respond to the word. In each case the exhortation occurs indirectly. The trace of an exhortation is seen, but it is only with the final example of the good soil that the trace of the exhortation emerges in the clearest possible way, yet occurring in a different manner in each of the evangelists.

2.3 Mark 4:3-10 and Mark 4:13-20 as intertexts

> Ever unfinished, the text is a 'permanent metamorphosis' which transforms reader into
> author and author into reader (Taylor 1982a:126).

There is one sense in which the historical-critical method and the deconstructive approach would be in agreement. The rereading or rewriting of the text is undoubtedly a natural progression in the handing on of any text. The parable as taught by Jesus is remembered by the three evangelists, and is rewritten into Greek with what appears to be minor adaptations from the words of the historical Jesus. Each one of the Synoptics presents the text in a very similar way. All texts are previous texts that have been rewritten (Taylor 1984:16).

A second stage in the handing on of the text is observed in the allegorising of the parable. Here, each synoptic writer gives an application of the text to the needs of his readers in his own way. Once again the process of rewriting is in evidence. In handing on the text of the parable each gospel writer rewrites the text in his own way. In this rewriting one also notes a transformation that takes place whereby the parable is reread according to new contexts or intertexts, giving it a different perspective in each of the evangelists.

In quite another sense the historical-critical method and the deconstructive approach would part company quite sharply over the very issue of meaning. It is in the quest for meaning that their undertakings go in quite different directions. For the historical-critical method the whole purpose of the undertaking lies in the quest for meaning within the text. All their strategies are geared towards the discovery or the unearthing of this meaning. Instead, the deconstructionists avoid any form of quest for meaning within a text. They illustrate how meaning and the traces that appear of this meaning are in fact deferred as each text is rewritten. Both the parable and the application offered to the parable show that meaning is deferred in each instance. In the case of the parable the trace that appears and disappears only to reappear again is that of the expectation and awaiting of the establishment of God's kingdom. In the allegory that developed from the parable, this meaning is deferred to focus upon another trace that emerges. The focus is placed now upon the seed in so far as it is identified with the word. The trace that occurs throughout is that of the exhortation to respond favourably to the words. This exhortation occurs indirectly and vaguely at first, only to emerge in a clearer and stronger way at the conclusion to each parable. At the same time the focus given to this exhortation takes on different perspectives in each Gospel: acceptance (Mark), understanding (Matthew), holding fast (Luke).

2.4 A deconstructive reading of the texts

> We must begin with absence, with silence, with the confession of the absence of word(s).
> And we must dwell with this silence until we can hear, hear how absence presents. Then we
> shall see, see that the word is absent when present, and present when absent (Taylor
> 1982a:124).

In the parable of The Sower no reference is made directly to the kingdom of
God. Its very absence is what makes its trace present. Through the intertexts of
the other parables recorded in Mark 4 appears the contrast that the parables
are presented as a means to illustrate by way of story what 'the kingdom of God
is like...'.

'A sower went out to sow. And as he sowed...'. The presence of the sower
soon becomes an absence. The sower is not mentioned again in the parable, for
the focus of attention falls upon the fallen seed; '...he is mentioned at the start
and thereafter ignored. The parable is about seed...Or, if one prefers, it is about
the absence and departure, the necessary self-negation of the sower' (Crossan
1980:50).

The presence of the seed on the path, on rocky ground, and among thorns
brought about its death and absence. The presence of the seed in good soil ultimately brought about its growth into a magnificent harvest. The presence of the
soil in the absence of a receptive foundation led to its annihilation, while the absence of any hindrance to the soil led to its presence in superabundance. Ultimately the immense harvest comes as a surprise: it is a miracle (Crossan
1973:51). The kingdom of God comes as a gift, its presence comes as a surprise,
it is worked by a miracle.

The kingdom of God is absent in the parable: it is not mentioned. Yet, as has
been indicated, the intertexts draw attention to the comparison of the kingdom
of God in all the parables. Ultimately the silence of the kingdom gives birth to
its presence in the extraordinary harvest that arrives. The advent of the kingdom
becomes present through miracle and gift.

The trace of the kingdom is taken up again in the intertext of the allegory of
the sower as the text of the parable is rewritten in the early church. Once again
the sower disappears into the background. This time it is the word that is sown.
Here again a trace of the kingdom appears: it is the word of the kingdom that
makes its appearance, its call to acceptance. In three different appearances
analogous to the presence of the seed it becomes absent. In the final appearance of the word, the kingdom truly becomes present in the acceptance of
the hearer. This time the presence of the kingdom and its magnificent growth
occur through the response of the hearer to the word. In the parable the trace of
the kingdom becomes present as divine gift; in the allegory the trace of the kingdom becomes present as human acceptance and bearing fruit.

> But be doers of the word, and not hearers only, deceiving yourselves. For, if any one is a

hearer of the word and not a doer, he is like a man who observes his natural face in a mirror; for he observes himself and goes away and at once forgets what he was like. But, he who looks into the perfect law, the law of liberty, and perseveres, being no hearer that forgets but a doer that acts, he shall be blessed in his doing (James 1:22-25).

In a different way the Epistle of James rereads the parable of The Sower in a different context. He issues the call to be a doer of the word and not just a hearer. 'But those who were sown upon the good soil are the ones who *hear the word and accept it and bear fruit...*' (Mk 4:20).

In the image of the mirror I am present, but when the mirror is absent, I too am absent. I forget about myself. It is a very similar experience to that of Estelle who says: 'I feel so queer...When I can't see myself, I begin to wonder if I really and truly exist. I pat myself, just to make sure, but it doesn't help much...I've six big mirrors in my bedroom. They are there. I can see them. But, they don't see me...how empty it is, a glass in which I'm absent! (Sartre 1964:20).

The subject is dead unless one is prepared to do the word, to make it present. The dissemination of the word is the very actualisation of the self. This involves an emptying of oneself. 'The Word became flesh'. The Word emptied himself of his divine qualities in order to diffuse himself. The *kenosis* of the word brought about the dissemination of the Word. In becoming man, in becoming flesh, the Word becomes a host, becomes a victim given over to the world of man.

This *kenosis* continues. The word is still becoming flesh. The word still proclaims the advent of the kingdom. The hearers of the word are issued with a challenge to consume the word, to imbibe the word, to make it their own. In doing so they too must act on the word, they must disseminate it.

Word becomes flesh: body and blood, bread and wine. Take, eat. Take, drink. To eat this bread and drink this wine is to extend the embodiment of the word and to expand the fluid play of the divine milieu. When freely enacted, the drama of the word proves to be self-consuming (Taylor 1984:120).

3. A retrospect

A retrospect looks back over the endeavour. The attempt was to illustrate the task, rather than simply to endorse it wholesale.

Writer calls to reader, 'Come.' Come on a search that is a research – a research for an impossible event that might be the strange nonevent of the Impossible. Such research is, of course, impossible. It fails, repeatedly fails. And what remains is the writing of this repetition. The only response to the writer's solicitation is to write (Taylor 1987a:353).

The reader thus becomes a participant in the dissemination of the word. The reader cannot remain a hearer only of the word, but must be a doer in which the text is handed on in ever new contexts and intertexts and in this way produces new rereadings of the text. Elsewhere I have drawn attention to a number of shortcomings of the deconstructive activity (Hartin 1987:53-54; 1988a:385-387), not least of which concerns the aspect of relativism. In the concept of the deferral of meaning the text is seen to remain always open to a new rereading of the text. When, however, the text is read in the context of the Scripture, the issue becomes a really burning one.

Richards (1987:119-124) provides an interesting reflection that helps to give a direction towards overcoming the problematic. The difficulty arises either in the exclusive identification of Scripture and text, or in the total separation of the two. This is, as Richards (1987:122) says, 'to misunderstand the difference between text and Scripture'.

One should rather see a movement taking place in which the perception of the reader passes from that of text to Scripture, and then from Scripture to that of text. It is this progressive interplay that brings about a movement not unlike that of a corkscrew, which is an ever spiralling and penetrating insertion into the heart of the text.

> The presence of the text discloses what cannot be enclosed in its presence and may participate in becoming scripture. In becoming scripture one realises the approximation and may return to the text discerning its incompleteness (Richards 1987:122).

Consequently, the choice is not to view it exclusively either as text or as Scripture, nor to see them in opposition, but to see them as perspectives enabling one to gain a deeper penetration of the writing through their interdependence on each other. In viewing the presence of the text it is necessary to turn to the absence of Scripture and to make it present. In viewing the presence of Scripture the need arises to make present again the text as text.

> Finally, what is the point of all this parabolic effort? Certainly the play of dialectic itself can give a rush of excitement; certainly the interplay of texts yields some measure of uncanny satisfaction in its own right. But, for Matthew's text and reader in its historical context intertextuality and discourse keep the tradition alive in the effort to unfold God's revelation. To read the text is to interpret the tradition and to participate in the revealing action of God in the world (Phillips 1985:137).

BIBLIOGRAPHY

Altizer, T. 1982. History as Apocalypse, in *Deconstruction and Theology*. New York: Crossroad, 147-177.
Barthes, R. 1972. *Critical Essays*. (Tr. by R. Howard.) Evanston: North-Western University Press.
Barthes, R. 1975. *The Pleasure of the Text*. (Tr. by R. Howard.) New York: Hill.
Barthes, R. 1977. *Roland Barthes*. (Tr. by R. Howard.) New York: Hill.
Barthes, R. 1979a. From Work to Text, in J. V. Harari (ed.). *Textual Strategies: Perspectives in Post-Structuralist Criticism*. (With an introduction by J. V. Harari.) London: Methuen, 73-81.

Barthes, R. 1979b. *Image-Music-Text*. (Tr. by S. Heath.) Glasgow: Collins.

Barthes, R. 1982. *Empire of Signs*. (Tr. by R. Howard.) New York: Hill.

Blanchot, M. 1985. *Vicious Circles*. (Tr. P. Austen.) New York: Hill.

Bloom, H. 1979. The Breaking of Form, in *Deconstruction and Criticism*. London: Routledge, 1-38.

Burms, A. & De Dijn, H. 1986. *De Rationaliteit en haar Grenzen: Kritiek en Deconstructie*. Assen: Van Gorcum.

Butler, C. 1986. *Interpretation, Deconstruction and Ideology*. Oxford: Oxford University Press.

Connick, C. 1974. *Jesus: the Man, the Mission and the Message*. Englewood Cliffs: Prentice Hall.

Crossan, J. 1973. *In Parables: The Challenge of the Historical Jesus*. New York: Harper & Row.

Crossan, J. 1980. *Cliffs of Fall: Paradox and Polyvalence in the Parables of Jesus*. New York: Crossroad.

Crossan, J. 1982. Difference and Divinity. *Semeia* 23, 29-41.

Crossan, J. 1987. Living Earth and Living Christ: Thoughts on Carol P. Christ's Finitude, Death and Reverence for Life. *Semeia* 40, 109-118.

Culler, J. 1981. *The Pursuit of Signs: Semiotics, Literature, Deconstruction*. London: Routledge.

De Man, P. 1979. Semiology and Rhetoric, in J. V. Harari (ed.). *Textual Strategies: Perspectives in Post-Structuralist Criticism*. (With an introduction by J. V. Harari.) London: Methuen. 121-140.

Derrida, J. 1975. The Purveyor of Truth. *Yale French Studies* 52, 31-113.

Derrida, J. 1976. *On Grammatology*. (Tr. by G. C. Spivak.) Baltimore: Johns Hopkins University Press.

Derrida, J. 1978. *Writing and Difference*. (Tr. by G. C. Spivak.) Baltimore: Johns Hopkins University Press.

Derrida, J. 1979. Living on: Border Lines, in *Deconstruction and Criticism*. London: Routledge, 75-176.

Derrida, J. 1980. *The Archaeology of the Frivolous*. (Tr. by J. P. Leavey.) Pittsburgh: Duquesne University Press.

Derrida, J. 1981a. *Dissemination*. (Tr. by B. Johnson.) Chicago: Chicago University Press.

Derrida, J. 1981b. *Positions*. Chicago: Chicago University Press.

Derrida, J. 1982a. Letter to John P. Leavey, Jr. *Semeia* 23, 61-62.

Derrida, J. 1982b. Of an Apocalyptic Tone Recently Adopted by Philosophy. *Semeia* 23, 63-97.

Detweiler, R. 1985. What is a Sacred Text. *Semeia* 31, 213-230.

Dodd, C. [1935] 1980. *The Parables of the Kingdom*. Glasgow: Collins.

Gadamer, H.-G. 1975. *Truth and Method*. (Tr. by G. Barden & J. Cumming.) New York: Seabury.

Gouws, A. 1988. The Post-Modernist's Progress or: Bluff your Way in Post-Modernism. *SAVAL Conference Papers* VIII, 145-157.

Hartin, P. 1986. Deconstruction and Theology. *Journal of Theology for Southern Africa* 54, 25-34.

Hartin, P. 1987. The Angst of Waiting: A Deconstructive Reading of Luke 12:35-40. *Journal of Literary Studies* 3, 42-56.

Hartin, P. 1988a. Angst in the Household: A Deconstructive Reading of the Parable of the Supervising Servant (Lk 12:41-48). *Neotestamentica* 22, 373-390.

Hartin, P. 1988b. James: *A New Testament Wisdom Writing and its Relationship to Q*. Pretoria: University of South Africa. (Unpublished DTh Thesis.)

Hartman, G. 1979. Words, Wish, Worth. Wordsworth, in *Deconstruction and Criticism*. London: Routledge, 177-216.

Hartman, G. 1981. *Saving the Text: Literature – Derrida – Philosophy*. Baltimore: Johns Hopkins University Press.

Harty, E. 1985. Text, Context, Intertext. *Journal of Literary Studies* 1, 1-13.

Havener, I. 1987. *Q: The Sayings of Jesus*. Wilmington: Glazier.

Leavey, J. 1982. Four Protocols: Derrida, his Deconstruction. *Semeia* 23, 42-57.

Leitch, V. 1983. *Deconstructive Criticism: An Advanced Introduction*. New York: Columbia University Press.

Liebenberg, W. 1988. Postmodernism: Progressive or Conservative? *SAVAL Conference Papers* VIII, 195-208.

Miller, D. 1987. The Question of the Book: Religion as Texture. *Semeia* 40, 53-64.

Miller, J. 1979. The Critic as Host, in *Deconstruction and Criticism*. London: Routledge, 217-254.

Myers, M. 1982. Toward What is Religious Thinking Underway? in *Deconstruction and Theology*. New York: Crossroad. 109-146.

Nethersole, R. 1988. Playing Nicely: A Critical Assessment of Post-Modern Thought and Criticism. *SAVAL Conference Papers* VIII, 247-261.

Niebuhr, H. R. 1963. *The Responsible Self: An Essay in Christian Moral Philosophy*. New York: Harper & Row.

Nietzsche, F. 1957. *Thus Spoke Zarathustra*. (Tr. by M. Cowan.) Chicago: Ragnery.

Norris, C. 1984. *The Deconstructive Turn: Essays in The Rhetoric of Philosophy*. New York: Methuen.

Phillips, G. 1985. History and the Text. The Reader in Context in Matthew's Parables Discourse. *Semeia* 31, 111-140.

Rasche, C. 1982. The Deconstruction of God, in *Deconstruction and Theology*. New York: Crossroad, 1-33.

Rasche, C. 1987. From Textuality to Scripture: The End of Theology of Writing. *Semeia* 40, 39-52.

Revised Standard Version of the Holy Bible. 1980. Cape Town: Bible Society of South Africa.

Richards, H 1987. From Scripture to Textuality. *Semeia* 40, 119-124.

Ricoeur, P. 1976. *Interpretation Theory: Discourse and the Surplus of Meaning*. Fort Worth: Texas Christian University Press.

Ryan, R. 1982. Post-Structuralism: Deconstructing Derrida, in R. Ryan & S. van Zyl (eds.). *An Introduction to Contemporary Literary Theory*. Johannesburg: Ad Donker.

Sartre, J.-P. 1964. *Nausea*. (Tr. by L. Alexander.) New York: New Directions.

Scharlemann, R. 1982. The Being of God when God is not Being God: Deconstructing the History of Theism, in *Deconstruction and Theology*. New York: Crossroad, 79-108.

Scharlemann, R. 1987. Theological Text. *Semeia* 40, 5-19.

Schleiermacher, F. 1978. *Hermeneutics: The Handwritten Manuscripts*. (Tr. by J. Forstman and J. Duke.) Missoula: Scholars.

Schneidau, H. 1982. The Word against the Word: Derrida on Textuality. *Semeia* 23, 5-28.

Smit, D. 1988. Responsible Hermeneutics: A Systematic Theologian's Response to the Readings and Readers of Luke 12:35-48. *Neotestamentica* 22, 441-484.

Soskice, J. 1987. *Metaphor and Religious Language*. Oxford: Clarendon.

Sykes, J. 1982. *The Concise Oxford Dictionary of Current English*. Oxford: Clarendon.

Taylor, M. 1982a. *Deconstructing Theology*. New York: Crossroad.

Taylor, M. 1982b. Text as Victim, in *Deconstruction and Theology*. New York: Crossroad, 58-78.

Taylor, M. 1984. *Erring: A Postmodern A/Theology*. Chicago: University of Chicago Press.

Taylor, M. 1985. Symposium: Deconstructing Theology. V masking: Domino effect. *Journal of the American Academy of Religion* 54, 547-555.

Taylor, M. 1987a. *Altarity*. Chicago: Chicago University Press.

Taylor, M. 1987b. Shades of Difference. *Semeia* 40, 21-38.

Winquest, C. 1982. Body, Text and Imagination, in *Deconstruction and Theology*. New York: Crossroad, 34-57.

Winquest, C. 1986. *Epiphanies of Darkness; Deconstruction in Theology*. Philadelphia: Fortress.

Wyschogrod, E. 1985. On Deconstructing Theology: A Symposium on Erring: *A Postmodern A/Theology*. *Journal of the American Academy of Religion* 54, 523-555.

P. J. DU PLESSIS

FUNDAMENTALISM AS METHODOLOGICAL PRINCIPLE

1. Introduction

For the past two decades New Testament research has concerned itself to an appreciable extent with questions concerning methodology and hermeneutics. This is particularly true of the South African scene (Combrink 1983:3-5). The pendulum has swung from immanent methodological research to a contextual approach concentrating mainly on socio-historical background evidence. The present publication is witness to this ever-widening field of methodology.

Within the framework of these dynamic processes the question of fundamentalism as a methodological principle is certainly worthy of attention. In our day of historical and literary criticism of whatever kind, it is more or less taken for granted that fundamentalism is no longer a matter of contention. The non-tiring James Barr with his fixation on debunking fundamentalism illustrates the issue (Barr 1984; Wells 1980). Despite the academic attitude towards the matter, it is remarkable to note that fundamentalism is either totally or partially practised, surprisingly, by more scholars than one would imagine, all over the world.

In South Africa the method is still widely practised despite its general dismissal in theological research. One can almost distinguish a certain dualism in this respect. Many scholars when publishing articles on methodology, for example historical criticism and related themes, at the end of the day retain a 'conservative biblical' point of view, viz. that the Bible is the inspired word of God (Combrink 1988:137; Du Rand 1984:45-63; Nortjé 1988:15-16). This is probably due to the traditionally conservative mind of these theologians. And this in turn is probably due to their confessional convictions. This factor is not always sufficiently recognised. In the past, and speaking in general, theology was and is an activity of scholars of the church. It is only quite recently that theology shed its close or formal ties with particular confessions and churches, although there still remains a very strong affinity.

Fundamentalism is, of course, no 'new' approach to the biblical text. It seems to have found its name and character in the early years of this century in America (Conn 1976:114). Although it has been severely criticised in the past decade or so, it has stood its ground and can be recognised in the background of so many exegetical publications that pretend to be wholly historical-critical.

To understand this reality one has to attempt an outline of what is meant by fundamentalism. Fundamentalism does not exist, at least not as a 'highly self-enclosing ideology', as James Barr puts it (1977:341). What we have is a mass of disparate religious and cultural material with identifiable common characteristics. In various parts of the world these phenomena are known by various names. They exist wherever the Bible is accepted as the word of God. One of the most basic traits common to religious fundamentalism is the totalitarian view of the Bible, i.e that the Bible is inspired and inerrant. Therefore it is beyond criticism and universally normative.

Concomitant with this point of view we find to a more or lesser degree theological themes, such as the universality of sin, the divinity of Christ, his virginal conception, personal and religious experiences, imminent judgement of the world, etc. When one or more of these concepts dominate to the point of becoming totalitarian, the resulting view of life is exclusivism. This in effect means a dualistic view of Scripture and life, viz. true as against nominal Christians, conservative as against historical-critical examination and application of the Bible and its message. These issues need to be considered in greater detail.

2. Facts and phenomena

It has already been said that fundamentalism is not a closed system of theological thought. We have to consider how the mass of material in this respect, which is characterised by an inner cohesion of facts and phenomena, is interrelated. We may identify the concept common to all phenomena, indicated as fundamentalism, to be a form or type of absolutising. In terms of Scripture interpretation it means a totalitarian view of the character of Scripture, i.e. conviction that all Scripture as such is inspired and therefore free of error. The exhaustive works of Barr illustrate the point (Barr 1973; 1977; 1984 cf. Conn 1976; Teeple 1982).

To do justice to the theme it is necessary to characterise some of the phenomena. By analysing the concepts we could imaginably arrive at a closer identification of the underlying principle that is the unifying force behind the phenomena. By exposing the system of application of interpretation within this framework it is possible to establish what fundamentalism is as a *methodological principle*.

3. Names and places

Fundamentalism is known in various countries by a great variety of names. As an historical phenomenon fundamentalism is essentially a twentieth century method of interpreting Christian texts. The term originated in the USA (Conn 1976:14). During the years 1909-1915 a series of essays and studies were published under the title *The Fundamentals* (Barr 1977:2). The term and its meaning spread rapidly. The need for alternative terminology soon resulted in the coining of terms more suited to express a wider range of meanings: evangelicalism, Biblicism, pietism, extreme fundamentalism, strict fundamentalism, obscurantism, puritanism, perfectionism and many others (Galbraith *s.a.*:5). In South-Africa the preferred term is still 'fundamentalism'.

4. General characteristics

When a description of the phenomena is attempted , it must of necessity be historically selective in terms of our preliminary viewpoint that fundamentalism is basically a form of absolutizing. We have to keep in mind that fundamentalism is also a term that is appropriated by instances other than those in a Christian-confessional context. Orthodox Judaism has fundamentalistic features, while Islam as such can be called a fundamentalistic religion. Apart from religious contexts we also find a secular fundamentalism in the fields of education, school systems, cultural and political fields. In this respect fundamentalism is a universal phenomenon.

One of the most important characteristics of fundamentalism centres on the question of the *inspiration of the Bible*, i.e. is the Bible the inspired Word of God, and if so, how? Machen, one of the system's foremost exponents, gives us the following definition:

> When we say that the Bible is the Word of God, we mean something very definite indeed. We mean that the Bible is true. We mean that the writers of the Bible, in addition to all their providential qualifications for their task, received an immediate and supernatural guidance and impulsion of the Spirit of God which kept them from the errors that are found in other books, and made the resulting book, the Bible, to be completely true in what it says regarding matters of fact and completely authoritative in its commands. That is the great doctrine of the full or plenary inspiration of the Holy Scripture (Machen 1965:14).

This description contains a most basic outline of fundamentalism, viz. that Scripture is completely true, that it has a supernatural origin under the guidance of the Holy Spirit and that these factors determine its infallibility. The choice of Machen's definition for quotation is by no means arbitrary. It contains the basic elements that are common to all systems and institutions with a fundamentalistic approach. Machen does in fact give us a concise account of the system. When considering this system of interpretation as a methodological principle, we shall have to address the basic issues that have been identified. It is simply not defensible to dismiss the whole system of thought because of its obvious deficiencies in comparison with the highly probable results of historical criticism and other methods.

What we need in terms of our theme is to determine whether fundamentalism rules out any form of criticism on Scripture from the outset. At first glance it does seem to be the case.

From this basic presumption of the character and validity of Scripture as in-fallibly inspired we need to understand how this basic view extends and develops into the highly divergent scheme of thought that it really is. Under-standably this would lead to a shift in accent and interpretation of textual evidence. Foremost in this regard is the doctrine of the origin of sin and the total corruption of mankind, the divinity of Jesus Christ, the virginal conception and birth of Jesus, his vicarious passion and death, personal experience of faith and conversion, dispensationalism, literal interpretation of the Bible, the rapture, the immanent end of the world and final judgement, world mission and evangelisation, creation over and against evolution, etc. The list is endless.

A characteristic particularly remarkable to scholars and followers of this con-viction is their personal attitude to others of a different or opposing persuasion. They manifest a distinctly hostile attitude. For this reason they find it necessary to 'grade' people and by doing so reveal their attitude as an extreme form of *ex-clusivism*. To them people are either true to Scripture, or they are critical of it. They can be found in many Churches and institutions because fundamentalism is not a closed system akin to one specific Church organisation.

There are a number of Church institutions where 'fundamentalists' would or could be at home. In the mainline Churches they would be the ones to preserve and uphold the *'conservative'* elements that are universally present. On the other hand their tenets and boundaries are so flowing that they could be termed *'evangelicals'* in a sense that is particularly prominent in Pentecostal-charismatic circles. This type of accentuation is not neutral or innocent, because the dualism between 'true-false'; 'conservative-critical' etc. is maintained to the point of being completely intolerant towards contrary viewpoints. Being *intolerant* to all views and interpretations except your own is typical of a 'closed' Church with inflexible views on Scripture and dogmatic issues. Contrary opinions are disapproved by labelling them 'liberalism', 'higher critisism', 'modernism', etc., while their own views are overtly defended as beyond criticism. This rigidity and aggressive apologetic are perhaps the most typical characteristics of fun-damentalism. James Barr's analysis is by and large the most thorough at our dis-posal. One cannot agree with him in all respects (that would no doubt alarm him!), but his conclusion is sound:

> If fundamentalism has to be specially studied, it is not because it is uniquely damaging (though that can at times be so) but because of its peculiar alienated and cut-off character (Barr 1977:337).

5. The Bible as Word of God.

The question of inspiration is not as such a question that concerns us here. What we need to understand is the functioning of the Bible within the frame-

work of the phenomena from which fundamentalism receives its particular character. There is one concept that continuously comes to the fore when discussing this theme, viz. the Bible has complete authority as the inerrant Word of
God.

How this principle functions in our context has to be indicated. Barr is quite
correct in saying that the problem does not lie with the Bible but with the
people who dominate the interpretation of the Bible by virtue of their own experience and background traditions. In this manner the Bible is manipulated to
become an instrument to maintain their own identity. This powerful hold on
Scripture is fundamentalism's most profound characteristic. It furnishes its adherents with an instrument to motivate the zealous and with which they
maintain their position as if it is dictated by Scripture, while it is in reality a
figment of their own creation (Barr 1977:11).

To maintain this stance necessitates the use of two hermeneutical techniques,
viz. to accept a continuous switch from literal to metaphorical interpretation
and *vice versa*. The real issue for these exponents is not whether a text is to be
interpreted literally or metaphorically, but how to maintain at all costs the inerrancy of the Bible (Strauss 1989:79ff). The argumentation is: If the Bible is not
'inerrant' it cannot lay claim to full authority and authenticity. Thus fundamentalism is a self-imposed defence and maintenance of the character of inerrancy
ascribed to the Bible (Roscam Abbing 1974:7ff). The hermeneutic problem we
are dealing with is the *absolutising of Scripture*.

5.1 Literal and metaphorical meaning

To uphold the inerrancy of Scripture recourse is taken to switching continuously
literal and metaphorical interpretations. The criterion for deciding when to
switch roles seems quite arbitrary. Barr cites Genesis 1 in the New Bible
Commentary as an example of this chop and change way of dealing with incon-
sistancies. The chapter is interpreted as a literal account of history, but the
'days' is considered to be clearly defined periods of time (Barr 1977:41), for obvious reasons.

What is striking in this and countless other instances is the fact that the resul-
tant interpretation is in reality a *re-interpretation* of the biblical text for the sole
purpose of maintaining the inerrancy of Scripture. When confronted by such in-
consistancies it is clearly a case of *non liquet* (Ridderbos 1968:66).

5.2 Harmonising

If one is inclined to vindicate at all costs the inerrancy of Scripture one is forced
to use all sorts of devices to smooth out unevenness. When two texts obviously

describe the same incident but in such a manner that one contradicts the other, then one's starting point demands that they be brought in harmony. Such instances of *harmonisation* are countless. Just as numerous are the motives for adopting such tactics.

As these phenomena are so well-known and generally practised, it hardly seems justified in a paper of this nature to fill page after page with random examples. At any rate one cannot escape a feeling of inadequacy when dealing with a subject of this kind. It is not to be moulded into a patttern exploring specific passages in terms of a formally systematised method. It is much more a way of dealing with the products of those studying the Bible from a set of preconceived suppositions. To identify the features manifested in their works is a prerequisite for understanding the mind of a fundamentalist. Such a perception could reveal the methodological basis of all who seek to interpret biblical texts. The bottom line of all methodology and interpretation is to arrive at the meaning of passages as we read them, as they make sense to us, the readers.

It should be clear in dealing with new approaches to biblical texts that they can never be formalised into a singular objective and valid explanation. The subjective basis of every interpretation should be recognised from the outset. The renewed and contemporary importance attached to the role of the reader illustrates the point (Culpepper 1983:199). In a fundamentalistic paradigm the mind of the interpreter sets the scene, pace and route of one's particular interpretation. It is therefore extremely difficult to judge such versions and approaches by standards not recognised in the mind of the fundamentalist. His motives cannot be questioned as though he is deliberately distorting the text to suit his own ends. We must recognise and respect the motivation of the fundamentalist mind, which is to preserve the sanctity of the transmitted text to its fullest possible comprehension. Fundamentalists do not, to take the argument a step further, set out to arrive at a congruent explanation by the most direct route. The serious and voluminous expositions of its advocates witness to this fact. Like all expositors of the Bible, fundamentalists have to contend with the serious communication problem between a text and its readers. This communication process is at times so severely battered by methodological problems and analyses that it scarcely survives the onslaught.

With these issues in mind we may deal with some examples of fundamentalist interpretation.

6. Some examples

It would not serve any useful purpose to discuss a few random examples. It seems more appropriate to discuss the rudiments of fundamentalist thinking as seen from their perspective on crucial issues in New Testament interpretation.

The *miracle narratives* have always been a bone of contention for querulants in the theological world. It has become somewhat of a platitude that the mind of modern men and women is to a great extent determined by their spiritual, intellectual and religious maturity. Since the *Aufklärung* reason became the decisive factor in understanding and relating to the world. The religious world demands that one accept only concepts that can be determined by reason. As miracles by their very nature are contrary to the natural law of cause and effect the miracle narratives, of the New Testament have always been stumbling blocks for religious experience and understanding. Günter Klein states, perhaps too boldly, that 'Wer also dem modernen Menschen einen Glauben an Wunder abverlangt, der scheint von ihm objektiv Unmögliches zu verlangen' (Klein 1970:15). To a more or lesser degree historical criticism would go along with this point of view. By explaining the element of the supernatural in terms of natural parameters, modern Bible criticism finds various ways of explaining the apparently inexplicable.

As far back as the 18th century J. J. Hess (1741-1828) 'explained' the healing of the demon-possessed in Matthew 8:28-34 as follows: 'The unfortunate men were the victims of some mental disease. The stampeding herd of pigs had such a shock effect on the deranged men that they were cured of their afflictions!' (Klein 1970:16). Such examples can be multiplied endlessly. 'Natural' interpretations include application of psychosomatic factors in some miracle narratives. Another useful tool is the theory of apparent death (suspended animation). By this means death and resurrection, particularly that of Christ, is 'explained' as events within natural confines.

Contrary to these rational approaches the fundamentalist mind incites its exponents to accept without doubt the miracle narrative as it is related in its supernatural presentation even to the point of accepting the absurd. Miracles, so it is said, are to be interpreted in a literal, very real manner even if it should demand a *sacrificium intellectus*.

Although there are degrees of rigidity in the literalness employed by the fundamentalist interpreter, by virtue of which some expositions become more acceptable than others, fundamentalism cannot be theologically vindicated or practised without reservation. It is on the whole 'eine aüsserste Gefahr' (Klein 1970:21). Driving out demons from a demon-possessed person can seriously jeopardise such a patient's chances of recovery, and could have long-term and disastrous effects. Despite occurences like these and the explanations given that are so much in dispute, it is surprising how widely and universally fundamentalistic notions are fondly harboured and boldly expressed. Considering the death and resurrection of Lazarus for instance, Hendriksen discusses divergent views, but concludes: 'We should adhere to the story as given in Scripture' (Hendriksen 1961:138).

Considering Hendriksen's views, representative of the larger body of kindred thinkers, it should be remarked that the miracle narratives are far more complex than these commentators would have us believe. By merely accepting them literally, i.e. on the story level, we still do not recognise the theological import of the story. Still bearing the Lazarus miracle in mind, its design and end are to be considered in its Johannine context (cf. Jn 11). An attempt at doing just this is done from an obviously historical-critical point of view, quoted by Hendriksen. It sets out from

> the assumption that Lazarus was still alive, and this not only when the messenger...reached Jesus, but also when he returned again; and that he found Lazarus still fully conscious, and intimated to him that he would be raised from the dead, so that he knew about this and was confronted by it before he died! (Hendriksen 1961:137).

Such a contention is not likely to be taken seriously by commentators any more. Far from being in a suspended state of animation (apparent death) or still alive (but seriously ill) when Jesus arrived, the story explicitly states 'Jesus told them plainly, 'Lazarus is dead" (Jn 11:14). The relatively positive value of the fundamentalistic interpretation is borne out by the insistence that the story (text) is to be accepted as it stands and how it obviously wants to be read: In this context as a real event.

Günter Klein formulates the fundamentalistic approach as follows:

> Den Mut, der eigentlichen Absicht der Texte standzuhalten, die Bereitschaft, uns von ihnen vor ein wirkliches Wunder führen zu lassen, dies ebenfalls können wir vom Fundamentalismus lernen, und das ist sein positiver Dienst an uns (Klein 1970:23).

It is beyond the scope of this paper to pursue these methodological issues.

'Time marches on' is a slogan used by the South African Broadcasting Corporation to caption a radio programme during World War II. It could quite easily caption the ever-increasing concern of so many church leaders who are struggling to free themselves from the shackles of a basic conflict between themselves and their churches and who still remain loyal to tenets of their church.

In Roman Catholicism scholars and laity alike were compelled to embrace some fundamentalistic convictions contrary to and in conflict with modern scholarship (Nowell 1981:259). All it accomplished after two decades of scholarship was 'a pious schizophrenia'. They had to accept as historical fact the first three chapters of Genesis (and many other passages and notions) while they had great difficulty in integrating faith and reason. A very prominent example is Hans Küng; remarks Nowell:

> Küng splendidly illuminates the significance of Jesus' miracles... Küng makes it quite clear why the Christian cannot be content with psychological and mythical explanations of the resurrection, but will insist with the reality of Jesus' new life with God (Nowell 1981:279).

The scene is ever changing. The incidence illuminates the point under discussion. Fundamentalism, however delicately it is articulated and applied, is never free from the fear of a religious schizophrenia. At this point we must leave the discussion.

7. The Old Testament in the New Testament

This matter has always been the subject of a fundamentalistic squabble. One example has to suffice. Zechariah 9:9 is quoted (partially) in Matthew 21:6-7, which in translation reads: 'They brought the donkey and the colt, their cloaks over them, and Jesus got on' (Good News Bible). Matthew speaks clearly of two animals: a donkey and a colt. Mark (11:7), Luke (19:28) and John (12:14) only mention one animal, which is indeed in accordance with the parallelism of the Zechariah text. Matthew complicates the problem by having Jesus ride on two animals at the same time.

Groenewald (1968:342) explains the Matthew text in terms of the Johannine passage despite the plural 'over them' of Matthew. He is no doubt harmonising the accounts for the sake of maintaining the consistency and inerrancy of Scripture. His exposition is a clear case of fundamentalism, as is indeed his book as such.

A new approach in historical-critical manner is attempted by Colwell, whose comments on this passage illustrates the weakness of fundamentalism. He says, justifiably, 'An ignorance of a literary form led Matthew to ask us to picture Jesus as riding two animals into Jerusalem' (Colwell 1967:125).

8. Synoptic inconsistency

Perhaps no other aspect highlights the problem so profoundly as the synoptic discrepancies in the narration of Jesus' death and resurrection (Baarda 1974:27-51). Considering the evidence carefully one is compelled to accept an entirely different complexion on the matter if fundamental harmony is rejected as hermeneutic model. Brown highlights the problem of synoptic inconsistency by remarking on the annointing of the body of Jesus after his death as follows (cf. Jn 19:38-42; Mk 16:1; Lk 24:1): One must reject the harmonisation theory that the preparations on Friday described in John were provisional and the women came to complete the task on Sunday (Brown 1983:57).

9. Summary and conclusions

The above examples have to suffice. In conclusion a short summary and important conclusion are called for.

Fundamentalism is not a single phenomenon in a particular church, but is a series of divergent theological phenomena. Its main feature is its insistence on the absolute inerrancy of the Bible as historically qualified truth and reality. It is not inherent to defined churches and associations. Some church organisations may demonstrate inclinations and leanings towards a fundamentalistic character. The demonstrations are universal and varying in degrees of rigidity. It is therefore difficult to assess fundamentalism as a collective designation for such a disparity of phenomena. Conversely not every instance of upholding the inerrancy of Scripture can be branded as fundamentalism. It is therefore necessary to distinguish carefully between the features discussed.

The bottom line is unquestionably that fundamentalism is a theological disease fraught with dangerous aberrations (Barr 1977:5). It infiltrates orthodox and heterodox organisations alike. In its extreme form it petrifies into presuppositions passing themselves off as Scripture authority which can lay claim to acceptance by the church organisation.

Fundamentalism is therefore, by definition, intolerant and exclusive. It shows very little regard for interdenominational discussion and communication. Whenever a line of contact is found it is always from a position of safe entrenchment. Therefore fundamentalism is by nature polemic and apologetic.

Fundamentalism is also a complex and profound system of phenomena that manifests itself in the most diverse areas of life: The church, culture, education, science, politics, etc. Caution in analysing these constellations of thought is of the utmost importance.

Fundamentalism is in the final instance not merely the postulation of the inerrancy of Scripture but also the practising of it as totally true and valid under all circumstances. It is tantamount to deification of Scripture. As such there is no 'positive' side to fundamentalism, only alternatives and other potentialities. It is possible to confess and accept the authority of Scripture and to live and experience biblical truth without surrendering to the dictatorship of fundamentalism.

10. Fundamentalism in South Africa

This is a matter not without risks and pitfalls. It is a sensitive undertaking, not only because it involves the mainline churches and other minor organisations, but also because it so seriously influences political thought, educational systems and the cultural plurality of this country. A basic question that dominates so much of South African thinking is the question whether and how it is possible for so many cultural and religious societies to live and work together, accepting the Bible as final authority whatever the ethnic and cultural background of its people may be.

Loader (1980:101ff) established a so-called Totius-model of fundamentalism. This type of thinking has and still does exercise a profound influence on the

South African, i.e. the Afrikaans speaking churches. In this model the authority and the inerrancy of the Bible dominates all theological thinking. It is upheld to such an extent that influential theologians, church leaders and organisations are forced into some kind of straitjacket.

The Totius-model consist of the following elements: A totalitarian view of the Bible as the inerrant and inspired Word of God, rejection of Bible criticism, rejection of dissidents as 'unbelievers', rejection of alternative interpretations of Scripture because they are considered as rejecting Scripture and Christ as well, the interchange of literal and metaphorical interpretations of Scripture passages and utilising archeological evidence to prove the truth of the biblical texts and narratives. Basically it boils down to an authoritarian view of Scripture, exclusivism and harmonisation of the Bible passages.

It would take us beyond the scope of this paper to discuss fully the historical incidence of fundamentalism in South Africa. Instead reference is made to some of its outstanding features. The important point to keep in mind is that South Africa in its Afrikaans segment is basically reserved in its political and theological thinking. This can be illustrated by referring to obvious incidences.

In a South African broadcasting program (Wat sê die Bybel: What does the Bible say) one can hear opinions like the following: Joshua 10: The sun literally stood still over Gibeon and the moon over the Ajalon valley; Noah's ark was big enough to accomodate all the animals of the earth and could cope with the problem of dung removal; the historicity of Samuel's ghost and Saul as the unbelieving one, and many other examples (Loader 1980:109-110). It must be mentioned that the participants to these programs are mostly all professors of theology of the three mainline Reformed Churches.

Beside the mainline churches we find a considerable number of charismatic churches and organisations in this country. These adherents are not fundamentalists in the original sense, as has been indicated above; they are the products, the offspring of fundamentalist thought. In some cases they are more extremistic than others. They share a common Bible criticism but they also reject extreme fundamentalism. They could be termed neo-fundamentalists. A typical example is the publication *SA Renewal*. In its publication no. 6, 1983, the inflexibility of the established church is justifiably highlighted. In this case formalism became empty opportunism.

James Barr censures such fundamentalist movements, of which there are abundant followers in this country:

> These types of religion are not absolutely tied to fundamentalism, and sometimes they spring up within quite other streams of Christianity. Healing and speaking with tongues both commend themselves fairly naturally on the grounds that they represent a recovery of the original state of the New Testament Churches: One should have a fresh and overwhelming experience of the Holy Spirit after one has been a Christian for some time, one should speak with tongues... (Barr 1977:207).

To what degree these notions have penetrated the church and secular societies is not all that clear. However, the publication of Van Huyssteen and Du Toit suggests that there are dynamic forces at work to move away from fundamentalism. They say that

> believing Christians can no longer afford to immunize themselves by seeking safety in group affinities, but should not hesitate to question and criticize established conceptions (Van Huyssteen & Du Toit 1982:1ff).

A final word is called for. There is a dynamic force at work in this country, to change established positions and to move away from fundamentalism. It is still mere indications of a beginning, but nevertheless it is there. By far the greatest contribution can be made by the church if it fulfills its calling, i.e. to let the Bible be what it should be: Universal and inclusive, a dynamic force as the ultimate communication between God and humankind.

BIBLIOGRAPHY

Baarda, T. 1974. De Opgestane en de Aardse Heer, in *Eigentijds Verstaan van de Bijbel*. Kampen: Kok.

Barr, J. 1973. *The Bible in the Modern World*. London: SCM.

Barr, J. 1977. *Fundamentalism*. London: SCM.

Barr, J. 1984. *Escaping from Fundamentalism*. London: SCM.

Brown, R. E. 1983. *The Gospel according to St John*, v. 2. London: Chapman. (Anchor Bible.)

Colwell, E. C. 1967. *The Study of the Bible*. Chicago: University Press.

Combrink, H. J. B. 1983. Die Pendulum Swaai Terug. Enkele Opmerkings oor Metodes van Skrifinterpretasie. *Skrif en Kerk* 4, 3-15.

Combrink, H. J. B. 1988. Strukturalisme – Is 'n Herwaardering Nodig? *Nederduits-Gereformeerde Teologiese Tydskrif* 29, 129-138.

Conn, H. M. 1976. *Contemporary World Theology*. Nutley, New Jersey: Presbyterian & Reformed Publishing Co.

Culpepper, R. A. 1983. *Anatomy of the Fourth Gospel: A Study in Literary Design*. Philadelphia: Fortress.

Du Rand, J. A. 1984. Die Leser in die Evangelie volgens Johannes. *Fax Theologica* 4, 46-63.

Galbraith, J. P. s.a. *Why the Orthodox Presbyterian Church?* Philadelphia: Committee on Christian Education.

Groenewald, E. P. 1968. *Handboek Bybelse Geskiedenis. Die Nuwe Testament*. Pretoria: HAUM.

Hendriksen, W. 1961. *The Gospel of John*. The Banner of Truth Trust.

Klein, G. 1970. *Argernisse. Konfrontationen mit dem Neuen Testament*. Munchen: Kaiser Verlag.

Loader, J. A. 1980. Ortodokse Fundamentalisme en die Gebruik van die Ou Testament in Suid-Afrika. *Hervormde Teologiese Studies* 35, 101-118.

Machen, J. M. 1965. *The Christian View of Man*. London: Banner of Truth Trust.

Nortjé, S. J. 1988. *Johannes die Doper in die Vierde Evangelie*. Johannesburg: Rand Afrikaans University. (Unpublished Doctoral Thesis.)

Nowell, R. 1981. *A Passion for Truth. Hans Küng: A Biography*. London: Collins.

Ridderbos, H. N. 1968. Feilloosheid, Onfeilbaarheid, Autoriteit. Over de Aard van het Schriftgezag, in *Het Woord, het Rijk en onze Verlegenheid*. Kampen: Kok.

Roscam Abbing, P. J. 1974. *Eigentijds Verstaan van de Bijbel*. Kampen: Kok.

Strauss, P. J. 1989. Die Bybel: Enigste Bron vir Gereformeerde Kerkregtelike Beginsels? *Hervormde Teologiese Studies* 45, 79-98

Teeple, H. M. 1982. *The Historical Approach to the Bible*. Evanston: Religion & Ethics Inst.
Van Huysteen, W. & Du Toit, B. 1982. *Geloof en Skrifgesag*. Pretoria: NG Kerkboekhandel.
Wells, P. R. 1980. *James Barr and the Bible. Critique of a New Liberalism*. Philippsburg, New Jersey.

W. R. DOMERIS

SOCIOLOGICAL AND SOCIAL HISTORICAL INVESTIGATIONS

For I believe, that in measure as we realise its surroundings so to speak, see and hear for ourselves what passed at the time, enter into its ideas, become familiar with its habits, modes of thinking, its teaching and worship shall we not only understand many of the expressions and allusions in the New Testament, but also gain fresh evidence of the truth of its history alike from its faithfulness to the picture of society, such as we know it to have been, and from the contrast of its teaching and aims to those of the contemporaries of our Lord (Edersheim 1876:v).

The concern for the details of the New Testament world is not new. Indeed it is as old as the Gospels themselves, and has continued over the centuries in the manifold attempts to write a life of Christ. Yet the present explosion of interest in the sociology of the Bible is not simply a continuation of this trend. Indeed many new elements have emerged within the last decade, making this approach to the Bible one of the most important phenomena of modern biblical studies. Several scholars (Smith 1975; Gager 1982; Hollenbach 1983; Gottwald 1983a; Scroggs 1983; Wilson 1984), myself (1988a) included, have described the recent sociological and social historical research of the Bible, and in some ways this article serves to update those works. At the same time, I intend to expose more thoroughly its historical roots, and by means of examples, make the method more accessible to non-specialists.

1. The roots of social and sociological studies of the Bible

Interest in the social history of the Bible arises out of a concern for the lives of the New Testament characters, particularly Jesus. The gospel writers, both canonical and uncanonical, began a process of documenting the life of Jesus within the double context of faith and history. Even before form criticism arose as a discipline, scholars had already seen an opportunity to distinguish the one from the other. The quest for the historical Jesus was born and the subsequent lives of Jesus through to the beginning of the twentieth century, were the result. Attention was also given to the social background of Jesus' time. Emile Schürer wrote his *Geschichte des jüdischen Volkes im Zeitalter Jesu Christ* in 1885 and Alfred Edersheim penned both *The Temple, its Ministry and Services as they were at the Time of Jesus Christ* and *Sketches of Jewish Social Life* before the close of the nineteenth century. Both writers made extensive use of rabbinic sources as well as Josephus, and so pioneered the modern social historical approach of the last few decades.

With the dawn of the twentieth century, the great Albert Schweitzer attempted to call a halt to the process, when he declared the historical Jesus to be an
enigma, and banished him to his own time. Then the form critics came and, with
scalpel in hand, they peeled away the layers of tradition so as to expose the historical roots. Far from leading to an increased interest in the social matrix of
Christianity, the opposite was true. Thus, for example, the existentialist philosophy of Rudolf Bultmann ruled Jesus' social and political milieu to be irrelevant,
and so laid the tombstone on the quest for the historical Jesus. But the engima
continued to plague the scholarly mind, and finally surfaced in the 1980's as a
veritable explosion of interest in Jesus and his social situation.

Sociological studies of the Bible date back to the late nineteenth century. In
1897 Shailer Mathews published his work on the social teaching of Jesus. This
was followed in 1914 by Shirley Jackson Case's *Evolution of Early Christianity* as
one the leading sociologists of the so-called Chicago school. The most important
of the early studies was the work of Max Weber. His essays on Judaism were
published in 1917-1919. Other German writers included Ernst Lohmeyer, whose
Soziale Fragen im Christentum appeared in 1921, and Oscar Cullmann, who in
1925 called for the creation of a special branch of sociology that would compli-
ment form criticism (quoted by Gager 1982:260). Apart from scholars like Ernst
Troeltsch and Case, Cullmann's call remained unanswered until the second half
of the century. Yet the sociology of religion grew apace, and the outmoded conceptions of the nineteenth and early twentieth century gave way to the critical
analyses of modern religious movements and sophisticated anthropological
investigations.

In 1960, when E. A. Judge published his study on the social patterns of Christian groups in the first century, he marked the beginning of new waves of interest in the sociological study of the Bible. In 1975, Gregory Baum wrote an
important, but much neglected book entitled *Religion and Alienation*, which was
a theological reading of sociology, in which he called for theologians to take
seriously the methodology of sociology. The same year, Jonathan Z. Smith was
able to catalogue the several different forms of social and sociological study that
had arisen in the interval, and in 1986, John Elliott listed no fewer than eighty-
one such works, which had so far appeared in the eighties (1986:1 note 1).

2. Trends in Social and Sociological Studies

Smith (1975) describes four possible approaches to what he called 'the social
description of early Christianity'. The first of these concerned the social facts
found in early Christian writings. The second was social history, and the third,
social organisation. The fourth is an analysis of 'early Christianity as a *social
world*, as the creation of a world of meaning which provided a plausibility structure for those who chose to inhabit it' (Smith 1975:21). The fourth, as Gager

(1982:258) quite correctly notes, is the only one that may properly be described as sociological or social scientific (involving the disciplines of sociology, anthropology or psychology).

Gager's distinction between social historical and sociological is an obvious one, although in recent times, as with Wayne Meeks' *Urban Christianity* (1983), scholars have tended to use some form of sociological model within their social histories. However, with this reservation in mind, I believe one can still make use of the distinction as a means of classification.

2.1 Social descriptions

Two factors contribute to make the present social descriptions of the early Christian communities a reliable pursuit. The first is the acquisition of a growing number of texts relevent to the New Testament social milieu from different parts of the Graeco-Roman world, ranging from agricultural lists to household codes. The second factor is the ongoing archaeological excavation of the eastern Mediterranean, and particularly the region of Syro-Palestine. Archaeology, freed from its role as 'the handmaiden' of biblical studies is now able to dedicate itself to its true task, namely the deeper appreciation of the life-context of people of old.

Social descriptions fall into two groups: those that deal with Jesus, and those that deal with the various early Christian communities. We shall consider these each in turn.

2.1.1 Social historical studies of Jesus

The social history of the Jesus movement is the focus of the work of scholars like Sean Freyne, Paul Hollenbach, Gerd Theissen and Albert Nolan. The general question behind most of the studies is, 'What were the political, economic and social concerns which obtained in Palestine, during the time of Jesus' ministry?' Apart from Edersheim's two books mentioned above and Frederick Grant's, *The Economic Background of the Gospels*, published in 1926, few of the earlier scholars had ventured even to ask such a question. Instead their concern was the religious milieu, which they often divorced from its greater context. Jesus was seen as a religious teacher, who interacted with a number of rival teachers (scribes and Pharisees) until they grew jealous and connived to have him executed. The political function of the high priest, the economic oppression by the Sadducees or the educational exploitation by the pharisees was left in the past.

The situation today is very different. We have the outstanding work of Joachim Jeremias on Jerusalem (1969), Sean Freyne on Galilee (1980 and

1988), Paul Hollenbach on Jesus and John the Baptist (1982), and John Stambaugh and David Balch (1986) on the social environment of the New Testament. Together they have uncovered many intriguing details vital to an understanding of the milieu of Jesus. For example, we are able to see how oppression was exerted on the common people of Palestine from two separate sources.

The first, and largely indirect source of oppression, was that of the Romans. The Roman pressure was felt in the form of the rising spiral of violence, as they ruthlessly suppressed any sign of Jewish resistance. Much of this resistance was not directed against the Romans, but against the Jewish authorities. Indeed, the direct oppressors of the time were the wealthy landowners, notably the high-priestly family of Annas. Through their ownership of the land and of the other modes of production, they were able to squeeze the peasant farmers dry. Their control of the temple, and the profits they made from its taxes, sacrifices and tithes seems to have been a further issue for the people of first century Palestine. But it was the debt records, which were stored in the Temple, which led ultimately to the capture of that place and the burning of the records, at the start of the Jewish Revolt in 66 C.E.

Some modern studies have addressed specific aspects of the milieu of Jesus, and in particular Jesus' reponse to the issues of his time. For example, D. Oakman has written a book entitled *Jesus and the Economic Questions of his day* (1986). Here he considers issues such as taxation, peasant farming, the rural-urban dialectic and other issues, and he shows how Jesus as an artisan responded to the economic pressures of his day.

George Pixley (1983) attempts to unravel the political strategy of Jesus, and so looks at the question of the aims of Jesus. Likewise Richard Horsley (1986 and 1987) chooses to focus upon the political milieu. Having dispelled the myth of the Zealots as a party that existed in Jesus' time, he goes on to show how the main resistance to oppression on the part of the common people was essentially non-violent until the outbreak of the Jewish revolt in 66 C.E. The exception was the social bandits (*sicarii*) who targeted the pro-Roman sympathisers, and set about disturbing the collection of taxes. They captured the temple in 66 C.E., and then held Masada until 73 C.E. The former action suggests that the real target of the Jewish revolt (66-70 C.E.) was the economic exploitation of the wealthy elite, and not primarily the rule of the Romans!

Freyne's most recent book (1988) looks at Jesus' teaching in its Galilean context. The question of Jesus and the poor in a situation of economic oppression is the focus of the work of Richard Cassidy (1978), and Luise Schottroff and Wolfgang Stegemann (1986). The practice of Jesus is dealt with by Hugo Echegeray (1984), and from Elisabeth Schüssler Fiorenza (1983) and Schottroff (1983), come studies on Jesus and women.

2.1.2 Studies of early Christian communities

The trend among those scholars who deal with early Christian communities has been to focus upon one particular community, or in the case of Paul, one set of communities. The purpose of the study may be a social history of the chosen community, a class analysis or even an overall structural representation of the community.

The most important work on the Pauline communities is the work of Wayne Meeks on *Urban Christianity* (1983). Meeks uses the various people mentioned in the letters of Paul to compile a breakdown of the various communities that the apostle visited. He has also uncovered a wealth of material concerning various aspects such as the social structure of the Roman world, and the average life expectation of the time. Meeks' work, together with the writing of R. Hock (1980), Robert Grant (1977) and Abraham Malherbe (1983; 1986 and 1987) among others, gives us a detailed picture of Paul's social context.

Studies of the Gospel communities have tended to focus on the Fourth Gospel. Here the clearest example of social history is revealed in the work of Raymond Brown (1979) and Louis Martyn (1979). On the basis of the Gospel and the First Epistle, they sketch the history of the Johannine community on its path from the Judaism of the synagogue to its independence as a Jewish-Christian sect and finally to the schism mentioned in the First Epistle.

The Matthean community is the focus of a commentary, published by the present writer, in the series Portraits of Jesus (1987). There is also an article by Robert Smith (1983) who has attempted, to my mind unsuccesfully (cf. Domeris 1988:384-5), to present a case for the middle-class nature of the Matthean community. His work illustrates the potential danger of all social descriptions, namely that of projecting one's own context onto that of the ancient community.

The observable trends among scholars of early Christian communities have been to focus on aspects like social structure, the crisis of the break from Judaism, the rise of heresies, and the general Roman milieu. Several studies deal with the class structure of early Christianity (Were they mainly rich or poor?), on the leadership of the first century communities (Were they egalitarian in structure?), and finally on the sectarian nature of these communities (Were they comparable to recent millenarian movements?). Such focii lead inevitably in some form of social analysis, resulting in the explicit or implicit use of some sociological model. For, the moment one moves from pure description (the what) to deducing cause and effect (the why or the how), one leaves the realm of social description or social history and enters that of sociological studies.

2.2 Sociological studies

Robin Scroggs (1983) details five types of sociological study, which had appeared in New Testament studies up to the time of his writing. I have chosen to develop these and to include four further areas:

2.2.1 Typologies

Scroggs includes here studies of the New Testament communities as religious sects, based upon the models of Ernst Troeltsch. The models are largely drawn from studies of new religious movements. The structure of the group is examined, as well as the role of the leader, the social status of the members and their reasons for joining the sect. The models enable one to make certain deductions concerning the structure and life of New Testament communities. One of the reasons put forward for the attractive nature of the early Christian communities was their development of a new symbolic universe, which allowed members to live out their anxieties in a secure environment. Scroggs' own study (1975) fits into this category with its discussion of the early Christians and unconscious social protest.

2.2.2 Cognitive dissonance

The term comes from the pioneering work of Leon Festinger and others (1964), who have studied contemporary millenarian groups. The theory of cognitive dissonance maintains that when a strongly held tenet of faith (like the date of the end of the world), is irrefutably shown to be false, the result is not the collapse of the sect, but a greater missionary drive. Thus a sense of cognitive dissonance is found between the non realisation of the sect's hopes that their evangelistic zeal seeks to redress. Robert Carroll (1979) has applied this to the Old Testament prophets, and John Gager (1975) to the early missionary zeal of Paul. Gager believes that when the *parousia* of Jesus failed to take place within the lifetime of the first apostles, this led not to a decrease, but to an increase in the missionary effort.

Meeks links this theory with that of status dislocation (cf. 2.2.3 below) and writes of the urban Christians:

> We might guess that people who have advanced or declined socially, who find themselves in an ambiguous relation to hierarchical structures, might be receptive to symbols of the world as itself out of joint and on the brink of radical transformation (Meeks 1983:174).

Both Gager and Meeks presuppose that there was a tendency to reduce the sense of dissonance as the sect and its members grew. A critique of this theory is found in Malina's study (1986a) of normative dissonance, which holds that a necessary aspect for the well-being of any community is some sense of dissonance. Far from attempting to resolve the inconsistency within their framework of varied and sometimes contradictory beliefs, early Christianity held them in tension. Malina argues that

> it was the dissonance itself along with the normative inconsistencies typical of early Christian movement groups that best accounts for the survival and growth of those groups (Malina 1986a:39).

Loss of such normative dissonance might well have been one of the causes of extremist groups in the ancient world and today.

2.2.3 Role analysis

Working essentially from psychological studies, role analysis studies the social role of a particular individual or group of individuals and the function of that role within the wider social context. Gerd Theissen has used this theory in his depiction of the social worlds of Jesus and of Paul respectively. He describes Jesus as a wandering charismatic (1978) and Paul as a community organiser (1982). Role analysis as used by Theissen works from a structural-functional perspective in contrast to the conflict perspective of historical materialism (Elliott 1986:11, cf. also p. 225 below).

Wayne Meeks' description of urban Christianity, and in particular his use of 'status dislocation or inconsistency' to explain the attraction of such Christianity, is a further example of role analysis. But where Theissen (1982) argues that high social status involves a high degree of consistency, Meeks opts for the opposite view (1983:70). Meeks believes that 'the strong' of Corinth were those of the congregation who were inconsistent in status (1983:70). For example large wealth (achieved status) and humble birth (perceived status) might destine an individual to such a sense of inconsistency. Yet within the circle of the church, he/she might find relief together with a new sense of belonging more in line with their 'achieved' status.

2.2.4 Sociology of knowledge

The work of Peter Berger and Thomas Luckmann (1966 and see Berger 1969) provides the groundwork here. The main idea is that the world in which we live is 'socially constructed and created, communicated and sustained through language and symbol' (Scroggs 1983:347). The advent of a new sect, like early

Christianity, implies the creation of a new 'symbolic universe'. Believers are inducted into the range of new symbols, or in some cases, old symbols with new content through the medium of their involvement within the new community. Meeks (1972), for example, shows how the Johannine community made use of the older symbol of a 'man from heaven' in their depiction of Jesus. They thus communicated a new idea in a guise long familiar to their Mediterranean audience.

The social construction of reality as a theory goes back ultimately to Ludwig Feuerbach and his thesis that religion is a projection of the mind, and the refinement of Emile Durkheim, who considered religion as the projection of a society. The projection model plays an integral part in sociological research and appears regularly in works that deal with the relationship between a group's beliefs and their identity (e.g. Gottwald 1979; Aune 1972; Domeris 1988; 1988a).

2.2.5 Marxist historical materialism

Marxist thinking operates from the starting point of the projection model outlined above and from Marx's famous statement that 'Being determines consciousness and not consciousness being'. Thus a tension is operative between matter (material) and the abstract or supernatural (idealism). Where the idealist scholar operates from the top down, the materialist scholar begins instead with an analysis of the social structure defining modes of production, and then moves on to superstructures and finally ideology. Norman Gottwald goes so far as to state that

> as long as we stay in the framework of idealism, there can be no sociology of religion for the simple reason that no lawful statements can be made about social phenomena, religion included, if they cannot be correlated and causally examined (Gottwald 1979:602).

Biblical scholars on the whole (e.g. Meeks 1972; Gottwald 1979 and Riches 1983) tend to use a dialectical model in which being and consciousness interact, so avoiding the danger of reductionism. In such a model space is given for the possibility that religious beliefs are not simply the reflection of the social being of the group, but in turn affect and alter the groups' patterns of behaviour (cf. Gottwald 1979:643).

Class conflict is the essence of historical materialism, as the work of De Ste Croix (1981), Belo (1976) and Clevenot (1985) illustrate. We should bear in mind, however, the caution voiced by Paul Hollenbach (1987:53), which reminds us of the dangers of foisting our own social consciousness upon the shoulders of the citizens of the first century. He argues that class was not in itself a sufficiently cohesive factor to sustain a full scale class conflict in the ancient world (following Carney 1975:198-199).

2.2.6 Legitimation

The process of legitimation is integral to Theissen's short essay on Corinth (1975), D. B. Woll's detailed examination of the leadership conflict in the Johannine community (1981) and my own study of the role of the Paraclete (1989). While Theissen and Woll speak of legitimation with regard to the rise of a new leader (Paul and the successor to the founder of the Johannine community respectively), I chose to develop this further by relating such legitimation to the belief that the Holy Spirit was operative in and through a particular leader (Domeris 1989:20). Thus the dominant ideology (held by the community) exercises an influence on the choice of a successor to the founder of the community. Conversely the leader is then able to utilise the belief in the Spirit to legitimate the leader's position in the community.

2.2.7 Community values

The pioneering work of the anthropologist Mary Douglas in the area of purity and symbolism, as this relates to the Old Testament (1966) has opened up the possibility of using her grid/group method on the New Testament. By ranking the relative ethics and values of a community, one can build up a picture of the community itself in comparison with the rest of the society of that time. So Leland White (1986) investigates the cultural values and social dynamics of the community behind the Sermon on the Mount. White concludes that the group was a strong one, with clear-cut boundaries between itself as the righteous remnant and those outside of the community, This low grid or mismatch with the prevailing norms, is further indicated in the apparent failure of the Matthean community to establish an hierarchy of leaders. A picture emerges of a small group secure within the parental protection of God, and living in tension with the prevailing ideologies.

2.2.8 Cultural anthropology

The name of Bruce Malina is synonomous for New Testament scholars with cultural anthropology. His two studies (1981, 1986b) have opened the way for biblical scholars to make use of the findings of cultural anthropologists. Of particular importance is his emphasis on status as independent of class, and of the wider context of 'the poor' as those suffering from relative deprivation rather than purely economic constraints. Unfortunately, Malina fails to come to terms with the harsh realities of political and economic oppression. By underplaying this dimension he falls short of creating an adequate ground upon which to build a reliable picture of first century Christianity. In spite of this, cultural anthropology remains an essential element of New Testament sociology.

2.2.9 Transformation of human experience

In his most recent book Theissen has suggested yet another approach to the social scientific study of the Bible. He combines three different psychological theories, that of learning theory, psychodynamics and cognition, to explain how religious symbolism can alter human behaviour and experience. He then applies these theories to different passages from the Pauline epistles. He looks at the function of the Jewish law, glossolalia and wisdom in his endeavour to develop a psychological form of exegesis. One of the more important of his conclusions is his belief 'that Christ is an avenue of access to the unconscious' (1987:396). Thus does Theissen seek to use this exegesis to describe and explain human behaviour in early Christianity (1987:1).

2.3 Models and perspectives

A criticism often levelled at those biblical scholars who employ social scientific methods is their lack of methodological preciseness. Malina (1983:239-240) speaks of 'vague implicit models and scholarly intuition' that results in 'theory proliferation and inconclusive 'conclusions' inaccessible to testing and validation'. Elliott (1986:6) calls for a clear statement by the respective scholars as to their choice of a model or models, together with a description of the chosen model. A good example of a scholar who does this is Gottwald in his *Tribes of Yahweh* (1979), and Malina in his article on normative dissonance (1986).

Elliott (1986:4) likens a model to a metaphor, as a means of comparison and for the purposes of using the known to explain the unknown. According to Malina (1983:14), 'a model is an abstract, simplified representation of some real world object, event, or interaction, constructed for the purpose of understanding, control or prediction'. Social scientists make use of what Carney (1975:11-12, quoted by Elliott 1986:5) calls homomorphic models, in contrast to the much more precise isomorphic model used, for example, in geography. An isomorphic model might be a scale model of a certain geographical feature, while an homomorphic model would represent something more abstract, such as the power hierarchy of a society.

A great variety of homomorphic models are open to one, but one's choice is often dictated by a prior decision, namely that of a perspective (Elliott 1986:7). Elliott distinguishes a model as a tool 'for transforming theories into research operations', from a perspective that represents a 'more encompassing' way or style 'of theorizing'. Such perspectives include structural-functionalism (as used by Theissen in his work on Jesus), conflict theory (basic to historical materialism), and symbolic interactionism (Berger's sociology of knowledge). Once the initial choice is made, one can move on to the choice of a model, which, as Malina (1983:22) points out, needs to be suitable for use of a first century situation.

Awareness of the differing perspectives enables the critical reader to understand why there remain major differences regarding the make up of the social class of early Christianity. Theissen (1978), for example, speaks of 'the poor' in the teaching of Jesus as those who have voluntarily chosen the path of poverty, as an expression of their radical itinerancy. He works within a perspective in which society is essentially stable and its structure and the functions of the different groups within that society are in harmony. His chosen perspective is that of structural-functionalism, in which society is in equilibrium, a collection of interrelated spheres and essentially static (cf. the critique in Malina 1983:16). By contrast, Hugo Echegaray (1984) works from the perspective of the conflict model, defining the means of production during Jesus' time, and drawing out the conflict between Jesus and the groups of his time as well as his concern for the poor and the marginalised members of his society. He works from the presupposition of a sustained conflict between different parts of society, such as between the ruling elite and the common people of the time. The conflict perspective visualises a society in motion (Malina 1983:17). Change is a normal part of life, and exists everywhere, except where some group uses its power to thwart change. So, for example, superstructures imply a degree of rigidity that results in conflict.

At an even deeper level the biblical scholar may be faced with a choice of a paradigm. Following Elliott (1986:7), a paradigm refers to 'the traditions, presuppositions, and methods of a discipline as a whole'. In the field of biblical studies one of the prevailing paradigms is that of the historical-critical method. Another would be literary analysis, such as structuralism.

The sociological study of the Bible necessitates a variety of choices, which ultimately affect the findings of one's research. By stating in advance one's choices, from paradigm through perspective to model, one opens one's work up to critical analysis. Only in this way can social science make its proper contribution to the study of the Bible.

3. Social History and Sociological studies in practice

We have considered at length the theoretical aspects of social histories and sociological studies of the New Testament. For a more detailed survey, I recommend Norman Gottwald's *The Bible and Liberation* (1983), and for the Old Testament, Robert Wilson's *Sociological Approaches to the Old Testament* (1984). We now turn to a study of two examples of exegesis utilising these methodologies.

3.1 A social historical study of John 9

The object of a social historical study of a particular book of the Bible is to read that book from the perspective of the community in which it came to fruition. Unfortunately there is a lack of supplementary evidence about the community. One is not in the same position as, for example, the student who examines the Dead Sea scrolls and who has access to the archeological data from Khirbet Qumran. In the case of the Johannine community, one is limited to the Gospel and the First Epistle, and a variety of indirect evidence in the form of late first century Jewish texts, the Nag Hammadi library, and the earliest papyri of the Gospel found in Egypt. To this one can add the investigations of possible locations for that community, varying from Ephesus, or Antioch (Brown 1984; Brown & Meier 1983) to Alexandria (cf. Domeris 1988:54). The bulk of the evidence for the community comes from the documents themselves. The scholar needs therefore to develop a sense of reading between the lines in order to map out the structure of the community, its symbolic universe and its history.

Martyn has proposed such a reading in terms of what he calls a two-level approach to the Gospel (Martyn 1979:129). He believes that the history of the community intrudes upon the Gospel's presentation of Jesus. To the critical eye, the Gospel may become transparent to that history. In my own work (Domeris & Wortley 1988), I have chosen to speak of the three horizons within the Gospels. There is the horizon of Jesus' own time, that of the community in which the Gospel was written and our own perspective that we bring as readers. Following Martyn, I believe it is possible, in some measure, to delineate these horizons.

John 9 tells a story of a blind man from birth. In its simplest form the genre of the story is that of a healing miracle, taken from the original Signs Source. But as it now stands it testifies to the drama of the exclusion of the Johannine community from their parent synagogue, and to their own quest for faith in Jesus (cf. Martyn 1979:24-62).

The chapter opens with the introduction of the blind man, and in verses 4 and 5 the theme of the chapter, namely spiritual light and darkness, is made manifest. 'Night is coming' prophesies Jesus in verse 4b, and he speaks of his departure. This word addresses directly the pain of the Johannine community, when they thought that Jesus had abandoned them, as the waves of persecution and opposition rose to engulf them. But Jesus did not leave them alone, and the community understands his new role as 'the light' in which the Holy Spirit remains as the *alter ego* of their Lord (Martyn 1979:145).

Jesus heals the man (6-8) and we hear his initial testimony, as he takes his first step towards belief. His knowledge, like the early Johannine community before the writing of the Gospel, is limited to the idea of Jesus as a prophetic wonder worker (cf. 17b). He is at this point at the level of the Signs Source. The man is questioned by the Pharisees, and we realise that the chapter is taking the format of a trial. The accused is not the blind man, but Jesus (cf. 24), with the man and his parents acting as witnesses in the proceedings. Yet the role of the witnesses is complicated, for a threat is levelled against them, the threat of excommunication (22, 23).

The parents are cowed, but not their son. He challenges the Pharisees (25), 'This one thing I know; once I was blind, but now I can see'. There is a pun on the word 'see', as the end of the chapter will show. The 'blind' man, like the Johannine community, can 'see' Jesus and his divine nature, whereas the educated elite of Israel cannot.

In verse 27 the man inquires of the Pharisees if they *also* wish to become Jesus' disciples. The 'also' is significant, for it indicates that the man has decided to follow Jesus. That is how the Pharisees understand his state (28), and they then insult him. But their insult has a hollow ring, and simply underlines their own blindness. They follow Moses, yet the evangelist has already shown that Moses, who wrote of Jesus (5:46), will be their judge (5:45). We sense the conflict between the Johannine community and the attempt to create an orthodox Judaism on the part of their parent synagogue. Verse 29 sums up the synagogue's view of Jesus, as they claim not to know from whence he comes. Indeed they are blind to his heavenly origin. We sense that the 'struggle between the two is one of words and arguments, of questions of authority and power and the major issue of the person of Jesus' (Domeris & Wortley 1988:70).

The once blind man, devoid of formal education, now faults the teachers of the law (30-33). Is there a clue here to the educational status of some members of the Johannine community? The Pharisees then cast the man out of the synagogue, in line with the later Twelfth Benediction against heretics in general (promulgated by the rabbis of Jamnia in about 85 C.E., and the key to the dating of the Fourth Gospel). In their eyes he is 'steeped with sin' (34, cf. the debate in 2), as a person without any formal education. But that is where they are wrong, for from the perspective of the Johannine Christians the real sin is the spiritual blindness of the judges (39-41).

The story moves beyond the walls of the synagogue, where Jesus meets the man, and reveals to him his divine nature (35-37) as the Child of Humanity (Son of Man). The man responds by worshipping Jesus. So we see his path to faith revealed, as his healing leads to his testimony to Jesus as prophet, the worker of miracles (17b), to his expulsion from the synagogue for accepting Jesus as Messiah (implicit in 34), and to the final acknowledgement of Jesus' divinity (37). This is the very same path that was followed by the members of the Johannine community as they moved from the prophetic faith of the Signs Source and their place in the synagogue, through the trauma of their excommunication in about 85 C.E., to the writing of the Gospel with its unequivocal testimony to Jesus' divinity.

From this short exegesis we see something of the way in which a social historian like Brown or Martyn rereads the Gospel from that perspective, and so

constructs and develops a social history. The main criticism against this
methodology is the lack of outside evidence to form some kind of control, and
the fact that the reconstruction is both developed and confirmed from the same
texts.

3.2 Sociological exegesis

The term Sociological Exegesis was coined by Elliott in his work on the First
Epistle of Peter (1981). The method is sociological in that it involves 'the employment of the perspectives, presuppositions, modes of analysis, comparative
models, theories and research of the discipline of sociology' (1981:8). The
method is exegetical in that it deals with the biblical text and utilises exegetical
subdisciplines so as to arrive at 'the meaning...of the text, within its various
contexts' (1981:8).

I have chosen the well-known parable from Luke 15, the Prodigal Son, in order to show how social science can benefit the exegete. In my choice of a model,
I have decided to move into the discipline of cultural anthropology and to apply
Malina's understanding of honour and status in the Mediterranean world of that
time, which is based in turn upon the model of structural functionalism
(1981:47).

'Honor', according to Malina (1981:27), 'might be described as socially proper attitudes and behavior in the area where the three lines of power, sexual
status, and religion intersect'. He goes on to speak in terms of one's value in the
eyes of oneself and others of one's social grouping. He writes: 'When you lay
claim to a certain status as embodied by your power and in your sexual role, you
are claiming honor' (1981:27). Conversely society accords one the place on the
social ladder that one's honour rating justifies. This is termed 'a grant of reputa-
tion' (1981:28). Failure to achieve this grant means that one's claim to honour is
regarded as 'foolish'.

The Mediterranean world of the first century was *agonsitic*, which means that
'every social interaction that takes place outside of one's family...is perceived as
a challenge to honor, a mutual attempt to acquire honor from one's social
equal' (1981:32). One may loose such a contest, in which case one's honour is
considered to be 'in a state of desecration' that would render a person 'socially
dishonored and dishonorable' (1981:35-36). If one attempts to restore one's
honour, then it is returned to the state of the sacred, even where such an
attempt is unsuccessful. The person is rescued from his or her shamefulness.

Honour is reflected in one's person (particularly the head) and one's dress.
Honour should be understood both individually and corporately: 'social groups
possess a collective honor' (1981:38).

We turn now to the parable and we note several significant details. In the
first place, it is the younger of the two sons who makes demands of his father

(Lk 15:12). Here is an implicit threat to the position of the older son, for the father cannot give the younger son his inheritance before attending to his first born. The father takes cognizance of this fact. We read that he gives both sons their inheritance, and so neutralises the conflict.

The riotous living of the younger boy results in his loss of wealth. He becomes poor, not in the sense that he joins a particular group or substrata of society (cf. Malina 1981:81), but in the sense that he is no longer able to maintain his status, as the heir of a land-owner. Verse 15 recounts his interaction with a 'citizen' of that country. The term 'citizen' (πολίτης) suggests, in the context of the story, a person of substance and of secure social standing in the land. In other words, here is someone of an equal or better social standing than the son. The scene is set for the challenge contest.

The son retains his status, even without the presence of his wealth and family until the moment he goes to feed the pigs (15b) as a hired worker. At that moment he loses the status challenge, for he is not accorded work that is befitting of his station. He is shamed by that society and his honour is desecrated. The actual presence of the unclean pigs seems to underline the depths of depravity into which he has fallen.

The shame is not limited to the boy as an individual, but reflects upon his family. Thus he speaks in terms of sinning against his father, and against the religion of his family (heaven), ultimately God. The corporate honour of his family has been dragged in the dust, precisely because 'the sin' has occurred in a foreign land. To be shamed by strangers was the greater insult.

In the pigsty, his honour in disgrace, the boy decides to return home. He has little faith that he will be accorded his original status, but he will nevertheless attempt to salvage something, if only to save his own life ('I am starving to death': 17). 'I am no longer worthy...' he will say to his father, and so give an accurate assessment of his state. Indeed he may no longer speak as son to the father, but as an hired labourer, a servant looking for work. The whole speech of the son is resonant with the ancient system of honour and shame.

The compassion of the father knows no bounds, for when he sees the returning son, he abandons dignity and rushes down the road. As with the two preceding parables, the joy and celebration seem out of all proportion to the occasion. Who celebrates for one coin or one lost sheep? Which father, who has suffered hurt and shame, runs down the road to find his prodigal?

In the father's eagerness he cuts short the prepared speech of the boy, and so reinstates him as his son and heir. The cloak and shoes speak of the restored status and authority, just as before their absence spoke of the lack of these properties. These were the elements lost by the boy because of his work and not because of his poverty. Barefoot and denied the honour of a cloak, the sign of a head of a household, he would have been seen as one of the many thousands of day-labourers who haunted the streets during Jesus' time. But now the father brings the best robe, one of his own, kept for special guests, and a ring, the symbol of authority and power. Nor does he stop there, for he orders the slaughter of the fatted calf, which by custom was kept for visiting dignitories, and visitors of high social status. Now it becomes the extravagent sign of the father's acceptance, and the upliftment of the prodigal.

The elder son, who represents in the parable the righteous teachers of the Law (Lk 15:2), is angry when he finds out what is happening in the house. He refuses to enter, and so undercuts the acceptance shown by the father. Justifiably he criticises the boy who has brought shame on the head of the family. He cannot understand why his father is acting in a manner out of keeping with social norms. The boy has squandered the father's wealth, and shamed them all, and even now has come back to live like a parasite on the estate of the elder brother. Yet the father celebrates. It does not make sense!

Does the father reward the boy because he has done the noble thing in attempting to regain his honour? The story suggests otherwise. The father is motivated by an overwhelming love, and a mercy that aparrently knows no bounds. He closes the door on his son's past and opens a new door right back into his former place of social esteem and honour. The honour once desecrated is now made pure and clean. The love of the father, and the Parent God, heals the ravages of sin.

The end of the parable is not disclosed, and we do not know what the elder son decides to do. Will he accept his brother as a brother or only as a servant? Here is the heart of the parable, by which Jesus challenges the Pharisees to accept the marginalised members of society (the poor, sinful and uneducated), as brothers and sisters in the community of God. Will they eat and feast with them as Jesus had done? By doing so, they will restore the honour of those to whom they have denied honour, by their carefully contrived walls of ritual purity and education.

Sadly, like the church leaders who will follow them, they seem reluctant to admit that God has declared all people to be joint-heirs of the reign of God. Tightly they hold onto the keys of the human social ordering with its castes, classes and levels of purity and education. So the parable retains its ability to speak into all societies where humankind erects barriers, by which some people are declared or perceived to be 'better' than others.

The note of judgment of the parable is softened by the father's words, as he assures the elder son of his love, and reminds him that all the father has, belongs to him. Indeed as the elder son, the right to the land is his. But the message to that son is also Jesus' reminder to the Pharisees of their special place as the elders of Israel.

4. Conclusion

We have considered the methods of social history and sociological analysis as they relate to the study of the Bible. What remains is to relate this to the urgency of the South African situation. Sociological and social historical methodologies provide us with some of the most important tools for the creation of a South African theology of liberation. In particular, a knowledge of the social history of Jesus' time can equip ordinary people to develop a contextual theology of their own, and to devise their own strategies for fighting oppression and injustice.

Such a process of contextualisation will not happen so long as academics hide themselves in ivory towers, and the truth of the Gospel and the insights of sociological exegesis remain in the preserve of the rich and powerful. The urgent task is then to awaken the people to the liberating message of the Bible. In this regard the challenge of the parable in Luke 15 might well have been addressed to university teachers, with their academic lines of ritual purity and defilement. The interpretation of the parable is, then, back in their hands.

BIBLIOGRAPHY

Aune, D. E. 1972. *The Cultic Setting of Realised Eschatology in Early Christianity*. Leiden: Brill.

Baum, G. 1975. *Religion and Alienation. A Theological Reading of Sociology*. New York: Paulist.

Belo, F. 1976. *A Materialist Reading of the Gospel of Mark*. Maryknoll, New York: Orbis.

Berger, P. L. 1969. *The Sacred Canopy: Elements of a Sociological Theory of Religion*. Garden City, New York: Doubleday.

Berger, P. L. & Luckmann, T. 1966. *The Social Construction of Reality. A Treatise in the Sociology of Knowledge*. Garden City, New York: Doubleday.

Brown, R. E. 1979. *The Community of the Beloved Disciple*. London: Geoffrey Chapman.

Brown, R. E. 1984. *The Churches the Apostles Left Behind*. London: Geoffrey Chapman.

Brown, R. E. & Meier, J. P. 1983. *Antioch and Rome*. London: Geoffrey Chapman.

Burridge, K. 1969. *New Heaven, New Earth: A Study of Millenarian Activities*. New York: Schocken Books.

Carney, T. F. 1975. *The Shape of the Past. Models in Antiquity*. Lawrence, Kansas: Coronado Press.

Carroll, R. 1979. *When Prophecy Failed*. New York: Seabury.

Cassidy, R. 1978. *Jesus, Politics and Society. A Study of Luke's Gospel*. Maryknoll, New York: Orbis.

Clevenot, M. 1985. *Materialist Approaches to the Bible*. Maryknoll, New York: Orbis.

De Ste Croix, G. E. M. 1981. *The Class Struggle in the Ancient Greek World*. London: Duckworth.

Domeris, W. R. 1986. Book Review of W. Meeks *The First Urban Christians*. *Journal for Theology in Southern Africa* 55, 72-74.

Domeris, W. R. 1987. *Portraits of Jesus. Matthew. A Contextual Approach to Bible Study*. London: Collins Liturgical.

Domeris, W. R. 1988. Christology and Community: A Study of the Social Matrix of the Fourth Gospel. *Journal for Theology in Southern Africa* 64, 49-56.

Domeris, W. R. 1988a. Social Scientific Study of the Early Christian Churches: New Paradigms and Old Questions, in J. Mouton, A. G. van Aarde & W. S. Vorster (eds.). *Paradigms and Progress in Theology*. Pretoria: Human Sciences Research Council (Human Sciences

Research Council Studies in Methodology 5), 378-393.

Domeris, W. R. & Wortley, R. 1988. *Portraits of Jesus. John. A Contextual Approach to Bible Study*. London: Collins Liturgical.

Douglas, M. 1966. *Purity and Danger. An Analysis of Concepts of Pollution and Taboo*. Baltimore: Penguin Books.

Echegaray, H. 1984. *The Practice of Jesus*. (Tr. by M. O'Connell.) Maryknoll, New York: Orbis.

Edersheim, A. 1876. *Sketches of Jewish Social Life in the Days of Christ*. London: The Religious Tract Society.

Elliott, J. H. 1981. *A Home for the Homeless. A Sociological Exegesis of I Peter. Its Situation and Strategy*. Philadelphia: Fortress.

Elliott, J. H. 1986. Social-Scientific Criticism of the New Testament: More on Methods and Models. *Semeia* 35, 1-33.

Festinger, L., Reicken, H. W. & Schachter, S. 1956. *When Prophecy Fails: A Social and Psychological Study of a Modern Group that Predicted the Destruction of the World*. New York: Harper & Row.

Freyne, S. 1980. *Galilee from Alexander the Great to Hadrian 323 B.C.E. to 135 C.E.: A Study of Second Temple Judaism*. Chicago: University of Notre Dame Press.

Freyne, S. 1988. *Galilee, Jesus and the Gospels. Literary Approaches and Historical Investigations*. Dublin: Gill & Macmillan.

Gager, J. C. 1975. *Kingdom and Community: The Social World of Early Christianity*. New York: Prentice Hall.

Gager, J. C. 1982. Shall We Marry our Enemies? Sociology and the New Testament. *Interpretation* 37, 256-265.

Gottwald, N. K. 1979. *The Tribes of Yaweh: A Sociology of the Religion of Liberated Israel, 1250-1050 B.C.E.*. Maryknoll, New York: Orbis.

Gottwald, N. K. 1983a. Bibliography on the Social Scientific Study of the Old Testament. *American Baptist Quarterly* 2, 142-156.

Grant, R. M. 1977. Early Christianity and Society. New York: Scribners.

Grant, R. M. 1986. *Gods and the One God*. Philadelphia: Westminster. (Library of Early Christianity.)

Hock, R. F. 1980. *The Social Context of Paul's Ministry: Tentmaking and Apostleship*. Philadelphia: Fortress.

Hollenbach, P. 1983. Recent Historical Jesus Studies and the Social Studies, in K. H. Richards (ed.). *Society of Biblical Literature 1983 Seminar Papers*. Chicago, California: Scholars Press, 61-78.

Hollenbach, P. 1987. Defining Rich and Poor Using Social Sciences, in K. H. Richards (ed.). *Society of Biblical Literature 1987 Seminar Papers*. Atlanta, Georgia: Scholars Press, 50-63.

Horsley, R. 1987. *Jesus and the Spiral of Violence. Popular Jewish Resistance in Roman Palestine*. San Francisco: Harper & Row.

Jeremias, J. 1969. *Jerusalem in the Time of Jesus*. (Tr. by F. H. Cave & C. H. Cave.) Philadelphia: Fortress.

Judge, E. A. 1960. *The Social Patterns of Christian Groups in the First Century*. London: Tyndale.

Malherbe, A. 1983. *Social Aspects of Early Christianity*. 2nd ed. Philadelphia: Fortress.

Malherbe, A. 1986. *Moral Exhortation: A Greco-Roman Source-Book*. Philadelphia: Westminster. (Library of Early Christianity.)

Malherbe, A. 1987. *Paul and the Thessalonians. The Philosophic Tradition of Pastoral Care*. Philadelphia: Fortress.

Malina, B. 1981. *The New Testament World: Insights from Cultural Anthropology*. Atlanta: John Knox Press.

Malina, B. 1983. The Social Sciences and Biblical Interpretation, in N. K. Gottwald (ed.). *The Bible and Liberation: Political and Social Hermeneutics*. Maryknoll, New York: Orbis, 11-25.

Malina, B. 1986a. Normative Dissonance and Christian Origins. *Semeia* 35, 35-59.

Malina, B. 1986b. *Christian Origins and Cultural Anthropology: Practical Models for Biblical Interpretation*. Atlanta: John Knox Press.

Martyn, J. L. 1979. *History and Theology in the Fourth Gospel*. Nashville: Abingdon.

Meeks, W. A. 1972. The Man from Heaven in Johannine Sectarianism. *Journal of Biblical Literature* 91, 44-72.

Meeks, W. A. 1983. *The First Urban Christians: The Social World of the Apostle Paul*. New Haven: Yale University Press.

Meeks, W. A. 1986. *The Moral World of the First Christians*. Philadelphia: Westminster. (Library of Early Christianity.)

Meeks, W. A. & Wilken, R. 1978. *Jews and Christians in Antioch of the First Four Centuries of the Common Era*. Missoula, Montana: Scholars Press.

Nolan, A. 1976. *Jesus before Christianity. The Gospel of Liberation*. London: Darton, Longman & Todd.

Oakman, D. 1986. *Jesus and Economonic Questions of his Day*. Lewiston, Queenston: Edwin Mellen Press. (Studies in the Bible and Early Christianity 8.)

Pixley, G. V. 1983. God's Kingdom in First Century Palestine: The Strategy of Jesus, in N. K. Gottwald (ed.). *The Bible and Liberation: Political and Social Hermeneutics*. Maryknoll, New York: Orbis, 378-393.

Riches, J. K. 1983. The Sociology of Matthew: Some Basic Questions concerning its Relation to the Theology of the New Testament, in K. H. Richards (ed.). *Society of Biblical Literature 1983 Seminar Papers*. Chico, California: Scholars Press, 259-271.

Schüssler Fiorenza, E. 1983. 'You are not to be called Father': Early Christian History in a Feminist Perspective, in N. K. Gottwald (ed.). *The Bible and Liberation: Political and Social Hermeneutics*. Maryknoll, New York: Orbis, 394-417.

Schottroff, L. 1983. Women as Followers of Jesus in New Testament Times: An Exercise in Social-Historical Exegesis of the Bible, in N. K. Gottwald (ed.). *The Bible and Liberation: Political and Social Hermeneutics*. Maryknoll, New York: Orbis, 418-427.

Schottroff, L. & Steggemann, W. 1986. *Jesus and the Hope of the Poor*. (Tr. by M. O'Connell.) Maryknoll, New York: Orbis.

Scroggs, R. 1975. The Earliest Christian Communities as Sectarian Movement, in J. Neusner. *Christianity and Judaism and other Greco-Roman Cults*, v. 2. Leiden: Brill, 1-23.

Scroggs, R. 1983. The Sociological Interpretation of the New Testament, in N. K. Gottwald (ed.). *The Bible and Liberation: Political and Social Hermeneutics*. Maryknoll, New York: Orbis, 337-356.

Smith, J. Z. 1975. The Social Description of Early Christianity. *Religious Studies Review* 1, 19-25.

Smith, R. 1983. Were the Early Christians Middle-Class? A Sociological Analysis of the New Testament, in N. K. Gottwald (ed.). *The Bible and Liberation: Political and Social Hermeneutics*. Maryknoll, New York: Orbis, 441-460.

Stambaugh, J. E. & Balch, D. L. 1986. *The New Testament in its Social Environment*. Philadelphia: Westminster. (Library of Early Christianity.)

Theissen, G. 1975. Ligitimation und Lebensunterhalt: Ein Beitrag zur Soziologie urchristlicher Missionäre. *New Testament Studies* 21, 192-221.

Theissen, G. 1978. *Sociology of Early Palestinian Christianity*. (Tr. by J. Bowden.) Philadelphia: Fortress.

Theissen, G. 1982. *The Social Setting of Pauline Christianity: Essays on Corinth*. (Tr. and ed. by J. H. Schütz.) Philadelphia: Fortress.

Theissen, G. 1983. The Sociological Interpretation of Religious Traditions: Its Methodological Problems as Exemplified in Early Christianity, in N. K. Gottwald (ed.). *The Bible and Liberation: Political and Social Hermeneutics*. Maryknoll, New York: Orbis.

Theissen, G. 1987. *Psychological Aspects of Pauline Theology*. (Tr. by J. P. Galvin.) Philadelphia: Fortress.

White, L. J. 1986. Grid and Group in Matthew's Community: The Righteousness/Honor Code in the Sermon on the Mount. *Semeia* 36, 61-90.

Wilson, R. R. 1984. *Sociological Approaches to the Old Testament*. Philadelphia: Fortress.

Woll, D. B. 1981. *Johannine Christianity in Conflict*. Chico, California: Scholars Press.

J. A. DRAPER

'FOR THE KINGDOM IS INSIDE OF YOU AND IT IS OUTSIDE OF YOU': CONTEXTUAL EXEGESIS IN SOUTH AFRICA

1. Historical framework of the debate in South Africa

Ordinary readers of the Bible in South Africa have remained, by and large, within a pre-critical, naive frame of reference. The Bible is read with little insight into either its historical context or the influence of the reader's context on the process of interpretation (Draper & West 1989). Ideologically loaded 'study guides', mostly from the United States, are often used without reflection on the differences in the relative socio-economic situations. This presents a major stumbling block in the way of a biblical contribution to the current South African debate.

1.1 Historical criticism

The problem of reading the New Testament in South Africa has been compounded by the hermeneutical traditions of the academic community in South Africa. Ministers trained within the churches originating from the English-speaking world have been heir to the historical-critical tradition of Western Europe, although this has made little impact on their congregations (Draper & West 1989).

The *diachronic* approach of historical-critical analysis has aimed at the elucidation of the genesis of the text, how it came to have its present form. Questions concerning the 'author' or the 'author's environment' (*Sitz im Leben*) have played a central role in such studies. Questions concerning the *meaning* of the text for today were bracketed off, and relegated to systematics or homiletics. This led to a fundamental hiatus in the interpretative process (Jeanrond 1988:1-8), which was recognised by Bultmann.

Bultmann was concerned above all

> to avoid their [historical-critical and history-of-religions schools'] mistake which consists of the tearing apart of the act of thinking from the act of living and hence of a failure to recognise the intent of theological utterances (Bultmann 1955:250).

Bultman's work of historical 'reconstruction' has been taught and used in 'English-speaking' circles in South Africa, without much understanding of or interest in his existentialist 'interpretation'. For Bultmann himself, however, the process of historical 'reconstruction' stands in the service of 'interpretation', 'under the presuppostion that they [the New Testament writings] have something to say to the present' (Bultmann 1955:250).

Bultmann's hermeneutic emerged out of an intense debate in Europe about the possibility of historical interpretation. Failure to recognise this has neutralised Bultmann's challenge and potential for the 'English-speaking churches', and their exegesis has remained a matter of theory learned in the academy with no impact beyond it.[1] Many in the English-speaking world have continued to insist on the possibility of 'disinterested and objective study in biblical criticism' (Davies & Allison 1988:xi),[2] in spite of a general agreement in the scientific community that 'all data are theory laden' (Hanson 1961; Barbour 1966:176-191). To a large extent, we see in the text what we expect to see there, and even the questions we ask of it and the answers we are prepared to consider are determined by our social context (Kuhn 1962; cf. Cone 1975:15; Ricoeur 1981:57-59; Downing 1987:10; Croatto 1987:66-67; Baum 1989[3]). The failure of the historical-critical exegetes in South Africa to acknowledge and analyse their social situation and preconceptions has meant that they reflect uncritically their own middle-class, white capitalist values.[4]

1.2 Text immanent approaches

The failure of the *diachronic* historical-critical method led to a new school of *synchronic* interpreters, who refused to go behind the present form of the text: structuralists, deconstructionists, narratologists and rhetorical analysts. This move from the 'author' to the 'text' has been hailed by some as a 'paradigm shift' in biblical interpretation (Crotty 1985:15-30), but it seems instead to be part of a wider process of questioning and redefinition.

This new hermeneutic was enthusiastically adopted by most biblical scholars within churches originating from the Afrikaans community. This has, in some

---

[1]   There are exceptions to this blindness to the implications of Bultmann's theory of *interpretation*, e.g. Professor J. Suggit (1987a; 1987b).

[2]   The starkness of this editorial statement of the I.C.C. was first brought to my attention by a paper given by L. Moore to the St. John's Theological Society in November 1988.

[3]   Professor Baum was to present this paper at the University of Cape Town, but was prevented from attending in person by the refusal of an entry visa by the South African government.

[4]   Bultmann himself, despite his acknowledgement of such 'pre-understanding' in exegesis (1955:234-261; 1961:289-296, 314-315), does not analyse his own captivity to his middle-class German socio-economic situation. The consequences of his existentialist position are an extreme individualism, which reduces the challenge of the gospel to pesonal decision, and ignores the challenge of social issues: 'Today the limitations of existentialist interpretation become clearer because the real unredeemed state of mankind looks different. Therefore, one must arrive at an ideological critique of this existentialist interpretation. But one must still keep in mind the concrete experiential content behind the outline of existence theology' (Moltmann 1968:318; cf.

ways, isolated the ministers trained within this tradition from the challenges of both the Enlightenment[5] and of the socio-political crisis. Nothing outside the text is allowed to intrude on the interpretative process. It has also had the effect of 'mystification' of reading the Bible, so that it becomes the property of the academic community. Narrative theories, in which the reader is envisaged as disappearing into the text, take on the nature of the snake swallowing its own tail (cf. Placher's critique of Frei and Lindbeck 1987:35-38).

'Interesting readings' abound in the New Testament Society of South Africa (e.g. the 1988 Conference Papers collected in *Neotestamentica* 22), but outside the gate stand the angry youth asking why they should read the Bible at all!

> What is the *point* of literary theory? Why bother with it in the first place? Are there not issues in the world more weighty than codes, signifiers and reading subjects? (Eagleton 1983:194).

Eagleton's challenge to literary criticism is that method is determined funda-mentally by what the critic wants to do, even when the critic does not want to acknowledge that fact:

> In any academic study we select the objects and methods of procedure which we believe the most important, and our assessment of their importance is governed by frames of interest deeply rooted in our practical forms of social life (Eagleton 1983:210-211).

In other words, every method of reading of the New Testament, including the text-immanent approach, is fraught with the preconceptions and socio-economic interests of the reader.[6] The only question is whether the reader is aware or unaware of them, open or covert in her/his interests (cf. Baum 1989; West 1989). The claim to be engaged in 'value neutral' research 'is actually a powerful ideological instrument that helps to reconcile the intellectual community with the existing social order' (Baum 1989:13).

Käsemann 1969:260-285 and Schottroff & Stegemann 1986:v-viii, 1-6).

5   The conservative religious revival in the white Dutch Reformed Church in 1860, following Andrew Murray's move to Worcester, led to the decline and eventual defeat of liberalism in the Reformed family of churches in South Africa, after the heresy trials of Ds. Kotze and T. F. Burgers (Hinchliff 1968:79-84).

6   For Paul Ricoeur, this follows from the fundamental conditioning of self-understanding by factors external to the self, so that 'the understanding of the self is always indirect and proceeds from the interpretation of signs given outside me in culture and history from the appropriation of the meaning of these signs' (Mudge 1980:12).

1.3 Explanation and Understanding

Both the historical-critical method and text-immanent readings, in their different ways, represent a failure of the hermeneutical endeavour. At least, if the purpose of a text is 'to say something to someone about something beyond itself', then it must be said that both methods end up saying nothing about anything beyond the text, certainly nothing relevant to the South African crisis:

> Any discourse purporting to 'say something to someone about something' presupposes the contextual closure that renders it intelligible. Otherwise it is not a message. There are no universal languages (Croatto 1983:164).

Here Croatto draws on the distinction Ricoeur derives from Dilthey between *explanation* and *understanding* (Ricoeur 1965:21-40; 1981:43-62). Neither the quest for historical origins nor internal linguistic analysis can, by themselves, produce a satisfactory reading of the text:

> The essential question is not to recover, behind the text, the lost intention, but to unfold, in front of the text, the 'world' which it opens up and discloses. In other words, the hermeneutical task is to discern the 'matter' of the text (Gadamer) and not the psychology of the author... We cannot stop at the immanent structure, at the internal system of dependencies arising from the crossing of the 'codes' which the text employs; we wish moreover to explicate the world which the text projects. (Ricoeur 1981:111).

Historical criticism and structural analysis of texts remain at the level of explanation, concerned with the text or its genesis and not with its references to a world beyond itself, to a meaning. This is the 'revelatory power' of the text to 'disclose a possible world' (Ricoeur 1981:19; cf. Croatto 1987:50). Neither of these methods is able to arrive at the place of understanding, where exegesis enables the reader to make an *appropriation* of meaning.

This 'Babylonian captivity' of the Bible has allowed it to become the tool of the oppressors in South Africa. The academics and clergy within the churches have remained methodologically silenced or immobilised, while the people have continued to read the Bible without any assistance from the South African academic community. This has served the interests of the *status quo*, what Nolan calls 'the system' (Nolan 1988:68-88), which continues to use the Bible to legitimate its domination and exploitation of the people (Draper 1988:30-41).

1.4 Reading from below

Questions were raised powerfully by the movement of black consciousness in the nineteen-seventies, concerning the ideological oppression of blacks by white culture. The Church was also sujected to ideological critique, and the mask of legitimation of the system was exposed for what it is. This movement finally bore fruit in the deliberations leading to the *Kairos Document* (in 1986), which was a provisional statement of a revolutionary new perspective for the Church in South Africa. The challenge of the *Kairos Document* to the Church is also a challenge to the exegesis of the Bible, since it represents its programme as an attempt to restore a genuinely *biblical* theology:

> To be truly prophetic, our response would have to be, in the first place solidly grounded in the Bible. Our KAIROS impels us to *return to the Bible* and to search the Word of God for a message that is relevant to what we are experiencing in South Africa *today*. (*Kairos* 1986:17).

The *Kairos Document* rightly asserts the importance of the people in the struggle for justice in South Africa, so that 'real change and true justice can only come from below, from the people – most of whom are Christians in our context'. The Bible has often been treated as a kind of specialist handbook, accessible only to the trained scholar. In Latin America, the rediscovery of the Bible by the people has had a powerful effect (Cardenal 1982; Mesters 1983), and there are signs that this is happening in South Africa today. Compared with the focus of historical-critical study on the production of the text, the focus of text-immanent studies on the text itself, the new focus on the *reader* constitutes a further paradigm shift (Lategan 1984:1-17). However, a return to a naive, pre-critical reading of the text will not solve the hermeneutical crisis. It has often been noted that 'the ruling ideology is the ideology of the rulers', and this is confirmed by preliminary research into how actual readers operate (Draper & West 1989).

Mesters and Cardenal are effective only to the extent that they can inculcate a liberative approach to the Bible:

> The Bible is ambiguous. It can be a force for liberation or a force for oppression. If it is treated like a finished monument that cannot be touched, that must be taken literally as it is, then it will be an oppresive force. (Mesters 1983:124).

The foundation stone of Mester's method may be described as a 'hermeneutics of suspicion' founded on Marxian economic analysis. This is the fundamental challenge our modern culture presents to the gospel message, and it must be faced not evaded (cf. Mudge 1980:4-5). However, the readings of the people in *The Gospel in Solentiname* bypass the question of whether a particular reading may be legitimate or illegitimate (Boff 1987:141).[7] They sever the text altogether from its historical roots, which also removes the possibility of critical dialogue.

---

[7]   C. Boff captures the danger in a graphic image drawn from Gregory the Great: 'Who jerks the teat, draws butter; who bites it, blood' (Boff 1987:299, note 56).

The appeal made by the *Kairos Document* to the Bible cannot, by itself, solve the crisis, since the interpretative methods currently taught and used in South Africa are not appropriate to the development of a liberation theology based on the Bible. T. A. Mofokeng has argued that 'the Bible itself is indeed a serious problem to people who want to be free' (Mofokeng 1988:37), and that historical critical study is the 'hermeneutical yoke of the oppressor' (Mofokeng 1988:39).[8] I. J. Mosala points to the problem of the 'oppresor in the text', since the Bible was written by the powerful and not the oppressed (Mosala 1987). For Mosala, the consequence is a radical questioning of the possibility of deriving liberative theology from the Bible, except by using it as a text-book of the class-struggle (Mosala 1987; cf. Croatto 1987:51-52).

In attempting to formulate a contextual hermeneutic for South Africa, I accept the reading of the Bible by ordinary people as the presupposition and goal of the whole enterprise (Mesters 1983:125-130; cf. Schottroff & Steggemann 1986:vi; Boff 1987:150). I have attempted to avoid an entirely subjective reading of the text, although the crucial question of 'truth' may remain elusive or even insoluble. I concur with Ricoeur in his determination to 'resist the temptation to separate *truth*, characteristic of understanding, from the *method* put into operation by disciplines which have sprung from exegesis' (Ricoeur 1981:19; cf. Bauckham 1989:16-17).[9] This paper is an attempt to respond methodologically to the challenge of the *Kairos Document* in the production of a contextual exegesis that can empower an appropriation of meaning from the New Testament text by those engaged in the struggle for democracy in South Africa today.

2. Methodological theses

2.1 The priority of event

Text and, indeed, all discourse is initially the interpretation of prior event or experience:

---

[8]   Mofokeng himself argues for a purely pragmatic use of Scripture in the struggle. C. Boff perceptively calls this approach a kind of 'hermeneutic improvisation' that forms 'an open door to a riotous carnival of meanings' (1987:136).

[9]   It should be noted that Ricoeur here locates 'truth' at the level of *understanding*, so that it is a part of *belonging*, but clearly does not subscribe to an entirely subjectivist position. Ricoeur admits the problem of distinguishing 'true and false testimony' in Biblical interpretation (1980:44), but his concept of the *fusion of horizons* allows him to locate truth in the interface between the objective and subjective. In his work *History and Truth* Ricoeur captures this with the expression a 'subjectivity of reflection' (1965:22). I would add the criterion of *praxis* as a way of distinguishing true and false 'testimony'.

To the extent that the narrative genre is primary, God's imprint is in history before being in speech. Speech comes second inasmuch as it confesses the trace of God in the event. (Ricoeur 1987:1-2, 37-40).

This is important, because it highlights the impossibility of ever returning to a historical event *in sich*. The very first statement about an event is already an interpretation, such that historical study can never get behind a declaration that this is a *significant* event. Jesus himself is accessible to us only through the interpretations of the earliest Jesus movement (Schottroff & Steggemann 1986:3-5), so that the quest for the 'historical Jesus' is fatally flawed.[10]

The priority of event to language is also important in defining the relation of *praxis* to interpretation. Each new interpretation of a particular text reflects, in its turn, an interpretation of further events or experience by the interpreter and his community, even though these may not stand in a causal or historical connection with the original event underlying the text. The new interpretation initiates further events, which demand further new interpretations of the text. There is thus a dialectic between *praxis* and interpretation.

2.2 The polysemous nature of language

All language is open-ended in terms of meaning, since every word and every combination of words in a sentence and beyond that into text has many potential meanings. Successful discourse depends upon a mutually understood context or horizon of understanding between a sender and a receiver, which closes down the range of meanings (Ricoeur 1981:43-44, 105-109; Croatto 1987:15-16). In spoken discourse the person gives us clues as to which of the possible meanings of the words s/he intends. Both the tonal inflection and gestures (*il*locution) and the situation (*per*locution) give us clues, so that we usually have no difficulty in catching his/her meaning. The meaning is rooted in a concrete situation or context, which is shared by the speaker and the hearer.

In the case of something written, these conditions are missing. We are not party to the concrete situation of the communication, we may not know the author and may not be the intended readers of the text at all. We are left with a text having many different potential meanings, even an infinite set of meanings (Ricoeur 1981:107-108; Croatto 1987:15-21). Does this mean that we cannot draw meaning from the text? Does it mean that we make our own meaning out of the text arbitrarily? Not necessarily, but it does mean that the process is not immediate or straightforward. It means that we have to re-contextualise the text: recreate the situational conditions of discourse.

---

10   This does not invalidate the quest entirely, but does severely limit its possibilities.

2.3 Explanation and distanciation

The first step could be called *re-construction* (Bultmann) or *explanation* (Ricoeur). Dilthey uses the term *explanation* to refer to the objective empirical explanation of the natural sciences, opposed to the psychological *understanding* of history (Ricoeur 1981:49). We have already seen that science can no longer be held to have the kind of objectivity claimed for it by Dilthey, nor need historical explanation be understood entirely on the basis of psychology (Ricoeur 1981:55-56).

Historical criticism is understood in this essay to belong to the process of *explanation*, whereby empirical data are analysed. This is the step by which we try to re-create the text within the real world in which it was written. There is no absolute objectivity nor any guarantee of meaning in such historical analysis, but it explores the projection from the text to a real world beyond itself. The distanciation involved in such a process invokes the 'the capacity to suspend our own prejudices, our own convictions, our own point of view, ultimately to put into parentheses our own desires' (Ricoeur 1981:295). Historical-critical studies help us to explain the reference of the text beyond itself to a world.

Traditional historical-critical method needs to be challenged and supplemented by the insights of the social sciences. Texts are the products of social and economic forces, and reflect the dynamics of intra- and inter-group interaction, which can be, to some extent, reconstructed with the help of social-scientific tools. Social and economic analysis help to recreate the real world in which and by which the text was produced. This might be termed socio-historical method.

These disciplines form part of *distanciation*, in that they place a certain distance between the text and the reader, enabling her/him to analyse it (Ricoeur 1981:110-111). They apply the tools of suspicion: what is going on inside or behind the text; what is the socio-economic dynamic; who is exploiting whom; what interest lies behind the production of the text? Yet in the process of *distanciation* there is a dialectic with belonging, 'our experience of *being* historical'. Paradoxically, history opens up the real towards the possible since 'the 'true' histories of the past uncover the buried potentialities of the present' (Ricoeur 1981:17).

The analysis of the structure of the text within itself is also a facet of *explanation*. It can help clarify the logical relations between linguistic components within the text. Structuralism serves a valuable purpose as preparation for *understanding*, but cannot itself provide *understanding* (Ricoeur 1981:111).

Socio-historical study and structural analysis can thus both be a valuable part of the preparation for interpretation, but they are not themselves interpretation. They do not convey the meaning of the text, nor do they constitute understanding.

2.4 Understanding and belonging

The essential polysemy of the text is only closed down into an univocal communication by the context of the reader. *Understanding* (Ricoeur) or *interpretation* (Bultmann) is discovering the meaning of the text for me in my situation. The goal of written discourse is attained when the reader 'owns' the text, makes an assertion of belonging. It is only when we read the Bible in our own specific context that the many meanings it could have are narrowed down into a specific meaning.

This is a consequence that is related to action: we act on what we own and believe (just as what we own and believe is related to how we act). Only then is the hermeneutical cycle complete (cf. Boff 1987:135-139). The event or experience that originated the discourse in the text is rediscovered in further event or experience. It is related also to community, because language is communal and religious event or experience is interpreted within a community of faith. Thus the choice of the community in which the text is read becomes crucial to the whole process.

The *Kairos Document* calls on the Church in South Africa to take the option for the poor, to choose the community of the oppressed over against the community of the powerful and rich. My hermeneutic also deliberately chooses to read the text within the community of the oppressed, because the fundamental paradigm of the Bible is God's *liberative* design for mankind (cf. Croatto 1987:40). Jesus seems to have deliberately chosen to identify himself with the landless poor of Palestine, although he had the option of the security of a trade and home (Draper 1989a; cf. Croatto 1987:52-53). The option for the poor forms the horizon of my understanding and belonging, yet it does not itself determine the process by which the text is interpreted:

> And so, strictly speaking, the word of God is not to be found in the letter of scripture. Nor is it in the spirit of the hearing or reading community. It is precisely *between* these two, in their mutual, dynamic relationship, in a back-and-forth that is never perfectly objectifiable (Boff 1987:136).

To sum up in the form of a diagram, there are two related bi-polar axes at work: explanation-understanding and distanciation-belonging:

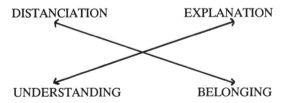

| DISTANCIATION | EXPLANATION |
| UNDERSTANDING | BELONGING |

These poles are in a dialectic tension with each other. Ricoeur rejects the Cartesian starting point of the self-consciousness, because the reader starts with a pre-understanding of the text that is derived from her/his cultural and communal context. Thus the reader moves from *understanding* and *belonging* to *distanciation* and *explanation*, in which the text confronts her/him with 'a proposed world, a world I may inhabit and wherein I can project my ownmost possibilities' (Ricoeur 1980:102). This confronts the reader as a 'call' or *kerygma*, which unmasks the 'false evidences of everyday reality' or the 'pretensions of the *ego*' (Ricoeur 1981:113). There is then a return journey to *understanding* and *belonging*, in the light of the possibilities opened by the text.

2.5 Text and correspondence

The choice of the context of the poor and the oppressed in which to read the text determines my understanding. Meaning, however, cannot be transferred from the text to the present on a 'one for one' allegorical basis. Even if it could be established that Jesus did this or that, it could not simply be assumed that this would be directly transferable to my own context. Scripture is not a blueprint, but a paradigm: 'Scripture appears as a model interpretation, and thus as an interpreting interpretation, a *norma normans ut normata*' (Boff 1987:140). The socio-economic conditions of Jesus' ministry cannot be recreated today, so that what we can derive from the gospel message is a 'correspondence of relationships' or a 'relationship of relationships' between the New Testament and its context and us and our context, which is the 'hermeneutic value for the work of the Holy Spirit':

> The key element in this model, then, is not this or that particular text of Scripture, in correspondence with such and such a precise situation... The key element here is the global, and at the same time particular 'spirit' (Boff 1987:140).

Albert Nolan's valuable book *God in South Africa* has described this correspondence between gospel and context as a matter of *shape* and not *content*:

> The gospel for us today is *shaped* by what the Bible says about God but its *content* is the latest news about the wonderful works of God in South Africa today (Nolan 1988:149).

This challenging terminology may be misleading, since it seems to concede too great a role to context over against text. On the other hand, it does capture something of the nature of a contextual reading of the Bible, which becomes the way we see the world:

Now word ceases to be simply text to be interpreted, and itself becomes interpretative code. Now word is no longer world to be seen but eyes to see, no longer landscape but gaze, no longer thing but light (Boff 1987:137).

2.6 Text and praxis

The possibilities opened up by reading the Scriptural text challenge the reader to a new creation of 'freedom in the light of hope' (Ricoeur 1980:155-182), to 'establish through the Gospel a life lived for others, and to anticipate, ethically and politically, a liberated humanity' (Ricoeur 1975:127). This hermeneutic encompasses the dynamic of *praxis*, the interface between action and reflection. It is here that truth should be located, at 'the convergence of reason and commitment', as Habermas asserts against technological positivism (Habermas 1974:281):

From this vantage point, then, textual exegesis is no longer only a peculiar concern of self-understanding which will occasionally conform with comprehension. It is more a matter of a special understanding of the text's concern which strives for practical congruence between the biblical tradition's horizon of concern and present circumstances (Moltmann 1968:314).

Nevertheless, the *kerygma* of the biblical text is not emptied by its social and political implications for a particular context, since religious discourse, like the metaphor, is characterised by the 'still more' of 'a quest that cannot be exhausted by any program of action' (Ricoeur 1975b:127).

2.7 The reservoir of meaning

This means that there is no one universal, timeless meaning of a text. It also means that material written in Britain, Germany or the United States may be completely inappropriate in South Africa. We must read the Bible again and again in our own contexts. The Christian community can provide some point of reference where individual readings can be tested, but even here, there is no absolute. If one thing is obvious in South Africa, it is that the lines of division in socio-economic crisis run through the Church itself. An infallible Pope located in Rome, no less than a Professor in Tübingen or Cambridge, is poorly placed to pronounce on the interpretation of the Bible in Latin America or South Africa. In any case, the text will always remain beyond the possibility of any final interpretation. It has the character of an enigma from which we have to tease out meaning on our own context, while its 'reservoir of meaning' is as inexhaustable as the number of potential readers (Croatto 1987:37-50; Boff 1987:138).

On the other hand, the historical context of the text is not 'ballast to be jettisoned' (*contra* Croatto 1987:35), nor a husk to be stripped off by demythologisation in order to leave the existentialist kernel (*contra* Bultmann), since distanciation remains as a control on the interpretation of the text. The historical, event-based, nature of the biblical text is part of its kernel, not its husk (cf. Culmann 1951:17-33). Historical reconstruction can make no absolute claims to truth, but this does not mean that we need despair of historical meaning and retreat altogether into subjectivity. Ricoeur appropriates Gadamer's concept of a *fusion of horizons*, without his subjectivism, to describe the possibility of combining the objective and subjective dimensions in a dialectic 'nearness of the remote':

> Another index of the dialectic of participation and distanciation is provided by the concept of the *fusion of horizons*... Communication at a distance between two differently situated consciousnesses occurs by means of the fusion of their horizons, that is, the intersection of their views on the distant and the open... Insofar as the fusion of horizons excludes the idea of a total and unique knowledge, this concept implies a tension between what is one's own and what is alien, between the near and the far; and hence the play of difference is included in the process of convergence (Ricoeur 1981:62).

We are caught up in history in such a way that its action upon us is part of us, part of our belonging; but the process of historical reflection already introduces the element of distance, which alienates us from our own past. In this 'paradox of otherness' it is the text which builds a bridge between the present and the unknowable past. It becomes in this process 'a call, a kerygma, a word addressed to me' (Ricoeur 1980:15).

This is the dialectic that I intended to capture with the provocative text in the title, cited from the Gospel of Thomas 3 (*NgH II.25-26*), 'For the kingdom is inside of you and it is outside of you'. The *kerygma* or 'good news of the kingdom' is both text and a world projected in front of the text; it meets the reader as a challenge to enter into the 'world of the text' in order that the possibilities of the kingdom might be opened also for the world of the reader.

As an example of the operation of the kind of hermeneutic I have suggested, I shall deal with the parable of the Fig Tree in Luke 13:6-9. This has the advantage that it is relatively self-contained and must rate as one of the least read parables in the New Testament, and also one where conventional methods of exegesis themselves seem to yield little fruit.

3. The parable of the Fig Tree: Luke 13:6-9

3.1 Literary context

The parable of the Fig Tree has its place in a rhetorical unit extending from Luke 12:1 to 13:9. It takes place in the same location at the same time, with a 'wandering perspective' between the crowds and the disciples. The unit is framed by the *inclusio* of warning concerning imminent judgement. Warning against the leaven of the Pharisees, specified as their hypocrisy (12:1-3), is balanced by the concluding warning of the felling of the unfruitful fig tree (13:6-9). Judgement, envisaged as the revelation of what is hidden, forms the horizon of the whole unit. It is significant, though, that the passage with which the parable of the Fig Tree is linked in this *inclusio* concerns the leader of Israel, rather than Israel in general. The inner logic of the unit may suggest a connection of the fig tree with the Jewish leaders.

Within this broad context, the parable forms the climax to a series of passages underlining the need for readiness in the face of judgement (12:49-13:9): Jesus' ministry brings fire and division, not peace (12:49-53);[11] the need to read the signs of the times (12:54-56 - linked to the preceding passage by the double 'flag' δὲ καί); the need to get ready in the face of impending judgement (12:57-59 - again linked by δὲ καί); the need for repentance in the face of sudden death (13:1-5 - the connecting δέ is reinforced by the phrase ἐν αὐτῷ τῷ καιρῷ[12]). These passages on judgement are climaxed by the parable of the Fig Tree (13:6-9), connected closely to what precedes by δέ. What follows (13:10-17) is again linked by δέ, but the theme, location and audience changes, with a controversy story of a healing on the Sabbath.[13]

Tannehill (1986:50-51; 144-145) sees the parable as parallel to the parable of John the Baptist in 3:9, as part of Luke's stuctural emphasis of the continuity between the ministry of Jesus and John. In Luke 3:9, however, the plural τῶν δέν-δρων seems to require an individualistic ethical application, which is absent from Luke 13:6-9. Tannehill also analyses this section of Luke as part of a group of passages (5:17-6:11; 7:29-10:37; 11:37-18:27; 19:39-23:43) setting out Jesus' conflict with the religious authorities (Tannehill 1986:169-199).

---

[11] This passage begins a new series, since it has no connecting particle, although the theme of judgment binds it to the previous section of discipleship.

[12] The choice of the connecting Greek words results in the fact that the theme of judgement is concretised in the fate of the unfortunate Galileans whose blood Pilate mixed with their sacrifices, and the fate of those on whom the tower of Siloam fell.

[13] Marshall (1978:509) sees 13:10-21 as part of the same rhetorical unit, but this seems unjustified.

3.2 Luke's redaction of the tradition

It seems that the combination of the series of texts from the hypothetical sources 'Q' and 'L' in Luke 12:49-13:9 is influenced by the destruction of Jerusalem by Roman armies in A.D. 70. Luke believes that this event was a punishment on Jews for refusing to believe in Jesus, God's Messiah, when God's special moment (καιρός 12:56) came. According to Luke, they have brought this terrible fate on themselves by their disobedience (cf. Lk 19:44; Draper & Cochrane 1987:66-72). He reflects the growing separation and hostility between the Christian and Jewish communities in his own day (cf. Conzelmann 1960:145-149). On the other hand, it is the Jewish leaders, the Pharisees in particular, on whom Luke sees the responsibility for the catastrophe resting (cf. Juel 1983:109-112). Such, at least, is the implication of the *inclusio* of the rhetorical unit. It is not 'Israel' as such that is rejected (*contra* Wilson 1973:75), since Luke emphasises the continuity between Israel and the Church in redemptive history (Conzelmann 1960:146). The same tendency to implicate the Jewish leaders as opposed to the people is discernible in Luke's account of the trial of Jesus and the persecution of the nascent Church in Acts (cf. Draper 1989b).

3.3 Form

Luke 13:6-9 is couched in the form of a parable, that is a fictional rather than a historical narrative. Yet, as fiction, in its 'imitation' of 'real' human activity (*mimesis*), it refers beyond itself to the historical condition of humankind in general and of first century Palestine in particular:

> Everything we have said about the mimetic dimension of fiction enables us to conclude that, by its mimetic intention, *the world of fiction leads us to the heart of the real world of action* (Ricoeur 1981:296).

The parable has thus a material reference to its own socio-economic environment, and a direct relevance to the socio-economic environment of its potential readers, for whom it opens up a 'new possible mode of being-in-the-world' (Ricoeur 1965:26-27).

On the other hand, account must be taken of the peculiar nature of the parable as metaphor, as having an inexhaustible 'reservoir of meaning':

> The thesis is that metaphor can also articulate a referent so new or so alien to consciousness that this referent can only be grasped within the metaphor itself. The metaphor here contains a new possibility of world and of language so that any information one might obtain from it can only be received after one has participated through the metaphor in its new and alien referential world. Remove the metaphor and you lose the referent. The metaphor is body, not cocoon. (Crossan 1973:13).

Parables have the particular function of representing the good news of the kingdom or rule of God in the preaching of Jesus. They have both a material dimension, located in the socio-economic dynamic of first century Palestine, and a universal metaphorical dimension, which is irreducible and inexhaustible (a *reservoir of meaning*).

3.4 Narrative structure

In the marginal food-producing region of Palestine, fertile and arrable land is precious. A vineyard utilises this land to produce food for the people. A fig tree stands like a foreign body in the vinyard; it is not a vine and does not belong there by right but only by the grace of the owner of the vineyard. Nevertheless, the fig tree is allowed to grow there because it, too, is a potential source of food for the people. The planting of fig trees in vineyards is not uncommon (Manson 1947:274; Jeremias 1972:170), but this tree is hopelessly barren. The fig tree first bears fruit only three years after planting, and this one has borne nothing for three years even after that (Jeremias 1972:170).

Now the fig tree is hardy and tenacious, but it draws huge amounts of goodness and moisture from the soil (Jeremias 1972:340; Marshall 1978:555); its spreading branches keep the sun from the vines. This might be acceptable if the tree bore fruit, but it bears no fruit. Land is scarce and food production all important. The fig tree has usurped the means of production and withholds them from the vines. The fig tree has become parasitic on the vineyard. The owner of the vineyard decides the tree must be cut down, so that the fertile land, the means of production, can be restored to the vines.

Suddenly, the unexpected figure of a gardener appears, pleading on behalf of the tree for a stay of execution: more labour, more fertilizer for the tree. (There are no other examples of such practice, and the seemingly independent account of this parable in the Apocalypse of Peter has βαλεῖν ὕδωρ in the place of βάλω κόπρια (or βάλω κόφινον κόπρων in D and the Old Latin.) This raises an ambiguity: we do not want the vines to be stunted any longer; is the interference well-founded or merely a delaying tactic, when the tree has had so long already?

Our ambiguity is recognised: the proposed stay of execution is very short; one year and then out comes the tree. Moreover, the ambiguity is intensified by the absence of the owner's response to the gardener's appeal, so that the possibility of destruction is still open.[14] The generous treatment proposed for the barren fig tree is out of the ordinary, not a part of the 'folk-tale element' of the parable

---

14 *Contra* Marshall (1978:555), who talks of a 'successful intercession of the vine-dresser'. There is no indication in the text as to whether the intercession is successful or not.

(Jeremias 1972:170). There is no evidence that fig trees were ever cultivated in this way (Jeremias 1972:170). Often what is out of the ordinary carries special emphasis in a parable. The course of action the gardener proposes interrupts what had seemed the inevitable destruction of the fig tree with the possibility that it may, after all, bear fruit, but only if the last possible measures are taken. Thus the text ends with the open ended-ambiguity of an unanswered appeal for one last short delay.

3.5 The underlying tradition

It is possible to dig underneath Luke's redaction to an earlier stage of the tradition. In particular, the use of the historic present ($\lambda \acute{\epsilon} \gamma \epsilon \iota$ vs. 8) indicates the presence of an older layer in the parable, since Luke consistently removes the historic present from material he edits (Jeremias 1972:183; Marshall 1978:555). The figure of the gardener could represent a Christological development, although this is not certain. The three years of the tree's barrenness could be a reference to the three years of Jesus' ministry, but could simply be a Semitic 'round number' (Marshall 1978:555). Both details are left sufficiently undeveloped, so that they could also plausibly reflect a parable in the preaching of Jesus (Schweizer 1984:220). This must be left an open question.

The parable has a background in the religious thought-world of the first century Palestine. It draws on the common Old Testament image of Israel as the vineyard of God and God as the owner of the vineyard (e.g. Isa 5:1-7; Mic 7:1; Jer 8:13; 24:1-10), which underlies several of Jesus' parables (e.g. the Wicked Tenants, Lk 20:9-19 par.; the Labourers in the Vineyard, Mt 20:1-16). Yet here it is not the vineyard that is the object of the owner's wrath, but the fig tree. The fig tree does not represent Israel, but an entity over against Israel.

The interpretation of the fig tree as the individual who does not live a life in accordance with Jesus' teaching, raised by Plummer (1896:339) and again by Wellhausen (1911), is a common popular understanding today. It moves the focus of the interpretation away from the concrete location of the parable in first-century Palestine and universalises it in a 'spiritual' and 'universalistic' direction. A clear example of the consequence of such an interpretation is provided by Manson (1949:273) in his comment on Luke 13:1-5, on which his interpretation of Luke 13:6-9 depends:

> Jesus is not to be drawn into criticism of the Roman governor or revolt against the Empire. Instead, He carries the whole matter out of the political into the religious sphere.

Such an assertion is unwarranted. Even if repentance is the theme of these pericopes, there is no justification for proceeding directly to an understanding of repentance and judgement in pietistic terms. It is not Jesus but the critic who carries the matter out of the political sphere. In Jesus' preaching, the breaking in of the eschatological kingdom, or rule of God heralds the eschatological reversal of the present social order – 'the first shall be last and the last first'.

3.6 Religionsgeschichte

The fig tree refers to the leaders of Israel, although not in an allegorical way. The key to this interpretation is provided by the use of the fig tree in Mark 11:12-14, 20-26. Here the parable is carefully woven around the account of the Cleansing of the Temple in Mark 11:15-17, and the Conspiracy of the chief priests and scribes in Mark 11:18-19. The cursing and withering of the fig tree here is a symbol of the failure of the Jewish leaders to produce the fruit of God required of them when his time came. Their corruption has polluted the temple and its cult, using it as a means of exploiting the poor and entrenching their own power (cf. Bauckham 1988:72-78). Jesus' threat to the *status quo* results in a conspiracy by the leaders of Israel to destroy him. For this reason they stand under the imminent judgement of God.

The other 'Q' sayings concerning the fig tree (Lk 17:6) or mountain (Mt 17:20) being uprooted and planted in the sea are probably echoes of the same tradition. The ambiguity of tree and mountain probably reflects the metaphor's primary reference to Jerusalem or the temple mount. (Cf. *Apoc. Pet.* where the parable of the Fig Tree uses the terminology of uprooting rather than of chopping down.)

A parallel to this usage may lie behind the Septuagint rendering of the Hebrew text of Hosea 9:10:

> Like grapes in the wilderness I found Israel.
> Like the first-fruits on the fig tree in its first season I saw your fathers,
> But they came to Baalpeor and consecrated themselves to Baal
> And became detestable like the thing they loved.

The text is constructed in Hebrew poetic form, in parallel lines, saying the same thing twice in slightly different terms: Israel as a vineyard in the first half is parallelled by the fathers as a fig tree in the second half. Later Rabbinic tradition understands both vineyard and fig tree to refer to Israel, so that the fig tree is a favourable image of Israel's growth (e.g. *Gen.R.* 46:11; *Ex.R.* 36:1).

The Septuagint changes the meaning under the influence of the second pair of parallel lines. It reads:

> Like grapes in the wilderness I found Israel,

> And like an inspection (ὅς σκόπον) of a fig tree early in the season I saw their
> fathers;
> They went in to Beel-phegor, and were shamefully estranged,
> And the abominable became as the beloved.

This understanding seems to envisage Israel as different from the fathers, who
are the ones involved in shameful activity. The fig tree may then refer to the
leaders of the community, not the community as a whole. God inspects the fig
tree early in the season and finds no fruit on it.[15] This mode of re-interpreting
the two halves of poetic parallelism in the Old Testament is not uncommon in
the *pesherim* of the Dead Sea Scrolls (e.g. *1QpHab.* 12:1-10; *4QpIsa*ᵃ; cf. CD
3:21-4:6: 4:13-19).

3.7 Sitz im Leben *Jesus*

One thing we know for certain about Jesus (at least, Jesus as he is portrayed by
the earliest 'Jesus movement') is that he preached the good news of the kingdom of God, and that he preached it particularly to the poor and outcast, the
sick and estranged (Jeremias 1971:108-121; Schottroff & Stegemann 1986:1-37;
Wengst 1988; cf. Brueggemann 1977:167-183). Jesus himself left home, family
and goods and identified himself with the vagabond poor. He taught them,
cared for them, healed them, gave them unity, dignity and hope. Above all, he
taught them the value of love, the solidarity in which they might find a new way
of dealing with their situation: no longer passive and captive, but free people
with a purpose (Schottroff 1984:129-147; Scottroff & Stegemann 1986:21-22).

The time in which Jesus preached was a time of growing distance between
the rich and the poor. The Maccabees and Herodian rulers had confiscated
huge tracts of land, which became royal estates, farmed by slaves to enrich
themselves (Grant 1973:47-50; cf. Oppenheimer 1977). The Romans sold off
these estates to the aristocrats who could afford to invest in land (Josephus *Ant.*
XVIII.2). This accelerated the empire-wide drift from small subsistance farming
of freehold farming families, towards the big slave-based estates (MacMullen
1974:15-25). This drove the poor off the land (ἀναχωρῆσις, cf. MacMullan
1974:34; Avilla 1983:31) and forced them into the wage market, where they
were helpless in the face of exploitation by the prospective employers (Mt 20:1-
16; Schottroff 1984:129-147; cf. Draper 1989a). The minimum living wage to
support a family in first century Palestine was about 200 *denarii per annum*

---

[15]   The Vulgate text has an interesting reference to the fig tree bearing its first fruit 'at the tree
top' or, perhaps, 'at the extreme end of the branches': *in cacumine.* This may indicate that they
were considered inaccessible. The phrase translates the difficult Hebrew *br'shyth*, which is simply
omitted by the Peshitta.

(Heichelheim 1938:158-188), but a labourer *in season* might only hope for a *denarius* a day (Mt 20:1).

Such poverty was widespread in Jesus' day and is reflected in many biblical texts. It was exacerbated by the system of double taxation by Rome and Jerusalem (Grant 1926:94-97), which meant a crippling burden of 30 to 40 percent. The exploitation of temple monopolies on sacrifices and the housing of the records of debts in the temple fuelled the fire (Freyne 1980:259-304; Bauckham 1988:72-89).

In this context the metaphor of the vineyard and the fig tree, which Jesus found already to hand in the Old Testament, is re-interpreted to analyse and comment on the situation of the unemployed and exploited of his day. Land is the basic means of production, in economic terms. The accumulation of land is the necessary precursor to the growth of the capitalist economy. Land is intended for the production of food to supply the needs of the people. It now becomes a source of enrichment for people not on the land at all, but for whom it provides a surplus to enable them to accumulate capital. Read against this background , the parable of the Fig Tree is a parable about the expropriation of land and the primitive accumulation of capital.

The Jewish leaders of Jesus' time have begun to usurp the land and the wealth of the people, with their added burdens of tax and tithe and their alliance with the Roman oppressors. They became parasitic on the people, taking all and giving nothing back. God has judged them for failing to bear fruit and for exploiting the poor in Israel.[16] The land, as the basic means of production, must be taken away from them and returned to the poor. Jesus' proclamation of the kingdom provides an undeserved, gracious, but ambiguous respite for the rich, in which they may repent: do his hearers, the poor and outcast, the victims of the depradations of the rich, really want such a stay of execution? Jesus acknowledges their ambiguous response: the stay will be for a short period only; the judgement is certain and final (cf. Plummer 1898:339).

4. Full circle

4.1 Analysis of the South African context for reading the parable of the Fig Tree

There can be no direct or allegorical connection between the parable and our modern industrial, post-Christian South African society. Yet the 'correspondence of correspondences' for the oppressed in South Africa is rich.

---

16   Luke gives one of the main charges against the Pharisees in this section as greed and hypocritical designs on the wealth of widows and the poor (Tannehill 1986:180-187).

We live in a society where an invading army and a colonising people conquered another society and subdued it to its will. The land, the primary means of production, has been taken away from the colonised people. They have been driven into over-crowded, non-economic reserves, so that they have been forced onto the labour markets. The pressure on the land and the dispossession of the people create a pool of cheap and to some extent docile labour (Wilson & Ramphele 1989; Christie 1989:7-15). The basic means of production confiscated from the conquered produced a surplus that has enabled the conquerors to accumulate capital and divert it into the creation of an industrial economy based on non-productive enterprises like gold and arms (Christie 1989:18). The enrichment of the conquerors is matched by the progressive impoverishment of the conquered. The conquerors have become parasitic on the conquered, taking all and giving nothing back. Land is at the heart of the South African crisis.

The 'correspondence of correspondences' between the parable and our society would suggest that the conquerors stand under the judgement of God who created the land for the production of food for the needs of his people, and who proclaims the good news that he takes the side of the poor and the oppressed. The good news of the kingdom for the oppressed would be that the time of their suffering is over, the time of their deliverance is at hand (cf. Nolan 1988:25-30). The means of production are intended to provide for the needs of all God's people. Where they are diverted unproductively into the hands of the few, for their own enrichment, then they will be taken away and returned to the people. We experience the present in South Africa as a time of historical ambiguity; the future of the conquerors hangs in the balance, but the certainty of God's justice is at hand. This says nothing to offset the role of the people in *their own* liberation, but promises that their struggle for social and economic justice is also God's struggle.[17]

4.2 The role of the Church

At this point the Church comes and says, 'Wait! The conquerors also have the potential to bear fruit, to contribute to the welfare of all. We must spend more energy conscientising the conquerors, teaching them and moving them. Perhaps they will change and become less parasitic'. There are many Christian voices, especially in the white churches, calling for the Church to be a *third force* in society. According to this view both the oppressors and the oppressed are at fault and need to be brought together and reconciled by an impartial Church. This effectively stiffles the struggle of the oppressed and tells them to be patient in

---

[17]   This is not to romantisise the poor or to give a *carte blanche* justification of the *means* the oppressed might use in the struggle for their liberation. It is rather to indicate their call to an active role, as opposed to passive pietistic waiting for God to do something.

their affliction; the *status quo* is left intact. The oppressed in South Africa are confused and angered by this sudden intervention: how long must they still wait?

4.3 Suspended judgement

Ambiguitiy is at the heart of our experience of history, as it is at the heart of the parable of the Fig Tree. The parable confirms the appeal for a respite of judgement but gives no response to the appeal. Only the certainty of judgement in the absence of repentance and the very limited time remaining are affirmed. Peace and reconciliation are not the priorities but just and fruitful use of the means of production for the good of all. The Church has all along in South Africa played the part of the gardener in the parable. It has tried to be a *third force*, brokering power on the behalf of the oppressed, but the time for its game is over. God is at work among the poor, bringing them the good news that power comes from below, that the system is coming to an end, that the Church belongs to them, that justice and peace are on the horizon! There *may* be a continued role for the fig tree, but its continued unfruitful monopolisation of the land is over.

BIBLIOGRAPHY

Avilla, C. 1983. *Ownership: Early Christian Teaching*. Maryknoll: Orbis.
Barbour, I. 1966. *Issues in Science and Religion*. New York: Harper & Row.
Bauckham, R. 1988. Jesus' Demonstration in the Temple, in B. Lindars (ed.). *Law and Religion*. Cambridge: James Clarke, 72-89.
Bauckham, R. 1989. *The Bible in Politics: How to Read the Bible Politically*. London: SPCK.
Baum, G. 1989. Religious Studies and Theology. Paper Presented *in Absentia* at the 20th Anniversary Celebrations of the Department of Religious Studies at the University of Cape Town, 11-13 April, 1989. Forthcoming in the *Journal of Theology in Southern Africa*, 1990.
Belo, F. 1976. *A Materialist Reading of the Gospel of Mark*. (Tr. by M. J. O'Connel.) Maryknoll: Orbis.
Boff, C. 1987. *Theology and Praxis: Epistemological Foundations*. Maryknoll: Orbis.
Brueggemann, W. 1977. *The Land: Place of Gift, Promise and Challenge*. London: SCM.
Bultmann, R. 1955. *Theology of the New Testament*, v. 2. London: SCM.
Bultmann, R. 1961. *Existence and Faith*. London: Hodder.
Caird, G. B. 1963. *Saint Luke*. Harmondsworth: Penguin.
Cardenal, E. 1982. *The Gospel in Solentiname*. 4 vols. (Tr. by D. D. Walsh.) Maryknoll: Orbis.
Christie, R. 1989. *A Critique of Contemporary Business Strategies in South Africa*. Paper Presented to the *Theology, Work and Labour* Conference, 28-31 March 1989 at FEDSEM, Pietermaritzburg.
Cone, J. H. 1975. *God of the Oppressed*. San Francisco: Harper & Row.
Conzelmann, H. 1960. *The Theology of Luke*. (Tr. by G. Buswell.) London: Faber.
Creed, J. M. 1965. *The Gospel according to Saint Luke*. London: Macmillan.

Croatto, J. S. 1983. Biblical Hermeneutics in the Theologies of Liberation, in V. Fabella & S. Torres (eds.). *Irruption of the Third World: Challenge to Theology*. Maryknoll: Orbis, 140-168.

Croatto, J. S. 1987. *Biblical Hermeneutics: Toward a Theory of Reading as the Production of Meaning*. Maryknoll: Orbis.

Crossan, J. D. 1973. *In Parables: The Challenge of the Historical Jesus*. New York: Harper & Row.

Crotty, R.B. 1985. Changing Fashions in Biblical Interpretation. *Australian Biblical Review* 33, 15-30.

Cullmann, O. 1951. *Christ and Time: The Primitive Christian Conception of Time and History*. London: SCM.

Davies, W. D. & Allison, D. C. 1988. *Commentary on St. Matthew*. Edinburgh: Clark.

Downing, F. G. 1987. *Jesus and the Threat of Freedom*. London: SCM.

Draper, J. A. 1988. 'In Humble Submission to Almighty God' and its Biblical Foundation: Contextual Exegesis of Romans 13:1-7. *Journal of Theology for Southern Africa* 63, 30-41.

Draper, J. A. [1989a]. *Christ the Worker: Fact or Fiction*. Paper presented to the *Theology, Work and Labour* Conference, 28-31 March 1989 at FEDSEM, Pietermaritzburg, in J. R. Cochrane & G. O. West (eds.). 1990. *The Threefold Cord: Theology, Work and Labour in South Africa*. (Forthcoming.)

Draper, J. A. [1989b]. Church-State Conflict in the Book of Acts: A South African Perspective, in C. Wanamaker & W. Mazamisa (eds.). *Reading the Bible in South Africa*. Braamfontein: Skotaville. (Forthcoming.)

Draper, J. A. & Cochrane, J. C. 1987. The Kairos Debate: The Parting of the Ways. *Journal of Theology for Southern Africa* 59, 66-72.

Draper, J. A. & West, G. E. O. 1989. Anglicans and Scripture in South Africa, in F. England & T. Paterson (ds.). *Bounty in Bondage: The Anglican Church in Southern Africa*. *Essays in Honour of Edward King, Dean of Cape Town*. Johannesburg: Ravan, 30-52.

Eagleton, T. 1983. *Literary Theory: An Introduction*. London: Blackwell.

Elliott, J. H. 1982. *A Home for the Homeless: A Sociological Exegesis of 1 Peter, its Situation and Strategy*. London: SCM.

Elliott, J. H. 1986. Social-Scientific Criticism of the New Testament: More on Methods and Models. *Semeia* 35, 1-33.

Fitzmyer, J. A. 1985. *The Gospel according to Luke*, v. 2. New York: Doubleday. (Anchor).

Freyne, S. 1980. *Galilee from Alexander the Great to Hadrian, 323 B.C.E. to 135 C.E.: A Study of Second Temple Judaism*. Wilmington, Delaware & Notre Dame, Indiana: Michael Glazier & University of Notre Dame.

Gottwald, N. 1983. Introduction, in N. Gottwald (ed.). *The Bible and Liberation: Political and Social Hermeneutics*. Maryknoll: Orbis, 1-8.

Grant, F. C. 1926. *The Econonomic Background of the Gospels*. Oxford: University Press.

Habermas, J. 1974. *Theory and Praxis*. (Tr. by J. Viertel.) London: Heinemann.

Hanson, N. R. 1961. *Patterns of Discovery*. Cambridge: Cambridge University Press.

Heichelheim, F. M. 1983. Roman Syria, in T. Frank (ed.). *An Economic Survey of Ancient Rome*, v. 4. Baltimore: John Hopkins, 121-257.

Hinchliff, P. 1968. *The Church in South Africa*. London: SPCK.

Jeanrond, W. 1988. *Text and Interpretation as Categories of Theological Thinking*. (Tr. by T. J. Wilson.) Dublin: Gill & Macmillan.

Jeremias, J. 1971. *Theology of the New Testament*, v. 1. London: SCM.

Jeremias, J. 1972. *The Parables of Jesus*. London: SCM.

Juel, D. 1983. *Luke-Acts*. London: SCM.

The Kairos Document: Challenge to the Churches. 1986. 2nd ed. Braamfontein: Skotavile.

Käsemann, E. 1969. Thoughts on the Present Controversy about Scriptural Interpretaton, in *New Testament Questions of Today*. London: SCM, 260-285.

Kuhn, T. S. 1962. *The Structure of Scientific Revolutions*. Chicago: University Press.

Lategan, B. C. 1984. Current Issues in the Hermeneutic Debate. *Neotestamentica* 18, 1-17.

MacMullan, R. 1974. *Roman Social Relations 50 B.C. to A.D. 284*. New Haven: Yale University Press.

Malherbe, A. J. 1983. *Social Aspects of Early Christianity*. Philadelphia: Fortress.

Malina, B. J. 1983. The Social Sciences and Biblical Interpretation, in N. Gottwald (ed.). *The Bible and Liberation: Political and Social Hermeneutics*. Maryknoll: Orbis, 11-25.

Malina, B. 1986. *Christian Origins and Cultural Anthropology: Practical Models for Biblical Interpretation*. Atlanta: John Knox.

Manson, T. W. 1947. *The Sayings of Jesus*. London: SCM.

Marshall, I. H. 1978. *The Gospel of Luke*. Exeter: Peternoster. (New International.)

Mesters, C. 1983. The Use of the Bible in Christian Communities of the Common People, in N. Gottwald (ed.). *The Bible and Liberation: Political and Social Hermeneutics*. Maryknoll: Orbis, 119-133.

Miranda, J. 1973. *Being and the Messiah: The Message of St. John*. Maryknoll: Orbis.

Miranda, J. 1974. *Marx and the Bible: A Critique of the Philosophy of Oppression*. Maryknoll: Orbis.

Mofokeng, D. 1988. Black Christians, the Bible and Liberation. *Journal of Black Theology in South Africa* 2, 37-39.

Moltmann, J. 1968. Toward a Political Hermeneutics of the Gospel. *Union Seminary Quarterly Review* 23, 303-323.

Mosala, I. J. 1987. *Biblical Hermeneutics and Black Theology in South Africa*. Cape Town: University of Cape Town. (Unpublished Doctoral Dissertation.)

Mudge, L. S. 1980. Paul Ricoeur on Biblical Interpretation, in P. Ricoeur (ed.). *Essays in Biblical Interpretation*. Philadelphia: Fortress.

Nolan, A. 1988. *God in South Afirca: The Challenge of the Gospel*. Cape Town & Johannesburg: David Philip.

Oppenheimer, A. 1977. *The Am Ha-aretz. A Study in the Social History of the Jewish People in the Hellenistic-Roman Period*. Leiden: Brill.

Placher, W. C. 1987. Paul Ricoeur and Postliberal Theology: A Conflict of Interpretations? *Modern Theology* 4, 35-55.

Plummer, A. 1922. *The Gospel according to Saint Luke*. 5th imp. Edinburgh: Clarke. (International Critical Commentary.).

Ricoeur, P. 1965. *History and Truth*. (Tr. by C. A. Kelbley.) Evanston, Illinois: Northwestern University.

Ricoeur, P. 1975a. Biblical Hermeneutics. *Semeia* 4, 29-148.

Ricoeur, P. 1975b. The Specificity of Religious Language. *Semeia* 4, 107-148.

Ricoeur, P. 1978. *The Rule of Metaphor: Multi-disciplinary Studies of the Creation for Meaning in Language*. (Tr. by R. Czerny, K. McLaughlin & J. Costello.) London: Routledge & Kegan Paul.

Ricoeur, P. 1980. *Essays on Biblical Interpretaion*. (Ed. by L. S. Mudge.) Philadelphia: Fortress.

Ricoeur, P. 1981. *Hermeneutics and the Human Sciences*. (Ed. by J. B. Thompson.) Cambridge: University Press / Maison des Sciences de l'Homme.

Schottroff, L. 1984. Human Solidarity and the Goodness of God: The Parable of the Workers in the Vineyard, in W. Schottroff & W. Stegemann (eds.). *God of the Lowly: Socio-Historical Interpretations of the Bible*. Maryknoll: Orbis, 129-147.

Schottroff, L. & Stegemann, W. 1986. *Jesus and the Hope of the Poor*. Maryknoll: Orbis.

Schweizer, E. 1984. *The Good News according to Luke*. London: SPCK.

Segundo, J. L. 1979. *The Liberation of Theology*. Maryknoll: Orbis.

Suggit, J. 1987a. *Kairos*: The Wrong Way on the Right Road. *Journal of Theology for Southern Africa*. 58, 70-74.

Suggit, J. 1987b. *Kairos*: Words or The Word? Elucidations. *Journal of Theology for Southern Africa*. 60, 73-75.

Tannehill, R. C. 1986. *The Narrative Unity of Luke-Acts: A Literary Interpretation*, v. 1. Philadelphia: Fortress.

Wellhausen, J. 1911. *Einleitung in die drei ersten Evangelien*. Berlin.

Wengst, K. 1988. *Humility: Solidarity of the Humiliated*. London: SCM.

West, G. 1989. *Interesting and Interested Readings of Sacred Texts*. Paper Presented to a Colloquium of the Department of Religious Studies, University of Natal.

Wilson, F. & Ramphele, M. 1989. *Uprooting Poverty: The South African Challenge. The Second Carnegie Inquiry into Poverty and Development in Southern Africa*. Cape Town: David Philip.

Wilson, S. G. 1973. *The Gentiles and the Gentile-Mission in Luke-Acts*. Cambridge: University Press. (SNTS Monograph Series 23.)

S. VAN TILBORG

IDEOLOGY AND TEXT: JOHN 15 IN THE CONTEXT
OF THE FAREWELL DISCOURSE

In the ongoing discourse about the interpretation and hermeneutics of texts few authors omit to bring in the concept 'ideology'. This is true, especially, with those authors who see a text as an open communication system. The need to separate various positions from one another – between author and readers, between narrator and narratees, between the narratively speaking and the narratively addressed characters – visualises (textual) differences in interest, in subject installation and in perspective. This brings the critics to speak about ideology as a global and ambiguously connected system of ideas, feelings and presentations which lies at the base of a concrete textual expression.

1. The three areas of science

With that we have a first definition of ideology. Many others are used (cf. Hamon 1984:7ff). Based on Althusser's position, I wish to present a definition that can be used as an analytical and research model. Actually it seems to me that the three scientific areas that exert the strongest influence on modern exegesis – sociology, psychology and narratology – are using their own different concepts. I think it important to bring these together in a single, more linguistically and semiotically oriented concept.

The concept of ideology belongs of old to sociology. In reaction to Marx Weber has given it a permanent place in the professional field. Theories of interest and of epistemology give it a special flavour that is not lost even in modern variations. It is accepted as a factor that, together with many other realities, co-determines human social intercourse. Its proper place in the totality of sociological models is a subject for discussion. Elliott's theoretical reflections, developed in connection with Theissen's socio-historical studies (Elliott 1986:14, 18) see 'the ideologies' as a sector that directly influences and is directly influenced by 'the culture' and 'the political-military legal system'. Ebertz's study (Ebertz 1987) places ideology as religion simply parallel to politics and economics. From the many sociologically oriented studies it would be easy but not very relevant to give other examples.

These studies are usually fascinating enough, but for an exegete who comes from the literary corner of exegesis, questions about the denotative force of the texts keep nagging. The texts speak about farmers, slaves, soldiers, leaders of the people, etc., but they remain texts. Even if the texts give a different impression and, seemingly in a direct way, speak about 'reality', the concrete persons of flesh and blood, the grain in the granaries, the surplus of the produce of the land are brought forward only as text.

This is a statement with a important implication. If ideology is a system that lies at the base of any concrete textual expression, this must be true for the totality of a text and, besides, for all texts. In short, it means that the access to the historical material reality which determines people's life and history, is given only via ideologies: in texts money exists only as embedded in economic ideologies; soldiers only as expression of military ideologies; the power of the state only as textual expression of political theories. Ideology is the base phenomenon, installed furthermore in all social factors. If the socio-historical studies want to retain contact with the literary branch of exegesis, they need to give ideology a much more central place than usually is done.

In psychology the concept is linked to Lacan, to the insight in the relation between the subject installation and language. Concrete sentences constitute the subject. The ego locates itself in time and space via a linguistical identification with a non-ego. In this way the ego fits into the language system that is culturally, socially and economically determined.

Lacan's rather esoteric language was no obstacle for an enormous impact on literary science. The socalled post-structuralist authors, especially, have taken it as a starting point to criticise, fundamentally, the whole western approach to subject-thought. The subject is not a hypostatic given. It is, rather, a disintegrated and ambiguous language construction that as a linguistic phenomenon participates in the ideological conflict situation in which people fight for their interests.

As far as I know, this complex of ideas does not yet play a real role in New Testament exegesis. The deconstructive exegetes will possibly teach us something here. Studies on particular issues that can link up with some work done in exegesis – one can think of studies on the 'titles' of Jesus; on the 'self-consciousness' and the 'historicity' of Jesus; on the group formation of the disciples; on Paul as a historical person – will determine the agenda of exegesis for the time being.

It is not surprising that the ideology concept is also widely used in narratology. There is a close relation between ideology, language and text. Texts that are structured communicatively function in their own quite complicated way as speech act in the communication between people. In the same way as the perspective from which one speaks and the voice with which one speaks determine the power-play of communication, in that same way this happens in texts: who is allowed to speak and who is not; who knows what s/he should say and what not and who doesn't; what is the authority with which a speaking character is presented and what is the result of his or her speaking.

But here too it is easy to misunderstand. The focalisation of possible characters in a text, parallel to or in contradiction with the evaluations of the narrator/author of a text (cf. Sternberg 1987:53ff, 129ff and *passim*) are sometimes seen as directly expressed ideologies. One states that the point of view of a text expresses the ideology of the text (Van Aarde 1988:239, 247) or one says that a difference in focalisation shows different ideologies (Culpepper 1983:32). That is not right (cf. Smit 1988:444). The concrete perspective and the voice of a text do not give direct access to the ideology of a text. They are ideologically determined, but the ideological content must be revealed in a (literary) analysis. Everything is ideologically determined in texts. The proper form that the focalisation and the perspective take on are ideological particularisations of linguistic phenomena that, in their own quite particular way, give form to the power-play of human communication.

2. Althusser's definition redefined

Our opinion as exegetes about ideology is, therefore, far more important than people usually think. Because of the different ideological interests (!) uniformity does not seem possible. Nevertheless, I would like to try to re-interpret Althusser's famous definition and thus to make a proposal of a definition that could be used as a literary model of analysis. Using examples from John 15 I will also show how this works exegetically.

It is possibly known that Althusser links up with certain marxist theories. In his formulation he is influenced by Lacan. I quote his most explicit statement:

> Every ideology represents – in a necessarily imaginary deformation – the imaginary relation of the individuals to the real productive relationships and its dependent relations. Ideology, therefore, does not represent the system of real relationships which affects the lives of individuals, but rather the imaginary relation of these individuals to the real relations under which they live (Althusser 1976:104).

There is a threefold structure: 1. the relation of the individuals to the real conditions of existence; 2. these relations are imaginarily expressed; 3. this imaginary expression is imaginarily represented.

I suppose that Althusser can see ideology only as deformation. That is possible, but what interests me is not an interpretation of Althusser but a concept of ideology that is exegetically-scientifically useable. The deformation theory is then worse than useless, because an apriori judging scale of values cannot be part of science. One can be ideologically critical and one can show which interests are defended in certain ideological manipulations at the cost of other interests, but it is not part of science to know apriori what is good and what is bad. That certainly does not belong to the department of literary science (*pace* Althusser). If we, furthermore, realise that Althusser's imaginary order is the order of language itself, I come to the following definition: 'ideology is the linguistic representation of the linguistic relations of the individuals to the real conditions of existence'. That means that, as far as ideology is concerned, it is better to speak of a double structure: there is the opposition between 'expressed in language' and 'real' as the opposition between language and reality; and there is the opposition between 'linguistic relation' and 'linguistic representation' as the opposition between content and communication.

The 'real relationships of individuals to the conditions of existence' remain, of course, the basis and the point of departure of all ideological expression. The fact that people are actually embedded in the totality of a socio-political structure that is economically determined decides how people will speak. That is as-it-were 'reality', 'brute fact' that in the final analysis determines the human conscious, cognitive and emotive activities. Communicative access to this 'reality' is possible only via the symbolic order of language. Such an access is, therefore, not reality itself; on the material basis of practices, rituals and organisations 'reality' is expressed, made present and communicated.

Such communication must be structured: the linguistic representation of the linguistic relationships. There is a double structure that must be seen as the double structure of all linguistic expressions: the joining of *enoncée* and *enunciation*, of content and speech act, of message and communication. Ideology is never 'sec'. It poses itself in factual speech acts.

In what follows I will limit myself to one concrete text (Jn 15) and show what must be done if one wants to bring out, interpretatively, the ideology of this text. That is not all that has to be done. Texts are speech acts that intervene in ever new contexts. They are signifiers that are part of the process of human semiosis. They receive new meanings that do not necessarily defend the same interests. A meta-text on a text participates in this. However relevant this may be, in exegesis we are still making our first steps. This study wants to make the first preliminaries.

3. The linguistic representative of the linguistic relations

Therefore, there are no sentences, pronouncements, stories that are 'pure ideology' as, in reverse, there are no texts that are not ideologically determined. The ideological bias of a text is not directly expressed but, at the same time, it is present in every textual expression. In this sense we can compare the ideology of a text with the presence of the subconscious in all our conscious activities. It does not express itself directly but it is present all the time. Linking this with the research description above, it is possible to distinguish three areas of concern.

3.1 The denotation

One can take the concept 'representation' in its literal sense. The linguistic representation 'represents' in language a multitude of other possibilities of expression. Because concrete sentences are written, other sentences are no longer possible. These sentences must, therefore, be seen as the effective representatives of the totality of the ideology which they defend: the one (representative) who speaks for the interests of the many.

Procedurally this deals with the principle of selection. If ideologies are socially conflicting, it is the selection of one ideology at the cost of the others. If it is a question of selecting within an existing ideology, aspects of enlarging *versus* minimising, re-enforcing *versus* weakening, affirmation *versus* condemnation will determine the procedure. Content and mode of selection will indicate which interests are given priority and how these interests relate to the denotative reality about which the text speaks.

How to describe this selection for John 15:1-16:4?

One must start with a division of the text in reading units on the base of ideological coherences. Clusters of sentences that are ideologically connected, should form the basic reading units. It appears that John 15 is a discursive text, composed out of quite different areas and interests.It is a phenomenon that characterises most of John's text. At the end of the reading the reader is supposed to reconstruct the coherence of the totality: after the deconstruction of the text – following the traces of the narrator as the first reader of the text – a careful reader's reconstruction is nequised.

John 15:1-6: The basic metaphor comes from the world of agriculture. It is really quite simple. The text starts from the natural fact of vine and branches that bear fruit or do not. The active subject is the gardener who cuts and trims (αἴρω and καθαίρω). If a branch is separated and dries up, it is gathered with other branches and thrown into the fire and burned (15:6). The branches that remain united to the vine bear fruit. Outside the vine the branches cannot bear fruit or survive.

The life-giving aspect is unique in this use of metaphor: the vine gives life to the fruits; outside of the vine there is no life. It is a representation that has made Bultmann (among others) think of the tree of life and that caused him to step aside to gnostic and Mandaean parallels with all their specific ideological implications. Today's exegesis does not go beyond a reference to the Old Testament texts that describe Israel as a vine (cf. Brown 1970:690ff; Onuki 1984:119ff). It is accepted that the typical extension of the metaphor is John's own contribution, which is linked with his christology. In this explanation the adjunct ἡ ἀληθινή (15:1) is very important: Jesus is the true vine who, under the guidance of the Father, gives his disciples the chance to live fruitfully (cf. esp. Jer 2:21 (Septuagint) with the opposition in the text between a good and a bad vine). Jesus is the vine who realises the ἀληθεία, the *emet*, of God (cf. Jn 1:17) and who brings forth in his disciples καρποί in contraposition to the wild-growth of the vine in Jeremiah (and Isaiah and Ezechiel). Through Jesus God planted an Israel that he himself has made fruitful. The selectivity is evident but also the polemic.

John 15:7-17: The discourse on friendship, which in John 15:13 reaches its zenith, is embedded in the *oikos*-ideology. It is a large *oikos*, an *oikos* with royal manners. The son lives in a loving and obedient relationship to the father. He chooses people who will be allowed into the intimacy of 'the house': he calls them his friends; he tells them everything he has heard from his father; he tells them what is going on in the house, and especially what the *kyrios* is doing; he allows them to ask the father in his name whatever they want. He tells them that they must love one another, and he has the right to demand this, because he is ready to lay down his own life for his friends. This means that a threefold love relationship is described: the love between a father and his son; between the son and his friends-disciples; and between the disciples among themselves.

This way of presentation links up directly (I do not say that it is referring immediately) with the reflections of Aristotle on the ἰσότης and the δικαιοσύνη in friendship: the regal friendship between God and his creatures, a king and his subjects, a father and his children; the aristocratic friendship between husband and wife; and the democratic friendship between children of the same family or the friendship between friends (Aristotle *Eth. Nic.* 8,10). God as father in relation to Jesus as son (a form of royal friendship); Jesus in relation to his disciples whom he can command κατ' ἀξίαν (a form of aristocratic friendship); the disciples among themselves (a form of democratic friendship). The *oikos* that Jesus realises with his disciples contains in itself the structure of a complete *polis* in which, according to the command of Jesus, democracy is the new law. I would think that in the context of a hierarchical class society, at the head of which a *kyrios-theos* is residing in Rome, this linking up with the classical ideal is not without meaning and interest.

John 15:18-16:4: It should be clear that I limit myself to the main points. The *agapè* of the Jesus group will call forth the hatred of the *kosmos*. Looking back at his own life Jesus starts to speak a prophetic language.
1. The basic mythology of the whole Gospel of John is elaborated. Not only Jesus (cf. Jn 7:7), but also the disciples will suffer the hatred of the *kosmos* (15:18-21). Jesus' life is memory and model for the fate which awaits the Jesus-group. Because, and in the same way as his own *oikos* was torn apart and had a Judas in its midst who was prepared to hand Jesus over to his death, in the same way it will be with the future Jesus-group (cf. the similarity between 15:20 and 13:16 and together with this that between 15:19-13,18; 15:21-13:19; 15:21-13:16, 20 and the ideological use of 'the life of Jesus' that follows from this).

2. It is a prophecy about the future that is strengthened by the prophet ideology that John 15:22-25 uses (cf. Rendtorff 1959:811). Via the cluster 'words-works-sin-accusation' Jesus is identified as a special prophet (cf. Mic 3:8: 6:13, 15; Ez 3:16ff; 18:24ff).

3. In the *paraklètos* saying the forensic-judicial context is further developed (cf. De la Potterie 1977:378ff).

4. The closing words (cf. 16:1,4) use the most explicit language. We find here the real polemical context: the disciples will be made ἀποσυναγώγους, a 'reality' that can only be thought of from a situation of conflict with 'the Jews'. Even an incidental murder is not excluded. If this means that the disciples will lose the protection of the law of the Jewish religion (cf. Hemer 1989:8ff), they will live without protection in a *kosmos* where people, because they do not adore the one true God, are haters of God (cf. the only places in the Septuagint where μισέω τὸν θεόν is used, *scil.* Ex 20:5; Dt 5:9 and Dt 7:9, 10). Notwithstanding the certainty with which all exegetes speak about the 'factual reality' of the persecutions for the hearers of John's Gospel, we must say that the text itself does not say much more than that there will be persecutions in the future. Here too the text draws ideologico-denotatively from the prophet ideology: Jesus is presented as one who foretells the future, the truth of which will become clear when his words become 'real' (cf. 16:4). Since John 16:1-4 refers to John 15:18-21 in content as well as literarily (see the similarity between 16:3 and 15:21 and the one between 16:4 and 15:20), the text contains a strange reading effect. Once arrived at John 16:1-14 the reader is sent back to John 15:18ff and so on *ad infinitum* (cf. Onuki 1984:138). John 15:18-16:4 is a text that is closed in upon itself and that with every 'realisation' strengthens the truth of Jesus' words.

3.2 The subject installation

A linguistic representation has also an aspect of 'presenting (itself)', of proposing a subject that is the origin and end-term of the linguistic expressions. It is one of Althusser's merits that he brought about a relationship between the concept of ideology and the concept of subject. Obviously he was not after psycho-analytical theories of origin. He wanted to stress that individuals are embedded in the totality of real forces of production via the concept of subject. He pointed to the triad of practice, ritual and organisation as intervening forces: concrete psycho-somatic activities that, *in actu*, going on as it were, install the individuals in their subjectivity: address them as subjects, constitute them as subjects, determine them as subjects. In fact, behind Althusser's triad a multitude of attitudes, activities and organisations are hidden that offer the individuals a full time task. It is on this level that ideologies about man-woman relations, about racism and anti-racism, about dictatorship and democracy take a hold of individuals: the white men's golf club over against the sewing center or the kitchen club.

Subjectivity is not a once-for-all reality. It realises itself in partial aspects that do not have to be homogeneous or reinforcing each other. Its consciousness, which originates out of the human activities, behaves like boulders dispersed in time and place.

Ideology brings it together in language, but, as I have said already, ideology does not present itself as an interconnected text or insight. We are always dealing with partial texts ever changing with the speaker, the time or the place: texts as signifying agents within the total process of semiosis. Research in ideology in relation to the subject installation tries to show the special way in which the subjectivity of the characters is constituted in this text: the interplay of the linguistically expressed somatico-psychical activities of the characters and the subjective consciousness. Modalities play an important role then: time and place; the knowing, wanting, having to, being able to; the desire and its fulfillment; accident and fate; all positive and negative evaluations that surround the subject (cf. Hamon 1984).

John 15 is, obviously, first of all about the person of Jesus, about how he, as a subject, is embedded in this moment of the text. Jesus is giving a long address, the longest in John's Gospel. He is at table with his disciples and by serving them as a slave he has confronted them with his death as a slave. That was not a great success. Judas left the group and Jesus started to talk with the disciples: conversations that in the privacy of the last supper discussed the coming journey of Jesus. The disciples do not have a clue what it is all about. In their ignorance and their anxiety they do not even listen. They do ask questions but these are mostly repetitions of what Jesus just told them. At this moment of the text Jesus begins his discourse. There is a danger of a break in communication between Jesus and the disciples. In what follows immediately Jesus deals with that: 'why does not anyone ask: where are you going?' (16:5). The discourse expresses Jesus' need for contact and his fidelity to keep his disciples with him; his readiness also to go all the way. It is as a still-photograph that through the meal will gain in strength. Even if the disciples will flee, Jesus will not drop them.

It is, then, not without reason that the discourse emphasises as to content the 'good now'. There is contact between the Father and Jesus and the disciples-friends: 'I am the vine; my Father is the gardener; you are the branches'. It will depend on the disciples whether this contact will be maintained. The group of disciples is also installed but, linguistically, this happens in a completely different manner than the subject installation of Jesus. It takes place in the form of imperatives: 'remain in me; love one another'; in the form of conditionals: 'if you remain in me; whoever keeps my commandments'; and in the form of futures: 'they will hate you; they will cast you out of the synagogue'. The central word is 'remain': a remaining notwithstanding the imperfect situation of the moment where ignorance and incomprehension predominate; a remaining notwithstanding a future of opposition and persecution. The subjectivity of the group of

disciples has an insecure base, i.e. the remaining itself is problematic: the group
of disciples who are at table with Jesus as a model for a future group of readers
that can be brought to remain faithful to Jesus' words only with exhortation and
fulfilled prophecy.

This subjectivity, which is above all future directed and, therefore, rather
weak internally, is surrounded by a subject installation that is even more polemical: the identification and non-identification of 'the Jews' and 'the *kosmos*'.
At the start it is not clear from the text itself that the hatred of the kosmos will
later on in the text be expressed in negative activities of Jews. The first indication is the expression: 'in their law it is written' (15:25), clearly indicating the
Jewish law. That 'the Jews' play a leading part in the hatred of the *kosmos* becomes clear only when it is said that 'they' will banish the disciples from the
synagogue (16:2).

Are 'the Jews', then, to be identified with 'the *kosmos*' with all its ideological
implications ? My answer would be yes and no. It is clear that John 8:23 links
'the Jews' and 'the *kosmos*' explicitly, but it is also clear that in the last occurrences of the word '*kosmos*' in John (18:20 and 19:37) there is a transition from 'the
kosmos' as the public arena of the Jews to 'the kosmos' as the area where Pilate
is in command. As with other central concepts (ἀλήθεια and ὥρα) the text of
John deconstructs itself. John 15:18-16:4 stays between Jn 8:23 and Jn 18:20;
19:37. There is identification but there is also openness to the larger *kosmos* in
which the God-haters, the people who reject the only true God, are in power
(cf. 15:23-24 and Ex 20:5; Dt 5:9 and 7:9-10 (Septuagint)). The text makes it
clear that the subject installation of 'the Jews' and of 'the *kosmos*' is in a truly
critical stage.

3.3 The focalisation and the voices of the text

The linguistic representation contains also an element of communication: the
linguistic expressions in connexion with the whole system of linguistic communication seen now in its meta-communicative aspect: the author's self-presenta-
tion, who takes for himself/herself the right to use that linguistic communication which seems to him/her to be the most apt. This omnipotence of the inter-
pretating subject (the all knowing narrator of a narrative) is dispersed in a poly-
phony of speaking voices, especially in narrative texts; i.e. there are characters
that determine the discourse of a text in different and often contradictory ways.
As I have said already, an ideologically oriented research cannot stop with the
analysis of the perspective and/or the analysis of the focalisation of a text.
Ideological interests are determined not by communication as such but by the
manner and the mode of the communication.

The real question is the question about the right to speak. While in a story
only the implicit narrator speaks, there is always room for other speakers: cha-

racters who speak for themselves and are or are not in agreement with one another; characters who give the point of view of the narrator and others who resist
that perspective and who, yet, narratively go scot-free.

The intensity of the conflict determines how far the narrator wants or can
make his listeners part of the social conflict that lies at the origin of the narrative. Different from what L. Goldmann thought, there is very seldom in literature a direct reflection, a direct relation between the discursive conflicts in the
text and the social conflicts outside of the text (cf. Goldmann 1955; 1964). Most
of the time there are broken mirrors – a reflection of a mirror-image – which allow the reader a glimpse of a few pieces of the reality (cf. Macherey 1966). It is,
therefore, not without meaning to ask the question about power: whose words
are spoken and who has an interest; which position of power is supported and
which words are rejected and why; how is the conflict verbalised and which solutions are being offered. It is usual to see the polyphonic character of a text as
dialogue. It is better, however, to speak about this text reality in terms of
communication as a process where, however distorted, the positions of power in
society reappear with all existing conflicts and unresolved taking of positions,
filled with opposed interests that give to the strongest the right to speak the first
and last word and that only in important literature – and the Bible is part of that
– creates space for the otherwise suppressed and not-heard word of the weak
and losing party.

This aspect of ideology shows necessarily real constancy. An author cannot
endlessly vary the way in which s/he maintains communication with the
audience. As far as John 15 is concerned, at least, three levels are important:
1. The narrator of the text has made Jesus' knowledge his own, a knowledge
that according to the text itself is of divine origin. As especially Sternberg has
shown (cf. Sternberg 1987), this literary phenomenon endows the Bible with a
very special character (also the New Testament, *pace* Sternberg). The narrator,
who lets his main character speak 'words of God', gives himself a divine authority. The literary effect is not nothing! The narrative is given a divine authority in
an even more explicit way than happens with texts involving an omniscient and
omnipotent narrator. However, some nuance is necessary. Because the narrator
stands at a distance from the events he talks about (in John 15 the event of
Jesus' discourse), his own privileged knowledge is in service of the privileged
knowledge of the main character, Jesus – who himself is in service of the still
greater authority of God himself (cf. 15:1, 2, 8, 9a, 10b, 15, 16d, 23, 24, 26; 16:2).
It is a linguistic authority structure whose consequences have as yet hardly been
thought about in exegesis.
2. But that is not all. On a 'lower' level, a level that is more embedded in the
text, words are spoken 'with authority'. In John 15 only Jesus speaks. Thus, there
are no differences in focalisation. Yet several 'voices' speak. The manner in
which this happens is very important ideologically. In the first place we have
Jesus as the obedient and loving son of the father-God and as God's prophet

who has the right to speak to his disciples, 'the Jews' and 'the *kosmos*' in the way in which it happens in the text. The positive acceptance by the narrator of this *oikos*- and prophet-ideology determines the manner of the exercise of this authority and its structure. This can have a negative effect, as appears e.g. in cultures where it is not self evident that a son remains obedient to his father all his life; or where the exclusive father-son relationship is seen as negative for women. Whenever the positive evaluation of the use of the *oikos*- (and the prophet-) ideology is contradicted, John's authority diminishes.

3. Centrally located *qua* content is the phenomenon that what belongs to biblical Israel is attributed to Jesus. This is done in such a natural way that many readers do not even notice it (as e.g. in the exegesis of Jn 14, cf. Beutler 1984). Few professional readers overlooked it in John 15: Jesus is the true vine, i.e. Jesus is the true Israel, the Israel to which God has given his own faithful trust. Because the group of disciples (notwithstanding 15:3!) receives the task to realise anew this fidelity of God, every sign of an idea of a 'new Israel', which would have succeeded the 'old Israel', is absent. In John's perspective Jesus is the manifestation of God's own fidelity to Israel. Whoever is not willing to accept this places oneself outside the covenant that God made with Israel. The text ascribes this negative behaviour to 'the Jews', respectively to 'the *kosmos*'. There is no need to listen to their voice (any longer). The ambiguous way in which the text deals with 'their law' (15:25) shows that even the narrator of John's Gospel – always seemingly so sure of himself – is subject to ambiguity. It is a word that is theirs , i.e. it is a word of the opponents and yet it expresses apparently a opinion that is worth quoting. In the margin of the text a conflicting truth has been hidden.

BIBLIOGRAPHY

Althusser, L. 1976. *Positions*. Paris: Maspero.

Beutler, J. 1984. *Habt keine Angst. Die erste johanneische Abschiedsrede (Joh 14)*. Stuttgart: Katholisches Bibelwerk.

Brown, R. E. 1970. *The Gospel according to John*, vol. 2. Garden City, New York: Doubleday.

Culpepper, R. A. 1983. *Anatomy of the Fourth Gospel. A Study in Literary Design*. Philadelphia: Fortress Press.

De la Potterie, I. 1977. *La vérité dans saint Jean*. Rome: Biblical Institute Press.

Ebertz, M. N. 1987. *Das Charisma des Gekreuzigten. Zur Soziologie der Jesusbewegung*. Tübingen: Mohr.

Elliott, J. H. 1986. Social-Scientific Criticism of the New Testament: More on Methods and Models. *Semeia* 35, 1-13.

Goldmann, L. 1955/1971. *Le dieu caché. Etude sur la vision tragique dans les Pensées de Pascal et dans le Théâtre de Racine*. Paris: Gallimard.

Goldmann, L. 1964. *Pour une Sociologie du Roman*. Paris: Gallimard.

Hamon, P. 1984. *Texte et idéologie. Valeurs, Hiérarchies et Evaluations dans l'oeuvre Littéraire*. Paris: Presses Universitaires de France.

Hemer, C. J. 1989. *The Letters to the Seven Churches of Asia in their Local Setting*. Sheffield: JSOT

Press.

Macherey, P. 1966. *Pour une Théorie de la Production Littéraire*. Paris: Maspero. (Translated into English, 1978: *A Theory of Literary Production*. London: Routledge and Kegan Paul.)

Onuki, T. 1984. *Gemeinde und Welt im Johannesevangelium. Ein Beitrag zur Frage nach der theologischen und pragmatischen Funktion des johanneischen 'Dualismus'*. Neukirchen: Neukirchener Verlag.

Rendtorff, 1959. προφητης. *TWNT*.

Smit, D. J. 1988. Responsible Hermeneutics: A Systematic Theologian's Response to the Readings and Readers of Luke 12:35-48. *Neotestamentica* 22, 441-484.

Sternberg, M. 1987. *The Poetics of Biblical Narrative. Ideological Literature and the Drama of Reading*. Bloomington: Indiana University Press.

Van Aarde, A. G. 1988. Narrative Point of View: An Ideological Reading of Luke 12:35-48. *Neotestamentica* 22, 235-255.

S. J. NORTJé

ON THE ROAD TO EMMAUS – A WOMAN'S EXPERIENCE

1.Introduction

1.1 Definition

Like all definitions feminism defies formulation. This also applies to terms like 'feminist', 'feminism', 'feminist theology', etc. This can probably be attributed to the extremely varied forms and perspectives on the subject. Sakenfeld (1988:5) defines feminism as follows:

> A feminist, broadly speaking, is one who seeks justice and equality for all people and who is especially concerned for the fate of women – all women – in the midst of 'all people'. Such a definition means that issues pertinent to racism, classism, and ecology, as well as peacemaking, are part of the purview of feminism.

To arrive at a 'biblical' or 'theological' feminism one has to ask questions of a feminist nature in the studyof the Bible. Feminists, in particular, are concerned with

> patriarchy as a pyramidal system and hierarchical structure of society and church in which women's oppression is specified not only in terms of race and class but also in terms of marital status (Schüssler Fiorenza 1984:37).

Later in this paper we shall deal with this more extensively.

1.2 Background

The Enlightenment of the nineteenth century greatly influenced the church and theology. This is also true of women in this century (Boerwinkel 1974:168-170), their interpretation of Scripture and particularly their status vis-à-vis ecclesiastical offices. Women came to realise their need to partake in the affairs of what has hitherto been a dominantly male pre-occupation. Ackermann (1988:14) recorded some pertinent examples of women who consciously recognise that this movement has, for example, opened the door to a feminist approach to and interpretation of the Bible. It was Sarah Grimke who pointed out the male biased interpretation of the Bible. Antoinette Brown (1857) studied the epistles of Paul by addressing feminist questions to the text. Elizabeth Stanton (1890) and some twenty other female scholars studied those parts of the Bible where women occur or are mentioned. These studies eventually lead to the publication of the so-called 'Women's Bible'.

It was only two decades ago that feminist studies really appeared on the scene. In 1968 M. Daly set the scene for modern feminism with a publication *The Church and the Second Sex*, which was soon followed by numerous publications, for example, those of J. Huber (1973), L. M. Russell (1974) and R. R. Ruether (Ruether (ed.) 1974). Since then the flow of publications on various aspects of the subject increased dramatically. It has become a difficult task even to attempt to draw up a list of selected and relevant publications. Jakobsen (1989:84-88) gives a selected bibliography on women's studies in the area of religion and theology.

1.3 Basic issues

Feminist theology is characterised by diversity. As already mentioned, feminism cannot be qualified or expressed by a single theological issue or perspective. Generally speaking, feminist studies have two basic viewpoints in common: *(a)* Feminists reject outright any model or scheme of theological thinking that is based on *patriarchal* presuppositions. Sadly this has been the case in the major theological works on the theology and the church for the past two thousand years. *(b)* To feminists the concept of *experience* lies at the core of their theological activities. Ackermann (1988:15-16) quite aptly describes experience as a hermeneutic tool as follows:

> ...what have been called the objective sources of theology, scripture and traditon, are them-selves codified human experience and that human experience is the starting point and the en-ding point of the hermeneutical circle. Feminist theology draws on women's experience which...has almost entirely been shut out of theological reflections in the past.

The various perspectives and dimensions within feminist theology can be divided into two main streams of thought, although such a division is by no means exact and exclusive.

The first part of this division has basically a single component: The liberation of women from male domination. As Graham says: 'The heart of FF (Fairness Feminism – my comment) is sexual equality' (Graham 1988:306). It is obvious that this type of feminism is exclusive in so far as the concept of liberation is only relevant to women. There is, however, a broader and more inclusive type of feminism that 'seeks liberation and a new vision for all of humanity' (Ackermann 1988:17). This calls for an operative liberating force in matters of racial discrimination, class distinctions, dehumanising of people, the disturbance and destruction of the ecological balance in nature. Bussmann (1985:149) reiterates that

men also suffer from the limitations placed on their lives that say they should manifest typical male values and norms: rationality, power, hardness, strength. Every human being should
accept and develop both the 'strong' and the 'gentle' qualities in order to become totally human.

What feminism did for women during the past decade cannot be overestimated.
In the past it was only some women who succeeded in achieving the highest
echelons of the male world. Now feminism, however, is opening doors to all
women to be part of the male-reserved-job market, giving them opportunities
for developing the necessary skills and abilities.

The question still remains of the credibility and reliability of feminist
theology and its influence on the status of women in the church. Through centuries the church had a well established male structure and women had to contend with challenging these male dominated institutions in order to obtain their
rightful place among men. Primarily, women studied those parts of the Bible
where women occurred (e.g. Bolkenstein 1982:80-113) or where they
transformed patriarchal structures to such an extent that they justified their
claims to gain in all church offices (e.g. De Groot 1978:35-41; Schüssler
Fiorenza 1983:68-95). According to Woodward (1989:38) feminist Christians
argue that

> mutuality is what Jesus taught and what his male successors subverted in creating a males-
> only power structure in the church. Thus, for feminist theologians, patriarchy is the Original
> Sin and root of all other social evils: sexism, racism, clericalism, ageism, classism,
> homophobia, hatred of the body, parental subjugation of children and mankind's
> technological rape of Mother Earth.

At present the issue is no longer equality of the sexes but the thorough transformation of the religious institutions (Woodward 1989:38), and women are determined to do this. In America for example, about twenty-one thousand ordained
women serve as ministers. Between 1977 and 1987 the number of women
graduating with Master of Divinity degrees increased by two hundred and
twenty-four per cent. That means that in the leading interdenominational
theological seminaries at least a third of the students are women and 'at Yale
and Harvard, they're more than half' (Woodward 1989:39).

This raises serious questions and problems for the future structure of the
church in America. As women increasingly take over church offices, to the same
degree men withdraw from the ministry to seek positions in other professions.
As Woodward (1989:39) says: 'pay scales go down, prestige goes down and the
men get out'.

The next phrase of Christian feminism was not to put more women in the
pulpit, but to aim at a thorough and comprehensive transformation of the
language, symbols and sacred texts of the Christian faith – and therefore of the
faith itself. This culminated in a feminist movement that committed itself to the

establishment of a 'women-church' – a movement of 'self-identified women and women-identified men...to reinterpret the gospel from the perspective of women's liberation' (Woodward 1989:40). Under the leadership of distinguished feminist theologians, like Elizabeth Schüssler Fiorenza and Rosemary Ruether this movement created its own life-cycle ceremonies: 'They include rituals to mark the start of menopause, the union of a lesbian couple, mourning for a still-birth and recovery from an abortion' (Woodward 1989:40).

It is at this point that feminist theology alienated itself and lost considerable support from women – and men. After all, feminist theology and christian feminists need to be accepted by the church and all its members – male and female. It is not a matter to be settled only by women in theological seminaries.

1.4 The situation in South Africa

Except for some individuals at more so-called 'liberated' universities, feminist theology has not really found appreciable support in South Africa. The reason for this can probably be attributed to the following considerations:

(a) In accordance with the predominantly conservative character of the white South African society and consequently their more conservative religious beliefs, women in this country, it seems, prefer to suffer male domination rather than question fundamental Scripture authority and traditional institutions. Within the black South African communities it seems that traditional cultural values are the inhibiting factors for black women in developing a sense of feminist awareness.

(b) Another closely linked factor could be the conservative policy and, more specifically, the system of apartheid in South Africa, which does not allow black communities and individuals to develop to the same extent as the white society. liberation theology started out as a protest movement against various forms of oppression in society, e.g. socio-political, racial, economic, cultural, sexual, etc. Consequently feminist theology has a strong political liberation connotation (Ackermann 1988:24-28). For black women, feminist theology has a white connotation, which apriori makes it difficult for them to fully appreciate and embrace the feminist movement. These factors are probably some of the main causes why feminist theology in South Africa has not yet found wide support.

1.5 Conclusion

Despite the excessive views of some of its leading protagonists, feminist theology has a positive influence on the overall position of women in society and the Church. This movement brought new challenges to biblical interpretation and theology. The merit of feminist theology is that it forced theology as such to ask once again whether it is still reliable for today's contexts. Lombaard (1989:55) asks questions like: What role should the Bible play in human liberation movements? (cf. Schüssler Fiorenza 1984:13). How should we use new interpretation technics, such as deconstruction, reception, rhetoric etc.? Can the current reader's perspective on the Bible and its narrations be normative for the interpretation of the Bible?

Bearing this in mind we cannot ignore the signs that feminist theology has come to a crossroad. To be significant in the church, to women and to men, the 'movement' should be more trustworthy in its biblical interpretation, hermeneutical tools, church ceremonies and gender-free religion than it has been to the present.

2. Practical illustration of a feminist approach and method

One of the basic issues of feminist theology in its interpretation of the Bible is *experience*. Two aspects of experience as hermeneutic tool are involved viz. the 'women's experience in their struggle for liberation' from male domination (Schüssler Fiorenza 1984:13) and experience as 'distant from the 'objective' (i.e. 'male' – my comment) sources of truth of classical theologies' (Ackermann 1988:15).

I will use the narration of the *two disciples on their way to Emmaus in Luke 24:13-35* to illustrate a woman's perspective on biblical narration.

The narration of the two 'disciples' returning to Emmaus and Jesus' appearance to them is unique to the Gospel of Luke. Luke narrates two appearances of Jesus. One story (Lk 24:36-49) coincides with the other Gospel appearance-traditions in which Jesus appears to Peter and the disciples. However, Luke's main story about the appearance of Jesus is the one narrating him on his way to Emmaus with two 'unknown' disciples (Lk 24:13-35).

This narration shows literary links with other stories in the Luke-Acts unity, viz. the Feeding of the Multitude (Lk 9:10-17), Philip and the Ethiopian (Ac 8:26-40) and Jesus' appearance to the eleven disciples (Lk 24:36-49). Scholars are divided on the issue of historicity of this narration, i.e. whether it is indeed a historical event or a literary composition by the author. Marshall (1978:890-891) discusses various viewpoints in this regard. It is not the concern of this paper to discuss this problem and I conclude this issue by concurring with Marshall (1978:891):

> ...we are justified in regarding this story as having a basis in tradition, and that this tradition can have a historical basis. The hand of Luke in the formation of the narrative cannot be denied, but he was by no means creating his story *de novo*.

The question that concerns us: Why does Luke have Jesus appear to these two unknown followers and let *them* share in the glory of his resurrection when in fact he mentions the appearance of Jesus to Peter and the rest of the disciples almost as a passing comment?

Similarly, there is no consensus among scholars as to the purpose of this narration. I quote only two views: O'Toole (1984:46) sees two main issues in this narrative, viz. 'the risen Jesus is present to the community through the Eucharist' and that Luke used it as didactic-paraenetic material to address the Christian community. Marshall (1978:891) thinks the main purpose is 'to guarantee the fact of the resurrection'.

2.1 The burning hearts

Reading the narration I came to the conclusion that a story is told here about two people who had experienced something that had a profound influence on their lives: 'They were talking...about everything that had happened' (Lk 24:14). What this *everything* was, we can conclude from what they tell the 'stranger' in Luke 24:19-24 and this is a summary of the ministry of Jesus as Luke describes it in Luke 2:40,52 to Luke 24:12.

What they experienced of this 'everything' is spelled out in the narration.

(a) According to the narration of Luke 23 and 24 the 'two of them' (Lk 24:13) were part of a wider circle of followers of Jesus who were present since the beginning of his ministry: 'But all those who knew him, including the women who had followed him from Galilee, stood at a distance, watching these things' (Lk 23:49, cf. also Lk 8:1-3 and 10:1). Jesus' powerful words and deeds were also well known to them (Lk 24:19).

(b) Like Simeon (Lk 2:25) and 'all who were looking forward to the redemption of Jerusalem' (Lk 2:38) these two, in accordance with their knowledge and experience of Jesus' words and deeds 'hoped that he was the one who was going to redeem Israel' (Lk 24:21). 'They saw the blind receive sight, the lame walk, those who have leprosy cured, the deaf hear, the dead raised, and the good news preached to the poor' (Lk 7:22).

(c) But their hopes were dispelled when Jesus was sentenced to death and crucified by the chief priests and the very rulers who were supposed to expect the redemption of Israel (Lk 24:20). Their hope for the redemption of Israel had come to a 'dead end'.

(d) They even waited for three days to see if, according to Jewish belief, the soul had left the body. On the other hand, they had 'possibly a dim memory that Jesus had spoken enigmatically of something happening on the third day' (Marshall 1978:895).

(e) Their experience was not only negative as to what had happened, but they were amazed and confused by the women, who said that Jesus is alive (Lk

24:23). The reason for their confusion may be that despite the rumours about Jesus being alive, they did not experience it. So they returned home. This information serves as a bridge to the next 'level' of experience.

(f) Jesus himself then appears on the scene as a stranger who evaluates their hopes and beliefs as 'foolish' and 'slow of heart to believe' (Lk 24:25). Thus despite the fact that they had followed Jesus during his ministry and witnessed his crucifixion, they still did not understand the way of God's redemption for Israel.

(g) Again (as in Lk 18:31-34) Jesus explains God's redemption, saying that the Christ has to (δεῖ) suffer to enter into his glory (Lk 24:26). If they knew Moses and the Prophets they would understand the mystery. A light is kindled but still they did not recognise Jesus by his exposition of Scripture.

(h) The narrator then introduces another bridge to the next 'level' of experience, viz. the two followers' inviting Jesus to stay with them. No further detail is given about the event because the key to understand this narrative lies in the subsequent events. At the table when *Jesus gave thanks, broke the bread and began to give it to them* their eyes were opened and they *recognised him*. This is really the denouement of the whole narration.

The question is: Why couldn't they recognise Jesus on the road, even while he was explaining the Scriptures, and why were their eyes opened only when he broke the bread? To answer the question we should take into account the micro-context of the narration as well as the macro-context of the whole Gospel. The problem these two followers had is that they failed to understand the suffering and therefore the death of Jesus.

Jesus' whole life, according to the Gospel of Luke, was a life of suffering and a life identified with those who suffered. Marshall (1978:36) says that 'Luke particularly stresses how this salvation is for all who are poor and needy...'. Twice Jesus announced his coming suffering and the disciples did not understand (Lk 9:44-45; 18:31-34). After the second announcement, Luke narrates the healing of the blind begger. What is striking in this narration is the contrast between the inability of the disciples to understand the coming suffering of Jesus and the desperate desire of the 'suffering' blind begger to be able to see: 'Lord, I want to see' (Lk 18:41). The failure of the two disciples to recognise Jesus 'is part of a larger spiritual blindness which must be cured...and is caused by a lack of insight into God's purpose...' (Tannehill 1986:282). In Luke 19:10 Jesus explained the purpose of the coming of the Son of Man '...to seek and to save what was lost'. This redemption came only through the death of Jesus.

To return to the people of Emmaus, it becomes clear that with the breaking of the bread they understood the suffering and death of Jesus. By understanding the death of Jesus they were then able to recognise the glorified Lord.

The question that concerns us next is, why the narrator mentions the burning hearts of the two disciples only after they had recognised Jesus in retrospect?

The reason could lie in the fact that the narrator intends accentuating the reality of the risen Lord, and the significance it has for the church (Marshall 1978:899). An aspect in understanding the 'burning hearts' of the two men is the information supplied in what follows directly after this, viz. 'They got up and returned at once to Jerusalem' (Lk 24:33). Their experience and recognition of the living Jesus inspired them to return immediately to the disciples in Jerusalem. A strange turn in the story is that the narrator has the disciples returning to Jerusalem just to find out that the Lord has already appeared to Simon and that the disciples already knew this (Lk 24:34). This took all the 'fun' out of the story. A rather disappointing ending to the Emmaus story.

Finally, to answer our question we must advance to the next 'level' of experience in the story, and this is precisely what the narrator wants us to do. Reading the resurrection and appearance story again we are lead to the conclusion that the Emmaus story is really an addition to the Gospel tradition. The main purpose of the story is not to serve as proof for the resurrection. The women, Simon and the disciples are assigned this witness (as in the other Gospels).

We should rather understand the 'burning hearts' as an *introduction* to the work of the Holy Spirit kindling faith in Jesus as Lord (cf. Marxsen 1970:139), and the Holy Spirit as the power behind the mission of the two disciples to Jerusalem, and therefore the believer. This is spelled out in Jesus' command to the disciples to be 'witnesses to these things' (Lk 24:48). The story of the two disciples on the road to Emmaus is repeated in a nutshell in Jesus' final words to the full complement of disciples (Lk 24:44-49).

And so the Emmaus story is really a summary of the story of Jesus. At the same time it serves as an introduction to the second part of Luke's record of the origin and expansion of faith in the risen Lord. In this sense the Emmaus story is as much a summary as it is a *bridge* to the *Acts of the Apostles*.

2.2 Conclusion

In conclusion I pose the question (as Ackermann 1988:26 also does): How do we white South African female oppressors and oppressed rediscover our *imago Dei* both in ourselves and in the others? The narration of Jesus' appearance to the two disciples on the road to Emmaus gives us some clue to the solution of the problem. As we have pointed out, two aspects are of major importance for the understanding of this narration, viz. the 'burning hearts' of the two disciples and Jesus becoming known to them by the breaking of the bread.

The transformation from one level of experience to another gives significance to the narration. Their 'burning hearts' in becoming aware of *The Other* (the stranger talking to them on the road) are transformed into a participation in *The Me* of the breaking of the bread. By understanding the suffering of Jesus (the breaking of the bread) as God's redemption of the world and the way he entered his glory, the two disciples are transformed from 'foolish' and 'slow of heart to believe' to witnesses of 'repentance and forgiveness of sin...to all nations, beginning at Jerusalem'.

With this participation, the suffering *Other/other* becomes the suffering *Me/ me*. In this we rediscover our *imago Dei* both in ourselves and in others!

When we discover Jesus as the Other, he becomes the suffering me. It is therefore fundamentally important and necessary to create structures within the church and society to bring this experience into actuality. These structures are by nature context-bound and cannot be transferred from the primitive context (biblical context) to our modern context on a one-to-one basis (Nortjé 1988:92). Liberation in the Christian sense has the opportunities and the possibilities to create new structures for all human beings – male, female, white and black – to rediscover their *imago Dei*.

BIBLIOGRAPHY

Ackermann, D. 1988. Feminist Liberation Theology. A Contextual Option. *Journal of Theology for Southern Africa* 62, 14-28.

Boerwinkel, F. 1974. *Einde of Nieuw Begin? Onze Maatschappij Op de Breuklijn. Een Informatie- en Werkboek*. Bilthoven: Ambo.

Bolkenstein, M. H. 1982. De Plaats van de Vrouw in de Vroeg-Christelijke Gemeenten, in M. H. Bolkenstein & H. J. Bolkenstein-Van Bindsbergen (eds.). *Vrouw Zijn in het Licht van het Evangelie. Een Bundel Feministisch-Theologische Studies*. Baarn: Ten Have.

Bussmann, M. 1985. Woman and Man in Church History. *Theology Digest* 32, 148-149.

Daly, M. 1968. *The Church and the Second Sex*. London: Geoffrey Chapman.

De Groot, M. 1978. Maria en Elisabeth, in C. J. M. Halkes & D. Buddingh (eds.). *Als Vrouwen aan het Woord Komen. Aspecten van de Feministische Theologie*. Kampen: Kok.

Graham, G. 1988. Two Types of Feminism. *American Philosophical Quarterly* 25, 303-312.

Huber, J. 1973. *Changing Women in a Changing Society*. Chicago: University of Chicago Press.

Jakobsen, W. 1989. Feminist Theology: A Selective Bibliography. *Journal of Theology for Southern Africa* 66, 84-88.

Lombaard, C. 1989. Eva nie die Sondaar. *Insig* February, 54-55.

Marshall, I. H. 1978. *The Gospel of Luke: A Commentary on the Greek Text*. Exeter: Paternoster Press. (The New International Greek Testament Commentary.)

Marxsen, W. 1970. *The Resurrection of Jesus of Nazareth*. (Tr. by M. Kohl.) London: SCM.

Nortjé, L. 1988. Die Vrou in die Vroeë Christendom, in C. Breytenbach (ed.). *Church in Context: Early Christianity in Social Context*. Pretoria: NG Kerkboekhandel.

O'Toole, R. F. 1984. *The Unity of Luke's Theology: An Analysis of Luke-Acts*, v. 9. Wilmington: Michael Glazier. (Good News Studies.)

Ruether, R. R. (ed.) 1974. Religion and Sexism: Images of Women, in *The Jewish and Christian Traditions*. New York: Simon and Schuster.

Russell, L. M. 1974. *Human Liberation in a Feminist Perspective: A Theology*. Philadelphia: Westminster.

Sakenfeld, K. D. 1988. Feminist Perspectives on Bible and Theology: An Introduction to Selected Issues and Literature. *Interpretation* 42, 5-18.

Schüssler Fiorenza, E. 1983. *In Memory of Her: A Feminist Theological Reconstruction of Christian Origins*. New York: Crossroads.

Schüssler Fiorenza, E. 1984. *Bread not Stone: The Challenge of Feminist Biblical Interpretation*.
  Boston: Beacon.
Tannehill, R. C. 1986. *The Narrative Unity of Luke-Acts: A Literary Interpretation*, v. 1. Philadel-
  phia: Fortress.
Woodward, K. L. 1989. Feminism and the Churches. *Newsweek* 113, 38-41.

E. H. SCHEFFLER

READING LUKE FROM THE PERSPECTIVE OF LIBERATION THEOLOGY

1. Introduction

To read the New Testament from the perspective of liberation theology has become increasingly important in recent years for a twofold reason. Firstly, fifteen years after the pioneering book of Gutiérrez (1973) was published, the influence of liberation theology has not diminished, but rather increased. Secondly, liberation theology has itself also become increasingly reflective about its own premises and position within the theological discipline at large. The use and interpretation of the Bible is part of this reflection (cf. I. Mosala 1986; 1987; Weber 1989).

Liberation theologians are sometimes criticised for using the Bible on a rather *ad hoc* and selective basis in order to find inspiration from *any* part of Scripture or scriptural traditions that seemed to support its cause (cf. Loader 1987). In particular they draw upon the Exodus and prophetic traditions from the Old Testament. As far as the New Testament is concerned, a great interest has been shown in a political interpretation of the historical Jesus. The Gospel of Luke (as Gospel for the poor), and especially Luke 4:18 also feature prominently (cf. Moltmann 1975:11-12; Boesak 1977:20-26; Tutu 1983:63,76; *Kairos document* 1986:25; Motlhabi 1987:7; De Villiers 1987b:55-56).

What I intend in this article may perhaps be some attempt to contribute to an honest process of liberation. It is not my intention to assert that one has to listen to the Gospel according to Luke in a fundamentalistic way in order to get the 'true biblical' way of doing liberation theology. My intention is rather to attempt to let the Gospel of Luke dialogue with liberation theology. Being one of Early Christianity's most comprehensive documents (even when the Acts of the Apostles is also taken into consideration – cf. Cassidy 1987), and having indeed a deep concern for the concept of liberation, it is my belief that such an interest and dialogue with Luke's Gospel can contribute to the refining of insights within liberation theology and the practice of liberation in a more liberative way.

In what follows I shall first of all attempt to give a short introduction to liberation theology (par. 2), before turning to my own reflections of the topic of Luke and liberation (par. 3).

2. What is Liberation Theology?

Gutiérrez (1988:174) summarises liberation theology as follows:

> The theology of liberation attempts to reflect on the experience and meaning of the faith
> based on the commitment to abolish injustice and to build a new society; this theology must
> be verified by the practice of that commitment, by active, effective participation in the
> struggle which the exploited social classes have undertaken against their oppressors.
> Liberation from every form of exploitation, the possibility of a more human and dignified
> life, the creation of a new mankind – all pass through this struggle.

Deist (1984:94) defines it as

> an interpretation of theology from the view point of the politically and socially oppressed ac-
> cording to which God is by nature on the side of the oppressed (cf. the Exodus event, Is 61:1-
> 3; Lk 1:46ff) and encourages them to liberate themselves from the oppressing powers in or-
> der to live as free human beings.

Although these definitions may be to the point, it should immediately be
pointed out that the question 'what is liberation theology' cannot be adequately
answered by means of a simple definition. What can be and is labelled as 'liberation theology' is simply too diverse for that (cf. Motlhabi 1987:1-6).

In order to obtain an insight into this diversity and complexity of liberation
theology, we shall therefore first of all place liberation theology within historical
context (origins), and thereafter brief attention will be given to the main propo-
nents and variations of the movement.

As far as *origins* are concerned, it should first of all be pointed out that liberation theology is not a totally new factor in Christianity. In fact it can be said
that the theology of the first Christians, who were politically, socially and economically deprived, was nothing else than one of liberation. When Christianity became the official religion of the Roman empire and spread among the rich, the
concern for the lower classes and their situation was actually abandoned.
During the dark ages the church had a lot of power and it had a firm grip on the
masses. The movement of Francis of Assisi (twelfth century) was a reaction
against the 'topdog'- position of the church, but it spelled no danger for the
Church at large. During the Reformation period the peasant revolt lead by
Thomas Münzer was an attempt at overthrowing the yoke of serfdom and
feudalism in Germany, but the movement was opposed by Luther and the
Church's marriage with the authorities continued (cf. Loader 1988).

Perhaps the Enlightenment of the seventeenth and eighteenth centuries
paved the way for the Church's position to be questioned by the lower classes.
Marx made the point very harshly that the Church's way in dealing with the
poor working class was nothing else than doping them with the gospel as *opium
for the people*. With the promise of a heavenly reward (pie in the sky) the
Church encouraged the suffering masses to accept their lot. Christianity as such

became at stake. A movement then arose that asserted that this need not be, because a social concern for the lowly was inherent in Christianity itself (e.g. Ritschl, Maurice, cf. Loader 1988).

The nineteenth century was also the century of colonialism, accompanied by extended missionary work. Although the gospel was widely accepted by Third World peoples and much charity was done by (amongst others) medical hospitals, Christianity was always presented in collaboration with the colonial powers and never as a force that would encourage its new adherents to arise against these colonial authorities. The emergence of liberation theology in the late sixties can therefore be regarded as a final reaction against the oppression of nineteenth century colonialism.

According to Motlhabi (1987) liberation theology can actually be regarded as three different theologies, namely Latin American liberation theology, Black Theology (American and South African) and Feminist liberation theology. To these I would also add 'European' liberation theology (*vide infra*).

The main exponent of *Latin American liberation theology* is Gustavo Gutiérrez whose epochmaking book *A Theology of Liberation* appeared in 1973 and has virtually become a classic. The actuality of this book was condoned in 1988 when a fifteenth year anniversary edition (with an update introduction from the author) was published (1988). In this book Gutiérrez addresses the social discrepancies between the classes in Latin America. Much emphasis is therefore laid on socio-economic suffering. Other exponents of Latin American liberation theology are José Miranda (1980), the Boff brothers (1984) and José Miguez-Bonino (1974).

James Cone (1969; 1970) is probably the main exponent of American *black theology*. In his work Christianity as related to black power and racism in America is sharply addressed. Roberts (1971) became Cone's main rival in the American movement, the dividing issue being that of reconciliation between black and white.

In South Africa the first book on black theology (Moore 1973) was initially banned. Various publications followed in which the *apartheid* system was rejected from a theological point of view (e.g. Boesak 1977; 1984; Tutu 1983; Mosala & Tlhagale 1986; *Kairos document* 1986; *Road to Damascus* 1989).

Feminist theology is connected to 'classical' liberation theology in the sense that it identifies with the desire for liberation from oppression. However, it goes further by exposing women's subordinate position in contemporary as well as biblical society. The Bible is therefore criticised in so far as it provides the basis for the oppression of women (cf. Motlhabi 1987:11). The main exponent of this movement is Ruether (1972; 1975; 1985a; 1985b), and black contributions are those of Thetele (1979), B. Mosala (1986) and Bennett (1986).

In North America Brown (1978) and Herzog (1974) represent the main exponents from the white section of the population. In Europe, Moltmann's emphasis on 'psychische Befreiung' (1973), 'kulturelle Entfremdung' and 'die vom

Menschen unterworfene Kreatur' (1975) adds specific dimensions to liberation theology that is pertinent to the First World.

Conclusion: Liberation theology reflects on faith in the face of acute human suffering, which is experienced in specific contexts. It focuses strongly on political oppression, but other forms of suffering also receive attention. In its political reflection, Marxist analysis (cf. Deist 1987; Miranda 1980) is used to a greater or lesser extent. Being contextual, liberation theology does not work with unchangeable and stagnated 'truths', but is open to criticism that would better its own cause and that of 'the lowly'.

3. Liberation from suffering in Luke 4:16-30

3.1 General remarks

Three South African black theologians have reflected on Luke's Gospel in their doctoral dissertations. According to Boesak (1977:20-26), traditional Western theology should be rejected for its spiritualisation of the concept of the poor. According to him the Gospel is in agreement with liberation theology's view of 'the wholeness of life' and 'total liberation' (1977:26).

Contrary to Boesak's positive use of the Gospel, Luke is criticised by Mosala for his 'ideological suppression of the social revolutionary class' (1987a:155). According to Mosala there lies danger in the direct application of the Bible in liberation theology. The suffering of the working class should be taken as a point of departure and oppressive ideologies within the Bible should be exposed.

Mazamisa's (1987) analysis of the parable of the Good Samaritan is more in line with Boesak's positive use of Luke. His book reflects the most recent trends in New Testament exegesis and as such represents a dialogue between 'traditional exegesis' and black theology. The behaviour of the Good Samaritan is interpreted as 'beatific comradeship' and therefore relevant for black experience.

In an article on Luke 12:35-38, Sebothoma (1988:325) views Luke's Gospel as an expression of the liberating force of the gospel comprehending the 'totality of the human person'.

A 'liberationist' reading of a text does not imply the reading of a text according to the strict rules of a specific exegetical method (e.g. structural analysis, literary analysis, historical criticism), in which the application of the method actually dominates the whole exegetical operation and in which the involvement of the reader is eventually choked. The analysis rather departs from a specific motif (liberation from suffering), which is believed to be present in the text and which is exploited by the reader. This does not at all mean that the 'liberationist' exegete is careless towards reading preconceived ideas into the text. It also does not imply that the reader is a *tabula rasa* who merely receives the imprint of the text while reading. The liberation theologian reads from the personal experience of suffering or from the personal experience of *solidarity with sufferers*. Such reading is therefore a reflection on the text, and it is honest because it is a conscious reflection in which one is aware of one's own situation. It is a dialogue with the text in the sense that one probes the text in order to find meaning for one's own situation. It can also be critical towards the text when the ideology of the text (cf. Van Tilborg 1988) appears to be *non-liberative*. As such it is also not against traditional exegetical methods in principle, because insights from the latter can throw light on the motif of liberation from suffering.

The motif of liberation (ἄφεσις) is clearly present in Luke's Nazareth pericope, especially in Luke 4:18e and g:

18 a The Spirit of the Lord is upon me
 b because he has anointed me
 c to preach good news to the *poor*
 d He has sent me
 e to proclaim *release* to the *captives*
 f and recovering of sight to the *blind*
 g to set at *liberty* those that are *oppressed*
19 a to proclaim the acceptable year of the Lord.

The motif of liberation from suffering in this quotation is underlined by two important factors. *Firstly*, because this is a quotation from Scripture (Is 61:1ff), the sympathy for sufferers expressed in it is not merely a subjective feeling of Jesus or Luke: it has authority within its religious context by being supported by tradition. *Secondly*, the concern for the liberation of sufferers is directly linked to Jesus' messiahship for he has been *anointed* by the Spirit to have this concern for sufferers. In Jesus' day (as is the case today) the function of the Messiah was a much debated point as to whether its meaning was *political* (liberation from Roman oppression), or *spiritual* (salvation from sins). In this regard Luke's perspective has great meaning: Jesus is the Messiah because he cares and acts to the advantage of those who suffer. He is the Liberator of sufferers. Neither political nor spiritual suffering is excluded – on the contrary, both, as well as *any* kind of suffering, are included. Jesus' messiahship means that he is merciful, even as his Father is merciful (Lk 6:36).

Luke 4:18-19a is often referred to in isolation (e.g. Moltmann 1975:11-12; *Kairos document* 1986:25). To exploit the motif of liberation from suffering to the full, it is, however, necessary to refer to the Nazareth episode as a whole, which also occupies an important place in the entire Gospel. When it is compared to Mark (which happens to be its source – cf. Busse 1978; Bultmann 1967:31; Dibelius 1964:106; Tannehill 1972:52; Haenchen 1974:290; Schmithals 1980:61), on the basis of sequence it should have appeared between Luke 8:56

and 9:1ff. Luke, however, transposes the pericope to the inception of Jesus' ministry, thereby communicating that from the beginning Jesus' ministry was a ministry for sufferers. What is said in the rest of the Gospel should therefore be interpreted in the light of this *programmatic* (cf. Busse 1978:28-29) episode. In our reflection on the pericope, the lines should therefore also be drawn from the Nazareth episode to the rest of the Gospel.

As has become clear from what has been said above, liberation does not imply an abstract idea, but is always related to the concrete situation of certain states of suffering. To get a clearer concept of what liberation implies, the various dimensions of suffering that are linked to liberation should therefore be discerned in the text. This may perhaps have a self-critical function within liberation theology and may counteract a 'reductive' view on liberation which in the end may – at least in certain respects – appear to be enslaving rather than liberating. In what follows, therefore, I shall investigate the various dimensions of suffering as they are manifested in the Nazareth episode, and in the process refer to the recurrence of the same dimensions in the Gospel as a whole (and, because of constraints of space, to a lesser extent also in Acts). The dimensions are discussed as they appear in the text and nothing is to be deduced from the sequence of my presentation.

3.2 Liberation from economic suffering

In Luke 4:18c the good news to the *poor* is mentioned. This good news surely has a liberative connotation. But who are the poor? As far as Luke's Gospel is concerned it is a highly debated issue (cf. Degenhardt 1965; Schmithals 1975; Hoyt 1977; De Villiers 1987 etc). Is *the poor* equivalent to the late Jewish concept of the *anawim*, which had a comprehensive meaning (*int. al.* religious – cf. Brown 1977:351; Dibelius 1964:59-60), or should it be interpreted spiritually (as is perhaps the case in Matthew, cf. Mt 5:3), or should it be interpreted as a generic heading for the other suffering groups mentioned in verse 18? Or is *the poor* a *terminus technicus* designating 'Christians', as would perhaps appear to be the case in Romans 15:26? Since the *poor* features prominently in liberation theology as an *economic* concept (especially as far as Marxist analysis is used – cf. Deist 1987), this question is highly relevant.

Since liberation theology strives not to be fundamentalistic in its use of the Bible, it has an openness for the possibility that within the New Testament, the reference of term πτωχός may be diverse. What is important for the reading of the Lucan text is therefore not in the first place how the term is employed in other texts, but how *Luke* uses it within his own Greek context. A good rule would also be to accept a literal designation of a term, except when it is relatively clear from the text that it should be interpreted otherwise (e.g. the *poor in spirit* in Mt 5:3 or *rich toward God* in Lk 12:21).

Luke uses the term πτωχός ten times in his Gospel (4:18c; 6:20; 7:22; 14:13,21; 16:20,22; 18:22; 21:3) and one is nowhere compelled by the text to interpret the term metaphorically or allegorically. On the contrary, in most of these instances (especially 16:20,22; 18:22 and 21:3) only a literal understanding is feasible (cf. Scheffler 1988:58-60 where all ten instances are discussed). Furthermore it should be kept in mind that the Greeks had two words for poverty: πτωχός and πένης. The first designated total poverty, even towards the point of begging ('bettelarm' – cf. Rienecker 1970:137; Louw & Nida 1988:564; Bammel 1959:886), and the latter relative poverty (people with a small income – cf. Schottroff & Stegemann 1978:26). Luke always uses πτωχός and never πένης. The most prominent example is that of the begging Lazarus in the parable in Luke 16. There it is clearly portrayed what Luke meant by poverty. It is used there in its most literal meaning, as it is also in all probability the case in the rest of the Gospel, since nowhere does Luke give an indication to the contrary. The call to give alms in Luke 11:41 is also an indication that the *begging poor* is thought of, even though the term is not used there (cf. also 18:35). This also integrates with his concern for those who suffer from physical hunger (3:11; 6:1-5; 6:21; 9:10-17, see below).

The question how the liberation of the poor takes place is not directly answered in the Nazareth pericope, except that the liberation is closely linked to the coming of Jesus (4:21). In the rest of the Gospel and Acts some clues are, however, given. The lot of the poor should be alleviated through the charity of the rich towards the poor (e.g. Lk 16) and through the followers of Jesus who share what they have (e.g. Lk 3:11; Ac 2:44-45).

It can therefore be concluded that liberation theology has a partner in Luke in its concern for economic poverty. It can even be said that the term should be taken more literally than is often done. Not merely relative poverty is implied, but such a poverty that causes the severest pangs of hunger. Although there often exists a link between political oppression and poverty, the suffering of the poor compels the practitioners of liberation theology to alleviate the lot of the poor even if political liberation has not yet been achieved.

3.3 Liberation from physical suffering

In Luke 4:18f Jesus says that he came for the 'recovering of sight to the blind'. The *blind* in this verse should also be interpreted literally, as would also be the case in Luke 18:35-43. The blind in verse 18f therefore proleptically refer to Jesus' ministry as healer of the sick and those who suffer from bodily defects. Because God is the creator of the human body, Jesus is not indifferent towards *physical pain*. This is underscored in the Nazareth episode by what is said in verse 23 and the reference to the leper Naaman in verse 27. Furthermore, the Nazareth episode is closely linked to the Capernaum episode (cf. 4:23,43) where healings occur on a large scale (4:31-41).

From the rest of the Gospel it appears that Jesus healed a wide range of afflictions: fever (4:38-39), leprosy (5:12-16; 17:11-19), paralysis (5:17-26; 13:10-17), a withered hand (6:6-11), death or near-death (7:1-10; 7:11-17; 8:40-42,49-56), hemorrhage (8:43-48), inability to speak (11:14), dropsy (14:1-6) and blindness (18:35-43). Sometimes Jesus' compassion with the sick is so intense that he defies Jewish religious laws (e.g. the keeping of the Sabbath) in order to accomplish the healings (6:6-11; 13:10-17; 14:1-6). The suffering of the sick is often pertinently portrayed (4:38; 5:12), and whenever Jesus' ministry is summarised by the author, the healings (together with the proclamation of the word) are mentioned as being characteristic of that ministry (cf. 5:15; 6:18; 9:11; 13:32; 24:19; Ac 10:37-38).

Besides sickness there are also other forms of physical suffering towards which Jesus reveals compassion. To be a neighbour implies assistance to those who have been *assaulted* physically, as was the case with the man who fell among the robbers in the parable of the Good Samaritan and the slave of the high priest who was healed by Jesus during his arrest (22:51). Great emphasis is laid on *hunger* as the physical consequence of poverty (1:53; 3:11; 6:1-5; 6:21; 9:10-17; 16:21) and even physical *danger* (8:22-25) can be mentioned in this regard.

The portrayal of Jesus' healings as being characteristic of Jesus' ministry refutes the idea – so often present in traditional Western Christian thought – that the gospel mainly consists of going to church on Sunday and listening to a sermon. The extraordinary emphasis on physical suffering in Luke's Gospel proves that for Luke the gospel is not merely a 'spiritual' or 'religious' matter. It is as mundane as the human body. The attitude of Jesus' followers towards the physical suffering of others is an important religious matter. Authentic religion implies compassion towards those who suffer and the practical implementation of Jesus' call: *go and do likewise* (Lk 6:36; 10:37).

In a recent publication that is highly relevant for the South African situation, Nolan (1988:49) probes the concept of suffering and remarks:

> Suffering is a painfully concrete reality... One dare not speak about suffering in general ... One dare not lump together the discomfort of a headache or the inconvenience of losing a mere luxury with the pain of a mother who sees her children dying of starvation or a person who is at the mercy of cruel torturers day and night.

One can conclude that Nolan's view is in accordance with that of Luke, since the physical suffering portrayed in the Gospel is very concrete and intense. It is therefore disheartening that Nolan in the rest of his (vivid) exposition concentrates mainly on suffering within the political context. Although physical deprivation is in many cases (and not least so in South Africa) the result of political factors, the fact remains that sickness is indifferent to social classes, knowing no difference between rich and poor, oppressed or oppressor, black or white. This is why it often happens that the racial prejudices of whites vanish when they are overcome by severe illness. It is also ironical that burials are mainly the occasions on which black and white worship together in South Africa. It is therefore appropriate for liberation theology also to focus its attention on various kinds of physical suffering, as has in fact also been suggested by West (1983:74), when he criticised 'earlier conceptions of black theology of liberation' for 'its tendency to downplay existential issues such as death, disease, dread, despair and dissapointment which are related to yet not identical with suffering caused by oppressive structures'.

3.4 Liberation from psychological suffering

The validity of West's remark mentioned above is underscored when further dimensions of suffering are discerned in Luke's Gospel. In Luke 4:18e and 18g the liberation of *captives* and the *oppressed* are referred to. In the original context of Isaiah this could have referred to the Babylonian captivity (cf. Westermann 1976:292), or to the poor oppressed people who had remained in Palestine and who were ignored by those who returned (cf. Hanson 1979:63-65; Le Roux 1987:39-43). In order to establish what Luke had in mind, we have to take the rest of Luke–Acts into account.

In view of the exorcisms in Capernaum which are reported directly after the Nazareth episode (4:31-39), the captives and oppressed of 4:18 most probably refer (*int. al.*) to demon possession. This is supported by Acts 10:38 where Jesus' ministry is briefly summarised (in a way strongly reminiscent of 4:18) and where reference is made to the healing of 'all that were oppressed by the devil'. A too hasty conclusion that the political oppressed is referred to (perhaps on the basis of the English translation) should therefore be avoided (cf. Boesak 1977:20-26). Political oppression is indeed an important motif in Luke's Gospel (cf. 3.5 below), but not the main reference of Luke 4:18g.

Demon possesion can be interpreted as a form of *psychological suffering* (cf. Lk 9:39 where the symptoms of an epileptic attack are actually described). In the rest of the Gospel much attention is devoted to liberation from this kind of suffering, which Jesus effected through his exorcisms (4:33-37; 6:18-19; 8:26-39; 9:37-43a; 11:14-23). In Luke's description of the exorcisms, emphasis is not laid primarily on the casting out as such or the 'mighty deeds' of Jesus. That the focus is on the victims of demon possession is clear from Luke's mention in 4:35 (contrary to Mk 1:26) that the demon came out of the man *'having done him no harm'*. Alleviation of the demoniac's suffering seems to be what it is all about.

Luke's emphasis on psychological suffering is, however, not limited to demon possession. Although the 'captives' and 'oppressed' of 4:18e and g refer concretely to demon possession in the Capernaum episode, the terms do not loose their generic meaning, which can refer to *any* form of affliction. Luke seems to be sensitive to the psychological effect that more specific forms of suffering can cause. His third beatitude (6:21b: *'blessed are you that weep now'*) testifies to this, as well as Jesus' sympathy towards the relatives of sufferers (cf. 7:13; 8:52; 9:41-42). Luke's Gospel also has a special interest for *old people* with their peculiar needs of life-fulfilment or 'ego-integrity' (cf. Hjelle & Ziegler 1976:76). The narratives about Zechariah and Elizabeth and Simeon and Anna (cf. especially Lk 1:36; 2:29-30,38) can be mentioned in this regard (cf. also Scheffler 1988:94-96).

To distinguish a psychological dimension of suffering in Luke's Gospel is by no means an attempt to spiritualise or generalise concrete forms of suffering. On the contrary, it underscores the depth of suffering and shows how concrete forms of suffering can have a devastating effect on human beings as a whole. What has been remarked above (cf. 3.2 above) with reference to a one-sided political or economic concept of suffering, also applies here. Furthermore, the medical and psychological professions are drawn squarely into the realm of liberation theology.

3.5 *Liberation from spiritual or religious suffering*

In traditional Western theology salvation is often understood as salvation from sin. Liberation theologians are often accused of neglecting this dimension. To the extent that this has been the case, such a neglect can be ascribed to the one-sided concentration on 'salvation from sins in order to inherit eternal life', which often dominates the soteriology of Western theologians. Nolan (1988:34, 48) correctly stresses the close link between sin and suffering and the fact that sin always causes suffering. Salvation from sin also implies forgiveness which means the eradication of the guilt caused by sin. Forgiveness or release from sin therefore also implies liberation from the suffering caused by it.

It is interesting to note that the term ἄφεσις, which in Luke 4:18e and 18g is translated in the *Revised Standard Version* by 'release' and 'liberty', is exactly the same term that is used in the expression ἄφεσις ἁμαρτιῶν (*forgiveness of sins* – cf. 1:77; 3:3; 24:47; Ac 2:38; 5:31; 10:43; 13:38; 26:18). It is therefore highly probable that with 'captives' and 'oppressed' Luke also had those in mind who suffered from the guilt of their sins. It is also important to note that in Luke's day psychological, spiritual and physical suffering were not always so sharply distinguished. In the current world view there was a close link between demon possession, sickness and sin (cf. e.g. Lk 5:17-26). It therefore poses no problem that the 'release of the captives' and 'liberation of the oppressed' could simultaneously refer to demon possession, sickness and sin. What is important for Luke is that forgiveness of sins is not something that merely happens in the mind of God: it has a liberating effect for the sinner (cf. e.g. the joyful experience of the prodigal son after the unconditional forgiveness of his father –

Lk 15:22-24).

In the rest of the Gospel Jesus' acceptance and unconditional forgiveness of sinners are accentuated time and again. Mention can be made of the acceptance and forgiveness of the sinful woman (7:37-50), the promise of paradise to the penitent robber (23:40-43), Jesus' prayer for his crucifiers (23:34) as well as Jesus' social acceptance of 'toll-collectors and sinners' (5:27-32; 7:34; 13:1-5; 15:1; 18:9-14; 19:1-10).

With the motif of social acceptance of sinners, Luke suggests that liberation for sinners implies both forgiveness from God and acceptance by fellow humans. Therefore Christians who claim forgiveness of their sins and thereafter continue to denigrate fellow humans do not act in a liberative way. The motif of forgiveness from sins also hints at the desired liberation of the inflicters of suffering (e.g. political oppressors, the exploiting rich, assailants etc.). A liberation theology that denies this aspect because of fear of weakening the 'cause' and becoming 'soft on the enemy', is in an ironic way busy to weaken its own cause, because its desired freedom will ultimately be attained only when the oppressors are also free (*int. al.* from their sin of oppression). Although the sins of the oppressor are fought against with all vehemence, the *person* of the oppressor is to be saved. The oppressor–oppressed relationship is not to be reversed, but to be abolished. Liberation theology no more prays for the scattering of its enemies (cf. Tutu 1979:168) but ultimately works for a stage of reconciliation (cf. Mosala 1987b:19) or 'complete communion' (Gutiérrez 1988:104) in which 'my enemy is my guest' (Ford 1984).

3.6 Liberation from political suffering

In the South African context the actuality of political suffering is expressed in the following words of Boesak (1979:171):

> In a white church, or on the radio, it is the most natural thing in the world for a white minister to pray for our Christian government: 'Thank God for the Christian government that we've got.' But when we black South Africans pray about the government, our prayer is for deliverance.

In Luke–Acts political suffering receives more attention than in any other Gospel. Cassidy (1980 and 1987) devoted two volumes to this motif and co-edited a third (Cassidy & Scharper 1983). Our presentation here would therefore be rather cursory (cf. however Scheffler 1988:75-85).

In the Nazareth episode the political motif is dominant and is communicated by the narrative as a whole. After Jesus has read from Isaiah he announces that on that very day 'this scripture has been fulfilled in your hearing' (4:21). He immediately receives positive reaction from his audience: 'And all spoke well of him, and wondered at the gracious words which proceeded out of his mouth'

(4:22). However, when in Luke 4:25-27 he cites examples of the gentiles' sufferings (the widow of Zarephath and Naaman the Syrian) being alleviated (and
not those of the Israelites) the Nazarenes – who had just before applauded him
– grew angry and tried to kill him. Their change in attitude clearly reveals their
repudiation of the gentiles (racism). A positive attitude towards the underdog
(4:18) is applauded by them, as long as they are at the receiving end. First century racist Jewish attitudes are vividly described by Bietenhard (1977:1319):

> Nach Auffassung des rabbinischen Judentums ist der Nichtisraelit, der goj, für Gott fremd
> und fern, für nichts geachtet... Darum sind sie rettungslos dem Gericht der Hölle verfallen
> und haben keinen Anteil an der zukünftigen Welt... Gott ist der Schöpfer aller – er liebt aber
> allein Israel... Grundsätzlich gilt, dass die Heiden unrein sind: sie selbst, ihre Frauen und
> Kinder, ihre Häuser und Länder (St.-B. I,540.571; II,838; IV,374f)... Die grosse Wende wird
> die Messiaszeit bringen: die Völker, die Israel geknechtet haben (vor allem Rom!), werden
> durch den Messias vernichtet und enden in der Hölle.

Luke-Acts reflects a totally different approach. Peter's experience with Cor-
nelius in particular communicates clearly that 'God shows no partiality' (Ac
10:34), and that the tradition that it is 'unlawful...for a Jew to associate with or
to visit any one of another nation' (Ac 10:28) was abrogated by the Jesus event
(cf. also Bertram 1950:364-366).

The rejection of racism and the advocacy of universalistic attitudes is therefore crucial for the elimination of political suffering.

However, the criticism of Jewish racism does not mean that there is indif-
ference about the Romans' *oppression of the Jewish nation*. Although he seems
uninterested in obtaining political power himself and does not commit himself
to direct political action or violence (cf. 22:35-38,49-51; also Ford 1984:120-
121), Jesus' resistance (Cassidy 1980:41) to the political authorities (as inflicters
of suffering) is expressed *inter alia* by the following:

(1) his words (Herod is called a fox, cf. 13:32, Cassidy 1980:51-52)
(2) non-cooperation (cf his attitude before Herod and Pilate – Cassidy 1980:65-
    71)
(3) his acceptance, contrary to Roman practice, of the poor and social outcasts
    (Cassidy 1980:50)
(4) the criticism of political relationships of domination and oppression implied
    in his advocacy of an attitude of humility and service amongst his followers
    (22:24-27; Cassidy 1980:39,60,201)
(5) his qualification that loyalty to Caesar should not exceed loyalty to God
    (20:25; Cassidy 1980:58).

According to Luke, political liberation is further accomplished through the love
of the enemy. The resistance against the authorities is therefore non-violent (cf.
22:47-51 and 23:34 where Jesus acts in accordance with his own instruction of

6:27-36). This is why Jesus is also critical towards the *hostility between the Jews and Samaritans*. When a Samaritan town refuses to receive Jesus (9:51-55), Jesus rebukes his disciples when the latter wanted retaliation. In the well-known parable it is also a Samaritan who shows mercy towards the assaulted man, and not the priest or Levite (10:25-35; cf. Mazamisa 1987:164-169). Something similar happened after the healing of the ten lepers: not a Jew, but a Samaritan (sarcastically called ὁ ἀλλογενής by Jesus – 17:18) expressed his gratefulness.

The question of *violence* is an often debated issue within liberation theology (cf. Boesak 1977:68-71; *Kairos document* 1986:13-15). Should the struggle for liberation be fought 'by any means' or only by non-violent means, as Martin Luther King, amongst others, advocated? According to Boesak (1977:70) the option for violence is 'so strongly reminiscent of the ideology of the ruling class that we cannot but reject it outright'.

Luke's position seems clearly to be one of *passive resistance* in which verbal criticism of oppressors, humble service, love for the enemy and the willingness to suffer oneself are the means to be followed. Resistance against suffering is a prerequisite for the alleviation of the latter. But because Luke has a comprehensive view on suffering, he is consistent in his rejection of violence, since that would imply that physical suffering is employed in order to eradicate political suffering. The vicious circle of suffering would therefore continue. Regarding Luke's 'pacifism', Ford (1984:137) remarks:

> ...this is one of the special features of Luke (and John). In the contemporary world, where terrorism, violence, crime, war, and poverty are the most important issues of the day, this aspect of Luke's Gospel is acutely pertinent.

3.7 Liberation from social suffering

When reference is made in Luke 4:25-26 to the widow of Zarephath, it is not only mentioned that she was a Syrian, but especially that she was a *widow* (for a more detailed argument, see Scheffler 1988:19-20). In the raising of the son of the widow of Nain (which is reminiscent of the widow of Zarephath) the alleviation of the sorrow of the widow is even more highlighted than the raising of the son itself. Evidence of Luke's positive attitude towards women (and especially widows, cf. 2:37; 4:25; 7:12; 18:3; 20:47; 21:2) as a social minority group is therefore clearly manifested in the Nazareth episode.

In the rest of the Gospel *women* receive such positive attention that Luke's Gospel is sometimes called 'the Gospel of women' (e.g. Schmithals 1980:13). Especially the peculiarly Lucan pericope on *Martha and Mary* (Lk 10:38-42) suggests a role contrary to that traditionally reserved for woman (cf. Brutscheck 1986:167). Narratives on men and women are also presented in complementary parallelism to indicate that they 'stand together and side by side before God'

(Navone 1970:224, cf. 2:25-38; 4:25-28; 4:31-39; 7:1-17; 8:1-3; 12:45; 15:4-10; 17:34-36; 18:1-14; 23:55-24:35; Acts 5:1-11; 9:32-42; 16:13-34; 17:34 – cf. Flender 1968:15). This positive emphasis on women is especially noteworthy in the light of a current thanksgiving prayer of men, which was well-known among Persians, Greeks and Jews, namely that they 'were not unbelievers, uneducated, women or unfree' (cf. Oepke 1953:776-77). It can therefore be concluded that as far as liberation theology campaigns for the liberation of women in a patriarchal society, it is in accordance with Luke's view.

Women are, however, not the only social minority group to which Luke gives attention. He also has a positive attitude towards *tax-collectors* who were despised by Jews for collaborating with the Romans and who asked more tax than they were entitled to (cf. Fitzmeyer 1986:469-470 and 3:13; 5:27-32; 7:29; 15:1-2; 18:9-14; 19:1-10). Other despised groups who receive attention are *shepherds* (who often stole cattle, cf. 2:8-20; 15:4-7), *soldiers* (who helped to sustain the Roman order, cf. 3:14; 7:1-10; 23:47) and *children* (who were looked down upon by parents, cf. 1:17; 18:15-17).

With his emphasis on *various* ostracised groups within the community (one can also add lepers, the poor, and persecuted followers of Jesus – cf. 6:22), Luke clearly indicates that he has *all* suffering groups and *all* forms of suffering in mind. He campaigns for the alleviation of the suffering of the poor, but if the tax-collectors are ostracised for being tax-collectors, he has sympathy with them. The tax-collectors' exploitation of the poor should be contested, but the tax-collectors themselves are accepted (3:13). This accords with the view expressed above that one form of suffering cannot be eliminated by inflicting another kind of suffering. Liberation is to be effected through the kind of love that the earthly Jesus has practised. In practice it means charity and solidarity towards the 'underdog', the rejection of oppressive deeds by the 'topdog', but acceptance of the topdog who is also in need of liberation.

Liberation theology benefits from the comprehensiveness of Luke's view of suffering in the sense that an identification with Luke's view safeguards it against a one-sided view of liberation. To see liberation only as salvation from *sin* may sound 'conservative', but has the effect that the acute concrete sufferings of people on many spheres of life are consciously or unconsciously ignored. To view liberation solely as liberation from *political* suffering may also have the consequence that oppressors instead of oppression are hated and that suppression of women and children (to whom in their defencelessness the kingdom actually belongs) within their own community are overlooked (cf. Gutiérrez 1988:xxii-xxiii).

3.8 Jesus the sufferer and liberator from suffering

We have already noted that an important place is assigned in the Nazareth episode to Jesus as the Messiah (cf. 3.1 above). In the pericope he also appears as the one who suffers. When he explains the *universality* of liberation from suffering to the Nazarenes, they grow angry at him and try to kill him (4:29). This attempt to kill Jesus expresses the resistance to his ministry that was present from the outset and that ultimately led to his final passion (cf. Busse 1978:28-29).

Luke portrays Jesus as a sufferer from the manger to the cross. He is born in humble and poor circumstances (2:7), at the start of his ministry he is rejected by his hometown (4:28), he is persecuted by the Jewish leaders (5:21; 7:34; 11:54; 13:14; 15:1-2), rejected by the Samaritans (9:51-56), persecuted by Herod (13:31), and is painfully aware of his impending death right through his ministry (9:22,44-45; 12:50; 13:32-34; 17:25; 18:31-34). Moreover, during the culmination of his suffering in Jerusalem he is forsaken, denied and betrayed by his own followers.

A feature of Jesus' suffering is that it is closely connected with the suffering of his followers. It is just as comprehensive as the suffering of his followers (economic, physical, social, political). But most important is the fact that he suffers because of his unwavering compassion for those who suffer: when he associates with tax-collectors and sinners, the Pharisees and scribes murmur (15:1-2), and when he heals the sick on the Sabbath, they became indignant (13:10-16). Jesus' suffering therefore forms part of the liberation of his followers. His death is therefore typified as a *service* to his followers (22:27). Even during the culmination of his own suffering he is still still concerned for the suffering of others: he prays for Peter (22:31-32), he heals the ear of the slave of one of his own captors (22:50-51), he directs the sympathy of the women who bewailed him to themselves (23:28), he prays for the forgiveness of his crucifiers (23:34) and promises paradise to the penitent robber (23:43).

On the cross Jesus is repeatedly ridiculed for his inability to save himself from the cross. This inability is part of his humiliation and, ironically and paradoxically, a condition for his exaltation and the salvation of his followers.

One last question remains: *how* does the Lucan Jesus' humble death effect liberation for his followers? During the crucifixion the penitent robber experienced salvation because he *realised* that Jesus was dying innocently (= in humiliation) and because he humbled himself and turned to Jesus. *Insight into the irony that it is a powerless, selfless, humiliated, dying Jesus who saves, effects salvation.* This is borne out by the reaction of the centurion. At the moment when Jesus *died* in utter selflessness (cf. his selfless cry, 23:46), the centurion *realised* that he was righteous. The same insight caused the crowd to beat their breasts (23:48), a sign of repentance which implies salvation (cf. 18:13).

We *conclude* that, according to Luke, it is not so much the blood of Christ that saves (cf. 22:19) as the humiliation of his death. *Both* the breaking of his body and the shedding of his blood are expressive of this humiliation and salvation – salvation not only from sin, but from all kinds of suffering. Those who assimilate this insight (e.g. Jesus' followers in Acts) continue to effect liberation through similar humble service to all who suffer.

4. Conclusion

Liberation theology could reflect on several further pertinent issues in the light of Luke's Gospel. The questions of violence, the object of liberation, liberation and development, reconciliation, white response to black theology, the aftermath of political liberation, existential experiences of nihilism, cruelty to animals and ecology can all be mentioned (cf. *int. al.* Ford 1984; Gutiérrez 1988:13-25; Roberts 1971; Van Niekerk 1982; Kritzinger 1988; Moltmann 1972:268-292). Being a contextual theology, liberation theology has the built-in potential not to be dogmatic and to stagnate, but to widen its horizons.

In the fifteenth anniversary edition of his *Theology of Liberation*, Gutiérrez added a new introduction entitled 'expanding the view' (1988:xvii-xlvi). In it he reflects on previous viewpoints (e.g. regarding the poor) and the position of women in the process of liberation. Suffering is ever increasingly probed, not only in its acuteness, but also in its comprehensiveness, complexity and diversity. Like love, liberation theology also 'grows deeper and changes its manner of expression' (Gutiérrez 1988:xlvi).

BIBLIOGRAPHY

Bammel, E. 1959. πτωχός, κτλ. *TWNT*.
Bennett, B. 1986. A Critique on the Role of Women in the Church, in I. J. Mosala & B. Tlhagale (eds.). *The Unquestionable Right to be Free*. Johannesburg: Skotaville, 169-174.
Bertram, G. 1950. ἔθνος, κτλ. *TWNT*.
Bietenhard, H. 1977. 'Volk'. *TBLNT*.
Boesak, A. A. 1977. *Farewell to Innocence: A Socio-Ethical Study on Black Theology and Black Power*. New York: Orbis.
Boesak, A. A. 1979. Liberation Theology in South Africa, in K. Appiah-Kubi & S. Torres. *African Theology en Route*. New York: Orbis, 169-175.
Boesak, A. A. 1984. *Black and Reformed: Apartheid, Liberation and the Calvinist Tradition*. Johannesburg: Skotaville.
Boff, L. & Boff, C. 1984. *Salvation and Liberation: In Search of a Balance between Faith and Politics*. New York: Orbis.
Brown, R. E. 1977. *The Birth of the Messiah*. London: Macmillan.
Brown, R. M. 1978. *Theology in a New Key: Responding to Liberation Themes*. Philadelphia: Westminster.
Brutscheck, J. 1986. *Die Maria-Marta-Erzählung: eine redaktionskritische Untersuchung zu Lk 10,38-42*. Bonn: Peter Hanstein.
Bultmann, R. 1967. *Die Geschichte der synoptische Tradition*. 7. Aufl. Göttingen: Vandenhoeck & Ruprecht.
Busse, U. 1978. *Das Nazareth-Manifest Jesu: eine Einführung in das lukanische Jesusbild nach Lk 4,16-30*. Stuttgart: Katholisches Bibelwerk.

Cassidy, R. J. 1980. *Jesus, Politics and Society: A Study of Luke's Gospel*. New York: Orbis.

Cassidy, R. J. 1987. *Society and Politics in the Acts of the Apostles*. New York: Orbis.

Cassidy, R. J. & Scharper, P. J. 1983. *Political Issues in Luke-Acts*. New York: Orbis.

Cone, J. H. 1969. *Black Theology and Black Power*. New York: Seabury.

Cone, J. H. 1970. *A Black Theology of Liberation*. New York: Lippincott.

Degenhardt, H. J. 1965. *Lukas Evangelist der Armen: Besitz und Besitzverzicht in den Lukanischen Schriften*. Stuttgart: Katholische Bibelwerk.

Deist, F. E. 1984. *A Concise Dictionary of Theological Terms*. Pretoria: Van Schaik.

Deist, F. E. 1987. How Does a Marxist Read the Bible?, in P. G. R. de Villiers (ed.). *Liberation Theology and the Bible*. Pretoria: UNISA, 15-30.

De Villiers, P. G. R. 1987. The Gospel and the Poor: Let us Read Luke 4, in P. G. R. de Villiers (ed.). *Liberation Theology and the Bible*. Pretoria: UNISA, 45-76.

Dibelius, M. [1921] 1964. *Der Brief des Jakobus*. 11. Aufl. Göttingen: Vandenhoeck & Ruprecht.

Fitzmyer, J. A. 1986. *The Gospel according to Luke I-IX: Introduction, Translation, and Notes*. New York: Doubleday.

Flender, H. 1968. *Heil und Geschichte in der Theologie des Lukas*. München: Kaiser Verlag.

Ford, J. M. 1976. *My Enemy is my Guest: Jesus and Violence in Luke*. New York: Orbis.

Gutiérrez, G. 1973. *A Theology of Liberation: History, Politics and Salvation*. New York: Orbis.

Gutiérrez, G. 1988. *A Theology of Liberation: History, Politics and Salvation: 15th Anniversary Edition with a New Introduction by the Author*. New York: Orbis.

Haenchen, E. 1974. Historie und Verkündigung bei Markus und Lukas, in G. Baumann (Hrsg.). *Das Lukas-Evangelium: die redaktions- und kompositionsgeschichtliche Forschung*. Darmstadt: Wissenschaftliche Buchgesellschaft, 287-316.

Hanson, P. D. 1979. *The Dawn of Apocalyptic: The Historical and Sociological Roots of Jewish Apocalyptic Eschatology*. 2nd ed. Philadelphia: Fortress.

Herzog, F. 1974. Liberation Hermeneutic as Ideology Critique. *Interpretation* 28, 387-403.

Hjelle, L. A. & Ziegler, D. J. 1976. *Personality Theories: Basic Assumptions, Research, and Applications*. New York: Mcgraw-Hill.

Hoyt, T. 1977. *The Poor in Luke-Acts*. Michigan: University Microfilms.

Kritzinger, J. N. J. 1988. *Black Theology – Challenge to Mission*. Pretoria: University of South Africa. (Unpublished DTh Thesis.)

Le Roux, J. H. 1987. Two Possible Readings of Isaiah 61, in P. G. R. de Villiers (ed.). *Liberation Theology and the Bible*. Pretoria: UNISA, 31-44.

Loader, J. A. 1987. Exodus, Liberation Theology and Theological Argument. *Journal of Theology for Southern Africa* 59,3-18.

Loader, J. A. 1988. Wat is Bevrydingsteologie? Johannesburg. (Paper read at the Rand Afrikaans University.)

Louw, J. P. & Nida, E. A. 1988. *Greek-English Lexicon of the New Testament Based on Semantic Domains*, v. 1: *Introduction & Domains*. New York: UBS.

Mazamisa, L. W. 1987. *Beatific Comradeship: An Exegetical-Hermeneutical Study on Lk 10:25-37*. Kampen: Kok.

Miguez-Bonino, J. 1974. *Doing Theology in a Revolutionary Situation*. Philadelphia: Fortress.

Miranda, J. P. 1980. *Marx against the Marxists: The Christian Humanism of Karl Marx*. London: SCM

Moltmann, J. 1972. *Der Gekreuzigte Gott*. München: Kaiser.

Moltmann, J. 1975. *Gott kommt und der Mensch wird frei: Reden und Thesen*. München: Kaiser.

Moore, B. (ed.) 1973. *Black Theology: The South African Voice*. London: Hurst.

Mosala, B. 1986. Black Theology and the Struggle of the Black Woman in Southern Africa, in I. J. Mosala & B. Tlhagale (eds.). *The Unquestionable Right to be Free*. Johannesburg: Skotaville, 129-133.

Mosala, I. J. 1986. The Use of the Bible in Black Theology, in I. J. Mosala & B. Tlhagale (eds.). *The Unquestionable Right to be Free*. Johannesburg: Skotaville, 175-199.

Mosala, I. J. 1987a. *Biblical Hermeneutics and Black Theology in South Africa*. Cape Town: University of Cape Town. (Unpublished PhD Thesis.)

Mosala, I. J. 1987b. The Meaning of Reconciliation: A Black Perspective. *Journal of Theology for Southern Africa* 59, 19-34.

Mosala, I. J. & Tlhagale, B. (eds.) 1986. *The Unquestionable Right to be Free*. Johannesburg: Skotaville.

Motlhabi, M. B. G. 1987. Liberation Theology: An Introduction, in P. G. R. de Villiers (ed.). *Liberation Theology and the Bible*. Pretoria: UNISA, 45-76.

Navonne, J. 1970. *Themes of St. Luke*. Rome: Gregorian University Press.

Nolan, A. 1988. *God in South Africa: The Challenge of the Gospel*. Cape Town: David Philip.

Oepke, A. 1953. γυνή. *TWNT*.

Rienecker, F. 1970. *Sprachlicher Schlüssel zum Griechischen Neuen Testament*. Giessen: Brunnen-Verlag.

Roberts, J. D. 1971. *Liberation and Reconciliation: A Black Theology*. Philadelphia: Westminster.

Ruether, R. R. 1972. *Liberation Theology: Human Hope Confronts Christian History and American Power*. New York: Paulist.

Ruether, R. R. 1975. *New Woman, New Earth: Sexist Ideologies and Human Liberation*. New York: Seabury.

Ruether, R. R. 1985a. *Women-Church: Theology and Practice of Feminist Liturgical Communities*. New York: Harper & Row.

Ruether, R. R. 1985b. *Womanguides: Readings toward a Feminist Theology*. Boston: Beacon.

Scheffler, E. H. 1988. *Suffering in Luke's Gospel*. Pretoria: University of Pretoria. (DD thesis.)

Schmithals, W. 1975. Lukas – Evangelist der Armen, in Dr. Michel (Hrsg.). *Theologia Viatorum XII: 1973/1974: Jahrbuch der kirchliche Hochschule Berlin*. Berlin: Die Spur, 153-167.

Schmithals, W. 1980. *Das Evangelium nach Lukas*. Zürich: Theologischer Verlag.

Schottroff, L. & Stegemann, W. 1978. *Jesus von Nazareth – Hoffnung der Armen*. Stuttgart: Kohlhammer.

Sebothoma, W. 1988. Luke 12:35-38: A Reading by a Black South African. *Neotestamentica* 22, 325-335.

Tannehill, R. C. 1972. The Mission of Jesus according to Luke IV 16-30, in W. Eltester, (ed.). *Jesus in Nazareth*. Berlin: De Gruyter, 51-75.

The Kairos Document: Challenge to the Church: A Theological Comment on the Political Crisis in South Africa. 1986. 2nd ed. Johannesburg: Skotaville.

The Road to Damascus: Kairos and Conversion: A Document Signed by Third World Christians from Seven Nations. 1989. Johannesburg: Skotaville.

Thetele, C. B. 1979. Women in South Africa: the WAAIC, in K. Appiah-Kubi & S. Torres. *African Theology en Route*. New York: Orbis, 150-154.

Tutu, D. M. 1979. The Theology of Liberation in Africa, in K. Appiah-Kubi & S. Torres. *African Theology en Route*. New York: Orbis, 162-168.

Tutu, D. M. 1983. *Hope and Suffering: Sermons and Speeches*. Johannesburg: Skotaville.

Van Niekerk, A. S. 1982. *Dominee, Are You Listening to the Drums*. Cape Town: Tafelberg.

Van Tilborg, S. 1988. Luke 12:35-48: An Interpretation from the Ideology of the Text. *Neotestamentica* 22, 205-215.

Weber, H. 1989. *Power: Focus for a Biblical Theology*. Geneva: World Council of Churches.

West, C. 1983. Black Theology of Liberation as Critique of Captalist Civilization. *Journal of the I.T.C.* 10, 67-83.

Westermann, C. 1976. *Das Buch Jesaja: Kapitel 40-66*. Göttingen: Vandenhoeck & Ruprecht.

W. R. DOMERIS

HISTORICAL MATERIALIST EXEGESIS

1. Introduction

Few approaches to the Bible arouse as much controversy as does that of historical materialism. Yet viewed from the perspective of the South African struggle,
historical materialism offers the possibility of both a relevant hermeneutic and a
new Christian identity.

> If a church of the oppressed is to be built and if the folly of the cross is to be taken seriously
> in politics, then there is need not only of bidding farewell to bourgeois religion and the
> church of the established classes, but also of forming a new identity. A materialist reading
> owes its existence to this need, springing from an altered practice, for a Christian-socialist
> identity and for an appropriation of the tradition of faith and its sources that will make this
> identity secure (Fuessel 1983:138).

2. The theoretical foundations of historical materialism

Two sets of influences make up the present usage of the historical materialist
study of the Bible. We shall distinguish between these by listing them as primary
and secondary theoretical considerations.

2.1 Primary theoretical considerations

Modern historical materialism, as utilised by biblical scholars of the order of
Belo, Clevenot, Gottwald, Myers and Mosala, can best be understood through a
study of some of the theoretical statements advanced by Marx and Engels.

2.1.1 The priority of the material over the ideal

Marx and Engels utilised the German for an old French philosophical term
'matere' to describe the primary essence of human activity. As expounded by
Marx and Engels, the distinctive nature of historical materialism lay, therefore,
in its assertion of the priority of material being over human consciousness.

> In direct contrast to German philosophy (idealist) which descends from heaven to earth,
> here we ascend from earth to heaven... We set out from real, active men, and on the basis of
> their real life-process we demonstrate the development of the ideological reflexes and echoes

of this life-process (Marx & Engels 1959:247).

One's material situation (for example, as a worker) determines one's consciousness. In the now famous dictum of Marx, 'Being determines consciousness, and
not consciousness being'.

2.1.2 Marxist social analysis

De Ste Croix (1981:35-36) offers the following six point outline of the social
analysis undergirding the historical materialism of Marx and Engels:

(a) The human being as an individual can only be correctly understood within
    the framework of his/her society.
(b) The prime need of human beings in a particular society is to organise the
    production of the essentials among other goods of his/her material world.
    This may mean internal production, such as the growth of crops, or the ex-
    ternal acquisition of such goods through trade and barter.
(c) This results in a system of social, political and economic relations, which
    Marx classified as 'the relations of production'.
(d) While the most primitive communities appear to have been concerned only
    to meet their immediate needs, later groups took steps to develop their
    community in the face of economic or political competition from rival
    groups. So a production surplus was necessary to free certain members of
    the group from the daily grind of subsistence farming, for their roles as ad-
    ministrators, professional soldiers and other non-productive roles in the
    community.
(e) In practice, the need for surplus became a demand and erstwhile producers
    (particularly those in an agricultural setting) found that they were being ex-
    ploited. Heavy taxation and high interest rates created a situation of op-
    pression by the rich in the face of the increasing poverty of the poor.
(f) The final step in the process is the class conflict that grows out of the situa-
    tion of oppression.

2.1.3 Mode of production

Basic to the understanding of such marxist social analysis is the concept of the
'mode of production'. The mode of production consists of two basic elements,
'the relations of production' (cf. c above) and 'the forces of production'.

The *relations* of production describe the relation of producers and non-
producers to each other, and in turn to the product. So one might inquire
whether a worker owns his or her tools, whether they have a share in the 'sur-

plus' or profits of the sale of those things which they produce, and whether they have the same access to such benefits that may accumulate as does management.

The *forces* of production concern the basic elements that make production possible. Such forces may be either 'the means of production' (those basic elements such as land, raw materials, capital and tools), or 'labour' (human activity).

Every society consists of these two basic elements, (the forces and relations of production) and a grasp of the way in which they function in a particular society (the mode of production) is indispensable to an understanding of the material nature of that society. Indeed the mode of production is the foundation or base of a particular society. If one pictures society as a triangle, then the mode of production would be the base, above it the superstructures (e.g. government, legal forces) and the apex would be the dominant ideology.

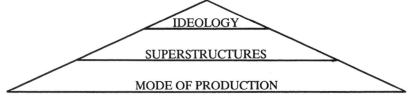

Marx sums up this perspective:

> In the social production of their life, men enter into definite relations that are indispensable and independent of the will, relations of production which correspond to a definite stage of development of their material productive forces. The sum total of these relations of production constitutes the economic structure of society, the real foundation, on which arises a legal and political superstructure and to which correspond definite forms of social consciousness. The mode of production conditions the social, political, and intellectual life process in general (Marx 1977:389).

This conditioning role of the mode of production, as Engels makes clear (cited in Posel 1982:130), does not mean that it is the only determining factor, as the dialectical materialism of the Communist Party supposed (Kolakowski 1978:329-354). Rather Marx and Engels believed that other factors might also play a causative if less significant role.

2.1.4 Ideology

The term ideology also plays a significant role in marxist discourse, although its precise definition is hotly disputed (cf. Williams 1983:153-157). For Marx and Engels, ideology implied 'false consciousness', a form of mind control utilised by the ruling class to secure their position of dominance (1959). Lenin (Letter to the Federation of the North cited in Williams 1983:157) and Mao Tse-Tung (1961:296), however, contended that different classes could produce different ideologies. So in an oppressive state, there would be the dominant (hegemonic) ideology of the ruling class and the revolutionary ideology of the working class.

For Marx (1977:389), ideology as a form of consciousness (albeit false) was a product of the material base of a society. However, Antonio Gramsci (1971:275, 326) argued for the possibility of a two-way (reciprocal) movement between the two forces (ideology and the mode of production). For marxist scholars of the Bible, such thinking leaves open the door for a theology/ideology of God as a force operative in human affairs.

2.1.5 Revolutionary practice

For Marx, 'revolutionising practice' formed the logical accompaniment to historical materialism. Thus he contradicted the clinical detachment and academic impartiality of much of German scholarship. Instead he grounded his critique firmly in the day-to-day life of the people, particularly the workers' struggle. This leads us to the secondary influences on the present use of historical materialism, namely the revolutionary context of its writers.

2.2 Secondary theoretical considerations

The use of historical materialism within the context of the Third World has been deeply influenced by the ongoing struggle against economic and political oppression. This has led to the following developments in the theological use of historical materialism.

2.2.1 The class struggle and the Bible

Historical materialism grows out of the dynamic of the class struggle, and as such is committed to wresting the Bible from the hands of the ruling elite and making it a weapon in the worker's struggle for liberation. Since much of the biblical text was written by members of the ruling elite, an historical materialist reading of scripture implies a process of excavation – a peeling back of its ideological veneer to expose the essence of the material situation, and in particular the class struggle that obtained in those days (cf. Mosala 1989).

2.2.2 A new hermeneutic

The linking of the class struggle of biblical days with our present struggle is for Itumeleng Mosala the key to developing a hermeneutic for black theology. In his critique of the social scientific approaches to the Bible he notes that both the Weberian 'ideal type' and the structural functionalism of Durkheim fail to take seriously 'the issues of class, ideology, and political economy' both of biblical and of modern times (1986:30). This failing, Mosala argues, makes these approaches unacceptable for creating a truly liberating hermeneutic within the context of the South African struggle. With approval, he quotes the words of Trevor Eagleton:

> Modern criticism was born of a struggle against the absolutist state; unless its future is now defined as a struggle against the bourgeois state, it might have no future at all (1984:124).

In his latest work Mosala (1989) utilises the socialist agenda of historical materialism in his development of an indigenous theology of the black worker struggle against apartheid. He clearly indicates in his reading of scripture that he perceives it to be the product of the ruling elite, which needs to be decoded in order to reveal the class struggle that ultimately gave it birth. Once this is accomplished, the Bible is free to be the tool of the liberation struggle.

2.2.3 Theology as ideology

Historical materialism as utilised by biblical scholars argues for an understanding of theology, and particularly theological literature, as ideology (cf. Gottwald 1979:65). Fuessel writes:

> Literary production is a form of ideological production. Like every other ideological production literary production is determined by the relation between basis and superstructure and by the class struggle. The production of texts is the privileged field of the conflict between rival ideologies at work on a social formation (1983:141).

This means that in order to develop an historical materialist critique of a piece of literature, such as the Gospels, one begins with the material conditions of the author and his/her audience. In this way one comes to comprehend the writing as an ideological product of those conditions.

2.2.4 The subversive nature of the gospel

Materialist studies of the Bible assume the subversive nature of the gospel. For example, Ched Myers writes:

In sum, the proper vocation of theology is the practice of 'ideological literacy', the critical discipline of political hermeneutics. It calls for discernment when liberating ideologies, including Christian theologies, become progressively hegemonic. This task is not conducted from a neutral site, but from the perspective of the gospel, which itself has an 'absolutely subversive' character that resists domestication and warns us against absolutizing any other ideological system (1988:21).

2.2.5 Praxis and faith

South American liberation theologians have used the term 'praxis' to describe Marx's 'revolutionising practice'. They believe that one 'does theology' through engaging in the struggle for liberation, for one's faith ultimately mirrors one's material being rather than one's religious convictions. Fuessel writes:

Revolutionary practice thus becomes the starting point for a comprehensive hermeneutic that not only makes possible a new interpretation of political and ideological reality in society but also becomes the basis for a new understanding of faith (1983:138).

2.2.6 The reign of God

The heart of the materialist endeavour, particularly within the realm of South African theology, is concerned with liberation. Correctly understood, liberation is a process, which leads to the creation of a just and equal social order. So in turn, materialist analysis (Echegaray 1984; Schottroff & Stegemann 1986; Ruether 1981; Schüssler Fiorenza 1983) understands the reign of God as coinciding with the establishment of such an egalitarian order. Ruether sums up this position:

Jesus' vision of the kingdom is one of radical social iconoclasm. He envisages a new era of God's justice and peace coming about only when all systems of domination of money, rank, and religious hierarchy are overthrown, when those who wish to be first are willing to be last and servant of all, and in which those who are nothing in this present system are lifted up (1981:17).

Divorced from his revolutionary and egalitarian praxis, the ideology of the church became by its very nature inimical to the teaching of Jesus. Ruether continues:

The Jesus who made himself one of the poor, one of the outcasts, and, finally one of the dead, in order to witness to the true conditions for entering God's reign, witnesses against this betrayal of his name. He flees from those who use his memory as a means of power and domination (1981:18).

3. The use of historical materialism in the study of the Bible

The era of the seventies and eighties has produced a number of significant works that utilise the method of historical materialism. We shall commence with the work of Gottwald, whose pioneering work in the Old Testament and his clear discussion of the theoretical implications of historical materialism serve also as an important preface to much of the New Testament study.

3.1 Historical materialism and early Israel

In 1979, Norman Gottwald published his monumental work, *The Tribes of Yahweh*, in which he rigorously applied the historical materialist critique to his study of pre-monarchic Israel. He understood the period of the settlement in Israel as a 'peasant revolt' in which a small group of escaped slaves from Egypt combined with the oppressed Canaanite peasants to overthrow the tyranny of the Canaanite feudal system.

The ideology of Yahwism was, according to Gottwald, a projection of the egalitarian community set up by the newly freed peasants. The covenant was their commitment to equality, in the face of the hierarchically ordered societies that surrounded them. 'From the start, Israel lived with a covenant charter which put optimum value on a people in egalitarian relations under one sovereign divine power' (1979:699). The law contained the necessary conditions to preserve the liberty and equality that they had found, and that were projected as the justice of God (1979:692).

3.2 Historical materialism and the early Jesus-community

Among the more popular books we find Michelle Clevenot's *Materialist Approaches to the Bible* (1985) and George Pixley's *God's Kingdom* (1981), which on account of their form avoid detailed theoretical discussion. Clevenot attempts indeed to provide a simple introduction to historical materialism and in particular to the complex writings of Fernando Belo. Pixley attempts to demonstrate the revolutionary nature of the kingdom of God, particularly within the unfulfilled mission of Jesus.

José Miranda's *Being and Messiah* (a study of John's Gospel) begins with a theoretical discussion of marxism and revolution. This opens the way for a presentation of Johannine Christianity as more radical and truly revolutionary (in the words of Miranda) than marxism.

Without a doubt, the most comprehensive materialist studies of the New Testament published so far are the works of Fernando Belo and Ched Myers.

3.2.1 Fernando Belo

In 1974, Belo published his materialist analysis of the Gospel of Mark. The
book, now published in English (1981), does not make easy reading, since it involves the reader in a host of difficult sociological and linguistic problems, particularly in his use of codes during the latter part of the book.

Belo's work is divided into three parts. The first part of the book deals with
the concept of mode of production (7-33). Belo is extremely thorough, and the
section is made up of no fewer than fifty-four hypotheses. In the second part,
Belo moves on to a consideration of the mode of production in biblical
Palestine (35-86). Here Belo discerns within the Old Testament two opposing
trains of thought. On the one hand is the Yahwist system based on gift and
concerned with equality and tribal self-rule, and on the other, a system based on
purity *versus* pollution, which is 'priestly, centralising and bureaucratic with its
focus in the exercise of sacral and royal power' (Fuessel 1983:135). Here is a
similar tension to that discerned by Gottwald (1979) and Brueggemann (1983)
between egalitarian early Israel and the later hierarchy of the monarchy.

In the third part of the book, Belo turns his attention to Mark. Here he
utilises various codes. Fuessel in his discussion of this section of Belo's book
refers to the pioneering work of Barthes:

> The mode of production peculiar to a text, and the structure that emerges from the text, are
> to be determined by deciphering the sequential codes used, whereas the insertion of the text
> into a particular situation can be known by the indicial or cultural codes (Barthes, cited by
> Fuessel 1983:143).

The indicial codes refer to the actors and their actions in the narrative (the
actantial code), their own analyses of the ongoing situation (the analytic code),
and the readers own evaluation of the behaviour of the actants in terms of the
attitudes they adopt toward each other. The cultural codes include such codes as
the geographical, topographical, chronological, mythological, symbolic and
social.

Leaving aside the complexity of the codes, we see in Belo's work a brilliant
analysis of the life of Jesus. For Belo, the teaching of Jesus, particularly his
scathing attack upon the temple of Jerusalem, led inevitably to his trial and
death. This is indeed the clear verdict of the three Synoptic Gospels. Scholarly
studies of the role of the temple as the point of economic power for the ruling
elite of Judaea (cf. Jeremias 1969 and more recently Evans 1989) show that
Jesus' action in 'cleansing' the temple courts, could not fail to bring the wrath of
the aristocratic Saduccees upon his head. The events in the temple have also
become crucial for other materialist attempts at determining the revolutionary
strategy of Jesus (cf. Nolan 1976:101-107; Pixley 1983:378-393; Echegaray
1984:31-41).

For Belo, the trial against Jesus centres on two rival ideologies – the prevailing ideology that grows out of the temple mode of production, and Jesus' ideological commitment to replace the temple, which arises out of his egalitarian life-style. (Here he refers back to the two ideologies he discerned within the Old Testament). In a similar way, Hugo Echegaray (1984) juxtaposes the non-capitalist mode of production of Roman Palestine (Belo calls it 'the subasiatic mode and slave system') with the egalitarian praxis of Jesus and his teaching concerning the presence of the kingdom of God.

In conclusion, then, we note that the basic elements of Belo's thinking revolve around the struggle between the two ideologies of the temple with its rules on purity and its hierarchy and the egalitarian concerns of the Jesus' community. However, the complexity of Belo's codes hampers his exegesis and so makes it difficult for the reader to follow his thinking into the pages of Mark's Gospel.

3.2.2 Ched Myers

Myers also chooses Mark for his materialist study. His five hundred page work consists of both a theoretical component and a sound exegesis of the Gospel. After a lengthy introduction to materialist exegesis and literary theory, Myers develops the social background, not just of the Jesus' events, but also of the evangelist. Unlike Belo, who contented himself with an understanding of the social situation in Roman Palestine, Myers recognises the fact that Mark's Gospel represents a different socio-political context, probably that of Rome. So the latter context impinges upon the presentation of the historical Jesus.

Myers uses the same clash of ideologies as that pinpointed by Belo, between Jesus and the temple hierarchy, but he sets it within the double horizon of the historical Jesus and the later writing of the Gospel. So while the Zealots may not be relevant to Jesus' time (following Horsley 1987), the defeat of the Jewish revolt was certainly a factor for the evangelist's presentation of Jesus. Myers' exegesis that makes up the bulk of the book is clearly written and particularly challenging.

4. A materialist study of Mark

The example that I have chosen to illustrate this method is based upon a section in Myers' book, entitled 'Challenging the ideological hegemony of priest and scribe' and concerns Mark 1:40-2:15. Myers writes:

> In the following series of stories, linked together by a variety of literary devices, Jesus launches his nonviolent assault upon the symbolic order of Jewish Palestine and the ideological hegemony of its stewards. Yet even as he challenges the social power and

exclusivity of the ruling groups, Jesus is simultaneously introducing an alternative social practice based upon inclusivity (1988:152).

The series commences with the healing of a leper (Mk 1:40-45). In terms of his
understanding of contending ideologies, Myers finds Jesus challenging the purity regulations laid down by Leviticus 13 and 14, and utilised by the priesthood as
part of their hegemony over the people. In the Jewish symbolic order the
disease was infectious yet Jesus touches the man, and far from himself
becoming unclean, the man becomes 'clean' instead (cf. Belo 1981:106). Thus
does Jesus subvert the old order, and he goes further. He does not tell the man
to 'show himself to the priest...', as most translations have it, but rather
according to Myers, 'Go back to the priest and make an offering ... as a witness
against them (1:44)'. In Myers' paradigm, Jesus does not 'cleanse' the leper in
the sense of heal, but he 'declares the man clean' in the Levitical sense. Thus as
a nonpriest Jesus subverts the symbolic order, as he declares the man pure and
in anger (1:41) he orders him back to the very priest who had refused to declare
him clean before.

The story that follows concerns the healing of a paralytic (2:1-12). Everything
in the scene, from the description of the dwelling to the poor man's bed,
indicates the poverty of the situation (Myers 1988:154). The man walks and then
Jesus makes his unusual pronouncement, 'Your debts (not sins, i.e. economic
not religious) are forgiven you'. The scribes are angry, for in their symbolic
order only God can remit debts (2:7), so they cry that Jesus blasphemes.
Correctly Myers realises that they are not defending God but their own social
power and financial interests. 'As Torah interpreters and co-stewards of the
symbolic order, they control determinations of indebtedness' (Myers 1988:155).
The introduction of the Human One (Son of Man) in 2:10, looks back to the
combat between Jesus and the scribes. 'The political struggle has truly commen-
ced: the Human One is wresting away from the scribal and priestly class their
'authority on earth" (Myers 1988:155).

In the third story Jesus is located among the crowd (ὄχλος), which Myers
(1988:156), following Ahn Byung-mu, understands as the equivalent of the poor
'people of the land' ('am ha'aretz). In this context the disciples are introduced
(2:14-15) as people who mix freely with 'sinners'. The reason is found in Jesus'
repudiation of the debt code, which has 'made everyone equal again before
God' (Myers 1988:157). In contrast to the Pharisees, who understood their identity in terms of exclusivity (the symbolic order or the clean and the unclean de-
lineated by Belo), the Jesus' community finds its identity in its inclusion of the
socially outcast.

The final story of the series concerns the actions of Jesus' disciples in the
grain field (Mk 2:23-28). When the Pharisees accuse the disciples of violating
the Sabbath, Jesus refers to the example of David who 'commandeered' bread
for his troops. The Human One has not only taken authority over the debt code,

but also the Sabbath code (Myers 1988:160). Idealist exegetes have seen in this story the issue of Jesus' divine authority, but the conflict is more material. A study of the laws regarding crops and land usage shows that the despised 'people of the land' were the victims of the wealthy Pharisees of Galilee and their iniquitous system of tithing. Therefore the action of Jesus can only be understood as a form of protest, of civil disobedience against the exploitation of the poor and oppressed. Myers' concludes:

> Jesus is not only defending discipleship practice against the alternative holiness code of Pharisaism, he is going on the offensive, challenging the ideological control and manipulation of the redistributive economy by a minority whose elite status is only aggrandized (1988:161).

So Myers introduces us to a materialist study of the praxis of Jesus, and shows how the 'spiritual' focus of idealist exegesis has consistently overlooked the 'material' concerns of Jesus, and his attacks upon the injustices of his time – the demonic hordes of Sadducean and Pharisaic hegemony.

5. A critical note

The use of the materialist method does not of necessity imply an uncritical acceptance of Marxist thinking. This is clear in the reservations expressed by writers such as Gottwald on Marxist practice and atheism, Clevenot on the church's role, and Myers on the place of the cross. In this final section, I would like to deal briefly with these issues.

5.1 Marxist practice and the problem of atheism

In his study of historical materialism, Gottwald deals with two key issues regarding the use of a methodology steeped in Marxist thinking. After confirming the method as 'he most coherent and promising understanding for developing research strategies in the social sciences' (1979:633), he goes on to distinguish between Marx's method and the implementation of his thinking in the years that followed (1979:634 and 697). He warns that we are not 'obligated to adopt without further examination his specific projections for the future, nor are we tied to any particular sociopolitical program described as Marxian' (1979:634).

Secondly Gottwald differs from Marx, who held that religion as a form of class justification would disappear with the end of the class struggle. Gottwald suggests instead that there exists a form of religious consciousness whose origins are 'anterior to social stratification' and which does not demand the denial of human selfhood (1979:637). With approval he cites the observation of Martin Buber, that Yahweh is not 'the personified spirit of the community', but rather as a power transcends the community, even exerts a changing influence upon it (1979:697).

5.2 The future of the church

Clevenot concludes his very readable study of Mark's Gospel with the question of the place of the church (1985:126-128). He writes:

> Is the church not...an idealist concept that covers, masks, beautifies, and therefore reveals under criticism an extremely diversified reality that is historically situated and always shot through with class struggle (1985:126-7).

Here is the dilemma faced by many Christians who have become involved in the struggle against political and economic oppression. Does one break from the church, or not? For Clevenot, the answer lies in the creation of an *ekklesia* separate from the Roman Catholic church 'which is hierarchical, clerical and often oppressive and repressive, and which we no longer want...' (1985:127). Such an *ekklesia* signifies 'the specific practice of these communities articulated at the economic, political, and ideological levels as faith, hope, and love' (1985:127), 'the place of messianic practice in the absence of the body of Jesus' (1985:127-8).

5.3 The place of the cross

The use of materialist criticism raises for Myers' the question of Jesus' strategy and in particular his death on the cross. The importance of this question cannot be underestimated for our reading of the Gospels, particularly in the context of oppression and state violence. Quoting Sobrino's view that Jesus dies in total discontinuity with his life and his cause, Myers asks:

> How is it that liberation theologians want the authority of a 'history of Jesus' when it comes to solidarity with the poor, but not at the point of the strategy of the cross?... It is ironic that the most indisputable political fact of the gospel story is depoliticized by liberation theology (1988:471).

For Myers the answer lies in a form of 'love over power' or nonviolent direct action, which provides a political hermeneutic that understands a sense of continuity between the strategy of Jesus and his death. There may be other solutions but one cannot do else than agree with Myers conclusion, 'Political readings can no longer skirt the implications of the cornerstone of New Testament faith – Jesus crucified as the justice of God' (1988:472).

BIBLIOGRAPHY

Belo, F. 1976. *A Materialist Reading of the Gospel of Mark*. (Tr. by M. J. O'Connell.) Maryknoll, New York: Orbis.

Brueggemann, W. 1983. Trajectories in Old Testament Literature and the Sociology of Ancient Israel, in N. K. Gottwald (ed.). *The Bible and Liberation: Political and Social Hermeneutics*. Maryknoll, New York: Orbis, 307-333.

Clevenot, M. 1985. *Materialist Approaches to the Bible*. Maryknoll, New York: Orbis.

De Ste Croix, G. E. M. 1981. *The Class Struggle in the Ancient Greek World*. London: Duckworth.

Eagleton, T. 1984. *The Function of Criticism*. London: Verso.

Echegaray, H. 1984. *The Practice of Jesus*. Maryknoll, New York: Orbis.

Evans, C. A. 1989. Jesus' Action in the Temple and Evidence of Corruption in the First-Century Temple, in D. J. Lull (ed.). *Society of Biblical Literature 1989 Seminar Papers*. Atlanta: Georgia: Scholars Press.

Fuessel, K. 1983. A Materialist Reading of the Bible: Report on an Alternative Approach to Biblical Texts, in N. K. Gottwald (ed.). *The Bible and Liberation: Political and Social Hermeneutics*. Maryknoll, New York: Orbis, 134-146.

Gottwald, N. K. 1979. *The Tribes of Yahweh : A Sociology of the Religion of Liberated Israel, 1250-1050 B.C.E.* Maryknoll, New York: Orbis.

Gramsci, A. 1971. *Selections from the Prison Notebooks*. (Ed. by Q. Hoare & G. N. Smith.) London: Lawrence and Wishart.

Horsley, R. 1987. *Jesus and the Spiral of Violence: Popular Jewish Resistence in Roman Palestine*. San Francisco: Harper and Row.

Jeremias, J. 1969. *Jerusalem in the Time of Jesus*. (Tr. by F. H. Cave and C. H. Cave.) Philadelphia: Fortress.

Kolakowski, L. 1978. *Main Currents of Marxism*, v. 2. Oxford: Oxford University Press.

Lapide, P. 1986. *The Sermon on the Mount. Utopia or Programme for Action?* Maryknoll, New York: Orbis.

Mao Tse-Tung. 1961. *Selected Works*, v. 1 (1924-1937). New York: China Books.

Marx, K. 1977. *Selected Writings*. (Ed. by D. McLellan.) Oxford: Oxford University Press.

Marx, K. & Engels, F. 1959. The German Ideology, in L. S. Feuer (ed.). *Marx and Engels. Basic Writings in Politics and Philosophy*. New York: Anchor Books.

Mosala, I. J. 1986. Social Scientific Approaches to the Bible. One Step Forward, Two Steps Backward. *Journal for Theology in Southern Africa* 55, 15-30.

Mosala, I. J. 1989. *Biblical Hermeneutics and Black Theology in South Africa*. Maitland, Cape Town: Struik Christian Books.

Myers, C. 1988. *Binding the Strong Man. A Political Reading of Mark's Story of Jesus*. Maryknoll, New York: Orbis.

Nolan, A. 1976. *Jesus before Christianity. The Gospel of Liberation*. London: Darton, Longman & Todd.

Pixley, G. V. 1981. *God's Kingdom. A Guide for Biblical Study*. Maryknoll, New York: Orbis.

Pixley, G. V. 1983. God's Kingdom in First Century Palestine: The Strategy of Jesus, in N. K. Gottwald (ed.). *The Bible and Liberation: Political and Social Hermeneutics*. Maryknoll, New York: Orbis, 378-393.

Posel, D. 1982. Marxist Literary Theory: Literature 'in the Final Analysis', in R. Ryan & S. van Zyl (eds.). *An Introduction to Contemporary Literary Theory*. Cape Town: A. D. Donker, 128-146.

Ruether, R. R. 1981. *To Change the World: Christology and Cultural Criticism*. London: SCM.

Schottroff, L. 1983. Women as Followers of Jesus in New Testament Times: An Exercise in Social-Historical Exegesis of the Bible, in N. K. Gottwald (ed.). *The Bible and Liberation: Political and Social Hermeneutics*. Maryknoll, New York: Orbis, 418-427.

Schottroff, L & Stegemann, W. 1986. *Jesus and the Hope of the Poor*. Maryknoll, New York: Orbis.

Schüssler Fiorenza, E. 1983. 'You Are not to be called Father': Early Christian History in a Feminist Perspective, in N. K. Gottwald (ed.). *The Bible and Liberation: Political and Social Hermeneutics*. Maryknoll, New York: Orbis, 394-417.

Sobrino, J. 1978. *Christology at the Crossroads*. Maryknoll, New York: Orbis.

Williams, R. 1983. *Keywords. A Vocabulary of Culture and Society*. London: Fontana.

CONTRIBUTORS

Dr. W. R. Domeris, Department of Religious Studies, University of the Witwatersrand, Johannesburg.

Dr. J. A. Draper, Department of Biblical Studies, University of Natal, Pietermaritzburg.

Dr. J. G. du Plessis, Department of New Testament, University of South Africa, Pretoria (formerly).

Prof. P. J. du Plessis, Department of Biblical Studies, Rand Afrikaans University, Johannesburg (formerly - Prof. died in 1990).

Prof. P. J. Hartin, Department of New Testament, University of South Africa, Pretoria.

Prof. B. C. Lategan, Department of Biblical Studies, University of Stellenbosch, Stellenbosch.

Prof. P. J. Maartens, Department of Biblical Studies, University of Durban-Westville, Durban.

Dr. S. J. Nortjé, Department of Biblical Studies, Rand Afrikaans University, Johannesburg.

Dr. J. H. Petzer, Department of New Testament, University of South Africa, Pretoria.

Dr. E. H. Scheffler, Department of Old Testament, University of South Africa, Pretoria.

Prof. A. H. Snyman, Dean of the Faculty of Arts, University of the Orange Free State, Bloemfontein.

Prof. A. G. van Aarde, Department of New Testament (Faculty A), University of Pretoria, Pretoria.

Dr. S. van Tilborg, Department of New Testament, Catholic University of Nijmegen, Nijmegen, The Netherlands.

Prof. W. S. Vorster, Director of the Institute for Theological Research, University of South Africa, Pretoria.

Prof. W. Wuellner, Department of New Testament, Pacific School of Religion, Berkeley, California, United States of America (formerly).

INDEX OF NAMES

INDEX OF BIBLICAL REFERENCES

NEW TESTAMENT TOOLS AND STUDIES

EDITED BY

BRUCE M. METZGER, PH.D., D.D., L.H.D., D.THEOL., D. LITT.

Vol. I
INDEX TO PERIODICAL LITERATURE ON THE APOSTLE PAUL, compiled under the direction of Bruce M. Metzger. 1960. xv + 138 pages.
Vol. II
CONCORDANCE TO THE DISTINCTIVE GREEK TEXT OF CODEX BEZAE, compiled by James D. Yoder, Th.D. 1961. vi + 73 double column pages.
Vol. III
GREEK PARTICLES IN THE NEW TESTAMENT, LINGUISTIC AND EXEGETICAL STUDIES, by Margaret E. Thrall, Ph.D. 1962. ix + 107 pages.
Vol. IV
CHAPTERS IN THE HISTORY OF NEW TESTAMENT TEXTUAL CRITICISM, by Bruce M. Metzger, 1963. xi + 164 pages.
Vol. V
THE EARLIEST CHRISTIAN CONFESSIONS, by Vernon H. Neufeld, Th.D. 1963. xiii + 166 pages.
Vol. VI
INDEX TO PERIODICAL LITERATURE ON CHRIST AND THE GOSPELS, compiled under the direction of Bruce M. Metzger. 1966. xxiii + 602 pages.
Vol. VII
A CLASSIFIED BIBLIOGRAPHY TO LITERATURE ON THE ACTS OF THE APOSTLES, compiled by A.J. Mattill, Jr., Ph.D., and Mary Bedford Mattill, M.A. 1966. xviii + 513 pages.
Vol. VIII
HISTORICAL AND LITERARY STUDIES: PAGAN, JEWISH, AND CHRISTIAN, by Bruce M. Metzger. 1968. x + 170 pages, + 20 plates.
Vol. IX
STUDIES IN METHODOLOGY IN TEXTUAL CRITICISM OF THE NEW TESTAMENT, by Ernest Cadman Colwell, Ph.D., Litt.D., LL.D., S.T.D., L.H.D. 1969. viii + 175 pages.
Vol. X
NEW TESTAMENT STUDIES: PHILOLOGICAL, VERSIONAL, AND PATRISTIC, by Bruce M. Metzger. 1980. x + 234 pages.
Vol. XI
STUDIEN ZUM NEUTESTAMENTLICHEN BRIEFFORMULAR, von Franz Schnider und Werner Stenger. 1987. viii + 191 Seiten.
Vol. XII
STRUKTURALE BEOBACHTUNGEN ZUM NEUEN TESTAMENT, von Werner Stenger. 1990. vii + 320 Seiten.
Vol. XIII
LIFE OF JESUS RESEARCH: AN ANNOTATED BIBLIOGRAPHY, by Craig E. Evans, Ph.D. 1989. xiii + 207 pages.
Vol. XIV
A KEY TO THE PESHITTA GOSPELS; vol. 1: ꞋĀlaph-Dālath, by Terry C. Falla, Ph.D 1991. xl + 136 + [21] pages.